Civil Rights in the Gateway to the South

CIVIL RIGHTS AND THE STRUGGLE FOR BLACK EQUALITY
IN THE TWENTIETH CENTURY

Series Editors
Steven F. Lawson, Rutgers University
Cynthia Griggs Fleming, University of Tennessee

Civil Rights in the Gateway to the South

Louisville, Kentucky
1945–1980

Tracy E. K'Meyer

The University Press of Kentucky

Scholarly publisher for the Commonwealth,
serving Bellarmine University, Berea College, Centre College of Kentucky, Eastern
Kentucky University, The Filson Historical Society, Georgetown College, Kentucky
Historical Society, Kentucky State University, Morehead State University, Murray
State University, Northern Kentucky University, Transylvania University, University
of Kentucky, University of Louisville, and Western Kentucky University.
All rights reserved.

Editorial and Sales Offices: The University Press of Kentucky
663 South Limestone Street, Lexington, Kentucky 40508-4008
www.kentuckypress.com

15 14 13 12 11   5 4 3 2 1

Maps created by Jeff Levy at the University of Kentucky Cartography Lab

The Library of Congress has cataloged the hardcover edition as follows:

K'Meyer, Tracy Elaine.
  Civil rights in the gateway to the South : Louisville, Kentucky, 1945–1980 /
Tracy E. K'Meyer.
    p. cm. — (Civil rights and the struggle for black equality in the twentieth century)
  Includes bibliographical references and index.
  ISBN 978-0-8131-2539-8 (hardcover : acid-free paper)
  1. African Americans—Civil rights—Kentucky—Louisville—History—20th
century. 2. African Americans—Kentucky—Louisville—Social conditions—20th
century. 3. Civil rights movements—Kentucky—Louisville—20th century.
4. Louisville (Ky.)—Social conditions—20th century. I. Title. II. Title: Louisville,
Kentucky, 1945–1980.
  F149K647 2009
  323.1196'07307694409045—dc22   2009000990
  ISBN 978-0-8131-3006-4 (pbk. : alk. paper)
  eISBN 978-0-8131-7335-1

This book is printed on acid-free paper meeting
the requirements of the American National Standard
for Permanence in Paper for Printed Library Materials.

Manufactured in the United States of America.

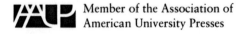

Member of the Association of
American University Presses

To Glenn,
with love

Contents

Illustrations follow page 178

Abbreviations

ACLU	American Civil Liberties Union
ACOH	Ad Hoc Committee on Open Housing
AFSC	American Friends Service Committee
BSU	Black Student Union
BULK	Black Unity League of Kentucky
BWC	Black Workers' Coalition
CAC	Community Action Commission
CAMP	Citizens Action for More Police; Community Action on Metropolitan Problems
COH	Committee on Open Housing
CORE	Congress of Racial Equality
EEOC	Equal Employment Opportunity Commission
FE	United Farm Equipment Workers
FEPC	Fair Employment Practices Commission
HEW	U.S. Department of Health, Education, and Welfare
HRC	Human Relations Commission
HUD	U.S. Department of Housing and Urban Development
IHM	Interracial Hospital Movement
JCSSA	Jefferson County Sunday School Association
JOMO	Junta of Militant Organizations
KBNA	Kentucky Bureau for Negro Affairs
KCIC	Kentucky Commission on Interracial Cooperation
KCLC	Kentucky Christian Leadership Conference
KCLU	Kentucky Civil Liberties Union
KUAC	Kentucky Un-American Activities Committee
LACRR	Louisville Area Council on Religion and Race
LBPOO	Louisville Black Police Officers Organization
LWRO	Louisville Welfare Rights Organization
MCM	Militant Church Movement

NAACP	National Association for the Advancement of Colored People
NLC	Negro Labor Council
PHTA	Public Housing Tenants' Association
PIE	Progress in Education
SCEF	Southern Conference Educational Fund
SCLC	Southern Christian Leadership Conference
SNCC	Student Nonviolent Coordinating Committee
SOCS	Save Our Community Schools
SRC	Southern Regional Council
UBPP	United Black Protective Parents
ULAB	United Labor against Busing
VISTA	Volunteers in Service to America
WCC	White Citizens' Council
WDC	Wade Defense Committee
WECC	West End Community Council
WEST	White Emergency Support Team
WILPF	Women's International League for Peace and Freedom
WLCM	West Louisville Cooperative Ministry

Acknowledgments

Over the years that I have been researching and writing this book, I have received financial, moral, and intellectual support from a number of institutions and individuals. The research could not have been completed without funding from the Louisville Institute, the Kentucky Oral History Commission, and the University of Louisville graduate school, College of Arts and Sciences, and Commonwealth Center for Humanities and Society. The content draws from and was fundamentally shaped by interviews with over eighty Louisvillians who graciously welcomed me into their homes and shared their stories of the movement. In particular, I am grateful to the Reverend James Chatham, Raoul Cunningham, Anne Braden, and J. Blaine Hudson for helping to identify narrators and make the contacts necessary to launch the interviews.

Once I moved on to writing, I benefited from the insights and suggestions of friends and colleagues. Catherine Fosl provided her perspective on Anne Braden and the Wade case. John Dittmer served as an extremely thorough and insightful external reader. And Kathryn Nasstrom not only was my sounding board over the years but read and gave extensive comments on the manuscript at various stages. I am profoundly grateful for their contributions.

Finally, I literally would not have been able to complete this work without the love, support, intellectual challenge, and editorial advice I received over the past decade from my colleague, partner, and husband, Glenn Crothers. While our other two coproductions—Colin and Norah—are more precious to our hearts, I trust he shares my satisfaction in completing this one.

Introduction

Gateway to the South

In the era of the civil rights movement and in retrospective accounts, white and black Louisvillians have often described their hometown as a "middle ground" between the North and South. In this border city, locals maintained, race relations were a "mélange of northern and southern attitudes," southern in the "approach to the Negro" but with a political culture and "relations between the two races" "similar to those found in northern communities."[1] To many observers, northern influences rendered Louisville, although still a southern city, a unique one. For example, Mark Ethridge, general manager of the *Louisville Courier-Journal* and *Louisville Times* from 1936 to 1963, wrote to a colleague, "I believe the Negro gets a better break in Louisville than in any southern city." Other residents and observers considered Louisville "exceptional among southern cities in its community efforts to solve racial problems" and concluded that, as a result, there was "more democracy" in the city than in the rest of the region.[2] However, black civil rights leaders and their white liberal allies at times charged that whites used Louisville's claim of relative progress compared to its sister cities in the South to quiet blacks' complaints. As Lyman Johnson recalled, "The white leaders would say, 'Look how good we are to you. Now, don't bug us too much.'" Other activists simply maintained that Louisville was not so different from the rest of the region after all. As black columnist J. C. Olden put it, many local whites held "Mississippi attitudes." Most often, however, black activists employed Louisville's border position to prod city fathers to action, contrasting local race relations with those in Cincinnati and Springfield, Ohio; Cairo, Illinois; and Washington DC. The "self-styled 'Gateway to the South,'" they

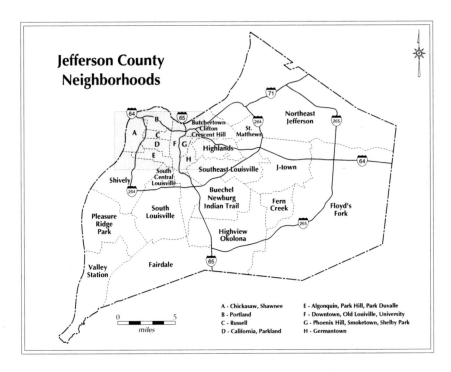

Jefferson County Neighborhoods

A - Chickasaw, Shawnee
B - Portland
C - Russell
D - California, Parkland
E - Algonquin, Park Hill, Park Duvalle
F - Downtown, Old Louisville, University
G - Phoenix Hill, Smoketown, Shelby Park
H - Germantown

argued, "is morally obligated to make even greater progress to justify its leadership claims."[3]

Echoes of these comments about Louisville's mixture of regional characteristics, and their meaning for race relations, could still be heard in 1995, when I moved to the city. Not long after my arrival, I was approached by a local minister, the Reverend James Chatham, to conduct an oral history project with the leaders of the sit-ins of spring 1961. In the course of those interviews, I heard assertions about the quality of local race relations and Louisville's relatively easy and certainly less violent mass movement for open accommodations. I also encountered skepticism about those claims and wry explanations of how local people liked to think of themselves as better without examining the more troublesome and frustrating parts of the struggle for equality. Intrigued about what history might lie behind these conflicting images of my new home, I decided to explore the story more fully. Other scholars have amply demonstrated the value of community studies in revealing how local contexts, cultures, and histories shaped the nature and outcome of the civil rights movement, in the process complicating the narrative of the national struggle. This study illuminates how the city's location

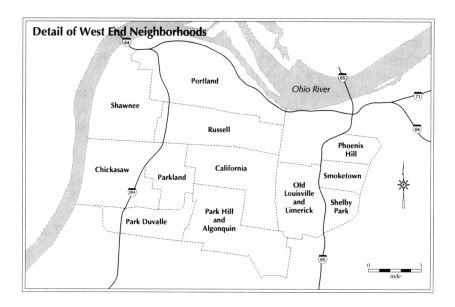

on the edge of the South, or as Louisvillians often put it, as a "gateway" between regions, shaped the local movement. More important, because the history of the struggle for racial equality in this border city contains many parts of the stories of other regions, it provides new ways of looking at the movement as a whole.

Historians and local commentators have called Louisville a gateway between North and South not only because of its location on the banks of the Ohio River, a traditional demarcation between the regions, but also because of its mixed economy, population, and regional identity. In its earliest history, Louisville was a frontier city, part of an undifferentiated "western country" of farmers and traders united by the Ohio River. Although in the early nineteenth century it was a slave city in a slave state and a center for a thriving trade in bondsmen and bondswomen, Louisville's commercial economy was linked to communities in the North and East by the river. By the Civil War, the city's identification with the North had grown stronger, as the number of slaves within its boundaries decreased to just 10 percent of the population, down from 25 percent earlier in the century. Louisvillians showed their independence from the South in 1861 by voting for John Bell of the Constitutional Union Party for president and then refusing, along with the rest of the state, to secede and join the Confederacy. Louisville provided some volunteers to the southern forces even after Kentucky formally joined the Union, but during the war it became more tied to the North, serving as a federal transportation hub, a host to Union troops, and a center for hospital facilities.[4]

After the war, however, Louisville's sectional orientation shifted again. As Omer Carmichael, school superintendent at the time of the *Brown v. Board of Education* decision, wrote in his memoir, "Louisville, like Kentucky, it has been said, seceded after Appomattox"—a colorful way to say that during and after Reconstruction, Louisvillians, at least white civic leaders, began to identify themselves more as southerners. Racial, political, and economic factors played roles in this shift. Many white Kentuckians, including those in the state's largest city, had supported both slavery and the Union, and they resented the Emancipation Proclamation as a betrayal of their loyalty. More generally, white Louisvillians reacted to the rising population of African Americans in the community, which doubled to fifteen thousand between 1860 and 1870 and continued to climb until, by 1900, it was just under forty thousand. Whites' fear of this growing community was compounded by their opposition to Radical Republican Reconstruction policies, which seemed to punish them while benefitting the freedmen. Politically, a majority of Louisville's white voters turned to the Democratic Party, which they viewed as their protector. When Reconstruction came to an end, Louisville's business community, looking to rebuild the economy, competed for access to new southern markets with merchants from Cincinnati and other midwestern and Ohio River valley communities. As historian Allen J. Share demonstrates, the ex-Confederates who returned to places of economic and political leadership in Louisville "recognized that the city's 'southernness' could be an important psychological weapon in the battle" for the "trade of the South." As southern resentment of Reconstruction and anything associated with the North increased, business leaders and their allies in the city "upped its claims to southern loyalties." As a result, by the turn of the century, when the city hosted the Southern Exposition, Louisville's civic leaders identified it as a southern place with cultural, political, and economic links to its sister communities in the former Confederacy. In 1895 city leaders provided the most visible evidence of this southern turn when they erected a Confederate memorial, ignoring in the process the city's Union heritage.[5]

A key aspect of this southern identity was the imposition of a system of Jim Crow segregation that limited the freedom of African Americans in nearly every aspect of social and economic life. In Louisville, as elsewhere, whites' efforts to accomplish the complete separation of blacks from whites and to relegate the former to inferior or no facilities did not all happen at once. Through the 1870s and early 1880s, the owners of some places of recreation and the city's social service institutions continued to admit black clients, but over time restrictions intensified. Theater owners began to bar black patrons completely; white-controlled sports facilities, including the baseball diamond and the Louisville Jockey Club, closed their doors. State officials segregated the reform schools, and most hospitals ceased to accept black patients. And at no point did city leaders consider letting white and black children attend school together, a policy that was confirmed in 1904 when the state legislature adopted the Day Law, which forbade the mixing of the races in any educational institution in Kentucky.

Yet the system of segregation in Louisville remained more fluid, less complete, than elsewhere—a fact to which Louisvillians still point today. The city passed no law, for example, that mandated separation in public accommodations. Consequently, individual white proprietors set their own policies, though the vast majority conformed to white public opinion and refused to serve blacks or did so in restrictive and humiliating ways. In 1871 the black community had succeeded, through a mass boycott, in convincing streetcar operators to allow them to ride unsegregated, and some Louisvillians boasted that their city allowed blacks equality on public transportation. According to historian George C. Wright, however, whites found "informal means" to enforce separation when they felt like it. Finally, although the parks remained open through the years when Jim Crow was solidifying, in 1924 city officials ordered blacks out of white spaces and into their own small, underdeveloped Chickasaw Park. Thus, although it was less complete, rigid, or backed by law, by the early years of the twentieth century, segregation existed in Louisville and restricted the life choices of African Americans much as it did in other southern communities.[6]

The system of segregation also encompassed private spaces such as housing. As the number of African Americans in the city swelled after the Civil War, the newcomers began to flood into the areas just west and east of downtown. Before World War I, blacks continued to live throughout the city on streets or alleys adjacent to whites in a checkerboard pattern. Often, these black residents lived near whites because they worked as servants for them. From time to time, whites suggested that a law be passed to force blacks into restricted areas or at least out of white ones, and in 1914 the city adopted an ordinance banning anyone from occupying property on a block on which the majority was another race. Ostensibly, the ordinance restricted whites as well as blacks, but in its first major campaign, the Louisville branch of the National Association for the Advancement of Colored People (NAACP) brought suit against the city for discrimination. In the 1917 *Buchanan v. Warley* decision, the U.S. Supreme Court overturned the law and made such city ordinances illegal, but that did not stop the hardening of residential segregation. Indeed, in the period between World War I and the civil rights movement, the black population became more concentrated in the Smoketown area, just east of downtown, and in the west end neighborhoods of the city. The pattern continued, and worsened, after World War II.[7]

Employment discrimination reinforced these residential patterns because low wages and insecure jobs ensured that most blacks could not afford to move out of the areas to which they had been restricted. From Reconstruction onward, African Americans in the city were overwhelmingly confined to service occupations in white homes and businesses, working as cooks, laundry workers, waiters, barbers, janitors, and drivers. Most employers excluded blacks from clerical, sales, and secretarial work because they assumed white customers would not accept African Americans in those roles. In construction and the growing industrial sector, blacks served as low-skill, seasonal, poorly paid laborers, shut out of white unions or confined to segregated locals. World War I did not alter this pattern significantly. As in other early-twentieth-century cities throughout the country, a separate black economy developed. Concentrated near black residential sections, small businessmen opened shops that served the African American community and depended on it for their success. Blacks also opened a few larger businesses, including Mammoth Life Insurance and two banks, though both banks failed during the Great Depression. Meanwhile, a growing population of black professionals—doctors, lawyers, ministers, and teachers—moved to Louisville from other parts of Kentucky and the South to tap into its larger black market. These men and a few women were likewise dependent on the black community for their livelihoods. The 1930s marked a few important advances as the city hired blacks for the first time in the police and fire departments, although it restricted their duties and confined them to black residential areas. Still, by 1940, 87.5 percent of African Americans who reported an occupation worked in service, common labor, or unskilled factory jobs.[8]

Louisville's Jim Crow pattern of segregation and discrimination contributed to contemporaries' sense that Louisville was southern in its "approach to the Negro," but the city nonetheless retained many characteristics more commonly associated with northern urban places. Louisville's economy was heavily commercial and increasingly industrial. Although the city's status as a trade and transportation hub, centered on the Ohio River and Louisville and Nashville Railroad, declined between the Civil War and the 1930s, the local economy revived during World War II as a result of new defense industries in chemicals, plastics, rubber, and munitions. The industrial expansion continued after World War II, and by 1950, 31 percent of the city's employed population worked in manufacturing. National corporations, including International Harvester, Ford Motor Company, and General Electric, established branch plants in the city, which also saw a growth in smaller, locally based manufacturers. The relationship among the larger plants, their national headquarters, and the federal government, and the interest of civic leaders in attracting more industry and investment, shaped the climate for the civil rights movement, bringing outside influences to bear in the city and encouraging local leaders to promote an image of peace and progress. Finally, unionization drives among Louisville workers by both the American Federation of Labor and Congress of Industrial Organizations provided potential allies for civil rights advocates. The CIO in particular pushed for antidiscrimination policies, but African Americans did not yet share equitably in the new jobs. A study by University of Louisville social scientists Scott Cummings and Michael Price showed that in the postwar era, 62 percent of white men were in white-collar skilled or supervisory positions, while the same percentage of black men remained in service and unskilled jobs.[9] Still, a mixed industrial economy and unionized workforce led the local movement to embrace strategies and allies and to confront issues and obstacles more often associated with northern cities.

Likewise, the relative religious diversity of the city distinguished it from its neighbors to the south. In the early twentieth century, Louisville had a small number of foreign-born citizens—approximately 2 percent of the white population—because such migration had taken place primarily in the mid-nineteenth century. But Louisville had relatively large Catholic and Jewish populations compared to other southern cities. Thus, while Protestants remained a majority, other religious faiths played an active part in the local community. A variety of organizations including the Young Men's Hebrew Association, the National Council of Jewish Women, and social service agencies coordinated by the Conference of Jewish Organizations gave Jewish residents a launchpad for civic engagement. Meanwhile, the liberalism of the Catholic Church hierarchy, including local bishops and the president of Bellarmine College, a Catholic institution of higher learning, provided support for clerical and lay involvement in interracial endeavors. Among Protestants, the Southern Baptist Theological and Louisville Presbyterian Theological seminaries became fonts of liberal thinking on race and social issues in the early and mid-twentieth century, breaking southern white church solidarity on Jim Crow.[10]

By midcentury both black and white civil rights advocates recognized these religious communities as the source of an influential group of local residents who provided support, at minimum, for amelioration of conditions for African Americans and, at times, for progress toward equal rights. The city's activists, including a small group of black leaders who were "much more aggressive than people" in nearby northern cities such as Indianapolis, and a smaller number of white and black radicals, worked within a climate established and to some extent controlled by a relatively liberal white intellectual and business elite. White labor and civil rights activist Anne Braden recalled her surprise when she moved to the city in the late 1940s and discovered that opposition to segregation "reached into high places in the community," most notably the offices of the *Louisville Courier-Journal* and *Louisville Times*. J. Harvey Kerns, in his 1948 study of social conditions in Louisville, reported that the editorial position of these papers "molds public opinion in favor of better race relations." Moreover, black leaders recalled the owner and publisher of the papers, Barry Bingham Sr., and businessmen Dan Byck and Harry Schacter as powerful friends to the African American community. Beneath this pinnacle of community influence, civil rights advocates found allies in seminaries, religious organizations, union leadership, and universities and among whites in the community who believed "we can't go on happily unless there are basic changes."[11] The visibility of white sympathizers in religious, civic, labor, and educational organizations set Louisville apart from other southern cities of its size. More important, they provided the basis for interracial cooperation with black leaders and groups throughout the movement era.

Diversity also characterized the black community of the city. By the immediate postwar years, the African American population had grown to just over fifty-seven thousand, or approximately 15 percent of the city's residents.[12] Although it composed a smaller part of the total urban population than in similarly sized southern cities, Louisville's African American community nevertheless produced a range of institutions, organizations, and leaders who brought to the movement a variety of ideological perspectives and approaches to change. For example, the African American population supported a number of large churches, including Quinn Chapel and Zion Baptist, that served as movement meeting places and organizing centers. Black professionals such as teacher Lyman Johnson, doctor Maurice Rabb, and attorney James Crumlin led the local branch of the NAACP. African Methodist Episcopal (AME) Zion Church bishop C. Eubank Tucker founded and led the Kentucky Bureau for Negro Affairs (KBNA). Journalists and editors such as William Warley, I. Willis Cole, and particularly Frank Stanley Sr. of the *Louisville Defender* became significant spokesmen for and leaders of the freedom struggle. Women such as Ruth Bryant and Murray Walls rose to leadership through social service organizations such as the Urban League Guild and neighborhood improvement clubs. Finally, church-based organizations such as the Militant Church Movement (MCM), led by the Reverend M. M. D. Perdue and J. C. Olden, and the Jefferson County Sunday School Association (JCSSA), led by the Reverend Daniel J. Hughlett, rallied grassroots support for antidiscrimination campaigns. These organizations cooperated throughout the civil rights era while maintaining separate identities that reflected their emphases on particular issues, the personalities of their leaders, and on occasion their political loyalties to the Democratic and Republican parties. As a result, the Louisville struggle for equal rights was never directed or dominated by one leader or organization but was rather a movement of constantly shifting alliances and ad hoc coalitions.

Arguably Louisville's single most important northern characteristic was that African Americans faced none of the typical Jim Crow restrictions on voting and indeed participated actively in elections and political party structures. Kentucky blacks gained the right to vote with the adoption of the Fifteenth Amendment in 1870, and although some

smaller communities across the state initiated poll taxes and other restrictive measures, in Louisville no organized effort overturned black
political participation. In the early years of the century, African Americans in the city remained a loyal constituency of the local Republican
Party; in 1921, for example, 99 percent of the twenty-five thousand
black registered voters belonged to the Grand Old Party. In 1917, in-
fighting among local Democrats enabled Republicans to come to power in the city and stay there until the 1930s. Composing 45 percent of
the Republican vote, blacks played a key role in the GOP's success and
could as a result win limited concessions by threatening to withhold
their support. In 1921, for example, black activists formed the Lincoln
Independent Party and attempted to woo voters away from the Republicans. The effort failed, but it convinced the administration to begin
hiring blacks in city government jobs. A few years later, Republican
leaders promised to open a campus of the University of Louisville for
black students in exchange for African American votes on an education
bond issue, a pledge that was fulfilled when Louisville Municipal College opened in 1931. Perhaps the most notable result of black support
for the Republican Party was the election of Charles W. Anderson to
the Kentucky General Assembly in 1935, the first African American
elected to a state legislature since Reconstruction.[13]

As in cities across the North and West, during the 1930s the Louisville Democratic Party began to gain black voters, in large part because of the direct economic benefits of the New Deal and the personal
appeal of Franklin D. Roosevelt. In 1936, Roosevelt won majorities of
the vote in black precincts, though with lower percentages than those in
other parts of the city. Thereafter, the Democratic Party courted African
Americans, sending a black delegate to the convention as an alternate,
airing political advertisements aimed specifically at blacks, and in the
late 1940s appointing an African American to chair the new City Colored Democratic Committee. Local Republicans continued to attract
support, however, and sought to keep it by increasing blacks' presence
on party committees. As a result, in the postwar period, blacks divided
evenly between the parties, with 47.7 percent registered as Republicans and 47.1 percent Democrats in 1956. In effect, African Americans
became a swing constituency, forcing each party to work to keep its
loyalists and recruit from the other side. The concentration of blacks in
particular neighborhoods and the delegation of aldermen and state representatives by district increased blacks' voting power and meant that

African American sections of the city could, and did, elect their own to city and state government. With these representatives in office and the potential of a black swing vote, African Americans could expect, at minimum, lip service to equality and a lack of racial demagoguery and, at best, the possibility of change through the political process.[14]

Finally, by the postwar era, many Louisvillians simply conceived of their city as more northern—or at least as less southern. More specifically, Louisville's civic leaders, both white and black, held a strong conviction that the city was more liberal and tolerant than those to the south and was a leader in racial progress. Moreover, they had some basis for celebrating the city's reputation for progress in race relations. The roots of this positive self-perception reached back to the successful protests that had integrated public transportation in 1870–1871. In the 1920s and 1930s, the black community, often working with white allies in the Commission on Interracial Cooperation, Urban League, and NAACP, won limited concessions that improved living conditions for blacks, opened a few doors in city government, and boosted black education by equalizing pay for black teachers and establishing Louisville Municipal College. Reflecting contemporary national patterns, much of this change took place within the bounds of segregation and thus did not directly challenge it. But limited successes kept lines of communication open between white and black leaders, set precedents, and led to the establishment of organizations that would contribute to more aggressive action in the future. Moreover, by World War II, the city could boast of African American elected and appointed officials, policemen, and firemen and a relative paucity of racial violence.[15] In the postwar era, white and black leaders pointed to a litany of such examples of progress, believing that they marked the city, because of its mix of regional characteristics, as a leader for the South. This positive self-image would play a central role in debates over the extent and pace of desegregation in the city.

Every local freedom struggle has its own story and a unique set of historical circumstances that shape the nature, process, and outcome of the movement. Louisville's border position and resulting mix of both southern and northern characteristics—its attachment to the South and that region's pattern of segregation combined with a more northern economy, population diversity, and politics—produced a particular civil rights struggle. Louisville lacked a dominant leader or group.

Instead, shifting alliances of people, organizations, and ad hoc coalitions conducted the struggle for black equality. The presence of liberal-minded whites in unions, in religious organizations, and among civic leaders ensured that these coalitions were often interracial. Indeed, activists persistently achieved change in the city through loosely connected interracial coalitions that organized around a particular goal while continuing to pursue different strategies and tap into different constituencies. The possibility of African American political influence convinced the activists in these coalitions to work within the political system and city government, believing they could secure legislation that could bring about equality. Finally, in campaigning for change, civil rights advocates often employed rhetoric that held the city to a higher standard, pointing to its northern character and its self-image as a model for its southern neighbors.

Local stories, while never fully representative of the movement as a whole, contribute to our understanding of it. The study of civil rights struggles in border cities that contain qualities of both northern and southern places has the particular potential for doing so because those cities' struggles serve as microcosms of the issues, strategies, and actions of the movement throughout the nation. Most scholarship on the civil rights struggle, however, has focused on southern locations or, more recently, on the North and West, and scholars have as a result paid relatively little attention to the border as a region. Nonetheless, a small number of studies that examine cities such as Baltimore, Cincinnati, and St. Louis reveal common themes and provide new insights about the national civil rights movement. First, the "gateway" cities of Baltimore and St. Louis, like Louisville, each possessed a mixed sectional identity, reflecting the presence of an industrial working class, political battles for the African American vote, and a black population that supported a large number of churches and institutions. As a result of this sectional mix, the movements in these border communities consisted of multiple leaders and organizations, producing divisions that both helped and hurt the cause. Most important, scholars have identified another sort of mixing in these communities: Civil rights advocates made few distinctions between economic and political goals and strategies. Activists did not regard these issues or efforts as separate but instead fought for equality in "concurrent contests over the various spaces." In short, in communities ranging from Baltimore in the East to St. Louis in the West—and Louisville in between—the on-the-ground and day-to-day work of civil rights activists displayed a "fluidity in ideology and practice."[16]

Because Louisville is a border city, its civil rights struggle linked northern and southern stories and thus provides insight into historiographical questions about the movement. Recent scholarship, for example, has portrayed a "window of opportunity" in the postwar South in the partnership of labor and civil rights organizations. Scholars who shift their gaze forward a few decades and to cities of the North and Midwest have demonstrated how union rules and the actions of the rank and file posed obstacles to black entry to certain trades and to government action to desegregate the schools. Louisville's story encompasses these two narratives and, in doing so, sheds light on the changing roles of labor as both an ally and opponent of the movement.[17] A number of scholars have discussed the role of southern white liberals and moderates in supporting the civil rights movement and helping to pave the way for integration, while other studies have traced the involvement of northern white clergy in promoting the cause.[18] Too often, however, these works underplay the role of white faith-based activism, particularly in the South after 1965. In Louisville, white citizens participated in the movement throughout its history—as moderates, liberals, and radicals—and their story can help scholars understand the impact of interracialism in the struggle after the height of the movement era. Finally, most literature on southern communities rightly focuses on attempts by blacks to gain the vote and on the fates of political leaders after the Voting Rights Act. In the growing literature on the struggle for racial equality in the North and West, scholars have explored black political activism, especially coalition building and the impact of black swing votes. The Louisville story provides a way to look at how activists used northern patterns of political behavior to grapple with southern problems in race relations and the extent to which they were successful in overcoming Jim Crow by doing so.[19]

Most significant, Louisville's border character and the civil rights struggle it shaped can point toward a new way of conceiving of the movement. A border can be understood not just as a dividing line but as a space where people, ideas, and experiences overlap and where differences blur. Border cities, where no single cultural or political pattern has hegemony, reveal that the distinctions between North and South, and the purportedly different racial problems in each, were not that great. The conditions pre–civil rights era African Americans faced in

Louisville, which they called a southern "approach to the Negro," were not confined to the former Confederacy. Rather, as recent scholars have amply demonstrated, de facto housing segregation, discrimination in employment, racially separate schools, and even limited access to public accommodations plagued black communities in the North and West—and these problems had existed all along, rather than emerging after 1965, when the attention of national leaders shifted there.[20] But just as problems in race relations did not neatly divide geographically into southern and northern, the manifestations of racism in housing, jobs, schools, and social relations were not separate. Instead, they were different expressions of a fundamental evil that needed to be fought and overcome concurrently.

In short, the Louisville movement demonstrates that the fight against racism and for racial equality could not be partitioned into separate battles. Instead, the coalitions working to overcome inequality, the issues they targeted, and the strategies they employed ran together into a long-term, interconnected struggle.[21] The Louisville story focuses our attention on the way civil rights activism was linked over time, replacing an image of discrete phases with a picture of multiple, simultaneous battles that proceeded in waves between periods of crisis and times of quieter organizing. That sense of connection applied across space as well, as Louisvillians claimed kinship with civil rights advocates in other cities. Equally important, collaborations among people and organizations of different races, political beliefs, and approaches to change characterized the Louisville movement. In part, interracial cooperation arose out of the city's unique history and the personalities and loyalties of the people involved, just as any local context shapes relations among activists. However, the persistent pattern of collaboration reveals that the people fighting for change did not divide themselves according to any particular ideology or identity but more often saw themselves and acted as part of a larger movement, cooperating or at least working alongside others with whom they may have differed on many points. Examining the struggle against racism over time in Louisville demonstrates that activists did not distinguish among its various manifestations and strategies to overcome it. Louisvillians saw the links among housing and schools, jobs and accommodations, the vote and direct action, fighting poverty and empowering black citizens. Moreover, they willingly combined strategies and moved from one purportedly separate movement—integration, black power, antipoverty—to another in the process of a long and, for many, ongoing struggle. The story of how they did so allows us not only to trace the different ideological perspectives at work during the movement era but also to understand how people who advocated a variety of approaches to change brought them together.

Conflict among the civil rights forces in Louisville certainly arose during this era. Activists differed in opinion and approach; they decided to work separately at times and sharply criticized one another at others. But even when they had exchanged hot words, it was not uncommon to see them then working on the same campaign, albeit in different ways. Factionalism, divided political loyalties, and generational antagonism existed, but the interconnections across time and space and among people and campaigns were in the end more characteristic of the Louisville movement. Though the connections that shaped the struggle differed in every community, the Louisville story suggests that directing our attention to such links helps to highlight the relationship among the diverse manifestations of racism, the compatibility of different strategies for overcoming it, and activists' sense of belonging to a larger and longer movement against it.

1

Postwar Campaigns for Citizens' Rights

One night in September 1950, three African Americans, Leroy Foley and Jessie Wallace of Louisville and John H. Smith of Lexington, went to Breckinridge County Hospital in Hardinsburg, Kentucky, after being in a car accident. There, they lay on the floor of the emergency room for three hours with no treatment except shots of morphine to ease their pain. Hospital officials called a black ambulance company in Louisville, seventy miles away, because, as one doctor explained, "We never admit a colored person." When Jessie Lawrence of Louisville arrived on the scene, he found that "they were lying on the hard concrete tile with not even a blanket under them. Their wounds had not been treated; the blood had not been wiped from their hands and faces." Foley died on the floor. Smith was still suffering from a broken back four months later.[1]

A few days later, when the incident was reported in Louisville's black newsweekly, the *Defender,* Mary Agnes Barnett, the wife of the chair of the local Progressive Party, read about it and declared, "This is one Negro that isn't going to put up with this any longer. We've got to do something about it." Enlisting her friend Anne Braden, a fellow Progressive Party member, she launched a drive to force hospitals in the state to accept patients without regard to race.[2] The campaign, a biracial effort from the start in the persons of Barnett and Braden, grew into the Interracial Hospital Movement (IHM), a coalition of over thirty black, white, and mixed organizations that pursued desegregation of medical facilities through appeals to the governor, legislation, and legal action. The IHM united militant integrated unions, the Progressive Party, students from white and black universities, church groups, and civil rights organizations from around the state but primarily from Louisville. They argued that African Americans, as voters and citizens, had a right to equal treatment in and access to the hospitals, as they did to other tax-supported facilities. Once won, the desegregation of medical institutions became part of a litany of achievements by which Louisvillians expressed pride in their racial progress and position as a leader for the South, and a justification for further advances.

The story of the IHM contains many of the elements characteristic of the early civil rights movement in postwar Louisville. There had long been organized pressure in the city for political recognition and improved conditions for blacks within segregation, but after the war black leaders and their white allies began to demand with increased assertiveness equal economic opportunity, nondiscriminatory access to public facilities, and a place at the legislative table. As in the IHM, a variety of black, white, and biracial worker, religious, youth, and civic organizations came together in ad hoc interracial coalitions to target specific problems, developing a tradition in the city of white and black cooperation in equal rights campaigns. In this period, Louisville activists argued that African Americans as citizens had the right to equal access to tax-supported jobs and facilities, identifying them as two linked manifestations of government-enforced Jim Crow. Piecemeal success in these areas laid the groundwork for the city's progressive self-image as a leader for the South in race relations, an image that played a significant role in struggles throughout the movement era. At the same time, frustrations over the limits and pace of change brought civil rights leaders to the edge of demanding integration in private spaces as well. Undergirding these efforts against Jim Crow and preparing the way for pressure for desegregation through city and state legislation was the increasingly active role of blacks in local politics. This period, then, helped to define the Louisville civil rights struggle as a movement of interracial coalitions strengthened by black political involvement that pressured government to end segregation.

The interracial cooperation that characterized Louisville's postwar civil rights movement took place in three overlapping coalitions: left-wing and labor organizations, secular and government-sponsored agencies, and church and youth groups. These coalitions were made up of a wide variety of organizations. The NAACP and Urban League were relatively enduring bodies with links to national headquarters, though they had periods of varying levels of engagement, depending on the officers' aggressiveness.[3] At times shorter-lived, indigenous groups such as the MCM took over leadership, though they lacked formal membership and—frustrating the historian—did not keep records. Of these local groups, a few, such as the KBNA and JCSSA, were the vehicles of charismatic individuals who brought people out for particular protest campaigns. Over the years, many smaller groups, such as the Committee of Fifteen and Committee of United Blacks, emerged, engaged in a particular campaign, and faded from the scene. Judging the size and composition of these various civil rights organizations is largely impossible. But what hampers the scholar often helped the cause. During periods of mass mobilization, representatives from these diverse groups came together in formal coalitions or committees that appealed to and united a large number of constituencies, utilized the skills of different leaders, and provided a wide base for the movement.

In the postwar era, the left-labor coalition involved the Progressive Party and a collection of CIO unions, including the United Farm Equipment Workers (FE) at International Harvester, transportation workers, furniture workers, and public workers. The MCM, an ostensibly religious group formed in 1951 to bring "the moral sanctions of the religion of Christ on the battle against segregation," initially focused on labor issues and joined the labor coalition. In addition, black activists quickly established the Louisville area Negro Labor Council (NLC) to push for jobs for African Americans in industry shortly after the national group's formation in Cincinnati in 1951.[4] Because of its base in working-class organizations, the coalition gave priority to fighting discrimination in employment. But members also challenged Jim Crow in the community: FE workers held integrated picnics; the Progressive Party propelled the effort to open hospitals to African Americans; and the MCM started agitating for the desegregation of public schools even before *Brown v. Board of Education*. Blacks and whites in these groups also went beyond civil rights issues to address cold war concerns including the H-bomb and the Korean War.[5]

The work of the Louisville labor–civil rights coalition exemplifies what some scholars have called a window of opportunity for change in the racial and economic status quo of the South. Across the region, the Southern Tenant Farmers' Union, the Southern Conference for Human Welfare, Highlander Folk School, and integrated CIO unions, among others, challenged the entwined problems of racism and the oppression of the working class. The rising anti-Communist crusade that beat back both unionists and civil rights advocates cut short the challenge, however.[6] In Louisville, for example, the FE lost the leadership of the International Harvester plant to the United Auto Workers after years of red- and race-baiting. Shortly thereafter, the city's red scare targeted white and black activists and cost the movement both personnel and energy.[7] Despite these setbacks, the militant community contributed concrete results in the integration of hospitals and parks, and component organizations within the coalition continued to fight segregation in collaboration with more moderate and liberal groups. Although its leadership was dominated by middle-class professionals, the local NAACP worked with the activist unions in desegregation campaigns, for example. Moreover, individuals in these coalitions continued to participate in local movement activity for the next two decades. For example, the Reverend M. M. D. Perdue, leader of the MCM; Andrew Wade of the Progressive Party; and IHM organizer and FE women's auxiliary member Anne Braden later formed the adult nucleus of the local Congress of Racial Equality (CORE). Finally, this labor and civil rights cooperation set a precedent for white radical–black militant cooperation that recurred periodically through Louisville's long civil rights movement.

While militant blacks and whites cooperated in labor and left-wing organizations, more moderate Louisvillians met in secular liberal groups, at times created or sanctioned by local government. Heightened interest in improved racial and religious relations at the end of the war gave rise to a burst of such activity. In late 1945, J. Mansir Tydings, a white Quaker who would be a leader of liberal interracialism in Louisville for decades to come, wrote to officials at the Southern Regional Council (SRC) boasting that Kentucky had thirty local biracial organizations. The Louisville leadership of this movement became more closely tied to a regional network when the Kentucky Commission on Interracial Cooperation (KCIC) joined the SRC in January 1946, pledging to follow that organization's agenda of improving "economic, civic, and racial conditions in Kentucky." Louisvillians hosted community forums and funneled proposed legislation through African American state representative Charles Anderson to the Kentucky General Assembly. The group also started working on issues related to the schools as early as 1947, with a series of programs on race relations for young people. The KCIC enjoyed the support of prominent whites in the community, including *Courier-Journal* publisher Barry Bingham and Hugh A. Brimm of the social service commission of the Southern Baptist Convention.[8]

In the immediate wake of the war, there also occurred an expansion of interracial activity within youth and church groups. In December 1945, a group of students from the black high school Central High, a Catholic youth group, the Young Men's Hebrew Association, the Young Women's Christian Association, and the Young Men's Christian Association came together to hold forums on "interracial and interfaith relations." After the first meeting, the young people pledged "to treat all men with the respect due them as children of God" and urged "equal economic and educational opportunities"—although they held back from condemning segregation per se.[9] The faith-based roots of this organization linked it to a broader phenomenon: the small but growing subculture among area churches promoting interracial fellowship. In the postwar South, this minority subculture developed mainly on college campuses, embodied in institutions such as the annual Brotherhood Week, when young people heard traveling ministers speak on new approaches to race and international relations.[10] White Louisvillians heard about these topics and met with their black coreligionists in weekly fellowship hours at Louisville Presbyterian Theological Seminary, monthly interracial interdenominational worship services, and "community clinics." The latter were workshops sponsored by the local units of the Federal Council of Churches and National Council of Christians and Jews during which participants engaged in "an interracial, interfaith process of community self-analysis," attempting to identify problems in race and religious relations and develop solutions.[11]

To a great extent, these meetings generated little more than talk. And, like the interracial work of unionists and leftists, only a minority of churchgoers participated in this subculture. But these encounters did put white and black Louisvillians together and gave them chances to share perspectives. Most important, these meetings and the relationships forged at them produced allies for campaigns to improve race relations. White Methodist women, for example, joined the Fellowship of the Concerned and promised to monitor the courts for mistreatment of blacks.[12] Some of these mixed religious organizations worked together to integrate the schools. Finally, like the more militant labor and left-wing coalition, the white-black fellowship of the postwar period set a precedent for faith-based interracial cooperation in major integration campaigns of the coming decades.

In the ten years after World War II, these coalitions, led by African American civil rights organizations, focused their attention on fighting discrimination in tax-supported jobs and public facilities. One of the primary concerns of African American leaders coming out of the war was guaranteeing black veterans and others access to good jobs. Despite increases in industrial employment and wartime efforts to ensure nondiscrimination in the defense industry, postwar surveys by the Urban League revealed a persistent gap between white and black economic opportunity. Since 1940 little had changed in the employment status of African Americans, largely because employers continued to resist hiring blacks, even veterans, and few unions allowed them to join as members. As a result, of the job placements recorded by the local office of the U.S. Employment Service by 1948, for example, blacks filled only 4 percent of the skilled jobs, while 42 percent of the service positions went to African Americans.[13]

Activists in Louisville first sought to challenge this pattern of discrimination by enacting a fair employment law. In 1945 and 1946, Louisvillians partnered with activists across the country to lobby for an extension of Franklin Roosevelt's wartime Fair Employment Practices Commission (FEPC). Local leaders sponsored rallies at area churches at which ministers, educators, and national speakers criticized southern senators' opposition to the FEPC and praised Kentucky senator Alben Barkley for supporting it. When southern senators filibustered to death the effort to extend the FEPC in February 1946, the local Franklin D. Roosevelt Independent Voters League, a black political club, vowed to press for its revival through petitions and mass meetings.[14] The issue rose again in 1952, when the NLC spearheaded a short-lived drive for a new FEPC. The FE at International Harvester circulated petitions and sent workers into the streets in biracial teams to knock on doors and gather support. The union urged strong worker participation because, it argued, "It is the duty of this union and every union in America to fight for fair practices on all jobs." The union's paper later boasted that nine of ten workers signed the petitions. Nevertheless, the measure failed again.[15]

Shortly thereafter, a coalition of Louisville organizations pressed the board of aldermen to adopt a city ordinance guaranteeing fair employment. Spokesman Chester Higgins, the executive secretary of the

Louisville NLC, argued that erasing racial discrimination in the workplace would benefit the entire community. He claimed the "southern differential"—the lower salaries in southern plants compared to those in northern ones—resulted from the lower wages paid to black workers and kept white pay low as well. In response, the board of aldermen used a technicality—the proposal had not been formally written as an ordinance—to stall. During the fall of 1952, the fair employment proposal garnered support from the FE and from H. A. I. Rosenberg, a white independent candidate for Congress who characterized job discrimination in Louisville as "vicious." Despite the efforts of the labor-civil rights coalition, the one black alderman, William Beckett, could not get the measure out of committee and onto the agenda for a vote. Fair employment legislation for the city thus languished and died.[16]

Stymied in the effort to secure equal opportunity through legislation, Louisville civil rights workers and community organizations focused their efforts on particular employers' policies, making the new General Electric plant one of the first targets. When GE decided to build in the area, executives promised that the plant, projected to build jet engines for the U.S. military, would employ up to fifteen thousand workers and would not discriminate by race. Within a year the company hired fifteen hundred employees, including only a few African Americans, none of whom held skilled positions. The MCM initiated protests a few months after GE began hiring, while the Urban League began negotiations with the company. When those organizations made little headway, others joined them. National officers of the NLC came to the city to lead rallies to pressure company officials; they feared that if GE did not hire African Americans early in the process, they would never acquire the seniority needed to provide them with job security. In addition, a short-lived local group representing black churches and white and black unions, the Citizens Committee on Fair Employment, tried unsuccessfully to get the company to guarantee blacks 15.2 percent of the skilled work, reflecting their proportion of the city population. GE responded that it did not keep records and thus could not say with certainty how many African Americans it employed.[17]

Despite these setbacks, some developments at GE in the early 1950s gave hope to civil rights activists. First, the International Union of Electrical Workers, CIO, won the right to represent the plant's workers and included in the contract a clause stating that the company and union would not discriminate based on race, religion, or national origin. In late 1953 the NAACP reported that GE had begun to hire additional African Americans. Continued discrimination, however, convinced officials in the Louisville NLC to ask the President's Committee on Government Contract Compliance to investigate the company's hiring policies. They argued that because the plant produced defense components, even if they were assembled elsewhere, it was in effect an agent for the government and therefore could not discriminate. The president's committee agreed to investigate, but the situation did not change. As of 1955, prospects for black workers had hardly improved. The campaign failed to achieve equal employment at GE but nonetheless illustrated a pattern that would be repeated throughout the civil rights era: a number of ad hoc and more enduring black and white organizations, including representatives from national groups, worked with and independently of each other toward a common goal.[18]

While these organizations targeted discrimination in industry, others focused on the civil service. In 1951 attorney Harry McAlpin, president of the Louisville NAACP, launched a protest against the practice of listing city jobs as "white only" or "colored only." Although the board of aldermen agreed and asked the civil service to change its practices, the director, Franklin Weir, declined, citing local custom and the fear that "more harm than good might be done" because white people were not ready for such a move. The local NAACP sponsored a rally of two thousand people in response to the rebuff. Black leaders continued to press the issue, drawing on the city's burgeoning progressive reputation by arguing that "the Louisville community, both Negroes and Whites, is far more advanced in its attitude toward right and justice" than the civil service board was giving it credit for. They also pointedly threatened political consequences for failure to act. As a columnist in the *Louisville Defender* put it, "We want to see some of these candidates we're voting for repay that support." Nearly three years later, the civil service department quietly removed the race designations from job listings. Denying that years of NAACP pressure had any impact, Mayor Andrew Broaddus claimed he made the change because "I just thought it was the right thing to do." There were some signs of improvement: the civil service office fulfilled a promise to hire black women as clerk-typists; the city assigned black firemen to white rather than segregated units; and the city safety director announced that police jobs would be filled "without regard for race." Yet not three months later, Broaddus defended a parks department decision to deny three African Americans jobs, stating he did not want to go too fast or be charged with "trying to change Louisville over night."[19]

Black leaders had some success in securing city jobs because they could bring political pressure to bear against government-sponsored discrimination. Likewise, they made limited headway in procuring industrial jobs because of the influence of unions. However, they made almost no progress with private business. The JCSSA, under the Reverend Daniel Hughlett, initiated a campaign to get Louisville Transit Company—a private company with a franchise from the city—to hire black drivers. The JCSSA had begun as a religious education group in 1925, but in the late 1930s under Hughlett, it began addressing race relations, particularly job discrimination. Its effort to gain transit company positions for blacks went nowhere, however, after the head of the company refused to "yield to pressure tactics" and showed no willingness to change his policies.[20]

The general manager of the phone company displayed similar intransigence, claiming it was "against public policy" to hire blacks as operators. In an early display of his assertiveness, Frank Stanley Sr. of the *Louisville Defender* urged people to pay their bills in pennies, discontinue their service, and generally engage in "persistent and intelligent harassment." On this issue and on others over the next two decades, Stanley would use the *Defender* to prod the black community to protest discrimination, making him one of the leading voices for civil rights in the community. Born in 1906, Stanley grew up in Louisville before moving to Atlanta and Cincinnati for school. After working as an English professor at Jackson College in Mississippi, he returned to Louisville to teach at all-black Central High School. In the early 1930s, he became a reporter for the *Defender*, and in 1936 he bought the majority of shares in the company, becoming the newspaper's owner, publisher, and editor until his death in 1974. Throughout his career he set the tone of the paper, using his column People, Places and Problems to articulate the demands of the movement and advocate for political and legislative solutions to the problems of Jim Crow.[21]

In 1956, phone company officials hinted at a change in policy when they interviewed African American women as operators. The company interviewed "scores" of black women but, despite a shortage of operators, hired none.[22] Such resistance convinced civil rights leaders to consider using the buying power of the black community to cajole retail businesses to integrate their staffs. In 1952 the NAACP and Urban League demonstrated that the A&P grocery chain depended on blacks for over 30 percent of its business. A year later, the *Defender* asserted that Louisville's African Americans spent $70 million a year on consumer goods. Most individual businesses recognized the significance of black buying power, but few made any changes. By the mid-1950s, continual failures left black leaders like Stanley despairing of the prospect for equal employment without a city ordinance making it "unlawful for any place open to the public . . . to deny Negroes full employment all the way up the line."[23]

Civil rights groups in Louisville made relatively greater progress integrating public facilities, though it took a combination of public pressure, legislation, and legal action, and success remained restricted to tax-supported and city-owned property. The first major coordinated public campaign began in fall 1950 when, as noted above, Mary Agnes Barnett and Anne Braden decided to work to ensure blacks access to the hospitals. Before 1951 Louisville's African Americans could use only the Red Cross Hospital, which was the "black" facility, and one segregated ward at Louisville General Hospital, the training hospital of the University of Louisville medical school. Segregated hospitals not only endangered the health of black citizens but also complicated medical education, since neither black nurses nor doctors could train in white facilities. The education situation began to change by the late 1940s, when legislators amended the state Day Law to permit integrated nursing programs. African Americans faced an even worse situation in small-town and rural Kentucky, where white-only hospitals routinely denied blacks access even to emergency treatment.[24]

Barnett and Braden began their effort with a petition drive, which Braden called a great "organizing tool." On her broken-down bicycle, she delivered petitions to grocery stores and drugstores and visited the Louisville Area Baptist Ministers and Deacons, a group of African American pastors of small black churches that would sporadically engage in civil rights advocacy over the years. Next, she enlisted the priest from the white Episcopal church she attended, the Reverend Albert Dalton. Students from the Southern Baptist Theological Seminary, Louisville Municipal College, and University of Louisville; unionized truck drivers and public workers; and black insurance agents soon helped circulate the petitions. The drive went so well that the organizers decided to launch an independent organization, the IHM, to coordinate it, cochaired by instigator Barnett and the Reverend J. C. Olden. A black

Baptist minister and leader of the MCM, Olden declared at the founding meeting, "We're going to stop people from dying because they can't get into the hospitals." To promote the campaign, the IHM sponsored the Brotherhood Rally, at which speakers from unions, churches, and local universities spoke to two hundred people who pledged "to deal with all human beings without prejudice." In January 1951 the drive culminated in a mass march in Frankfort, Kentucky, where protesters presented Governor Lawrence W. Wetherby with petitions containing over ten thousand names collected by over thirty organizations in fifty-six towns and cities across the state.[25]

Success came to the IHM in increments. Shortly after receiving the petitions, the governor opened Louisville's Hazelwood Tuberculosis Sanatorium to blacks, and by the end of the spring, other sanatoriums around the state followed suit. Next, the governor opened state-operated hospitals, though they represented less than one-third of the 144 hospitals in Kentucky. To prod private hospitals to follow that example, the IHM called for enforcement of the federal Hill-Burton Act, which outlawed discrimination in hospitals that received federal money, and enlisted NAACP lawyers to help with "laying the groundwork" for legal action. Shortly thereafter, the all-white Kentucky Medical Association called for the state legislature to open all hospitals to blacks. In the face of such pressure, the state assembly passed a law in February 1952 opening all state-licensed hospitals to African Americans.[26]

Throughout the campaign to gain African Americans' access to hospitals, the IHM argued that tax-supported institutions could not discriminate and that the Kentucky constitution specified that tax money could be "used for public, non-exclusive purposes only." Thus when any tax-supported institution served only one part of the public, it did so illegally, and the governor had a responsibility to stop it. After the movement succeeded in getting state-operated hospitals opened, leaders took the argument a step further and asserted that all tax-exempt institutions could not discriminate. In a legal brief for the IHM, Alfred Carroll, a black World War II veteran and lawyer for the NAACP, and white attorney Robert Zollinger highlighted a section of the state tax law that prohibited "special privileges" to argue that private hospitals could not get tax exemptions if they "refuse charity to a segment of the public." The IHM had a case it could take to court to force the desegregation of such facilities, but the new state licensing law made a lawsuit unnecessary.[27]

Activists used the argument that tax-paying African Americans had the right to equal access to public places as a key weapon in the battle to desegregate other city- and Jefferson County–owned facilities—though with mixed results. In early 1953 the KBNA, led by Bishop C. Eubank Tucker of the AME Zion Church, launched a letter-writing campaign to gain equal access to all facilities in county office buildings. Born in the British West Indies, Tucker grew up in Jamaica and came to the United States to study at Lincoln and Temple universities. He became a minister in the AME Zion Church in 1918 and served pastorates in the South as well as in Pennsylvania and Indiana before coming to Louisville's Stoner Memorial Church. By the 1930s he had become a bishop in the church and conducted a successful law practice defending black clients around the state. In one case, he confronted a threatening mob while defending an African American accused of killing a white farmer in Elizabethtown. He also became involved in Republican Party politics. After complaining that local Republicans did not nominate black candidates, he ran unsuccessfully in 1933 for the same seat in the Kentucky legislature that Charles Anderson won two years later. The incident did not diminish his loyalty to the Republicans, however, and he envisioned the KBNA, which he formed in 1940, as an alternative to the Democratic-leaning NAACP. By the early 1950s, the organization's pledge to conduct a "militant fight against segregation" attracted over three thousand members in the state. In the campaign to obtain black access to county facilities, Tucker achieved near immediate success; "white" and "colored" signs came down in county offices within a month.[28]

The NAACP's long fight to desegregate the city-owned Memorial Auditorium turned out less well. Immediately after the war, the group, joined by the black teachers' organization, decided to target the tax-supported facility, picketing at and boycotting particular shows with black performers such as Sugar Chile Robinson and black casts such as *Carmen Jones*. However, the protests made little impact. The state attorney general and the city argued that the auditorium had the right to segregate. Over the next decade, the city assumed the position that although the facility was tax-supported, the private business interests that produced the programs could choose to separate their audiences.[29]

In the late 1940s and early 1950s, civil rights activists spent more time on attempts to integrate public parks than on any other public facility other than schools. Louisville had an extensive park system designed early in the century by Frederick Law Olmsted's firm. The parks had originally been open to all, but in 1924 the parks commission had decided to set aside Chickasaw Park for African Americans and make the remaining city parks white-only. Although the commission's decision lacked the force of law, city police enforced the rule by forcing blacks and mixed groups to leave white-only parks. Between the end of World War II and the desegregation of the parks in 1956, local activists in a variety of organizations combined informal direct action, political appeals, and legal action to alter the policy.[30] Interracial organizations and those aligned with the Progressive Party sparked the first postwar attempts to desegregate the parks. In July 1946, Youth in Action, an "inter-faith and inter-racial" group of students inspired by the pluralistic rhetoric of the war years, wrote to director of parks and recreation T. Byrne Morgan and Mayor Leland Taylor asking permission to hold a biracial picnic in a park. The mayor turned down the students' request, arguing that such an event would create racial strife. A few years later, another group of young people, the New Voters for Wallace, asked the new mayor, Charles Farnsley, to change park policy, without success. One member, John Stubbs, a veteran and student at Louisville Municipal College, committed his own act of civil disobedience by playing tennis in a white-only park, for which he was arrested and fined. Older members of the Progressive Party joined the cause when its civil rights committee announced its intention to hold its own mixed picnic. Opponents of integration called the move a mere political gambit to draw attention to the Wallace campaign. More ominously, the committee received word that individuals associated with the Republican Party were threatening to use the picnic to stir up violence and use the violence to hurt the Progressives' political campaign. Meanwhile, city safety director David A. McCandless announced that he had it on good authority that "a communist goon squad" planned to incite a riot at the picnic. In response, the civil rights committee decided to cancel the event.[31]

After the failure of these efforts, the NAACP tried legal action. In 1947 an African American dentist, P. O. Sweeney, backed by the local branch, filed a suit in Jefferson Circuit Court to end segregation in the parks. The suit argued that it was unconstitutional for the city to deny African Americans the use of tax-supported parks. The Kentucky Court of Appeals decided against Sweeney, ruling that he had sued for a private rather than constitutional right. Undeterred, in March

1950 the NAACP launched a new suit, this time in federal court, with three plaintiffs: Sweeney, who had been barred from a white-only golf course; Mona Carroll, the fourteen-year-old daughter of civil rights lawyer Alfred Carroll, who wanted to fish in a white-only park; and James Muir, who had been denied entry to a performance at the amphitheater in white-only Iroquois Park. In each case, there was no "separate but equal" facility for blacks.[32] Some African Americans grumbled about the decision to focus on integrating the golf courses, which one man said was just a way for professional "big Negroes" to set themselves apart from other blacks.[33] Benjamin Shobe, the attorney on the suit, explained that the NAACP looked for issues it could win, and that meant focusing on obvious differences in facilities. The plaintiffs did not have a burning desire to use a golf course, but they sought a clear case of inequality and trusted that the city would rather integrate than build new facilities. Shobe hoped that a victory would lead to similar outcomes in other areas.[34]

The park issue followed a long and tortuous path toward resolution, in part because the city fought to maintain as much segregation as possible. From the beginning, city officials, including director of parks Morgan and a string of mayors, defended park segregation by warning that mixing would lead to violence and damage local race relations. In response to the civil rights committee's plan to hold an interracial picnic, Mayor Farnsley claimed he had received letters "displaying active hostile sentiments against the Negro race" and threatening a riot. Safety director McCandless suggested the issue be resolved peacefully through the courts, but the city responded to the lawsuits in a similar fashion. When Sweeney launched his first challenge, the city's law director, Gilbert Burnett, vowed to fight. He insisted Louisville had "the best race relations of any large city," and he intended to keep it that way by avoiding "flare-ups" that would result from a change in policy. Local officials also claimed that the city possessed equal facilities for blacks, that the amphitheater itself was privately owned and thus they could not control its policies, and that no court had ruled segregation unconstitutional. Most commonly, however, city officials claimed they had to continue separation to preserve Louisville's good relations and "protect" blacks. Louisville's reputation for good race relations, then, required that the city deny African Americans equal access to the parks.[35]

Black leaders turned such arguments on their head. Louisville's progress in race relations and its position as a leader for the South, they retorted, argued best for integrating parks. In making their case, civil rights advocates invoked Louisville's border position, linking it with similarly situated communities and emphasizing its difference from communities in the South. If whites and blacks could mix in Cincinnati, Indianapolis, and St. Louis—northern and nearby border cities that the civil rights community consistently used as benchmarks, where the relationship between the races was "not better than it is in Louisville"—then certainly they could do so in Louisville. Indeed, black spokesmen expressed indignation at the insult implied in officials' fear of riots. "Louisville is too fine a city," black leaders insisted, for such a thing to happen there, and by predicting violence, officials made local citizens look like the "hoodlums of South Carolina, Georgia, and Florida." Louisville had already proved itself better than that, they insisted. Editorial writers and civil rights spokesmen repeatedly pointed out that in many public spaces, including Churchill Downs, streetcars, county offices, and libraries, blacks and whites mixed without incident. Now it was time for the city to take the next step.[36]

In fall 1951 federal district court judge Roy Shelbourne heard the NAACP lawsuit and issued a temporary ruling allowing blacks access to city park golf courses. Instead of opening the white courses immediately, the city decided to build a course in the black park. However, in January 1952, following a precedent established by a Texas case, Shelbourne ordered the immediate integration of the golf courses.[37] City officials reluctantly relented but fought to limit the ruling by convincing the judge to drop Mona Carroll's case because of the existence of a fishing pond at the black-only park and James Muir's case because of the private management of the Iroquois Park amphitheater. The NAACP appealed the amphitheater decision, arguing that the city built the facility and thus the private managers could not discriminate there. Two years later, although the case was still pending, the Louisville Park Theatrical Association, which managed the theater, decided on its own to admit blacks. This was the decision of a private body; the city had not conceded any additional integration. Nevertheless, because it was the one example of "voluntary" change that could be pointed to, the Louisville Courier-Journal latched onto it as proof that "events are moving toward fairness and reason." In a less congratulatory response, the Louisville Defender pointed out that black access to a facility built with public funds still depended on the "whim" of a private owner.[38]

More important, the parks as a whole were still segregated. Blacks could drive through Iroquois Park to get to the amphitheater but could not stop to have a picnic on the way. Compounding the problem, city officials made plans to build new swimming pools in white-only parks. And in a move that seemed guaranteed to provoke reaction, director of parks Morgan reversed a standing policy and ordered that there could be no more racially mixed sporting events even in the black park, thus denying Central High School's teams a venue for their games. A flurry of lawsuits resulted. Harry McAlpin, former president of the local NAACP, tried a novel approach. On behalf of Hyburnia Moorman, a light-skinned African American with blue eyes who claimed she did not know whether she could gain admission to the park, he sought an injunction against police enforcement of segregation. McAlpin argued that if the city could not enforce the policy against Moorman, it should not exclude anyone. The circuit judge ruled against her. Meanwhile, C. Eubank Tucker filed a suit on behalf of Andrew Wade Jr. to prohibit the use of tax funds to build segregated pools. The judge dropped the suit, ruling that no African Americans had yet been denied admission to the unbuilt pools. Finally, the NAACP, inspired by the 1954 *Brown v. Board of Education* decision, and after failed appeals to the new mayor, Andrew Broaddus, filed a suit on behalf of a group of black parents charging that segregation in the parks was unconstitutional.[39]

In November 1955 the U.S. Supreme Court agreed, ruling in a case from Richmond, Virginia, that the segregation of public parks was illegal. The *Louisville Courier-Journal* hailed the decision as the "death knell for racial segregation in all places supported by public funding." But the city dragged its feet as Mayor Broaddus and director of parks Morgan declined comment and waited for further instructions from the court. Within a month, the Kentucky Court of Appeals followed the new precedent and ruled in favor of the NAACP. Responding to this final nail in the coffin for the city's public park policy, the mayor announced that, a year before, he had instructed the police not to enforce segregation. He asserted he had done so without making an announcement because "we wanted this change to grow gradually" and to avoid violence. Unimpressed, the president of the local NAACP suggested the mayor would have deserved credit if he had acted before pending court decisions forced his hand. As for the likelihood of violence, in early June the *Defender* boasted that there was not "a single untoward incident interracially" when the swimming pools opened. Just two weeks later, however, a mob of twenty whites attacked two park employees supervising a game between white and black softball teams in Shively, a new suburban subdivision that would soon be at the forefront of racial tension in the metro area.[40]

Although the *Louisville Courier-Journal* praised the "voluntary" opening of the Iroquois Park amphitheater and the mayor insisted that the city had opened the parks on its own—just very quietly—the real force behind the integration of these public spaces came from federal court decisions. The federal case from Texas broke the golf course impasse, and *Brown v. Board of Education* provided momentum as black leaders eagerly read in it the unconstitutionality of segregation in any public facility. Taunting local officials, the *Louisville Defender* editors linked the two issues: "Once our schools become mixed all sensible people will see how ridiculous separate parks are." Lower federal courts apparently agreed. The U.S. Court of Appeals for the Fourth Circuit ruled in a case from Virginia that "segregated parks, like segregated schools, are unconstitutional," a decision that further discouraged private leasers of public parks from discriminating. A similar case a few months earlier had integrated a private amusement park in nearby Cincinnati. In an attempt to postpone what was clearly inevitable, city officials maintained that the court of appeals' decision did not apply to Kentucky and was thus irrelevant. Not long thereafter, the Supreme Court park ruling concluded the long local battle. Despite last-minute city resistance, the NAACP's legal strategy had succeeded.[41]

The state's public universities constituted another category of tax-supported facility that Louisville and other Kentucky civil rights activists worked to desegregate through legal pressure backed by federal court action. At first, African American leaders sought to achieve the integration of higher education in the state through legislation. During the war, an effort to end segregation in graduate and professional schools made surprising headway in Frankfort. In February 1944 Charles Anderson introduced a bill to amend the Day Law to allow blacks to attend graduate and professional schools. Invoking the goals of the global war, Anderson urged, "If we are to speak of democracy to the world, then let us have democracy at home." In more practical terms, he pointed out that in light of the Supreme Court's insistence that postgraduate training for blacks be equalized or integrated, allowing African Americans into the University of Louisville or University of Kentucky would save the state the estimated $1 million it would take to upgrade the state's institution for African Americans, Kentucky State College in Frankfort. The *Courier-Journal* endorsed the measure, the KCIC made it the centerpiece of its work, and one state legislator declared it part of the fight "for the four freedoms of democracy." The state house of representatives passed the measure forty-one to forty, a move hailed as the "first favorable effort in any legislature of the South to abolish segregation and discrimination in education by legislative action."[42]

When supporters geared up to fight for the measure in the state senate, however, they hit a surprising roadblock. The first sign of trouble appeared when the Louisville NAACP branch voted to support the bill. Two members of the executive committee, however, William Warley, the editor of the *Louisville News* and an antisegregation leader since his role in the 1917 *Buchanan v. Warley* case, and Stephen A. Burnley, supported a rival bill to raise the funding of Kentucky State College and make it the equal of the University of Kentucky. Through his newspaper, Warley argued that the Anderson bill would allow Kentucky blacks to languish in unequal schools through college and would benefit only the small number of African Americans who sought postgraduate degrees. Improving Kentucky State, he maintained, would benefit a greater number of blacks. Both bills died in senate committees. The cosponsor of the Anderson bill reported that the apparent division in the black community gave opponents an excuse to vote against both measures.[43]

After the war, activists around the state redoubled their efforts to improve and integrate higher education. Early victories in the legislature increased out-of-state tuition grants and funding for nurses' training and Kentucky State. Most important for establishing momentum in the fight against educational exclusion, the legislature amended the Day Law to allow hospitals to admit black doctors and nurses for training. Then, in 1948, in the wake of a court order that the University of Oklahoma School of Law admit an African American, the local NAACP, under its president Lyman Johnson, decided to press for admission of blacks to Kentucky professional schools, preferably by persuasion but through legal action if necessary.[44]

At that time Johnson was a history teacher at Central High School. Born in Columbia, Tennessee, Johnson as young man considered Louisville a future home because he believed it might be more liberal than any place in his home state. After receiving a master's degree in history from the University of Michigan, he moved to Louisville in the 1930s to begin a long career in education. He also became an activist almost immediately after he arrived in the city. In 1939 he became president of the Louisville Association of Teachers in Colored Schools and helped to spearhead a campaign for the equalization of teacher pay. Then he got involved in the NAACP and, with an eye to the trend on the Court, decided it was time to push the University of Kentucky to open its doors and offered himself as a plaintiff.[45]

Johnson applied for admission to the graduate program in history at the University of Kentucky. Initially the state tried to avoid integrating by proposing a joint University of Kentucky–Kentucky State College program in which black students would take their classes at the latter school. African American leaders rejected the idea and filed suit against the university. In March 1949 federal district court judge H. Church Ford ruled that the state's flagship university had to admit all races until such time as truly equal facilities existed elsewhere. University trustees briefly considered resistance, but the trend of Supreme Court decisions convinced them to acquiesce to the admission of African Americans.[46]

With this victory in the Johnson case, the Louisville NAACP turned its attention closer to home, to the University of Louisville. A municipal institution, the university had grown from a collection of professional schools and, in the postwar era, expanded in both total number of students—it hovered just under ten thousand in the decade after the war—and academic programs. The NAACP first tried to negotiate integration but, when that failed, began investigating angles for a lawsuit. At the same time, university officials debated the issue behind the scenes. Based on his personal belief in the unconstitutionality of the Day Law, Wilson Wyatt, the wartime mayor and now a trustee, moved that the school open its doors to African Americans. Other trustees objected, but the deans of the different colleges supported the move, as did many faculty, who submitted a petition in favor signed by forty-five professors. As a result, the university investigated the possibility of a test case of the Day Law and began to work for an amendment that would allow colleges and universities to make their own policies.[47]

Meanwhile, outside the university, public pressure for change was building. Civic leaders, including the publisher of the *Courier-Journal,* expressed "qualified support" for open universities. A more direct endorsement came from the head of the Kentucky Federation of Labor, who pointedly asked the trustees to integrate. The main barrier to change was shattered in the spring of 1950, when state legislators amended the Day Law to give colleges and universities the right to open their doors to both blacks and whites. Thereafter, a wave of desegregation swept the city. Local Catholic colleges and seminaries began accepting black students, and the University of Louisville pledged to integrate its graduate programs in the fall of 1950 and its undergraduate programs one year later.[48]

As part of the plan to open the school to black students, officials decided to close Louisville Municipal College and accept those students, should they choose to transfer, into the University of Louisville. This decision sparked an immediate controversy because of its impact on the municipal college's faculty. Initially, University of Louisville officials, who had authority because Louisville Municipal College was a branch campus, planned to fire all of the municipal faculty and give them two months' severance pay. Understandably, the professors objected, and they hired Harry McAlpin to pursue a lawsuit against the university, charging breach of contract. While local black leaders criticized the university's decision and called on the school to hire black faculty, they also declared this "sacrifice for posterity" necessary for the cause of integration. Students weighed in on the side of the professors, however, asking administrators to hire at least some black faculty to make the climate at their new school more welcoming and their transition easier. The newly hired University of Louisville president, Philip Davidson, sought to diffuse the tension by hiring faculty member Charles C. Parrish Jr. of the sociology department at Louisville Municipal College and arranging yearlong fellowships for the others. Only two refused the plan, but Davidson secured a deal in which they were paid a year's salary and were helped to find teaching positions elsewhere. With the matter disposed of, the university welcomed Parrish as its first, and for a long time only, black faculty member and opened its doors to the municipal college students who wanted and could afford to attend. The controversy was a harbinger, however, of a later crisis at the university over its reluctance to hire, and its treatment of, African American staff.[49]

A final battle in which federal pressures buttressed the work of local activists was the integration of transportation facilities. Because city buses were not segregated, activists paid little attention to the situation on the actual carriers, though local people did participate in suits against trains and buses leaving Louisville for other southern states.[50] Instead, local groups worked to open waiting rooms and lunch counters in terminals. Because these were operated by private businesses, this campaign directed the movement away from targeting tax-supported institutions and toward attacking private segregation. After leading the coalition that opened the hospitals, the MCM tried a persuasive approach, asking Greyhound bus company officials to end segregation in their facilities. When the division manager refused, explaining that "the people in this section seem to demand it [segregation]," MCM spokesman Reverend Albert Dalton tried, in vain, to convince him that in Louisville "opposition to segregation is growing among white people." The group then shifted tactics and urged people to ignore the segregation rules, citing as justification recent court decisions outlawing discrimination on buses as well as Louisville's record of progress. At this point Tucker's KBNA got involved. Tucker went into the terminals trying to convince blacks to move into the white-only section; his organization and the NAACP offered legal assistance to anyone who would do so. After the arrest of one African American who strayed into the white section, the police changed their course. Police chief Carl E. Heustis announced that because no law mandated segregation, thereafter his men would not enforce the policies of the terminals—a pledge that he repeated during later confrontations over segregation in private businesses. To test the pledge and pressure terminal owners, in December 1953 Tucker and a handful of KBNA members conducted a sit-in in the white waiting room, the first organized sit-in in the city. They remained for twenty minutes, undisturbed by police or company officials. The station manager remained unfazed. "Negroes flaunt the custom [of segregation] all the time," he acknowledged, but he refused to abandon the policy.[51]

In early 1955, after a lapse of two years, the NAACP revived the issue, threatening to sue Greyhound to force the company to open the terminals. The *Louisville Defender* supported the suit, citing the opening of other local facilities and the potential damage to Louisville's reputation when visitors were forced into the separate, and entirely unequal, facilities, an argument that would be used when the fight broadened to include dining establishments elsewhere in the city. Such segregation, the editors argued, belied the assertion that "race relations are good in Louisville." "The truth is," the paper continued, "they are too good for the white man who wants to keep the Negro under foot, but they are cruel and painful to Negroes." The Interstate Commerce Commission resolved the issue when it ruled that Jim Crow must end in facilities that served interstate travelers.[52]

Concurrent with pressure on bus and train terminals, NAACP attorneys and their allies used similar lines of reasoning to challenge segregation at the airport. When Frankie M. Freeman, a St. Louis attorney visiting Louisville, was denied service at the airport lunch counter in November 1954, she authorized state NAACP official James Crumlin to sue on her behalf. Freeman had a history of involvement in civil rights cases in Mississippi and had participated in the effort to force St. Louis hotels to accept black patrons. In the short term, Crumlin succeeded. Heustis reiterated his pledge not to enforce private segregation policies, and airport officials announced that after closing for repairs, the snack bar would open to everyone. One year later, however, the Dobbs House Restaurant took over the airport franchise and began sporadically barring black patrons. African Americans quickly sued to end the capricious treatment. The city-county airport authority responded by terminating the Dobbs House Restaurant's lease and signing a contract with a new company that did not discriminate, thus rendering the suit moot.[53]

In the five years between the beginning of the IHM and the resolution of the airport snack bar question, movement leaders had moved from demanding black access to tax-supported institutions to calling for the integration of private businesses with links—in the form of leases—to government. In the parks the federal circuit court decided that leasers could not discriminate. In bus and train transportation, the Interstate Commerce Commission denied private businesses that operated in terminals the right to segregate. Each case revealed how federal policies influenced local leaders' actions. The local government had now been convinced not to give a contract to a company with exclusionary practices. Each step brought the movement closer to demanding that government force all private businesses to open their doors. In March 1954, the *Defender* editor, Frank Stanley, argued that only a civil rights law could stop private businesses from segregating "on a whim." Stanley envisioned a law, modeled on statutes passed in Ohio, Illinois, and Indiana, that would "make it unlawful for any public place"—defined as any business serving the public—to discriminate.[54]

To get such a law passed on a local level, African Americans would have to assert themselves politically. A presence in city politics had long produced some consideration for the black community by local officials. Several factors in the postwar era amplified African Americans' political voice and gave them legislative leverage. African Americans were divided evenly between the two political parties, making them the target of recruitment efforts by both the local Democrats and Republicans. In addition, although blacks made up just under 20 percent of the voting population, residential segregation concentrated them into a small number of wards and districts, which increased their ability to elect African Americans to some offices. After Eugene Clayton became the first black alderman in 1945, at least one African American served on the board until the 1960s, when the number increased to two and then, in the 1970s, three of a twelve-person body. At the state level, the fifty-eighth state assembly district, which was 90 percent African American, sent the first of an unbroken succession of black legislators to Frankfort in 1936. In 1948 an African American was elected in the forty-second district, followed by the fortieth in 1964 and forty-first in 1966. Within concentrated black neighborhoods, political participation lagged just slightly behind that of the area's population as a whole. In 1947, for example, 65 percent of the population voted, and 60 percent of blacks voted; a year later those numbers rose to 74 percent and 66 percent. Voter registration numbers showed a similar pattern. For example, in 1952, 58 percent of the eligible population registered to vote, just slightly more than the 53 percent of blacks. Thus, though slightly less engaged in politics than the white population, Louisville's black community was able to and did take a more active political role than African Americans in any comparable southern city.[55]

However, with the exception of nonpartisan races and contests with a single black candidate, the city's black voters usually divided by party rather than acting as a racial bloc. Benjamin Shobe, the NAACP lawyer, state senate candidate, and eventual judge, recalled that "people who were trying to change things politically" organized through either the race-based Third Ward Republican Club or the Democratic Club. These groups pressured city and county officials and "the people in charge" of the parties—the political bosses and legislative district chairs—for concessions. Shobe remembered that Lenny McLaughlin, a white party operative, could pull strings with the county judge or mayor to win political favors for the black community. Beyond appealing to powerful whites, African Americans held a few positions of power within segregated party committees and thus had influence over campaigns and jobs. In the immediate postwar elections, for example, the Republicans established a new headquarters for the Colored Republican Campaign Committee and a Negro Personnel Committee to ensure blacks got access to the patronage jobs, while the Democrats hired an African American to chair the Colored Division of the campaign headquarters.[56]

Such active involvement did not mean local African Americans were always happy with their parties. Rather, they often expressed disgruntlement, pressured party officials for additional consideration, and at times jumped to the opposition. Celebrated local black Republican Charles Anderson, the first African American state legislator, assistant commonwealth's attorney, and a party club organizer, announced after eighteen years that he was leaving the GOP because it had failed to appoint a black delegate to the 1952 national convention. Anderson's supporters argued that "the Republican Party must offer something to Negro voters to keep their loyalty," noting that "there's always been a Negro delegate, why should we act like Republicans in Georgia or Texas?"[57] Black Democrats complained more frequently about their party during this period, however, angered by the disparity between the "Roosevelt position" of the national party and the seeming neglect from local leaders. Black leaders regularly criticized the shortage of blacks in the party organization, particularly on the city-county executive committee and as campaign organizers, and repeatedly pressured Democrats to include an African American on their slate of candidates. Indeed, in the 1947 election, black Democrats organized their own slate when Mayor Leland Taylor failed to include a woman or an African American on his aldermanic slate. Though endorsed by the Franklin D. Roosevelt Independent Voters League, the African American–led slate went down to defeat.[58] Still, such episodes demonstrate that blacks increasingly expected positions of power within the party and in legislative office and that they were willing to move between the parties to get them. This threat of party mobility gave the black community additional potential for influencing policy.

Dissatisfaction with the Democrats and Republicans did not mean that large numbers of African Americans were ready to abandon them for independent candidates or movements, however. The local Progressive Party, a key component of the city's labor–civil rights coalition, formed to support Henry Wallace's 1948 campaign and remained active through the 1952 elections. The party united unionists from FE at International Harvester and the local branch of the NLC, whites and blacks interested in peace issues and racial equality, black students from Louisville Municipal College, and a few students and professors from the University of Louisville. In addition the party supported the congressional campaign of Alfred Carroll, a local black attorney who did frequent work for the NAACP.[59] The Progressives failed to attract large numbers of black voters, however. In the 1948 election, the party gained less than 2 percent of their support, largely because the Truman campaign, led by the Kentucky Civil Rights Committee for the Election of Truman and Barkley, made a concerted pitch to keep black Kentuckians in the Democratic fold. Although Wallace attracted support from militant blacks and whites, most African Americans refused to invest their votes in what many considered a losing campaign.[60]

Thus, despite periodic disappointment, local blacks threw their energy into running African American candidates on established parties' slates and using black voting power to influence white office-seekers. The latter tactic achieved some results, reflected in white Democrats' and Republicans' promises to aid the black community. In 1952, for example, local candidates for Congress tried to outdo each other with pledges of headquarter jobs and support for civil rights. Democratic mayoral contender Andrew Broaddus announced in 1953 that in his administration there would be "equal protection under the law for all our citizens, regardless of race, creed, or any other circumstance."[61] By the early 1950s, both parties also regularly ran a number of black candidates for positions as judges, state representatives, and aldermen. The concentration of the black community, however, meant that many of these candidates ran against each other. A 1956 study of black voting behavior in Louisville concluded that "party considerations, not race, seem to be all-important in determining victory" in aldermanic races. Still, as increasing numbers of blacks entered political contests, they campaigned not just on their party records but on promises to champion civil rights legislation more vigorously.[62]

Political competition sometimes created dissension within the civil rights community. Much of the conflict centered around accusations about the real or supposed partisan affiliations of the major civil right organizations. In fall 1952, African American attorney and Republican Charles Lunderman resigned from the legal redress committee of the NAACP because he believed that the organization had become a "fifth wheel of the Democratic Party" by supporting Adlai Stevenson for pres-

ident. Shortly thereafter, C. Eubank Tucker also attacked the group for
its alleged Democratic Party affiliation. Tucker and Lunderman were at
the time in the process of reviving the KBNA, claiming it would "meet
the needs of the man in the street," as they charged the NAACP had
failed to do. NAACP officers dismissed Tucker's accusations as "a publicity stunt" for a "one man operation." A year later, attorney Harry
McAlpin also denounced the Democrats and joined the Republicans.[63]
McAlpin and Tucker soon became the nucleus of a faction associated
with the KBNA and Republican Party that opposed more recognized
civil rights leaders affiliated with the Democrats and the NAACP. This
factional split, the root of a longer-term divide among black leaders,
resurfaced periodically throughout the civil rights era. Though at times
a source of conflict, these factions gave rise to a diverse range of leaders
and organizations in the city and prevented any individual, organization, or approach from dominating the local movement.

In the realm of political power, participation in party organizations and elections enabled blacks to assert both direct and indirect
influence on public affairs. African Americans held appointed positions
in decision-making agencies that included the housing commission and
the mayor's legislative committee. In the county, blacks served as deputy sheriffs and deputy county clerks. Over time, African Americans expected to fill certain slots, such as assistant commonwealth's attorney,
a position held successively by Charles Anderson, Harry McAlpin, and
Benjamin Shobe. Moreover, black elected officials such as Representative Felix Anderson, who held the forty-second state house district seat
from 1954 to 1960, and Alderman William W. Beckett used their positions to keep equal rights on the legislative agenda. Indirectly, the black
vote prompted campaigning white politicians to promise greater racial
equality, as Broaddus did in the 1953 mayoral race. In short, black
political participation in this period resulted, at a minimum, in gaining
whites' lip service to equality and, at times, in securing a black voice in
the process of governing. Influence within the parties and the threat to
switch their votes enabled African Americans and their white allies to
approach elected officials through persuasion and petition and reasonably expect a positive response. More important, black participation in
political life gave African Americans a sense of entitlement to the fruits
of citizenship, from public offices to expanded rights.[64]

By the mid-1950s, on the eve of the *Brown* decision and the resulting sea change in both the local and national civil rights struggles,

Louisville's black community could boast of modest gains against racial discrimination. African Americans gained election to the state legislature and city board of aldermen and appointments to city agencies and the office of the commonwealth's attorney. Both parties increasingly solicited black voters by offering jobs within their organizations and patronage positions. Moreover, concerted campaigns had brought about the integration of publicly funded facilities, including hospitals, government offices, and parks. In the area of employment, activists had made some headway against discrimination in civil service jobs and with some major industrial employers. Each year the *Louisville Defender* published an "honor roll" of individuals and organizations working for progress. The list included movement stalwarts like the NAACP and its officers and lawyers, James Crumlin, P. O. Sweeney, and Benjamin Shobe. The paper also listed African American "firsts" like the appointment of O. M. Travis as the first black member of the state board of education and Colonel W. George Matton as one of the first blacks in an integrated firemen's unit. Finally, the *Defender* pointed to white individuals and interracial organizations that had joined the fight. These summaries of accomplishments reminded readers of the struggle to "make Louisville one of the most progressive cities in the entire nation."[65]

By 1954 many observers—locals and outsiders, blacks and whites—saw Louisville as being at the forefront of racial change, especially in comparison to other southern cities. National civil rights leaders regularly praised Louisville for being "exceptional among southern cities in its community efforts to solve racial problems" and for having "done better" in that regard "than any other city in the South." Local branches of national groups, such as the Louisville Urban League, won commendations for their work, and the community as a whole earned praise for its "traditional freedom." Local blacks at times echoed these sentiments, pointing out that when problems arose, they could be solved "a little easier here than you could at some other places further South." Indeed, white and black observers quickly pointed out the gains Louisville made that were firsts among southern cities.[66]

Still, black leaders and more militant white allies regularly and sharply debunked this optimistic view of the community's progress. Early in the postwar period, the editor of the *Louisville Leader* raised the issue of the city's reputation. "We have boasted that the relationship between the races in Louisville was finer than any southern city," but segregation in the parks, he argued, belied this self-image. For J. C. Olden of the MCM, not only did the city fail to be better than its southern neighbors, but in some areas, "she outstrips Georgia and South Carolina in race hatred." Nearly a decade after the *Leader*'s critique, the *Defender* argued that the community could not boast until "a Negro can go to a theater, hotel or restaurant of his choice in Louisville; or get a job for which he is best qualified, build a home in any section of the city; send his child to the school nearest his home." Throughout the period, black leaders repeatedly pointed out the reasons that the city should not be so proud of itself. In a series of letters, for example, Charles T. Steele of the Urban League urged the National Council of Christians and Jews not to give Louisville an award, citing a range of continuing problems that included limited access to public accommodations, segregated schools, and discrimination by the community chest and YMCA. He further warned that such an award might make "the white leadership in the community tend to become complacent and say we have moved far enough and fast enough for the time being."[67]

For equal rights advocates, the changes that had taken place were too slow and too small. The city had made only "accommodative" progress that failed to alter the framework of segregation. In May 1956, T. R. M. Howard, a civil rights leader from Mound Bayou, Mississippi, spoke to one thousand people at Zion Baptist Church. He criticized the complacency of Louisville's civic leaders, saying that the city, and Kentucky more generally, had "indulged in half measures and slow progress" and then interpreted a few "general privileges" as signs of real success. The *Louisville Defender* and local black leaders gave his speech a rousing endorsement. The "general privileges" gained, moreover, affected only a small part of the population. "The weakness of Louisville's advances toward desegregation," Anne Braden later wrote, "was that they affected only a few people—and didn't affect them much." While small pockets of racial mixing existed in library stacks, on golf courses, and in the county offices, most blacks saw few "obvious achievements" in their "day-to-day activities." For the majority, behind their walls of separation—to use Braden's metaphor—segregation remained as firmly in place as anywhere in the South.[68]

2

Confronting School and Residential Segregation during the Cold War

On Thursday, May 20, 1954, the *Louisville Defender* front page carried dramatic headlines about two seemingly unrelated events that triggered the decade's biggest stories about Louisville race relations: "We Intend to Live Here or Die Here" and "Public School Bias Ruled Out." On Monday, May 17, the U.S. Supreme Court had issued the *Brown v. Board of Education of Topeka, Kansas* ruling, declaring segregation in public education unconstitutional. Most Louisvillians and other Kentuckians responded to the decision with moderation and even sympathy, but in the newly developed suburb of Shively, a violent confrontation over residential segregation brewed. A black family, Andrew and Charlotte Wade and their child, had moved into a home on Rone Court on May 14, and in the succeeding days, they faced a rising wave of harassment and intimidation. Over the next few years, the Louisville Board of Education, with support from a wide range of community groups, peacefully integrated the public schools, achieving national and even international praise. During the same period, the Wades struggled to hold on to their home in the face of financial and legal pressure, while in a climate of anti-Communist hysteria, a local grand jury indicted seven of their white friends for sedition and conspiracy.

From the start these two episodes were linked in important ways. They both took place in the context of a sectional reaction to *Brown* that merged with and gave new energy to a southern anti-Communist and anti–civil rights crusade. In both episodes activists relied on interracial cooperation to challenge the racial status quo, and the resulting events garnered national media attention that shaped Louisville's reputation. Most important, however, the issues at the core of the events—educational and housing segregation—were inextricably linked because, as in most communities, Louisville tied school attendance to residence. The widely disparate reactions to the *Brown* decision and the Wade house purchase reveal that in Louisville, most whites grudgingly accepted the desegregation of public, tax-supported spaces while remaining openly hostile to the breakdown of Jim Crow in private spaces—especially housing. Finally, the two stories suggest that broad community support for the desegregation of the schools in fact rested on the assumption that the racial barriers that restricted access to housing would not be broken.

The momentum resulting from the gradual opening of public facilities during the postwar era helped shape Louisvillians' response to *Brown*. Even before the Supreme Court's decision, activists in the city and state tried to use that momentum to desegregate primary and secondary schools. In 1953 the Militant Church Movement, fresh from its success in leading the Interracial Hospital Movement, initiated a mass petition campaign to urge Kentucky lawmakers to integrate the schools and continue their record of progress and leadership of the South in race relations. In response, in January 1954 state senator C. W. A. McCann of Louisville introduced senate bill 6, which would repeal the Day Law outright. A coalition of black and white liberal organizations, including the United Electrical Workers, Louisville Area Baptist Ministers and Deacons, and Women's International League for Peace and Freedom (WILPF), and student representatives from area colleges and seminaries rallied around the measure. To press for the bill, the coalition brought two hundred people, "equally divided Negro and white" and representing "every section of the state," to the senate for a hearing on the measure, during which no one spoke against it. After the event, organizer Anne Braden concluded, "We gave a very graphic demonstration of the support that exists in this state for non-segregated schools."[1]
  Despite the evidence of public support, one legislator hinted that the bill did not have "a ghost of a chance." Indeed, only nine of the thirty-six members of the committee holding the hearing bothered to attend, reflecting widespread antipathy to integrated schools. More-

over, the McCann bill faced another obstacle: just days after it was introduced, the Reverend Felix Anderson, an African American legislator from Louisville, proposed a halfway alternative to amend the Day Law to allow local school districts to make their own policies. "Some legislators won't vote for complete repeal," Anderson argued, and "if we can't get all we want, we can just keep cutting it [the Day Law] down until it won't amount to anything." His move raised the ire of those working for the stronger legislation, and they redoubled their efforts to support senate bill 6. Near the end of the session, Governor Lawrence W. Wetherby predicted that neither measure would come to a vote because Kentucky legislators would wait and let the Supreme Court make the decision. Wetherby's predictions proved correct; the legislature let both Anderson's and McCann's bills die in committee.[2]

When the Supreme Court announced its decision in *Brown,* Kentucky officials pledged to abide by the Court's directive and, in the words of Governor Wetherby, "do whatever is necessary to comply with the law." Other southern governors, including Francis Cherry of Arkansas and James Folsom of Alabama, also promised that their states would comply with the ruling. In two of Kentucky's border states, Missouri and West Virginia, leaders went further and announced their intention to implement the decision immediately. A region-wide backlash against school integration would shortly swamp this initial, moderate reaction, but at least for a time, some potential for orderly, if unenthusiastic, compliance existed.[3] In Kentucky, for example, the state attorney general, J. D. Buckman Jr., announced that the *Brown* ruling "knocks out the Day Law" and "nullifies" all requirements for segregation.[4]

Louisville officials believed the city's record of progress made the prospects for integration good. As the principal of Madison Junior High School put it, "Louisville is one city where desegregation would be accepted without any great problem" and thus will "serve as a pattern for other southern cities." Still, hints of potential problems arose in the midst of the predictions of success. Both Louisville school superintendent Omer Carmichael and Jefferson County school superintendent Richard Van Hoose, while praising *Brown* and pledging compliance, noted that the residential concentration of blacks might mean some schools would continue to have students of only one race, foreshadowing the ways in which residential segregation would for decades plague efforts to integrate the school system. Carmichael added that administrators retained the right to place teachers where they wanted. Both comments indicated barriers to the full implementation of *Brown,* but few noticed in the swelling tide of optimism.[5]

One month later, the Kentucky Board of Education put the brakes on any immediate change. Noting that the Supreme Court had promised a second ruling on the implementation of *Brown,* the board decided that the state still operated under the Day Law and would not pursue school desegregation in the 1954–1955 school year. The lone African American board member, Albert E. Meyzeek of Louisville, endorsed the decision, warning, "We should not lose our head and begin a fight right away." Following the state board's lead, the Louisville Board of Education "decided to stick with segregation" for the year and await the Court's promised second ruling. Carmichael explained that he had no choice because the state controlled the local boards, making them subject to its "directive" to wait. The only forward movement came from the governor, who in July appointed an interracial advisory committee to investigate how to accomplish integration. Otherwise, state officials stalled, awaiting direction from the Court.[6]

Local activists, in contrast, wanted immediate action. The *Louisville Defender* began a series of attacks comparing Kentucky's inaction to the progress made in other border states. In Baltimore, the paper noted, school officials modified an existing student choice plan to allow black students to choose to attend white schools in September 1954. Despite white resistance and limited results—a year later, only 3 percent of black students attended schools with whites—African American leaders praised the speed of Baltimore's actions. In St. Louis, the school board had within a month of the Court's decision produced a plan to integrate all its public schools by September 1955 and, despite a few stumbling blocks, effectively met that goal. In West Virginia, meanwhile, county school systems began integrating in 1955, with resistance appearing only in a few southern coal-dominated counties. While Kentucky leaders debated, in short, other border states moved ahead.[7]

In the face of state and local obstruction, the *Defender* recommended, "We should organize citizens committees, draw up proposals for complete desegregation," and pressure board members. A week later the NAACP and black parent and teacher organizations formed the Citizens Committee on Desegregation, which prepared a list of recommendations for the state, including steps that could be taken before a second Supreme Court ruling. Organized pressure to integrate the schools came to a head after *Brown II.* In the summer of 1955, representatives from NAACP branches across the state met in Louisville and decided to press their local school boards to produce definite plans for integrating by that fall. Twenty parents signed the Louisville petition, demanding "immediate steps to reorganize the public schools on a non-discriminatory basis" and agreeing to serve as plaintiffs in a lawsuit if necessary. In response to the NAACP petition, school officials announced that planning was under way to integrate the schools, not by fall 1955 but one year later.[8]

Indeed, school staff had already made some progress toward that goal. City school superintendent Omer Carmichael, a native Alabamian who had led school systems in his home state, Florida, and Virginia before coming to Louisville in 1945, laid the groundwork for implementing *Brown* when he ordered teachers, principals, and parent-teacher associations to discuss the potential problems of desegregation and produce written reports of their concerns and suggestions. His approach met some skepticism. One school board member wondered whether "asking for problems admits there are some" or at least invited people to concoct them, while the *Defender* asserted that "sometimes the best way of learning is just to do it." But white civic and educational leaders and many black civil rights spokesmen accepted Carmichael's approach as a start. In retrospect, Carmichael argued that the discussions gave people a chance to air concerns and gain information, and thus they smoothed the way for integration when it came. However, Carmichael did not anticipate an immediate transition; he predicted at one point that integration could take as long as five years. Still, once the Court issued *Brown II,* he pledged to begin preparing in earnest to be ready for mixed schools in fall 1956.[9]

In November 1955, Carmichael announced his plan. As he explained in his memoir, he proposed a "simultaneous system-wide change" to avoid problems that might result from gradual or partial integration. Carmichael's plan redrew the entire school system's district lines without "gerrymandering or other establishment of unnatural boundaries." Residence would determine student placement in schools, with only an "eye to convenience and the capacity of the buildings." In cases where two schools were very close, they would be in a joint district, and parents could choose between them. High school students could attend the school in their district or request a transfer to any other. School officials estimated that, under this plan, ten schools would remain all white, eleven would be mostly black, two would be approximately evenly divided, and the rest would be majority white. Carmichael also planned to close five black elementary schools. The greatest potential for significant integration existed in the upper west end and just east of downtown, neighborhoods where whites and blacks lived in close proximity. In contrast, little integration would occur in the almost exclusively white suburbs in the farther east end. Despite evidence that some segregation would remain, caused primarily by residential segregation, some black leaders conceded that there were positive aspects of the overall plan and that it seemed to follow the "letter and spirit of the Supreme Court decision."[10]

The key feature of Carmichael's plan was a pupil transfer option. Under this provision, the parents of a student assigned to a school in which he or she was in the minority had the right to request a transfer to a school in which the child would be in the majority. In other words, the school board would force no one to go to a school predominantly of the other race. Carmichael's transfer option bore some resemblance to "freedom of choice" plans promulgated around the South in response to *Brown*. Such plans, cast officially in race-neutral language, allowed parents to request a transfer for their child out of the school to which he or she was assigned. The authors of these plans reasoned that the *Brown* decision had eliminated procedures requiring segregation but had not ordered new ones guaranteeing integration. In other words, all school officials had to do was to give parents and students a choice. The federal district court in South Carolina buttressed such reasoning when it ruled in 1955, in the so-called Briggs dictum, that while schools could not deny any person the right to attend, boards did not need to take proactive steps to ensure the mixing of students. In most cases, local authorities drew school districts to maintain racial separation. White parents kept their children in white schools, and the onus was on black parents to overcome bureaucratic obstacles, as well as social and economic pressure, to arrange for the transfer of their children to previously all-white institutions. Louisville's plan differed from this pattern in that it assigned students to relatively more integrated schools, and parents had to request transfers to return their children to more segregated ones.[11]

The transfer option, however, immediately caused a storm of debate. Although black leaders accepted most aspects of the plan as a reasonable start toward integration, they almost uniformly opposed the transfer feature. George Cordery, president of the local NAACP branch, put it mildly when he noted, "It would have been better if they had left out the provision for flexible transfers." Kentucky Board of Education member Meyzeek predicted that the plan would allow white parents to "take their children and place them in schools to avoid integration." State NAACP head James Crumlin argued that "students must not be permitted to transfer from one school to the other solely because of race." Carmichael defended his transfer option, insisting that, without it, "you'd make integration compulsory." Carmichael almost directly quoted the South Carolina federal district court when he maintained that *Brown* had only forbidden forced segregation. His plan gave students the option of integrating but did not force them to do so. In his memoir, the superintendent admitted that he had hoped the transfer option would reduce opposition by allowing die-hard segregationist parents to opt out. Months of debate failed to convince Carmichael to modify his plan. Faced with little alternative, civil rights advocates begrudgingly accepted the transfer option and began to work to implement integration.[12]

Carmichael announced his plan in the midst of a broader community discussion about how best to integrate the schools. For example, Youth Speaks, an interfaith and interracial group of high school students, held periodic workshops and panel discussions to express their support for *Brown* and let their parents know they were ready to integrate. Meanwhile, the Eastern Council on Moral and Spiritual Education, a parents' organization from the rapidly expanding east end suburbs, where the paucity of African American families meant relatively little actual integration, organized forums for "people with an interest in smoothing the way for desegregation to get together to talk about it." One participant hoped the conversations would "pave the way for others to get interested too." The organization also published and circulated a pamphlet containing information about the desegregation plan, a schedule of community meetings to talk about it, and a list of reading material. Community leaders also got involved. Kentucky State College president Rufus Atwood and University of Louisville president Philip Davidson gave lectures around town urging people to welcome school desegregation and help make it successful. And white and black clergymen "discussed it with their congregations to get everybody to lose this fear of what's going to happen."[13]

While community groups tried to foster a welcoming climate,

school administrators and staff prepared to implement the plan. Carmichael recalled that he spoke to about sixty meetings, engaging in two-hour question-and-answer periods to increase parents' comfort level. Individual teachers and principals also organized education groups for both white and black parents to explain the rules and try to calm fears. With her school scheduled to receive large numbers of white students because of its proximity to a white public housing project, black principal Evelyn Jackson met with her teachers to discuss how to handle any tensions that might arise among the children. Sometimes groups of teachers from neighboring schools met to get to know each other and hear about each other's students. On a more formal level, the Louisville Education Association and Kentucky Education Association, all-white professional associations for teachers, voted to accept black members. And in the months before the scheduled date for desegregation, the black and white parent-teacher associations merged. The test run for integration came in June, when the summer program at Manual High School included twenty-eight black students in a student body of one hundred. With the preparations made, teachers ready, and summer classes deemed a success, school officials announced that "a favorable climate for the change has been created," and all expectations were for a successful transition.[14]

As Louisville prepared for integration, across the state and region, opposition mounted into what historians have called massive resistance. Whereas some southern state officials had quickly professed willingness to comply with *Brown,* others from the start made clear their hostility to the decision and intent to avoid or subvert it. Over time, such voices grew louder. Encouraged by President Dwight D. Eisenhower's silence, by the Court's willingness to let local white leaders set the pace, and by widespread popular support for resistance, southern politicians rallied around a pitched defense of segregation. The tide of opposition across the South forced most white moderates and supporters of integration into silence and gave the green light to local school officials to delay action on *Brown.*[15] In Kentucky, resistance never reached the level of hostility and violence seen in other states, but in many small and midsize cities, tensions simmered and opposition to integration festered. Despite initial promises by officials that the commonwealth would follow the Supreme Court's ruling, when James Crumlin and other NAACP officials toured the state in 1955, they met audiences of "ugly and sullen" whites, boards of education that had not even discussed integration, and blacks who faced economic pressure for raising the subject.[16]

The worst incidents of opposition in the state came just days before the Louisville school board planned to open its integrated schools. On August 31, 1956, eight African Americans signed up for classes at the all-white high school in Sturgis, Kentucky. On the first day of school, in a scene that foreshadowed Little Rock a year later, a crowd of three hundred angry whites blocked the black students' path and forced them to go home. Governor Albert B. Chandler ordered the state National Guard to escort the students through a mob that swelled to one thousand. For a week the students attended school while half of their white classmates boycotted. Faced with this opposition, the school board and principal, backed by the state attorney general, ended the experiment and told the students they had to go back to the all-black school. Smaller confrontations erupted in other parts of the state as well. In Clay, white elementary school students boycotted class to protest the enrollment of two African Americans. Though no mobs formed, the National Guard patrolled the school, and the state attorney general ordered the black children to go home. In Henderson, the White Citizens' Council (WCC) led four hundred elementary school students in a walkout, starting a boycott of the schools that collapsed only after the intervention of two white ministers. Little violence occurred in these cases, but boycotts and threats to students convinced local and state officials to stop integration. With the *Louisville Defender* providing high-profile coverage of these events, the specter of potential resistance to school integration in Louisville loomed as the opening day of the fall semester approached.[17]

Despite early professions of optimism and myriad community efforts to show support, signs of resistance to integration appeared among school personnel, parents, and others in Louisville. Parents and teachers peppered school officials and integration advocates with hostile comments at their various meetings. Parents demanded to know whether the students would be expected to socialize together, betraying their fear of racial mixing. Carmichael recalled that some white teachers complained that "it seems that the Negroes are dictating to the white people," while others thought it a "bitter dose" or "simply repulsive" that they must teach black children. The extent of parents' opposition became clear when the school district sent out notifications about where the students would be assigned in the fall. Within a month, 45 percent of parents of black pupils assigned to majority-white schools requested transfers, while an estimated 85 to 90 percent of parents of white youths assigned to black schools did so. The parents of white children assigned to Virginia Avenue Elementary School and Duvalle Junior High School were particularly vocal. They requested wholesale reassignments, saying, "We fear all our children will be stigmatized socially because of their attendance at schools with a predominating Negro element."[18] Unlike their counterparts in other southern communities, however, white Louisvillians did not at this point rush to private or parochial schools. In this respect Carmichael was prescient; the transfer option gave parents who opposed integration an option within the public schools for avoiding it.[19]

The most vocal and visible opponent of school integration in Louisville was Millard Grubbs. Grubbs had joined the Ku Klux Klan in Georgia, and in 1948, after moving to Kentucky, he helped organize the local States' Rights Democratic Party. In the 1950s Grubbs began to link resistance to integration to the fight against communism. In 1953, he launched a newspaper, the *American Eagle,* that declared the "fight of the Negroes" to be a "communist inspired program to mix, mongrelize, and destroy the white race." Three years later he incorporated a WCC for Kentucky, joined by James and Delores Rone, who by then had surfaced as key players in the housing segregation drama in the Louisville suburbs. The local WCC denounced civil rights as subversive, equating school integration with a "forcing of associations" that was "part and parcel of communism." In August 1956, the WCC launched a lawsuit against the Louisville Board of Education, charging it with violating the Day Law. School officials and civic leaders acknowledged this opposition but downplayed its importance, noting that "there were no important citizens of the community that took such a stand." As African American school official Milburn Maupin more colorfully put it, opposition "came from groups that were kind of kooky."[20]

Although they considered the opposition neither numerous nor dangerous, officials kept "a close eye on" potential troublemakers because of incidents and rumors of planned WCC activity before the school year began. At registration at Eastern Junior High School, a "sidewalk fuss" erupted between white and black students during which name calling escalated into a shouting match. More ominously, opponents of integration burned a cross in front of Parkland Junior High School, adding a sign that warned blacks to stay away. On the eve of integration, someone burned three more crosses on school property. Grubbs threatened to picket Male High School, one of the oldest and most prestigious public schools in the city, but instead he and five followers protested at the Louisville Board of Education office and city hall, carrying signs supporting states' rights and opposing the "communist-based Court opinion." Still, these incidents paled in comparison to the mob confrontations that occurred in other Kentucky communities and those that would make international headlines for Little Rock and New Orleans in the not too distant future.[21]

On the morning of September 10, 1956, Carmichael got up early to go to Male High School to watch his handiwork unfold. As he described it, a "throng of reporters and photographers" milled about, waiting for a confrontation. As the time for the first bell approached, about two hundred students gathered outside the building, milling about like typical teenagers before going to class. "The big difference," Carmichael noted, "was that some were Negroes, some were white." The bell rang; the students went into the building; and school integration in Louisville officially began.[22] Describing the first day of school integration in Louisville, *New York Times* reporter Benjamin Fine wrote, "When the history of this proud southern city is written, this day will undoubtedly go down as a historic landmark. . . . Even in the South, it was shown here, integration can be made to work without violence."[23]

With these words, Fine set the tone for the national and even international response to school desegregation in Louisville. The press showered praise on the city and its superintendent, cementing Louisville's image as a progressive leader for the region. By the end of the first week, the story caught the eye of President Eisenhower, who reportedly remarked, "I think Mr. Carmichael must be a very wise man. I hope to meet him and I hope to get some advice from him as to exactly how he did it." Eisenhower got his wish: Carmichael traveled to Washington the next week for an extended private meeting in the White House. Soon, interest in the Louisville story came from even farther afield. The U.S. Information Agency filmed a story about Louisville's school desegregation as part of its effort to publicize positive developments in American race relations. As a result, representatives of the South African Institute of Race Relations traveled to Louisville in late 1956 to study its progress. Even the national NAACP recognized the city's success, complimenting the integration effort as "an outstanding example of what can be done to effect an orderly transition to desegregated schools in the South." Soon thereafter the national office gave the Kentucky branch of the NAACP an award for its role in the process. Outside the black community, however, the lion's share of the credit went to the superintendent, perhaps because of the apparent anomaly of a white native Alabamian's leading the integration of schools in a southern city. Whatever the reason, within a year Carmichael had received awards and honorary degrees from cities and schools across the country and abroad.[24]

In contrast, many local activists questioned the extent of integration in the schools and whether it qualified as success. School officials released reports in October 1956 and one year later stressing the positive. One month after the celebrated desegregation of the Louisville schools, 73.6 percent of young people attended facilities with a "mixed" student body. A year later, that number increased to 78.2 percent. Breaking the numbers down, school officials noted that there were no longer any all-white high schools and only one all-white junior high school. To illustrate the success of the integration plan, they boasted that one previously white elementary school now had 135 whites and 166 blacks. But there were also signs of the limitations of integration almost immediately. For one, the transfer option had resulted in less integration than school officials had predicted. The previously African American Phyllis Wheatley Elementary School, for example, had expected 32 whites, but only 3 or 4 registered. In fact, the number of white students attending formerly black institutions remained extremely low—only 95 out of more than 32,000 whites in the system, according to one count—although, compared to the rest of the South, where few white students attended formerly all-black schools, this represented some progress. Moreover, after a year of integration, at least ten schools in the system continued to be all white, and eight remained all black. In many cases, "mixed" student bodies included a handful of blacks in a majority-white institution. In all, approximately 20 percent of black students attended formerly all-white schools, but that number obscured the fact that in some schools, they made up less than 1 percent of the student body, while in others, they were close to half. In reality, most black students who moved to formerly white schools became part of a small minority.[25]

Despite these limited gains, the small segregationist opposition to integration continued to press its case and cause trouble for officials. One problem arose at Male High School when a white transfer student from Michigan, Billy Branham, announced his desire to enroll at the school and his intention to organize opposition to integration from within. Branham moved to the city from Detroit and lived with Millard Grubbs until his parents found a house. Although Grubbs maintained that neither he nor the WCC had invited Branham to the city, he clearly supported the young man and his efforts. Though Branham offered to pay nonresident tuition, Carmichael refused to admit him to the school. The youth responded by filing suit against the schools, claiming that he was denied entry because of his beliefs. When officials reluctantly allowed him to attend the school, Carmichael warned him that if he "tried to interfere with integration he'd be suspended." A week later Branham landed in trouble, arrested for breach of peace after a meeting he organized—in a hall rented by Grubbs—got rowdy. For the remainder of the spring, he battled school and city authorities, but he left Male in June and did not return.[26]

In their effort to rouse opposition to school integration in Louisville, Branham and Grubbs reached out to a regional subculture of militant segregationists. In late 1956, they contacted John Kasper, who led the WCC in Clinton, Tennessee, and had served a year in jail for his part in the desegregation turmoil there. Kasper came to Louisville to "offer his services to local segregationists" and unite opposition to school integration. Indeed, in spring 1957, he declared Louisville his "next target" and vowed to bring down "Carmichael's house of cards." Some evidence indicates that he hoped to bring Branham back to Tennessee to organize a youth WCC. Grubbs and Branham, meanwhile, held a series of recruitment meetings to interest teenagers in the organization. Branham also took to the road, giving speeches around Kentucky about his experiences with black students in the North. During the summer, the Kentucky WCC held meetings calling for the impeachment and even assassination of Supreme Court justices for "giving aid and comfort to the communists."[27]

None of these events attracted the crowds of hundreds seen at WCC and other segregationist gatherings in Mississippi and Kentucky's other southern neighbors. Twenty-eight people attended one event; others attracted crowds of forty to fifty-five. The local WCC inspired so little fear that a group of thirteen black college students, after seeing posters at the University of Louisville, attended a meeting in October and managed to stop the proceedings while Grubbs unsuccessfully tried to get the police to remove them. By late 1957 the WCC faded from view in Louisville, though sporadic Klan activity continued. Grubbs sponsored a conference and tried to bring national organizers to the community. In 1959 Louisville became the headquarters of an effort to use opposition to school integration to revive the Klan in Ohio, Kentucky, Indiana, and Illinois. According to local media reports, however, the group had little success and resorted to a mail campaign to recruit members.[28]

Most white and black Louisvillians, in short, at least publicly accepted school integration. Still, ongoing problems rendered it incomplete and caused tension and turmoil in the community. Meanwhile, desegregation in the county made far less headway. In the 1950s, the city and county systems and their boards were separate, though officials communicated and tried to work together. Two months after Carmichael unveiled his plan, county superintendent Richard Van Hoose released a much less ambitious one. His proposal applied only to elementary school students, because the county had no black junior or senior high schools. Those students continued to be bused to schools in the city. Under the county plan, no white children attended formerly black schools, and only small numbers of African American students were assigned to formerly white schools. The limited nature of the plan became obvious when the county released the results one year later. While 78 percent of students in the city attended school in mixed facilities, only 47 percent did in the county. In fact, a majority of Jefferson County students did not attend integrated schools until 1958. Even then, the vast majority of students went to schools that were overwhelmingly of one race, and conditions in the black schools deteriorated with overcrowding. Most important, the county continued to bus black students past more modern facilities to reach older, black-majority schools. Not until the 1970s would the county schools adequately address the lack of integration.[29]

For Louisville's black leaders, the most obvious weakness in the city's desegregation effort was its failure to mix faculties. The question of what would happen to black teachers arose immediately. Across the South, black teachers greeted the *Brown* decision with some ambivalence. As the process of desegregation slowly worked out across the region, it became clear that white school officials would resist placing black teachers in front of white students, resulting in a loss of jobs.[30]

Anticipating such an outcome, the NAACP leaders in Kentucky, who praised the *Brown* decision, pledged to build a "war chest to fight for the rights of Negro teachers." They had cause to worry, because from the beginning of the integration process, Kentucky school officials resisted teacher integration. As the state superintendent of schools warned, "The same parent who might not object to his children attending school with colored children might object to having them taught by a Negro teacher." During the planning that preceded integration in Louisville, officials assured black teachers that they would not lose their jobs. But after the release of Carmichael's plan, and with the organizing of new school districts under way, the *Louisville Defender* reported that twenty-five black teachers had already received dismissal notices and predicted that one hundred more would lose their jobs as a result of the closing of black schools. In the summer of 1956, the state NAACP briefly considered filing a lawsuit to protect tenured black teachers but decided to hold off to see what action officials would take in the new school year.[31]

The status of black teachers became a controversy that marred the first months of integration when superintendent Carmichael made disparaging remarks about their qualifications in *U.S. News and World Report.* When asked about desegregating faculties, Carmichael responded, "The average white teacher is considerably superior to the average Negro teacher." He continued, "How can a person come out of a slummy, crime ridden area of the city, with poor churches and few of the things that go to enrich life—how can a person [who] come[s] out of such a background be the equal of one who comes out of a more cultured home in a more cultured community?" Outraged, black leaders demanded an explanation. At a meeting at Duvalle Junior High School attended by three hundred blacks, Carmichael said he regretted that his comments had been taken out of context. He asserted that they did not reflect his opinion of Louisville's blacks but were based on his interaction with their counterparts in Alabama, Florida, and Virginia. Not only did this tepid explanation let stand the insult to African Americans in those states, but Carmichael also refused to rescind his statement that "being taught by a Negro" could hurt a child.[32]

As it became clear that Carmichael would not budge on teacher integration, the NAACP, the *Defender,* and Central High School history teacher Lyman Johnson, the plaintiff in the suit that desegregated the University of Kentucky, launched a campaign to pressure the schools to change policy. The NAACP approached the Louisville Board of Education in July 1957, demanding a teacher integration plan. Carmichael delayed, arguing that he wanted to wait for student desegregation to be firmly established. The next spring Johnson revived the issue in a letter to the editor of the *Defender*, citing the psychological harm done to black students who did not have black teachers and arguing that tax-supported public schools could not discriminate so blatantly in employment. Carmichael responded that white parents would not yet accept black teachers. Rising to that challenge, the *Defender* undertook a series of unscientific polls of white parents and teachers and reported that 105 of the 131 parents interviewed claimed to have no opposition to integrated teaching staffs. The teachers expressed more reluctance; only 50 percent said they would work with blacks, and 20 percent said they would not. The remainder declared themselves undecided. Such polls had little impact on members of the board of education. Indeed, one board member predicted it might take ten years to accomplish faculty integration. As frustration among black leaders rose, the *Defender* published a steady stream of articles lambasting the results of teacher segregation. Though school officials remained unmoved, by 1959 the campaign on behalf of black teachers gained the support of liberal organizations such as the Kentucky Civil Liberties Union (KCLU) and the Louisville Area Baptist Ministers and Deacons, both of which endorsed teacher integration.[33]

On the eve of the new school year in 1959, Carmichael and the Louisville Board of Education finally announced that some school faculties would be desegregated. But only token integration took place. The Louisville plan resembled those in other states where school officials handpicked black pioneers to please whites and minimize conflict. Carmichael explained that he would choose ten black teachers based on "professional competence and personal qualities which we think will insure their success." Specifically, the teachers could not be "too aggressive on the race question" and had to possess "good poise, judgement, and consideration for fellow workers." Carmichael assigned them to formerly white schools that had high percentages of black students. Though he warned that he would not proceed with teacher integration at "breakneck speed," he boasted of the move's success, announcing that he had not received a "single call from a single parent." To keep the pressure on Carmichael, the NAACP pledged to pursue strategies to end all employment discrimination in the schools and to ensure that officials assigned teachers to duties without regard to race. Despite this limited progress, the *Defender* praised school officials for finally making Louisville more deserving of the title the "South's most desegregated city."[34]

At the same time that the city prepared for and celebrated its peaceful integration of the schools, Andrew Wade struggled to keep his home while his white friend Carl Braden fought sedition charges for helping him buy it. When Wade moved into a previously all-white subdivision, he joined a long history of confrontation over Jim Crow in housing. Although the 1917 *Buchanan v. Warley* decision had ruled city laws mandating residential segregation unconstitutional, policies of government agencies, financial institutions, and real estate professionals, together with public pressure, kept whites and blacks living apart and limited African Americans' housing options. In the postwar period, white Americans, aided by the GI Bill and other government loan programs, started an exodus from cities to suburbs.[35] Across the South, African Americans, enjoying increased income in the wake of the war but facing a housing shortage, began to push against old barriers and seek homes in formerly all-white areas. In response, whites sought to hold the line by enforcing old ordinances and covenants and forming block associations and purchasing cooperatives to prevent sales to blacks. When those tactics failed, whites resorted to violence, and by the early 1950s, a wave of house bombings stretched from Dallas to Norfolk.[36]

In Louisville, African Americans faced similar conditions and resistance. In 1948, when the Supreme Court ruled restrictive covenants—clauses in deeds prohibiting the sale of property to African Americans or other minorities—unenforceable by law, the *Louisville Courier-Journal* estimated that such agreements covered 75 to 80 percent of land in the city. Although city leaders announced that the decision meant blacks could live anywhere, a *Courier-Journal* investigation two years later showed that local lenders still honored the old restrictions.[37] Moreover, real estate agents, bankers, and builders followed "unwritten rules" not to sell new homes to African Americans. One study concluded that, as a result, blacks had access to only two hundred of the approximately twenty thousand new homes built in the postwar era in the Louisville area.[38] Faced with these barriers to new housing, African Americans crowded into the city's older neighborhoods. Some remained in the old east end, which consisted of a few blocks of public housing and dilapidated and overcrowded houses on streets bordering the central business district. Others moved to the west end, the area from Sixth Street on the western edge of downtown to the Ohio River. The west end was historically white and, by the postwar era, was mainly working class. In it, blocks of single-family, well-maintained bungalows mixed with poorer neighborhoods of older, subdivided homes and ramshackle cottages. As white families moved out, African American families began to move in, initiating the area's long transition from primarily white to majority black.

White residents remaining in the west end did their best to forestall change. In 1950, one hundred white families formed the Shawnee Foundation and raised fifteen thousand dollars to buy a house and stop its sale to African Americans. Not long after, four hundred residents formed the Shawnee Homeowners Association to enforce deed restrictions against black immigration to the area. Sometimes white west enders took more direct action against black newcomers. In 1953, two weeks after a black man moved into a home on Grand Avenue, vandals threw rocks through the window, began turning garbage cans over every night, and burned a cross in the yard. An unexploded bomb and a placard reading "Nigors git [sic] out this is your last chance" accompanied the cross. The message was signed by the Ku Klux Klan. On other occasions, angry mobs gathered outside homes that African Americans showed interest in buying or renting and harassed whites who contemplated selling to blacks. Louisville did not see the waves of arson and bombings that greeted blacks in changing neighborhoods in cities such as Birmingham and Atlanta. But the speed with which white west enders and other white Louisvillians used the threat of violence to keep blacks from crossing strictly defined racial lines foreshadowed the antagonism that greeted Andrew and Charlotte Wade.[39]

A black World War II navy veteran and electrician with a family and personal history of involvement in progressive causes, Andrew Wade maintained that he wanted to buy a house in a formerly white neighborhood not as a crusade but to give his children a nice home. The experience of fighting for democracy in the war galvanized Wade, as it did other black veterans. When he returned to Louisville, he joined the Progressive Party, not out of any radical political inclination but because it was one organization in that period in which whites and blacks met as equals. He left the party after the 1948 Henry Wallace campaign because, as he explained later, he felt overcommitted with work, school, and starting a family. Wade and his father both had confrontations with racist authorities and segregation that brought the Wade name to public attention before the younger man even contemplated buying a house. In 1951, police arrested Wade and charged him with disorderly conduct for being "sassy" during a traffic stop. And, during Wade's efforts to secure a home, his father, Andrew Wade Sr., acted as a plaintiff in a lawsuit to desegregate the public pools. Thus, though neither took leadership positions in the local civil rights community, each demonstrated a willingness to challenge the racial status quo.[40]

Andrew Wade and his wife Charlotte approached Carl and Anne Braden for help in buying a house when they repeatedly encountered white resistance to allowing blacks past the residential color line. The Wades had one child and another on the way, and they wanted a new house with space for their children to play outdoors. They had begun shopping in black neighborhoods, following the advice that they should look where they were "designated to buy." Andrew visited a number of new developments in Louisville and in nearby southern Indiana, but he and his wife could not find a home for sale to blacks that fit their needs. Eventually, the couple decided to pursue a purchase through a white "front." They contacted some white acquaintances, who turned them down for fear of the consequences. Andrew was acquainted with the Bradens from their involvement in the Progressive Party and because he and his father had done work on their house. He later recalled that he approached the Bradens because "they had always been known as staunch fighters for civil rights and better conditions for any group of people."[41]

By 1954 Anne and Carl Braden had indeed earned that reputation. Born in Louisville and raised in Anniston, Alabama, Anne returned to her birthplace after college and a few years as a journalist to become a reporter for the *Louisville Times* in 1947. Carl was born and raised in the white working-class neighborhoods in the west end of Louisville, and by the time he met Anne, he was an openly sympathetic labor reporter. They soon became friends and allies, sharing readings and conversations about labor and other issues of the time, and they married in 1948. Over the next couple of years, they stood at the center of the city's progressive community and of interracial efforts to overcome Jim Crow. They did public relations work for a group of left-wing labor unions, and Anne joined the women's auxiliary of the FE and women's peace groups. They also helped to organize and direct the lobbying of the IHM, campaigned for the Progressive Party, and got involved with early legislative efforts to overturn the Day Law. As participants in the left wing of the early civil rights movement, they moved in the same circles as Andrew Wade. As Wade predicted, the Bradens lived up to their reputation, agreeing to help immediately.[42]

In early May, the Wades found the home they wanted on Rone Court, a small development in Shively, an incorporated suburban town on the southwestern edge of Louisville. The builder, James Rone, would soon join Millard Grubbs in founding the local WCC. He lived in an older farmhouse near the property, and his son, James Rone Jr., owned the lot next to the house the Wades wanted. The Bradens visited the house, negotiated a buying price through a real estate agent, and secured a mortgage from South End Federal Savings and Loan. On May 10, 1954, they signed the contract to purchase the home, and three days later, they signed the deed over to the Wades, legally transferring the property. The Wades moved in the next day. Wade soon attracted the attention of James Rone Jr. while working on the house and yard. When Rone asked if Wade planned to rent the property, Wade explained that the Bradens had deeded it to him, and his family would be living there. On the evening of May 15, the first rock and threat arrived through the front picture window of the Wades' dream house.[43]

Serious harassment of the Wades and Bradens began immediately. The night after Wade's conversation with Rone, about twenty cars parked nearby as white residents came and went from the latter's home, though no one approached the Wades. Instead, a motorcade drove into Louisville to confront the Bradens. Though Carl successfully turned the crowd away, over the next several nights the Bradens received a barrage of phone threats, including one that "promised to blow up" their home. Meanwhile, on Rone Court, the Wades had suffered through their first night in the house. In the predawn hours on May 16, shortly after the rock came through the window, shotgun blasts tore into the home, and a cross was burned on the yard next door. In response, the police agreed to increase patrols, and for three nights no incidents occurred. But other forms of pressure started. On May 21 Wade's insurance company canceled his coverage, and he scrambled to find a new policy. A month later, South End Federal Savings and Loan sued to have the mortgage due immediately and to force Wade to surrender the property. After six weeks of simmering tension, harassment, legal threats, and violence, a bomb went off underneath the Wade home in the middle of the night of June 27, tearing apart one side of the house.[44]

The white moderates and liberals who so readily praised Louisville for following the Supreme Court edict to integrate the schools voiced little sympathy for the Wades and even less for the Bradens. When Anne Braden tried to elicit support for the Wades from clergymen in the area, for example, local Catholic priests would not acknowledge that Rone Court was in their parish. Most ministers privately lamented the violence but refused to address their congregations about it. Just one priest, while avoiding taking a position on the Wades' right to live in Shively, wrote to the local paper that it was wrong to "smash windows, to threaten people with a burning cross, or to fire bullets into a man's home." And when the popular radio program *Moral Side of the News* aired a forum of clergymen discussing the case, each of the panelists spent more time condemning the Bradens for their role in the purchase than denouncing the violence. With little support from the religious community, the Bradens turned to labor, a common ally in the postwar struggle for equal rights. "This is a hard issue to sell to our membership," one leader responded. "We can talk about equality on the job and things like that. But in housing it's different. They've [the members] got pretty set ideas. This gets into social equality and they don't believe in that." Local unions would not be a dependable friend in this case.[45]

Likewise, the voice of moderation and support for school de-segregation, the *Louisville Courier-Journal,* voiced little sympathy for residential integration. In an editorial published on May 18, the paper took just two lines to criticize the segregationist violence committed on Rone Court. Then, referring to the white residents of the development, the paper added, "They are entirely within their rights, we believe, in protesting the purchase of property in their subdivision by Negroes." With this, the editors invoked an argument that would re-surface throughout battles over residential segregation: that whites had the right to exclude blacks from their neighborhoods and, by exten-sion, other property and institutions. More significant in the short run, the paper blamed the entire crisis on the Bradens. The city's progress in integration, the editors argued, came from "careful, steady community effort." In contrast, the Bradens' "artificial and contrived" action was designed only to "force the issue," and it had caused the problem. As Anne Braden later noted, this editorial transformed the story, focusing on the Bradens' role and giving local white liberals an excuse to abandon the Wades and the cause of residential integration.[46]

While liberals vacillated and found excuses to look the other way, black leaders, civil rights organizations, and a few white allies came to the Wades' and Bradens' defense. Contradicting the notion of a white right to exclusivity, the Wades' sympathizers championed their right to acquire the property—specifically the home—of their choice. This was a "test of democracy," the *Louisville Defender* maintained, and "the Bradens and the Wades are to be praised rather than maligned" for "fighting a battle for all of us." Echoing that patriotic rhetoric, Nathaniel McKenzie, president of the Louisville NLC, called on working people to "unite in defense of democracy" by supporting the Wades. Likewise, the president of the local NAACP, George Cordery, declared that the organization stood "squarely behind Mr. Wade's right to live wherever he chooses" and called on others to do the same. Lillian Elder, a Progressive Party activist who probably knew both couples through her political work, chastised the *Courier-Journal* for suggesting that whites had the right to keep Shively just for themselves. Furthermore, she pointed out, the Bradens and Wades had committed no crime, in contrast to those who harassed them. Picking up the theme, I. O. Ford, a labor activist, asked why police failed to arrest the perpetrators and called on them to protect both the Bradens and Wades against "gangs of terrorists."[47]

In late May, the Wades' supporters established the Wade Defense Committee (WDC) to defend the couple's right to own the house and to provide protection for them. The organization brought together representatives from the NAACP, the NLC, the MCM, the KBNA, the *Louisville Defender,* and the radical labor and civil rights community that had coalesced in the Progressive Party. The Reverend M. M. D. Perdue chaired the group, and Frank Stanley, Harry McAlpin, and George Cordery served as financial trustees. Organized to help the Wades withstand the financial, legal, and physical attacks on their home, the WDC set up a twenty-four-hour vigil at the house to watch for trouble and unsuccessfully pressed local judges to order daytime police protection of the property. The committee also organized "Andrew Wade Day" in early July, when local black ministers raised money to help the family pay the mortgage and end the foreclosure suit. The WDC worked through the summer to press for a grand jury hearing to investigate the violence perpetrated against the Wades' home.[48]

While the WDC organized physical protection and legal and financial aid for the Wades, segregationists began accusing the Wades, the Bradens, and their allies of subversion. On May 20, the editor of the *Shively Newsweek*, John Y. Hitt, published a column questioning the motives of both couples. He labeled the deed switch a "sneaking" and "furtive" move designed to place blacks in the neighborhood with the ultimate goal of causing "panic and bloodshed." Hitt raised the red flag, asking, "Is he [Wade] really looking for a house or is he a pawn for the cause of communism?" Hitt closed with a call to his readers to protect democracy, not by ending Jim Crow but by allowing the white majority to decide who should live in their neighborhoods. Almost immediately, Millard Grubbs, the nemesis of Louisville's school integration, jumped into the fray, turning his attention from the threat of "mongrelization" in the schools to what he called the Wades' and Bradens' effort to establish "a black beachhead in every white subdivision." He argued that, like school integration, this campaign was part of a Communist plot to weaken America and deprive whites of their rights. Though he was a marginal figure during school integration, Grubbs's arguments this time resonated and had significant impact on the future handling of the case.[49]

By raising the threat of a Communist plot, Grubbs and Hitt, and eventually city officials, tapped into the national red scare that accompanied the cold war and the tide of anticommunism that swept the South in response to the *Brown* decision. At times civil rights activists used cold war rhetoric about the need to protect democracy to raise support for greater racial equality. According to legal scholar Mary Dudziak, "Concern about the effect of U.S. race discrimination on Cold War American foreign policy led the Truman Administration to consider a pro–civil rights posture as part of its international agenda to promote democracy and contain communism." While the Wade case brewed, the State Department promoted the *Brown* decision overseas as evidence of the strength of the American system. Indeed, officials broadcast the success of Louisville's school integration abroad in part because it confirmed State Department arguments about the progress taking place in American race relations. Likewise, local leaders of the Urban League and KCIC often based their calls for equal treatment for blacks on the need to stand up for democracy against foreign tyranny.[50]

Far more often, however, and especially in the South after *Brown*, the cold war atmosphere led to accusations about the Communist leanings and potential threat of progressive leaders and organizations. Hearings held by Mississippi senator James Eastland and the Senate Intelligence Committee harassed old New Dealers, labor leaders, and civil rights advocates such as Myles Horton, Clifford Durr, and Virginia Foster Durr. Such tactics drove organizations that fought for racial and economic equality, like the Southern Conference for Human Welfare and the Highlander Folk School, out of business, at least temporarily. Others, including the conference's progeny, the Southern Conference Educational Fund (SCEF), became tainted and were held in suspicion for years. Meanwhile, state investigative bodies such as the Georgia Bureau of Investigation and Mississippi State Sovereignty Commission began witch hunts that associated any fight against Jim Crow with subversion. Most white southerners assumed that segregation was the natural order and linked democracy to the right of whites to maintain supremacy. As a result, they considered anyone who questioned Jim Crow unstable at best or Communist at worst. In this atmosphere, the Wades' move into an all-white neighborhood, and even more the Bradens' efforts to enable it through "sneaking" methods, came under fire as subversive of the southern way of life.[51]

When Hitt and Grubbs hinted that Wade and Braden might be influenced by Communists, they borrowed a tactic that had already been used against civil rights advocates in Louisville. In 1952, members of the Progressive Party and others working for a permanent FEPC had come under attack. First, supervisors at the Jeffersonville (Indiana) Quartermaster Depot, which was affiliated with the U.S. military, fired veteran Frank Grzelak because the federal loyalty-security hearing board decided his wife's membership in the Progressive Party made him a risk. Two weeks later, the depot suspended Walter Barnett, another veteran and chair of the local Progressive Party, for circulating petitions for a federal FEPC. Labor, liberal, and civil rights groups rallied to their defense with letter-writing campaigns and legal advice. The actions against the men, their defenders argued, were "part of a general drive to deprive all of the people their rights" and a "movement against the Negro people." After appealing the charges, Grzelak regained his job, but Barnett lost his.[52] These incidents were part of a broader pattern of harassment of Progressive Party members that ranged from heckling at public events to veiled threats against staff to police raids of meetings and arrests for petty offenses such as noise violations and insulting officers.[53]

When the local commonwealth's attorney, A. Scott Hamilton, finally got around to launching a grand jury investigation into the attacks on the Wades' house, the national and regional red scare and the local history of anti-Communist attacks on interracial organizing laid the groundwork for Louisville's own McCarthy-style witch hunt. After months of pressure from the WDC, Hamilton announced in early September that he would bring the house bombing incident before the grand jury. The WDC had reason for optimism. Over the summer, police chief Carl Heustis had informed members that the police had evidence of who had committed the bombing, though not enough to prosecute. When the hearing convened, Hamilton opened by proposing two explanations for the crime: either those "inflamed with hatred because the Negro family moved into the neighborhood" had committed the violence, or Communists had plotted the bombing to incite racial tension.[54]

Once the questioning of witnesses began, it became clear that the only theory that interested Hamilton, and the only one he pursued, was that a group of Wade's white associates, led by Carl Braden, had used him and had plotted to bomb the home to provoke a racial crisis as an entry for Communist influence in the community. After perfunctory questions about the events on Rone Court, Hamilton grilled witnesses about their political activities and associations. Both Anne and Carl Braden refused to testify about their political work, membership in the Civil Rights Congress and other organizations, and reading habits. Andrew Wade declined to confirm that he was in the Progressive Party. Hamilton challenged Vernon W. Bown, one of the volunteers who stayed at the Wade house, about a radio that he had brought into the home with him, which police believed set off the explosion. He also had to explain the "communistic material" seized from his home during a warranted search. "It more or less convinces me," Hamilton declared after Bown's testimony, "that this thing was communist inspired." With red scare hysteria building outside the courtroom, the grand jury indicted seven of Wade's white supporters for violating the state's law against advocating sedition: Carl and Anne Braden; Vernon Bown, a Teamster and WDC member; I. O. Ford, Bown's roommate; Louise Gilbert, a social worker and a member of the WILPF who had written to Wade's neighbors on his behalf; Lewis Lubka, the secretary of the WDC; and Larue Spiker, Gilbert's roommate and a friend of the Wades.[55]

On November 29, 1954, the state began presenting its case against Carl Braden, who was targeted first by the commonwealth's attorney's office after the defendants won the right to separate trials. Anne Braden later recalled that the commonwealth's attorney's case rested on proving that Carl was a Communist and that Communists sought to create racial tension. Hamilton relied on reading material of a supposedly Communist nature found in the Braden home, the couple's membership in various progressive organizations, and the testimony of former Communist FBI informants who described Communist Party tactics used to stir up racial hatred to document Braden's alleged beliefs. In his testimony, Andrew Wade denied membership in the Communist Party, being enticed into joining it by the Bradens, and belonging to the Progressive Party while they did, but the court treated his statement almost as an afterthought. Alberta Ahearn, a white woman who had been a member of the WDC, provided the dramatic high point of the trial. She announced on the stand that she was an FBI informant who had attended Communist Party meetings at the Braden home and that Carl had sold her Communist literature. Though she never mentioned the Wade home, her testimony had a clear impact on the jury. Anne recalled that while she and Carl waited for the outcome, there was "never any doubt in my mind . . . what the verdict would be." The court found Carl guilty of sedition and sentenced him to fifteen years in prison.[56]

Within a month, Carl had new attorneys, provided by the American Civil Liberties Union (ACLU), who began working on an appeal. After months of fund-raising, Anne paid the forty-thousand-dollar bond, and Carl was released from prison. His lawyers filed his appeal in December 1955, but the Kentucky courts took no action because the U.S. Supreme Court had agreed to hear a Pennsylvania case challenging state sedition laws. In April 1956, the Court ruled all such laws unconstitutional in *Pennsylvania v. Nelson*. At first, Kentucky authorities tried to resist the implication of the ruling and refused to release Braden, but opposition soon crumbled, and the state court released Carl in the summer of 1956.[57] Hamilton did not want to give up so easily on the case. He initially tried to launch a grand jury investigation into communism in the community, then in fall 1956 decided to prosecute Bown for bombing the Wade house. The charges did not get very far, however, because Bown had sworn affidavits from three witnesses placing him in Milwaukee at the time. Barred from renewing the anti-Communist tone of the initial prosecution, Hamilton gave up and dismissed all charges against the defendants.[58]

Though safe from legal prosecution, all the codefendants suffered because of their association with the case. Spiker lost her job as a social worker and moved to Maine. Gilbert relocated to Philadelphia and worked for the WILPF. Bown moved to California, as did Ford. Lubka had careers as a welder, city planner, and professor at various places around the country.[59] Only the Bradens remained in Louisville to face the full consequences of the charges. For years they suffered hate mail and harassing phone calls as well as financial trouble and difficulty finding jobs. They felt abandoned by white liberal friends, trade unions, and black civil rights organizations. Over the years, moreover, the couple faced a continuing cycle of accusations based on the Wade house case, on their participation in SCEF, or simply on the fact that they had been accused and investigated before. In Louisville, they remained a lightning rod for segregationist anticommunism, enduring long-lasting personal and political demonization.[60]

The anti-Communist hysteria surrounding the sedition charges and Braden's trial turned attention away from the plight of the Wades, who continued to fight legal and financial efforts to force them from their home. Throughout 1956 and into 1957, the foreclosure suit moved through the court system. Meanwhile, money from the insurance on the damaged house remained tied up while the court decided which party—Rone, the mortgage company, or the Wades—should receive it. In 1957, the court ordered the money to be put toward the mortgage, leaving Wade with nothing to make repairs. Soon thereafter, the mortgage company declared the entire debt due in full. The Wades held on to their home briefly when a couple from Chicago provided the money to cover their bills. However, six months later, citing fear for the safety of his wife and children, Wade sold the house and moved his family to the west end. He participated briefly in CORE demonstrations in the early 1960s but withdrew thereafter into private life.[61]

The Wades' continued insecurity in their home and eventual need to abandon it point to the part of the story most ignored at the time: the ongoing resistance African Americans faced when they tried to move to white residential sections. Indeed, the violence against the Wades and the city's reaction to it exacerbated both African Americans' fears and the barriers they faced. Black leaders pointed out that as long as those who committed the violence against the Wades' house remained unpunished, blacks would hesitate to buy in new areas.[62] In addition, Hamilton had to squelch rumors that his office threatened to prosecute for sedition or otherwise treat as "another Wade case" any African American who bought a house in a white neighborhood. Not long after, Maurice Rabb sued a white home seller who, when he discovered Rabb was black, had backed out of the deal because he did not want "to stir up another Rone Court situation." More generally, black real estate agents reported evidence that white realtors and financial institutions continued to discriminate in housing sales. One survey revealed, for example, that only "2 of 9 lending institutions would make a loan to a Negro buying in a white neighborhood." Other lenders made a policy of refusing GI Bill and Federal Housing Administration loans to blacks. Finally, increasing signs of blockbusting appeared in the west end. The combination of these practices contributed to an ongoing, and even worsening, lack of black housing options and the segregation of African Americans in the west end.[63] No organized campaign against such practices would take place until the mid-1960s; for the time being, the rigid separation of white and black neighborhoods remained secure.

Although the plight of the Wades and Bradens made no significant dent in housing segregation, the sedition case did have both short- and long-term impacts on the Louisville community and the civil rights struggle in the city. Anne Braden remembered that black organizations abandoned her and her husband, but there were some exceptions. During the grand jury investigation and trial, some African American leaders and organizations spoke on the Wades' and Bradens' behalf. The Reverend Tucker, who served as legal counsel for Braden and other defendants, immediately went on the attack against the indictments and accused Louisville officials of using Communist charges to avoid prosecuting the real perpetrators of the violence. The WDC, on the defensive because of its close association with the alleged conspirators, nevertheless promised to fight the hysteria in the community and defend the Wades' and others' rights. Similarly, the Louisville NLC, though accused of subversion itself, criticized the witch hunt as an effort to divide the races and called the case a chance to "work together for democracy." More surprising, the more politically moderate *Louisville Defender* regularly published columns on behalf of the Wades and Bradens. The editors always emphasized Wade's predicament, but they also stood up for Braden as an example of a white citizen persecuted for being "too friendly to Negroes." Furthermore, the paper, while insisting it was "against communism," also declared, "It will be a bad day for this country when, in the witch hunting hysteria, we forget the canon that a man must be presumed innocent until proven guilty."[64]

The NAACP reacted more ambiguously to the case, revealing the wariness of many civil rights groups toward the Bradens. In fall 1954, when the indictments were announced, the executive board of the local branch released a statement saying that while they might be "more discreet and selective" in choosing their allies, the case would not "have any effect on the militant action" of their group. A week later, however, a few members of the board suggested that the group adopt a loyalty pledge to reduce the threat of Communist subterfuge by the Bradens, their associates, and members of the NLC. James Crumlin, president of the state conference of branches, denounced such "waving [of] the red flag" and argued against the proposal. The membership voted down the loyalty pledge, resulting in the resignation of four people.[65] The local branch, though it thus refused to purge itself of purported Communist influences, distanced itself from the case and pursued other matters, mainly school integration and open accommodation. Likewise, the national headquarters disavowed any involvement with the Bradens—noting that it did so at the couple's suggestion—and urged local members to steer clear of other potentially tainted organizations. But the Louisville NAACP did not become more conservative in its activism. Although never a leader in the field of housing, the organization continued its jobs campaigns and stepped up its activity in the sphere of accommodations.[66]

At the same time, the Braden sedition trial and the violence against the Wades inspired the birth of a primarily white liberal organization, the KCLU. In 1955, a small group of local members of the national ACLU, including Arthur Kling, Louis Kesselman, Patrick Kirwan, and Lee Thomas, started a campaign to form a Kentucky chapter. At their initial meeting, they heard the left-wing white attorney Grover Sales discuss the Braden case and warn that "the group would probably be investigated for communism." They decided to go ahead because, as University of Louisville political science professor Louis Kesselman put it, "Had this organization been in existence two years ago, we might not have gone through quite as bad a period as we have had." The KCLU became an active supporter of civil rights causes and a major channel for white participation in the movement, beginning with its support for teacher integration in 1959 and continuing in later fights against discrimination in accommodations, housing, and schools. The KCLU added a civil libertarian element to the local movement and a new connection among the battles against the diverse manifestations of Jim Crow.[67]

The national response to the Wade and Braden cases had a less direct impact on the community, but one that nevertheless helped to shape the direction of the local movement in years to come. At a time when the city was being praised for its peaceful and apparently successful integration of the public schools, national civil rights and progressive organizations and media outlets focused on the violence directed at a pioneering black family and the persecution of the white citizens who had tried to help them. In her fund-raising for Carl's appeal, Anne Braden spread word of the trial and its civil liberties implications through national liberal circles. In particular, the Emergency Civil Liberties Committee, a leftist alternative to the ACLU founded in 1951 and by 1954 headed by southern progressive Clark Foreman, publicized the defendants' plight and helped raise money through its Bill of Rights Fund. Other groups helped with moral support in the forms of sympathetic resolutions, letters to the governor, and offers to provide amicus briefs for the appeal.[68] The picture painted of Louisville in this coverage, and in the publications and pronouncements of liberal organizations across the country, contradicted the image of a forward-moving leader in southern race relations and instead put the city in the spotlight for persecuting those who tried to bring about integration. More important, interest in the case forged a connection between, on the one hand, the Bradens and the city they steadfastly refused to leave and, on the other hand, a national left-wing, civil libertarian, and civil rights network that in the future funneled attention and activists into Louisville's movement.

Finally, two principal actors in the house bombing and sedition trial drama saw significance in its relationship to the issue of school integration. Andrew Wade, speaking to the Interdenominational Ministerial Alliance, stressed the connections between the problems of discrimination in the schools and in residential options. "There will never be complete integration of schools in Louisville," Wade concluded, "until neighborhoods and public housing are integrated." After the charges against Carl were dismissed, Anne Braden wrote to friends in New York, "Many people feel that the determination with which decent Louisvillians rallied to the task of making school integration work resulted at least in part from the lessons learned here in the Wade case." She believed that the initial anger of the segregationists inspired by the *Brown* decision got spent on her family and the Wades. Once that spasm had passed, "people of good will recognized what happens when they remain quiet" and determined to make school integration happen without a crisis.[69] Yet this oversimplifies the reasons that white moderates and liberals, the same people who shunned the Bradens and their associates, largely accepted and even praised school integration. The long track record of gradual integration of public and tax-supported spaces, the determination of civic leaders to maintain Louisville's progressive image by following the law, their use of the transfer option to limit opposition and thus help to keep the peace, and the concerted effort by the school system and civic organizations to pave the way also helped ease that process. In retrospect, however, the Braden case apparently channeled anti-Communist agitation away from the school issue, protecting desegregation from the full force of the red scare that affected the process elsewhere. Put simply, Grubbs and his ilk, while opposing school integration, spent their energy against the Wades and Bradens and the challenge to Jim Crow in housing.

The question remains, Why did anti-Communists focus on the Bradens' efforts to help the Wades move into a white neighborhood? Why did whites find residential integration more threatening than school integration? In her memoir, Anne Braden provided one explanation with her description of the *Courier-Journal*'s response to the house purchase and its aftermath. The publisher and editors preferred gradual change directed by responsible civic leaders, but in this case an African American family and their white allies had taken the initiative. In short, Andrew Wade's audacity in moving into a white neighborhood threatened the white civic elite's control of the pace of change. The response of labor leaders to Carl Braden's search for allies in his time of trouble indicates another reason that the house case raised more ire than school integration. By the mid-1950s, radical unionists had faced similar anti-Communist smear campaigns and had become less involved in civil rights issues. Moreover, while liberal union leadership may have had some sympathy, the rank and file were not ready to move beyond the principle of equal rights in the public sphere and workplace and into the possibility of sharing the private spaces of home and neighborhood. Wade's actions brought integration literally too close to home. Thus as the civil rights struggle heated up, the links between these events displayed the limits of acceptable integration. Whites acquiesced to racial mixing as long as it remained confined to public space and did not touch on the daily experiences and decisions of the white majority in their private lives.

Finally, Andrew Wade may have come closest to identifying the linkage between his difficulties and the much-praised ease of school integration. With housing securely segregated, white Louisvillians could accept school integration in principle because residential segregation and the transfer option ensured that few of their children would be affected by it. If Wade and others like him succeeded in moving into formerly white neighborhoods, mixing in the schools might be accomplished on a broader scale. Segregationists focused on Braden because his effort to help Wade buy his home represented the greatest threat to Jim Crow. The volatile mixing of housing and schools would recur twice in Louisville's long struggle for racial equality, demonstrating the persistent link between these two manifestations of Jim Crow and the impossibility of understanding the fight against them in isolation from one another.

3

Open Accommodations in the All American City

On May 14, 1963, the Louisville Board of Aldermen passed an ordinance making it illegal to discriminate based on race in any place of business open to the general public, the first such law, according to Mayor William O. Cowger, "in any major city in the South." Passage of the ordinance, like the peaceful school integration of 1956, won Louisville national acclaim as an "All American City" and marked the high point of its reputation as a regional leader in race relations. This historic legislation did not arise in a vacuum; rather, the Louisville open accommodations struggle coincided with a region-wide wave of mass demonstrations for jobs and freedom, as the slogan of the 1963 march on Washington put it. The young people who led the sit-ins saw themselves as part of a larger movement, an identification reinforced by the relationship between Louisville activists and civil rights organizers in other communities. Moreover, they and their adult partners saw the demonstrations as only one part of a broader arsenal of tactics to accomplish the goal of integration. Indeed, in the nearly ten years between the *Louisville Defender*'s first call for civil rights legislation and the adoption of the ordinance, African American leaders employed as complementary and concurrent strategies both the new forms of mass nonviolent direct action being developed around the South and bloc voting akin to black political activity in the North. Finally, although Louisville won praise as being a "city that integrated without strife" after the victory in open accommodations, local activists saw it as one step in a continuing march.[1] The story of the open accommodations battle of the early 1960s thus illustrates how Louisvillians pursued change and the effort necessary to get it, but also the embedment of the campaign in both a larger regional movement and a longer struggle.

In the late 1950s, African Americans in Louisville faced the same restrictions as did African Americans elsewhere in the South in their day-to-day experiences of shopping, seeking recreation, and moving about the city. Yet segregation in the city lacked the rigidity of segregation elsewhere in the South; it was instead characterized by an uncertainty that caused frustration. For example, after the chamber of commerce and Louisville Hotel Association admitted that discrimination in hotels cost the city convention business, some of the major downtown establishments began relaxing their rules and accepting black convention participants as diners and overnight guests. But then new owners abruptly changed policies, prompting rumors about whether the hotels had opened their doors to African Americans or not. The waiting rooms at the train stations kept the Jim Crow signs up, but the management said it would make no effort to enforce the policy. In contrast, the city-owned auditorium insisted it had no "color problem" and "there has been no segregation here for several years," yet in reality the sponsors of individual programs could and quite often did bar blacks from attending. Most pertinent to the imminent demonstration campaign, downtown lunch counters showed no consistency in their policies. For example, Taylor Drug Store served black diners on Saturday but turned them away the following Monday. The "confusing picture" that resulted, concluded Nat Tillman of the *Defender,* left "Negroes open to embarrassment" as they tested each establishment and risked rejection.[2]

The situation, black leaders concluded, revealed that, contrary to the city's reputation in the wake of school desegregation, race relations in Louisville were worse than whites and outsiders imagined. According to the *Defender* editors, the capriciousness of Louisville's Jim Crow meant that, while blacks constantly heard that "race relations are good in Louisville," the "unpleasant pinch of discrimination can be felt at any time if you happen to be Negro." Beyond bursting the bubble of self-admiration among whites, black leaders sought to waken their own people from complacency and call them to action against these conditions. Again, the *Defender* argued that in light of the "far from commendable" record in public accommodations, "the decent citizens of the city who fail to protest vigorously are just as guilty as the perpetrators of discrimination." Criticizing black complacency inspired

by the few privileges Louisville's uneven segregation allowed, the editors argued that, since "we have a shorter distance to go," Louisville's
African American community had an obligation to forge ahead "full
steam" for complete integration, lest their "deep southern brothers"
get ahead of them.[3]

Such references to the stirrings of protest activity elsewhere in the
South gave Louisville's African American community inspiration and a
sense of belonging to a larger movement. The *Louisville Defender* carried extensive coverage of the Montgomery bus boycott, Emmett Till
murder, and Autherine Lucy case. Local African Americans also got
news from national black media outlets, such as *Jet*, from which two
future sit-in demonstrators, Runette Robinson and Arminta Poignard,
learned about the Till murder. Poignard recalled, "My first encounter
with racism was when Emmett Till was killed. That was my big one.
That just broke me down, up, and every which way when I saw in *Jet*
magazine about that young guy."[4] These news stories reinforced what
local African Americans heard firsthand at mass meetings sponsored by
churches and civil rights organizations. The NAACP and Urban League
brought in national leaders like Herbert Hill and Lester Granger to give
the keynote addresses that kicked off their annual membership drives.
Ruby Hurley came to talk about the Till murder; a "preacher for the
Montgomery boycott" spoke to an NAACP gathering; and Fred Shuttlesworth visited the city to stimulate "local activism and support for
the Alabama Christian Movement for Human Rights." Shuttlesworth's
speech, devoted in part to decrying the treatment of Anne and Carl
Braden, also showed that people elsewhere knew of Louisville developments.[5] These speakers left an impression on the young people who
conducted Louisville's largest sit-in campaign. Raoul Cunningham, for
one, attributed his awareness even as a fourteen-year-old to attending
NAACP meetings where his mother and others discussed the events in
Montgomery.[6] While black Louisvillians clearly had access to information about activism elsewhere, they also demonstrated a sense of mutual responsibility by contributing to the NAACP fund to investigate
the Till murder. Finally, Louisvillians referred to other communities as
models of how they should fight segregation in their own city. As the
Louisville Defender put it, "We need people who will follow the example of Montgomery."[7]

Louisvillians followed two models in this period, reflecting the
city's position on the border between North and South. Civil rights

activists sought to pass civil rights legislation, as had been done in mid-western and northern border cities, and organized direct action, as had been done in the South. The *Louisville Defender* called for legislation to force integration of public accommodations as early as 1954, citing examples in Ohio, Illinois, and Indiana.[8] Then, in the fall of 1957, the board of aldermen considered the first public accommodations ordinance. Submitted by civil rights leaders, the ordinance included the first full statement of the scope of their goals, asking for prohibitions against discrimination in both businesses open to the general public and employment by utilities, transit companies, and firms with franchises from the city. The aldermen immediately referred the bill to the city law department for review, where it languished into the spring of 1958. Acting law director William E. Berry suggested that the measure would need to come from the state legislature. In response, Felix S. Anderson, an African American state representative from Louisville, introduced three bills in the General Assembly in February 1958 that together would give cities permission to pass civil rights laws.[9]

In the meantime, the proposal had become an issue in the 1957 mayoral election. Speaking to the members of the Frontiers, an African American men's club, Democratic candidate Bruce Hoblitzell criticized attempts to "force" changes in race relations. He drew on Louisville's progressive image, saying, "We've already accomplished a lot and without animosity." Pressing the issue, however, would "upset the nice progress that is currently being made." Republican candidate Robert Diehl, in front of a hostile audience at a meeting of the Louisville Area Baptist Ministers and Deacons, reportedly spoke in favor of the measure, although he later asserted that he did not believe in legislating the policy of private business. The *Louisville Courier-Journal* weighed in at this point. Noting that both candidates refused to commit to the ordinance, the editors concluded that pursuing legislation at this time "is a mistake." They continued, "We see only danger to progress in the effort to force desegregation by statute in private business," because doing so moved past the issue of rights and into the "cloudier realm of social acceptance." Shut out by candidates and civic spokesmen, black leaders despaired of getting support from the leaders of the tickets.[10]

As noted above, the city law department concluded that the state needed to pass enabling legislation, but Anderson's bills failed in the assembly. After his election, Hoblitzell established a committee on human relations to investigate voluntary means of increasing integration.

The committee saw its role as trying to prevent potential disorder that might arise from the issue by meeting with businessmen. However, within a year, black leaders complained that the "committee is nothing more than window dressing." Moreover, Hoblitzell reaffirmed his opposition to forced integration, stating that businessmen "should do [it] out of their hearts." The *Louisville Defender* and civil rights leaders did not give up on the issue, proposing in the next few years several similar ordinances. But in the meantime, black activists looked for more direct ways to fight Jim Crow.[11]

Between 1956 and 1960, the NAACP Youth Council, CORE, and others made sporadic efforts to use direct action to end segregation in public accommodations. Organized in 1955 under the adult leadership of Muriel Gregg, the Youth Council soon had eighty members. Lacking enough interested students at the University of Louisville to have a separate college chapter, the council included high school students as well. Raoul Cunningham explained that the Youth Council planned "a lot of cultural activities, some educational type programming, discussion of issues, awareness, and education." Regionally, Youth Councils became the part of the NAACP most attracted to and influenced by the new direct action techniques. The Louisville group reflected this trend, adopting a program "to work on the integration of sit-down lunch counters in five and ten cent stores."[12] In 1956 Central High School teacher Lyman Johnson led a small group of students in sit-ins at drugstore lunch counters. Two years later, after a local Walgreens refused to serve the visiting mayor of Kingston, Jamaica, the NAACP public accommodations committee and Youth Council started a new campaign. That effort fizzled, however, when it failed to arouse community support.[13]

The Youth Council decided to try demonstrations again in late 1959, leading stand-ins at the Brown Theatre. Raoul Cunningham recalled, "We were in a meeting which must have been [in] November. The Brown had started advertising that the film *Porgy and Bess* would be opening on Christmas Day. It was mail order tickets. . . . We put our money in and sent for tickets. We all got tickets. So the next thing is we are going to demonstrate." Fifteen young people went to the theater, presented their tickets, but were turned away. They immediately launched a picket line. The adult NAACP branch organized the protest, and thereafter two people a day picketed for thirty minutes before and after each show, joined by a small group of white citizens from the Unitarians for Social Action. When members of the Youth Council attended Mayor Hoblitzell's weekly "beef session" to confront him on this issue, he admitted the immorality of segregation but refused to change his opposition to a law mandating integration. The campaign culminated when an interracial group went on a bus trip, organized by the Unitarians for Social Action, to see the film at a theater in Indianapolis owned, ironically, by the same company that managed the Brown.[14]

Within a month, the new furor over downtown accommodations pushed city government to respond, after a year of inactivity by all official bodies, including the mayor's committee on human relations. At a January 7, 1960, public meeting to discuss the Brown Theatre dispute, the mayor "half-shouted" that he would not talk to theater managers about changing their policy because "I wouldn't want to be party to anything that would cause trouble." He did not think it his place to tell people how to run their businesses. In mid-February, he met with his human relations committee for twenty-two minutes, after which the chair, the Reverend Frank Taafel, concluded, "We felt we had come up against a solid wall and that further meetings were useless." A month later, however, another city body, the civic and religious advisory committee, broke the impasse and agreed to call a meeting of hotel, restaurant, and theater representatives to discuss voluntary integration. Members claimed they had been trying to make such contacts for a year but only the restaurant owners association had responded. At that point the mayor agreed to support the call for a meeting, though he reiterated that on this issue citizens and not the city government should take the lead.[15]

The mayor may have softened his position in an effort to head off a new proposed ordinance mandating integration. An NAACP committee headed by Charles W. Anderson once again drafted a bill prohibiting discrimination in public facilities and wrote to Alderman William Beckett, asking him to introduce the measure. Simultaneously, the committee convinced African American representative William Childress to submit a "home rule" bill to the General Assembly, which would enable Louisville to adopt the ordinance. Beckett introduced the measure in early February, and the board referred it to the rules and grievance committee, with a vote scheduled, at the earliest, in two weeks. It immediately became clear that the mayor and the heads of the city and county Democratic organizations opposed the measure.

Supporters did not expect the aldermen to act on the measure quickly, but on February 23, 1960, the board considered and defeated the bill by a voice vote of the majority. Alderman Clifford Haury reported for the rules committee that they had determined that "the board of aldermen has no jurisdiction in this matter" because "it has no control over private property rights nor can it pass any laws in conflict with constitutional guarantee [*sic*] of private property rights." With this the aldermen joined the growing chorus of conservatives who grounded their opposition to civil rights legislation in a defense of white property rights, or, as massive resistance spokesman James Kilpatrick more bluntly put it, the "precious right to discriminate." Haury added that he believed that the Louisville "community would eventually voluntarily remedy the situation."[16]

Black leaders responded that voluntary action simply could not accomplish the job, even in a racially progressive city like Louisville. James Crumlin pointed out that previous negotiations had failed. The editors of the *Defender* expressed frustration with the emphasis on voluntary integration, arguing that no major gains had come in that fashion but rather had come through court action or threatened court action, or, as one black minister added, "by force and threat of force." The *Defender* praised Louisville's "almost perfect near ten-year record since the integration of local and state colleges" but argued that the record revealed an ability to adjust peacefully to change when it came rather than a willingness to undertake change without force. The defeat of the measure brought exclamations of anger and cries for retribution. Angry blacks labeled the board of aldermen's hasty action a "slap in the face" and a sign that neither the mayor nor the aldermen were "concerned about Negroes." Charles Lunderman concluded, "We should make sure none of them get re-elected."[17]

Eventually, the black community would act to achieve that result. In the meantime, Beckett went back to the existing board, setting off a flurry of antagonistic responses. During the debate over the ordinance, Beckett had asked the Kentucky attorney general, John B. Breckinridge, for an opinion on the constitutionality of such a law. When he stated that the city could pass a civil rights bill, Beckett revised the ordinance and reintroduced it despite rules against reconsidering a failed measure without majority consent. At the next meeting, the aldermen ended Beckett's effort, adopting by a vote of eleven to one a resolution declaring, "We, the board of aldermen, are opposed to any ordinance which takes away the right of an owner of a private business to select his or its customers or clientele." Beckett's proposal for the creation of a human relations commission met a similar fate, losing in April by the same vote. Shortly thereafter, the aldermen stepped up their opposition and considered a measure that would strengthen trespass laws in such a way as to prevent sit-in demonstrations. The mayor did not support the measure, however, and asked that it be withdrawn to prevent further tensions.[18] Nevertheless, it revealed the extent of the board's hostility and convinced many blacks that the Democrats on the board posed an obstacle that they needed to remove. It also convinced them to try other means to achieve integration.

While Louisville's aldermen dithered over a law to end segregation in public accommodations, around the South young men and women took direct action to reach the same result. After the Greensboro demonstrations triggered region-wide sit-ins, black Louisvillians considered how to follow suit. The *Louisville Defender* covered news of the North Carolina protest; demonstrations in Lexington, Kentucky; and events in all the hot spots across the South. A month into the new movement, the editors warned, "It can happen here," and advised the mayor and board of aldermen not to "underestimate the dissatisfaction of Negro Citizens." NAACP Youth Council members remember how the movement in Nashville inspired them. "Nashville was the largest mass movement," recalled Youth Council leader Raoul Cunningham. "When they did the mass demonstrations, that was the first real city to grab national headlines. There was great documentation on it on TV." In late April the Reverend James Lawson, the organizer of the Nashville sit-ins, told Louisvillians about the campaign at an NAACP conference. By the end of the meeting, the organization voted to support lunch counter demonstrations to show the city government "we mean business."[19] Louisville did not, however, immediately join the region-wide sit-in movement. Anne Braden criticized this failure as a sign of complacency and a result of the "veneer of liberalism" that "tends to discourage militancy." More likely, protesters delayed action in response to Beckett's plea to postpone demonstrations until his legislation could be considered.[20]

Once the smoke from the board of aldermen battles cleared, a new direct action group, a local affiliate of CORE, began to organize. In late April the Citizens Movement for Peaceful Integration, a short-lived local group headed by the Reverend M. M. D. Perdue, invited

CORE's national field secretary, Len Holt, to the city to hold workshops on nonviolent protest. At the end of the training, the group endorsed sit-ins led by CORE.[21] Perdue's group became the heart of the new CORE chapter, which conducted sporadic demonstrations throughout the spring and summer of 1960. The group included adult members Bishop Tucker and George Kimbrough, a white doctor living in the west end who became involved in social action through the Unitarian Church. Two white students, Lynn Pfuhl and Brigid McHugh, and two African American students, Beverly Neal and David West, were the first officers. They focused initially on the restaurant in the Kaufman-Strauss department store. Ray Gardner, the store's executive vice president, told CORE spokesperson David West that, while he personally opposed segregation, he had to do what was "for the good of the company" and continue discriminating. To support the young people, three black civic organizations—the local chapter of the Alpha Phi Alpha fraternity, the Louisville Links, and the Independent Improvement Association—decided to boycott the store and cancel their credit cards. In contrast to comparable protests in communities across the South, however, these demonstrations did not spark mass daily demonstrations accompanied by nighttime rallies and arrests.[22] In late July, when CORE began another stand-in at Kaufman-Strauss, Gardner told them they were "wasting their time." He closed the lunch counter for repairs and informed a visiting CORE official that he intended to tear it out. He proposed starting a citizens' committee to discuss the problem, and CORE decided he "should be let alone for a little while."[23]

While CORE maintained small-scale picketing, a new organization, the Non-partisan Voter Registration Committee, pursued the goal of marshaling black voter strength against their enemies in city government. Cofounder Woodford Porter recalled, "It was an attempt to build some political strength. Frank Stanley Jr., Neville Tucker, and I formed that group. Neville was a Republican, Frank was a Democrat, and I was an Independent. What we wanted to do was to get masses of black registrations so we could produce masses of black votes." In the early 1960s, student activists and their adult allies in the regional movement often debated the relative merits of direct action and voter registration as a focus for activity, at times portraying these as separate paths to change; indeed, the question became an early bone of contention in the Student Nonviolent Coordinating Committee (SNCC). In Louisville, however, where African Americans had access to the vote, activists regarded the two strategies as necessarily linked. As the *Defender* put it, the failure of blacks to vote "lead[s] to humiliations like the denial of the public accommodations ordinance." Over the summer the new committee sponsored a block-to-block registration campaign, culminating in a rally and visit by Martin Luther King Jr. By the end of the summer, the group claimed it had registered an additional twenty-two thousand voters.[24]

During the fall other groups started demonstrating. In September an interracial group of bowlers organized by Andrew Wade picketed the new alleys in the Algonquin Manor shopping center, located near the majority-black housing projects Southwick and Cotter Homes. They quickly expanded their demands to include black access to non-menial jobs in the stores of the shopping center and circulated over ten thousand flyers asking people not to "purchase where you can't get first class accommodation." After a week of picketing, violence broke out. On September 8, "iron pole–wielding white youths" attacked the demonstrators, who were of both races and were mostly teenagers. One black youth used a picket sign stick to retaliate against an attacker, sending him to the hospital with a cut in his stomach. Except for a broken car windshield and cigarettes thrown at the picketers, a peaceful night followed. The adult spokesmen for the group insisted they would continue to fight for the right to picket and, if necessary, stand up for themselves. The group briefly suspended its pickets to allow the NAACP to talk with the shopping center's management, but when negotiations failed, the pickets resumed, and the boycott effort was redoubled with NAACP support. By the end of the year, the campaign reported 95 percent effectiveness in the nonbuying effort.[25]

In late 1960, CORE made an effort to rejuvenate its own demonstrations, once again targeting the segregated lunch counters of downtown stores. This time it chose Stewart's Dry Goods Company because it was "the bulwark of segregation here." "We believe," student leader Lynn Pfuhl stated, "that if we can achieve integration here, we shall eventually be able to integrate all of Louisville." The campaign began on November 10 and continued with stand-ins every day, but like earlier efforts, this campaign seemed as if it would fizzle out without results.[26] In December, Pfuhl reported to national CORE official Marvin Rich that the demonstrations at Stewart's were "disorganized, uncertain, and . . . largely ineffective." The Louisville CORE affiliate was always relatively weak and unstable, in part because the city's NAACP

Youth Council, which had already engaged in protests at drugstore lunch counters and theaters, had attracted many activist-minded black youth. CORE's reputation as an organization dominated by "white radicals" and "affluent blacks," in the words of Lyman Johnson, also hurt its efforts. Whatever the reason, in November 1960 the organization had only ten reliable members and four people turning out to picket.[27]

Meanwhile, adult leaders of the NAACP such as the Reverend W. J. Hodge hesitated to get involved. Hodge had grown up in rural south Texas, attended college in Baton Rouge, Louisiana, and later received a divinity degree from Oberlin College. After his first pastorate in Virginia, he came to Louisville in 1957 to become the minister of Fifth Street Baptist Church, a venerable institution in the black community with an activist history. Buoyed by support from his congregation, he soon joined the local NAACP branch and by 1961 had risen to leadership in it. He doubted, however, whether sit-ins would work in Louisville. As he later recalled, "We felt at the time that in most cities where they had been effective, there was a black college. . . . Well, at that time Louisville had no black college, and we were fearful that because of the lacking of this . . . we couldn't get the kind of support" necessary to succeed.[28]

In late January, CORE member Beverly Neal reported that some of the black students at Male High School might join in a demonstration soon. Her informant was Raoul Cunningham, Louisville born and raised. When he was a teenager, Cunningham's widowed mother had moved with her only son to an all-white block in the west end. In his memory, he associated his first real interest in the NAACP with the experience of watching that block turn quickly majority black—the result of blockbusting and panic selling. His mother bought him an NAACP membership, and he joined the Youth Council, serving as an officer in the organization by the time of the *Porgy and Bess* demonstrations. He attended Male High School, a majority-white school that nevertheless had the second-largest number of black students, after Central High School. Through his church, the YMCA, and other social and educational activities, he maintained social ties with black students in other schools and neighborhoods, including Beverly Neal. Their conversations about the protests convinced them to ignore the "hang-ups" of adult leaders—concerns about bail money and whether the small number of black college students could carry off sit-ins—and go forward with demonstrations on their own. Cunningham brought an infusion of Youth Council high school members to the floundering CORE protests and transformed them into a truly mass campaign.[29]

On February 9, 1961, young people from CORE and the NAACP Youth Council began demonstrations at Kaufman-Strauss and Stewart's. On February 20, police arrested Cunningham and four other teenagers. Unlike previous efforts, the arrests at Stewart's made it into the pages of the *Courier-Journal* and the broader community consciousness. More important, the next day, seventy-five young demonstrators picketed the stores, unfazed by the arrests. Soon the numbers of protesters began to grow, and the local demonstrations started to resemble the sit-ins that had rocked the South over the last year. Within a week, daily protests of ten to fifteen people targeted the department stores, the Blue Boar Cafeteria, and the theaters, resulting in more arrests. By the third day, police had arrested fifty-eight protesters.[30]

These young people joined the mass demonstrations because of a sense that their generation had to take the lead in challenging segregation. As Cunningham recalled, they were inspired by young activists in Nashville and elsewhere, trained by visitors such as James Lawson and Len Holt, and linked through traveling speakers and fund-raisers to a network of activists around the region. Just as important, they saw their participation in the movement as growing seamlessly out of their experiences in an interconnected web of youth organizations and social relationships. Many were friends through church and school, which Runette Robinson described as the "center of our activities," while also belonging to a small set of organizations that promoted leadership, such as the High Y, a program sponsored by the YMCA. As Deanna Shobe Tinsley, daughter of NAACP lawyer Benjamin Shobe, later noted, "That program was designed to allow students to participate in political processes. . . . Although we didn't have classes, we met to learn and to acquire parliamentary procedure, to practice public speaking, to discuss issues." The core who launched the demonstrations recalled that sharing experiences and learning about politics and problems facing their community in these organizations inspired them to participate in the sit-ins. They saw the protests as a logical outgrowth of their experiences and viewed their efforts as part of a larger movement.[31]

As the number of demonstrators escalated, adult leaders stepped in to coordinate them, organizing a mass rally the Sunday after the first week of demonstrations at Zion Baptist Church, the largest in the black community. At that meeting, adult and youth leaders formed a steering committee to coordinate strategy, handle fund-raising and legal support for those arrested, and conduct negotiations with the city and downtown businessmen. The initial members of the group included students Beverly Neal and Sam Gilliam of the Youth Council, and participants in the demonstrations later recalled others such as William Summers III and Arthur Smith. The ministers of churches the young people attended, including NAACP leader Reverend W. J. Hodge, Bishop Tucker, and the Reverends D. E. King and F. G. Sampson, also took part, as did older leaders such as KBNA member Charles Lunderman. Finally, representatives of an up-and-coming generation of leaders joined, most important the young lawyers Frank Stanley Jr. and Neville Tucker, who attracted the admiration of the high school students. The formation of the steering committee and its role in the ensuing battle reflected the lack of a single dominant civil rights leader or organization in the community and ensured that different factions felt invested and represented in the open accommodations battle.[32]

In conjunction with the demonstrations, adult leaders at the NAACP launched Nothing New for Easter, an effort to hit downtown businesses with an attack on the pocketbook. They urged African Americans not to shop at downtown businesses before Easter to protest both segregated facilities and discriminatory hiring policies. NAACP branch president and steering committee member Hodge predicted that the seventy-five thousand black customers in the area could potentially cost businesses $18 million. Whether the boycott specifically changed merchants' minds remains unclear, but demonstrators believed it had an impact on downtown businesses, and at least some businesses reacted when white customers began to stay away from the area. As young demonstrator Gerald White remembered, "[The boycott] was the only reason it was integrated. Everybody was losing money. Blue Boar couldn't make any money. Everybody was worried because nobody could make any money." By the end of February, both Stewart's and Kaufman-Strauss opened negotiations, leading protesters to assume that they would take the lead and integrate by the end of March. Several downtown stores even placed ads beckoning blacks to patronize their business with slogans such as "Bob Brady's has been integrated for seven years" and "Comer's Pharmacy practices Democracy." But success did not come so quickly. The boycott continued over the next months of demonstrations and negotiations. The steering committee officially extended it beyond Easter and called it off only in early May, after the 1961 Kentucky Derby.[33]

As the demonstrations grew, so did the reaction to them on the street. Although the community responded mildly compared to other cities, confrontations occurred on the picket lines. In one incident, a spectator "grabbed" a white woman who had joined the demonstrators. In late March, an older white man was convicted in police court and fined for shoving his way through a picket line. Store employees adopted tactics that were more potentially dangerous and humiliating. Gerald White recalled that, as a marshal for the demonstrations, he kept an eye on the sky for the bottles, ashtrays, and other objects that rained down on the picketers from upstairs windows. In April at the Blue Boar Cafeteria, for example, an ashtray "narrowly missed" campaign leader Frank Stanley Jr. Runette Robinson recalled another common tactic: "We were sitting right there at Fifth and Chestnut; there was a restaurant there. A guy came out and dumped this nasty water with whatever I don't know what was in it, all on us."[34]

According to contemporary news reports, most of the violence on the picket line came at the hands of employees of the targeted businesses, especially the merchants' security guards. During the first week of mass demonstrations, Stewart's employees "knocked down" and "pushed around" demonstrators to get them to disperse, while nearby, at one of the theaters, a guard "jabbed" a young woman with a nightstick.[35] The use of force escalated in late April, particularly at the Blue Boar, as tensions over the continued demonstrations rose. Protest leaders claimed one guard regularly shoved people to the ground and that one young man was "kicked repeatedly." In other incidents guards struck a girl in the breast—she ended up in the hospital—and threw a male student through a plate glass window. Some of the violence took place when cafeteria-employed guards aided the arrest of demonstrators and got overzealous in their use of force. As Gerald White remembered, "They had a paddy wagon at Fourth and Walnut. . . . They would drag you, head bumping, to Fourth Street, in the street, by two legs, to the paddy wagon."[36]

Demonstrators faced a daily chance of detention. After the initial arrests at Stewart's on February 20, the numbers climbed steadily, and 175 protesters had been taken into custody by March 15. A second wave of mass arrests occurred in late April, including a one-week total of 332. By April 27, more Louisvillians—685 in all—had been incarcerated during demonstrations than anywhere else in the nation to that point.[37] Initially, protesters were uncertain about how city police would respond. The previous chief of police, Colonel Carl Heustis, had ordered his officers not to use their authority to enforce segregation by arresting demonstrators. In one early incident at a theater, Captain Carl Dotson refused to arrest stand-in demonstrators, saying, "These kids aren't doing anything wrong." However, the new chief, William Bindner, soon established a different modus operandi. He characterized the pickets as "mob violence" and not only ordered his officers to arrest demonstrators but encouraged proprietors and merchant police to swear out warrants and detain them.[38]

Police charged demonstrators under eighteen with disorderly conduct and took them to the juvenile center, where they were held until they could be released to their parents. Ultimately, juvenile court judge Henry Triplett, a former member of the board of aldermen who had voted against the ordinance and against creating a human relations commission, heard their cases. In contrast, adults were taken to police court, where they faced charges not only of disorderly conduct but also of loitering, contributing to the delinquency of minors, and breach of peace. The NAACP provided legal support for all the demonstrators, but the judicial process quickly fell behind events. By the first week of March, after the arrests of 72 people, only 14 teenagers and 7 adults had been formally charged. In April police court judge Hugo Taustine heard some of the adult cases and found 11 defendants guilty of disorderly conduct, fining them twenty dollars each. At the end of June, however, Triplett surprised demonstrators when he dismissed the 597 pending juvenile cases, noting it "was not in the best interest of the child nor the welfare of the community" to pursue them. The judges' decisions left 49 adult cases in limbo.[39]

Mayor Hoblitzell responded to the crisis by appointing a new emergency committee to meet with African American leaders and downtown proprietors. For the next two weeks, the emergency committee engaged in a dance with the steering committee. The mayor's group pushed for a promise to postpone demonstrations and asked for time to prepare local businessmen for integration; the movement leaders repeated that ending the demonstrations hinged on the extent of progress, demanded a definite date for desegregation, and pushed to have the charges dropped against those arrested.[40] Initially both sides expressed optimism. The *Courier-Journal* predicted, "Louisville Negroes are apparently near a major victory in their fight against segregation in the downtown area," and the mayor reported after his meetings with proprietors, "Everybody we've talked to is sympathetic." Over the next several months, as negotiations and demonstrations seesawed, white civic leaders focused on the victories, no matter how small, because any forward movement represented hope that voluntary action could work. At first, black leaders shared that hope. Frank Stanley Jr. spoke for the steering committee early in the negotiations when he declared, "We expect the complete desegregation of downtown Louisville within a month." The NAACP agreed, reporting that the "entire community, Negro and white, are friendly to what is going on and have expressed hope that something concrete will come out of the meetings." Indeed, at the end of one meeting, the steering committee and emergency committee "reportedly" agreed that integration would take place by April 1, 1961.[41]

The optimism and negotiations broke down after the release of the emergency committee's report at the end of the first week of March. The committee boasted that, in only two weeks of work, it had made much progress. "We have spoken to several groups of businessmen," the report stated, and "issued public statements urging integration." The committee also claimed that it had met with religious groups and had convinced the "largest department store" as well as other shops to integrate. All the agreements, however, were "confidential in nature and cannot now be publicly disclosed." Progress was in the eye of the beholder. The steering committee immediately responded that the report "did not indicate enough definite progress." Appealing to the civic leaders' pride in the city's role as a leader for the South in race relations, civil rights spokesmen added, "If Atlanta, with its previous rigid segregation pattern will desegregate by September, Louisville, in light of its past and present atmosphere of good race relations, should be able to desegregate immediately." In light of the failure to produce concrete results, demonstrations resumed, beginning with a 250-person march through downtown.[42]

Recriminations and questions about the future of negotiations began at once. The emergency committee's report blamed black leaders' "impatience with delay and a determination that immediate progress be accomplished" for hampering "the progress which the committee could otherwise have hoped for." The *Courier-Journal* took up the same line of attack, warning that further demonstrations could provoke a crisis that would make things worse. In public statements, black leaders did not specifically blame the emergency committee, saying, "They have given themselves wholly and unreservedly," but privately, CORE leader Lynn Pfuhl wrote that the negotiations deteriorated because the committee members did nothing but "condemn sin and tell each other how virtuous they are."[43] In the midst of this atmosphere of blame, the resumption of negotiations seemed uncertain. Governor Bert Combs broke the impasse when he intervened and encouraged both sides to return to the table. Tensions eased somewhat when steering committee members agreed to a period of two weeks of calm, though they warned that demonstrations could resume if they made no progress.[44]

While young blacks marched and adult leaders negotiated, individuals and organizations in the broader community weighed in on the debate over integration and a public accommodations ordinance. Ever since the Christmas 1959 Brown Theatre demonstrations, some white Louisvillians had expressed their support for integration. At the time of the early demonstrations, Ray Bixler, a professor of psychology at the University of Louisville, surveyed white attitudes and found that a slight plurality of Louisville whites believed blacks should have access to facilities. He reported that 54.7 percent of his respondents would attend a movie with blacks and 47.5 percent said blacks should be allowed into restaurants. But they rejected an ordinance making segregation illegal, with 66.9 percent opposed and 25.2 percent in favor.[45] The positions of white religious organizations reflected these statistics. In 1960, the local Catholic diocese declared that, although "segregation represents a pattern of life" antagonistic to democracy and Christianity, forced integration would foster hostility. At the same time, black clergy could not convince the interracial Louisville Ministerial Association to move beyond support for voluntary integration before all such options had been exhausted.[46] Slowly, however, some groups began to go a bit further. The KCLU went on record supporting both integration and an ordinance. In June 1961 the Greater Louisville Central Labor Council reminded officials of the broader issues involved when it asked the city to create a human relations commission, pass an open accommodations ordinance, and establish a fair employment program.[47] These actions and resolutions indicated that, within Louisville's religious, labor, and civic organizations, some sympathy existed for integration and a law mandating it.

Of course, not all whites in Louisville were sympathetic toward either the demonstrations or their goal. In spring 1960, Millard Grubbs, the opponent of school integration, led a new local group called the Citizens National Law Enforcement Commission, which smeared the leaders of the movement as Communists and called for their arrest. The WCC went further, calling on its members to bypass city law enforcement and take up arms themselves "in defense of private rights and property." Fortunately, no significant group of white citizens responded to the group's call.[48] Business owners expressed the strongest opposition to an ordinance. In late April, members of the Louisville Tavern Operators Association organized the Committee for Business Freedom. Spokesman Jack Lowery, who also served as an assistant commonwealth's attorney, said the group did not oppose integration per se but rather government orders to change policy. Like ordinance advocates, he invoked Louisville's good reputation and record in school desegregation—but with a twist. He called the demonstrations "blemishes on Louisville's splendid accomplishments in harmonious race relations" and argued that provisions similar to the transfer option that enabled people to opt out of school integration should be included in the open accommodations ordinance. The group quickly filed a suit to prohibit demonstrations and "disorder" at its members' establishments. It would later provide the main source of resistance to the implementation of the law.[49]

During the lull in demonstrations, Hoblitzell took the unexpected step of arranging a visit to St. Louis to learn from its leaders how they had accomplished integration. The *Defender* had held sister border city St. Louis up as a model for Louisville for over a decade, and steering committee leaders reinforced that connection. "Our expectation of desegregation in Louisville is not unrealistic," the committee stated, "when you consider that in a three week period St. Louis desegregated 200 downtown restaurants." The mayor's travel plans did not indicate any sympathy for the movement. He maintained his position, first articulated during his election campaign, against a public accommodations ordinance. Before the planned trip got under way, moreover, a new round of demonstrations began, accompanied by nearly 150 arrests and escalating violence. The mayor revealed his lack of sympathy again when he toured the demonstrations and, after viewing one protest outside the Blue Boar, declared, "This looks like a mob."[50]

In late April 1961, just days before Hoblitzell's trip, Martin Luther King Jr. visited Louisville to voice his support for the movement.

King gave five lectures around town, including to groups of fourteen hundred and five hundred at events at Southern Baptist Theological Seminary, where he praised Louisville's "inspiring example" but called for more progress.[51] King's visit was just one instance of the moral encouragement national movement organizations and figures gave to the Louisville struggle. The community's strong ties to activists throughout the region bore fruit in such visits and in advice and offers of support. Local CORE members, for example, kept in close contact with national officers, receiving instruction on negotiation strategies. James Farmer came back to town and gave another workshop during the demonstration moratorium in April. The NAACP sent its national youth director, Herbert White, to the city to pledge support in the forms of legal aid and money. Finally, SNCC held a meeting and workshop in town.[52] These visits not only provided concrete aid in the forms of advice and offers of funds—though the latter were turned down—but also helped reinforce the connections between Louisville and the movement elsewhere.

When the mayor returned from his visit to St. Louis, he announced a "new plan" for integration. Although he claimed that Louisville "has gone further in desegregation than any other city, including St. Louis," he nevertheless borrowed a model from that city. He called on downtown restaurants to desegregate by May 1. He asked black leaders to suspend demonstrations until then and to help him to conduct a testing campaign that would send small groups of blacks to targeted establishments after that date. One-on-one negotiations would follow the tests. Black leaders asked Hoblitzell to show his support for desegregation by asking the police not to arrest protesters. The *Courier-Journal* endorsed the plan as "the best chance for a solution" and called on recalcitrant restaurants to "yield to the inevitable." With the Kentucky Derby just around the corner, the paper wanted to prevent further demonstrations, which would obscure the city's progress.[53]

Unfortunately, like all previous efforts at moral persuasion and voluntary action, the mayor's initiative failed. Teams of two or three people visited fifty-seven restaurants and received service at twenty-six, frequently with rude treatment and higher prices. The steering committee pointed out that, since the demonstrations began, ten places had integrated voluntarily or through negotiation, twenty-four had integrated in response to sit-ins, and twenty-six had integrated in response to testing. When the black community and leaders met in the first week of May to decide what to do next, the issue became whether to demonstrate over Derby weekend. They decided to cancel protests for the weekend for several reasons. Some believed that demonstrators faced an increased risk of violence from drunken segregationists. Lawyers worried that a police force stretched thin by Derby festivities would provide inadequate protection and that court processing would be slowed down. The *Defender* argued that the movement wanted to create a "beloved community" in Louisville and therefore would show restraint for the good of the city.[54]

But movement leaders also expected some reward for that restraint, namely the passage of an open accommodations ordinance. The *Defender* argued that voluntary action, pleas from the mayor, and support from "considerable citizens" had not worked; only a law could effect change. Black leaders urged the mayor to introduce an ordinance making it illegal for restaurants, theaters, and hotels to discriminate, and they threatened to renew demonstrations if Hoblitzell and his committee did not support the law. Predictably, the mayor refused to do so. His emergency committee expressed its opposition to "forced desegregation" and disbanded. In response, the steering committee pledged to take the issue directly to the board of aldermen, submitting a proposal in late May modeled on a new law in St. Louis. While waiting for the board to act, black activists conducted a city-wide test and reported that 98 percent of restaurants and theaters in the city—not just those downtown—remained segregated. To show support for the measure, the steering committee planned a two thousand–person march to the next meeting of the board, and it earned the endorsement of eighty white citizens for the protest.[55]

The board of aldermen also responded in a predictable fashion, given its hostility to previous efforts. On June 13, Beckett introduced two measures, the public accommodations bill and a proposal to create a human relations commission. William Milburn, the president of the board and the Democratic candidate for mayor, spoke first. "It appears to me, Mr. Beckett, that the position of this board is so well known to you, that you can have no hope of success on this second trial," he opened. He hypothesized that Beckett was being used by "our political opponents, who wish to get as much political mileage as possible out of the racial discord that has developed here." Milburn saw the measure simply as a Republican election ploy. He decried the "attempt to gain desired legislation by demonstrations of potential mobs" and closed by asserting his continued opposition to any law that forced "private persons to handle their private affairs in a manner they resist." Following Milburn's speech, the board passed a resolution nearly identical to the one of the year before that put it on record against any public accommodations ordinance.[56]

One week later, demonstrations again erupted in the city, but they took place outside downtown and were met by more violence. On June 19, fifty-eight demonstrators picketed outside the gates of Fontaine Ferry, a private amusement park in the west end. Fontaine Ferry was a sore spot for the black community. Originally surrounded by a white working-class community, the park attracted the attention of black youngsters moving into the changing neighborhood. But, as Mervin Aubespin explained, it was also a more dangerous target. "Fontaine Ferry was most active at night," Aubespin recalled, "so we were marching in the evenings. The other thing was it was in a neighborhood where there were a lot of young people and in order to get here you had to go through the white neighborhood. . . . They waited for you and that made it really rough. Because at night you can throw a bottle or a brick and nobody knows where it came from."[57] On the first night of protests, five hundred white "spectators" surrounded the demonstrators. Cars bearing Confederate flags cruised by while whites carrying signs stating "Tickets Back to Africa" and "2-4-6-8 We Don't Want to Integrate" mingled with the crowd. Opponents threw cups full of rocks and flash bulbs at the demonstrators, and crowds of between fifty and one hundred whites pushed through police lines. In the end, police arrested twenty black youths, two black adults, and seven whites.[58]

The new demonstration and the arrests sparked renewed legal conflict. The park asked for and received an injunction prohibiting CORE and the NAACP from demonstrating at its gates. Meanwhile, Judge Henry Triplett sentenced the youths to probation, contingent on the promise that they not participate in any further demonstrations, and established a code of behavior that demonstrators had to follow or risk being jailed. Black leaders cried foul, accusing Triplett of coercing the young people to relinquish their constitutional right to protest. Frank Stanley Jr. declared the judge's dictatorial "code of behavior" put "property rights above human rights." Triplett's decision did not stand. Late in the summer, the circuit court voided the probation orders and the convictions of those arrested at the Fontaine Ferry demonstrations.[59] The park, however, remained segregated and was a target for summer demonstrations and legal suits for several years.

The brief renewal of demonstrations coincided with a new effort by white civic leaders to reestablish negotiations. The mayor's civic and religious advisory committee gained an African American member, Murray Walls, and met once with the Kentucky Commission on Human Rights, which was formed in 1960. Mayor Hoblitzell also formed yet another civic committee, a biracial committee on human rights, in lieu of a legally mandated local human rights agency. Its white members came primarily from the religious community rather than from downtown businesses and the chamber of commerce. But, the *Louisville Defender* quickly pointed out, none of the committee's black members held leadership roles in the protest movement. Nevertheless, the group made a sincere effort to revive negotiations in a strained atmosphere. Its goals were modest: to cultivate an understanding of the damage discrimination was doing to the community, to serve as a clearinghouse for information, and to publicize successful integration.[60]

By this time, the black community no longer trusted the Hoblitzell administration or the Democratic Party organization that he, the majority of aldermen, and Judge Triplett belonged to. In the summer and fall of 1961, black leaders turned their attention to voter registration and to defeating the incumbents on the board and the Democratic candidate for mayor, William Milburn. Black opposition to Milburn's candidacy, evident early in the primaries, stemmed from his role in the board of aldermen's 1960 refusal to enact a public accommodations ordinance or create a human relations commission. The Jefferson County Sunday School Association, the NAACP, and the Louisville Interdenominational Ministerial Alliance passed resolutions opposing him, and the Reverend D. E. King of Zion Baptist Church announced that Milburn's "defiant affront" to the black community could not go unchallenged.[61] Milburn did not give blacks any reason to change their minds over the course of the campaign. His position remained clear: he opposed any effort to force integration by legislation.

Milburn's main competition, Republican Party candidate William O. Cowger, refused to state his position clearly. He criticized Hoblitzell's handling of the sit-in crisis but also declared that integration should not become "a political football." He clarified his position at a June meeting of the Greater Louisville Central Labor Council, asserting that he supported voluntary integration, that he would neither propose nor work for an open accommodations ordinance, but that he would not veto one either. He also promised to create a human relations commission to work for voluntary desegregation. The *Louisville Defender* at first despaired that neither candidate would respond to the black community's demands, but Cowger's promise not to veto a civil rights law held out a slim ray of hope. Consequently, the editors of the paper and civil rights leaders mobilized the black community to vote the existing board of aldermen out and elect a mayor and new board who would pass a law.[62]

The Non-partisan Voter Registration Committee launched into action during the summer and fall of 1961. At the kickoff rally for the drive, Frank Stanley Jr. made the connection between the sit-in campaign and the election, arguing, "The greatest demonstration that can be staged at this time is a 'vote-in' for freedom." The drive culminated with a parade featuring Eartha Kitt and the Harry Belafonte Singers.[63] After registration, black leaders had to mobilize the voting power of their community. Since the 1950s, local blacks had drifted toward the Democratic Party, though some African Americans still worked as Republican Party activists. In this election, however, the community decided to vote as a bloc to swing the election. Mervin Aubespin described the process:

> Everybody decided we were going to vote Republican. . . . I saw people come to the poll and they had their Democratic buttons on, but they'd tell you, "You know what we're going to do." And they got in Cowger. . . . They cleaned house and it's the first time it's happened. It shows the power that the black community coming together could in fact have as a swing vote. It actually happened and that was a great day. . . . The word was "You know what we're supposed to do," and it went out to the churches, it went out to the network, the clubs. "We're going to clean house." And they did. They even brought in two black Republicans; Louise Reynolds was one of them. [The other was] a guy named Russell Lee.[64]

Election returns indeed showed a decisive switch in heavily black wards that helped the Republicans storm into power for the first time in twenty-eight years. The bright, pleasant day, the high level of interest in the campaign, and the voter registration drive brought out a record number of voters in the city for a local-only election, with an increase of more than eleven thousand voters over the previous record. Cowger and the Republican slate of aldermanic candidates swept the election, as did GOP contenders in the county races. In fact, at the end of the day, only one Democrat, the city controller, was left in office. The Democratic casualties included Alderman Beckett, who had incurred the wrath of the black community for endorsing Milburn. Black votes clearly contributed to Cowger's win and the Republicans' margin of victory. The eighth through eleventh wards, which were the heaviest in black registration, had previously revealed their Democratic preference in the last mayor's race, in 1957, by voting for Bruce Hoblitzell with margins of 600 to 800. This time, however, all the majority-black wards tipped Republican. In one, the eleventh, the margin changed to 958 for Cowger, a switch of approximately 1,500 to 1,700 votes.[65]

Significantly, white leaders from both parties and the editors of the *Louisville Courier-Journal* still hesitated to give credit to the African American vote for the election results. When asked to explain his loss, Milburn replied, "Evidently the people were ready for a change and the twenty-eight year cycle [of Democratic Party domination of city government] ran its course and caught me at the end." He also hinted that he believed, based on his own tour of the city, that voter turnout in the west and south, traditionally Democratic areas including the heavily black neighborhoods, was low. That observation was not borne out by election returns. Meanwhile, Cowger gave credit to his Republican precinct workers and the organizational efforts of his party. He also noted that Democrats must have crossed over to vote for him and reiterated the theme that people were ready for a change. The *Courier-Journal* raised the issue of whether Republicans benefited from a switch in black votes because of Milburn's and the Democratic aldermen's position on open accommodations. While the paper pointed out that the predominantly black wards did switch to the Republicans, however, it downplayed their significance, emphasizing that the margins of victory there were smaller than in some other places in the city.[66]

African American leaders at the time and since have, on the other hand, trumpeted the role of the black vote in the election results. Like Mervin Aubespin, who boasted that "they cleaned house," Raoul Cunningham recalled that all the young demonstrators voted against

Milburn, and along with them the black community "switched its allegiance from the Democratic Party to the Republican Party." The result, he maintained, was the public accommodations law. The Reverend W. J. Hodge added that blacks had not done it alone. Whites had also voted Republican because they "became upset about the way Hoblitzell handled things" during the sit-in crisis downtown.[67] The *Louisville Defender*'s commentary on the election presaged these memories. Frank Stanley Sr. praised the community for putting "first class citizenship above party affiliation" in their votes. Moreover, he reported, "Today, on almost every corner, and in every gathering, the topic of conversation is that 'we did it.'" Indeed, the paper emphasized again and again, citing the switch in the vote in the black wards, that African Americans had brought the margin of victory.[68]

The newly elected administration began by acceding to one of the movement's demands. In his first press conference, the new mayor announced that, while he still supported voluntary integration rather than legislation, he would seek an ordinance establishing a permanent commission on human relations. In late March he did so, and the board of aldermen created the Human Relations Commission (HRC) with no opposition and no debate. The new commission was composed of eleven members appointed by the mayor, plus a paid professional director and staff. Its main responsibility was to "act as a conciliator in controversies involving inter-group and inter-racial relations."[69] The commission decided its first order of business would be to conduct a citywide survey of public facilities to determine the extent of segregation. In the fall, small teams of African Americans were sent to a random sample of restaurants with instructions to ask to be served and to document their experiences. Meanwhile, the HRC attempted to negotiate some voluntary integration, with few successes. By January, the three black members of the commission, the Reverend D. E. King, Lois Morris, and James Crumlin, complained that the group was achieving little. When the survey showed clearly that only approximately half of restaurants and other facilities were integrated, the rest of the commission concurred. Mrs. Leopold Fleischaker put it bluntly: "We have accomplished virtually nothing through voluntary compliance."[70]

In 1962, while the HRC studied the problem and brought little result, CORE launched a series of demonstrations that inspired an increasingly hostile reaction from the city. In early May, the group began picketing at the West End Theatre, located in a black neighborhood on the west end of town. Within a week, a judge issued a restraining order requiring them to stay at least twenty-five feet from the theater's entrance. CORE would not play a significant role in Louisville's movement again and would disband a few years later. But a new Louisville affiliate of SNCC, the Student Nonviolent Action Council, which existed only for the duration of these demonstrations, stepped in, claiming that, since it was not affiliated with CORE, the injunction did not apply to it. Immediately, circuit court judge Charles M. Allen issued an injunction barring them from demonstrating at all. Five members— Nancy Pennick, Lynn Pfuhl, Clarence Glenn, and Margaret and Bishop Tucker—violated the injunction and were arrested.[71] During the demonstrations and arrests, the protesters were knocked to the ground, punched, and had their arms and hands twisted. Pennick was "pushed against a steel wall and suffered a concussion." A white sympathizer, Paul E. Duffy, was punched by police after he tried to help the student demonstrators gain admittance to the theater. Both he and Bishop Tucker compared their treatment to the violence against activists in the Deep South, saying the police "would make good cops in Mississippi." The confrontations proved to participants that "Louisville is comparable to Jackson, Mississippi, [and] Albany, Georgia."[72] Most frightening, the arrests and brutality raised the possibility that the city might see the violence that was then plaguing Deep South communities.

The theater manager's response to the demonstrations provoked a new round of discussions about an open accommodations ordinance. During the June demonstrations, the manager said he would not integrate until everyone else did but would do so if a law forced him to. J. Mansir Tydings, the former leader of the SRC affiliates in Kentucky who had been chosen as the executive director of the HRC, reported that, in conversations with other businessmen, he found a similar sentiment. Black leaders used this as an opportunity to revive the call for an ordinance. By January 1963, community leaders were insistent that a law be passed that year, even that spring, and were threatening renewed mass demonstrations if that did not happen.[73] By this time, they had allies on the HRC's subcommittees, who now believed that "a lot of what we have been doing has been a waste of time" and that, although voluntary integration was appreciated, "a law is needed." In light of this broadening support within a city agency, the *Louisville Courier-Journal* polled the aldermen and found that four of the twelve favored an open accommodations law "under certain circumstances."

That four would consider a law was progress. Moreover, even among those who opposed it, there were signs of a softening of positions, as some of them admitted that integration was a "moral responsibility" or said that they supported a law but thought it should be on the state level.[74]

In this seemingly more receptive environment, the subcommittees of the HRC began to prepare a draft ordinance and debate its provisions. After two months of delay because of disagreement over the penalty provisions and negotiations among members of the commission, the board of aldermen, and civil rights groups, the ordinance was completed and on April 9 was formally introduced. The final version called for a fine of up to one hundred dollars for a violation. After three violations, the city could seek an injunction to stop the discriminatory practice. Reflecting the interest in conciliation, under the law, after a complaint was made, a new antidiscrimination division of the HRC would investigate for ten days and attempt negotiations for twenty. Upon receiving the ordinance, the president of the board of aldermen, Kenneth Schmied, referred it to a subcommittee for study. Initial reaction from the aldermen was mixed. John W. Young wondered whether it was constitutional. Harry Korfhage said he did not want to force anything on businessmen. Others wanted to study the issue further and to assess the public reaction before making up their minds.[75]

While this open accommodations ordinance was being considered, the editorial board of the *Louisville Courier-Journal* shifted its position. When the possibility of a law was raised in January 1963, the paper adopted a clear policy of supporting it, a change from its previous endorsement of the various mayoral committees' efforts at change only through negotiation. The editors explained that the "voluntary approach has exhausted its possibilities" and that "it is doubtful that at this late date persuasion can induce the relatively few holdouts" to go along with the progress exhibited so far. The paper invoked Louisville's good record in race relations and called the final push for full integration unfinished business that needed to be attended to if that record was to be maintained. Moreover, the paper began to follow the *Louisville Defender*'s lead and cite other cities like St. Louis as models.[76] Thus, just as it had during school integration, the city's main daily paper, through its coverage and editorial policy, helped to create an atmosphere in which a change in race relations was seen as acceptable, desirable, and for the good of the city.

On the eve of the board of aldermen vote on the public accommodations ordinance, the *Courier-Journal* raised one additional reason for
passing it. The paper declared that failing to enact the ordinance would
invite the kind of disorder being witnessed in the Deep South. Specifically, the paper warned, "The lesson of Birmingham is clear, Negroes
are no longer content to let the white community decide when they will
be given certain rights." This column revealed one of the major factors
that helped to bring about the passage of the city's historic open accommodations law: fear of the racial violence in places like Birmingham.
This specter was raised by the HRC when members declared that the
law would be "the most effective means of insuring Louisville against
the dangers of demonstrations and boycotts." Closer to the vote, white
minister Ted Hightower invoked the connection between local activists
and those in other cities, warning that "people who are willing to go
from Louisville to Birmingham to demonstrate could easily do it here."
Indeed, Louisville blacks had already demonstrated their feeling of kinship with the protesters in that southern bastion of segregation. In late
April, just as the Birmingham campaign was getting under way, Bishop
Tucker led sympathy picketing at downtown stores. Meanwhile, area
ministers heeded Martin Luther King Jr.'s call to go to Birmingham and
participate in demonstrations there. Finally, in the weeks surrounding
the board of aldermen vote, local groups were planning and advertising
a visit from Southern Christian Leadership Conference (SCLC) leaders
Fred Shuttlesworth and Wyatt Tee Walker. Supporters of the law made
the connection explicit. The social action committee of Temple B'rith
Sholom wrote to the mayor and president of the board of aldermen, explaining its support for the ordinance: "We would hate to see the kind
of demonstrations that have been happening in Birmingham" erupt in
Louisville.[77]

The fear of a Birmingham-like crisis in Louisville seems to have
influenced the mayor, who in turn influenced the board of aldermen.
On May 9 Cowger declared his support for the law after receiving a
telegram from Lyman Johnson of the NAACP calling for immediate
action on the bill, and the speculation at the time was that Cowger
decided to push for passage to avoid new demonstrations. Indeed, in
a national publication a few months later, Johnson provided some details about his exchange with the mayor and its role in his decision. In
Look magazine, Johnson explained, "Everything the Negro has won in
Louisville has been won by fighting. Not by violence, but by insistence.

I was ready to bring out my people for demonstration in Fourth Street against what was going on in Jackson and Birmingham. I told the mayor we would come marching on Saturday, and he said could you hold it off till Tuesday, that's when the board of aldermen meets. We did hold it off, and that Tuesday, the aldermen passed the anti-bias ordinance. That's how things can happen everywhere there's trouble."[78] In the mayor's public statement announcing his change in position, he revealed concerns about events elsewhere and for Louisville's reputation, saying, "The present news stories of violence in other cities should make all of us proud to live in Louisville. We enjoy national prestige for sane and sensible race relations. I hope we will not tarnish this reputation." The next day, he met with members of the board of aldermen for two hours. Then, on May 14, the aldermen considered the bill and, with no debate, passed it by a voice vote. A later count showed that eight voted yes, one was absent, one abstained, one voted no, and one would not say how he voted. The law, which would go into effect in 120 days, would be the "first of its kind in Kentucky or probably in the South" to prohibit discrimination in public places.[79]

In the wake of the adoption of the open accommodations ordinance, the city was once again, as in the aftermath of school integration, the subject of accolades from its own citizens and from national and even international observers. Much of this praise placed Louisville's historic moment squarely in the context of the racial crises around the region and thus helped to bolster the city's image as a leader for the South. National columnist Drew Pearson set the tone when he wrote in a guest column in the *Courier-Journal* that "while national and international attention was focused on the police dogs and water hoses of Birmingham, a very quiet and little noticed vote took place" in Louisville. Avoiding the "riots in Birmingham," Louisville chose a different path and, in the words of Reuben S. Turner of Columbia, South Carolina, as a result "has proven itself to be a standard setter." Other cities rushed to follow that standard. In the month after the law passed, people in forty-five communities wrote to the HRC asking for advice on handling integration. In addition, the national and international media, including *Look, The Today Show,* the British Broadcasting Corporation, the U.S. Information Agency, and the *New York Times,* publicized Louisville's success. Hedrick Smith, writing in the *New York Times,* called Louisville "a city which is making effective progress in race relations without fanfare or the public turmoil which has gripped other southern cities." He continued, "The city government is committed to an active program for progress in civil rights. Its approach is to head off trouble before it occurs." This outpouring of admiration culminated a year later in Louisville's winning the All American City Award from the American Municipal League, specifically for being the first city in the South to adopt a public accommodations law.[80]

Members of the civil rights community expressed reservations about this fulsome praise. The *Louisville Defender* chastised the mayor for taking too much applause for himself and the community. After all, the paper argued, it was not as if "Louisville was just waiting for this to happen." Unrelenting pressure for over two years had forced the community to make this change, which now was treated as if it had always been "universally accepted." Charles Parrish wrote to his colleagues on the SRC, asking them not to be fooled: "Louisville is always more impressive to outsiders than it is to those of us who are close to the situation." Moreover, it was dangerous to let this seeming victory and the praise received for it lead to complacency. African Americans had reason to be suspect of all this enthusiasm for public accommodations and Louisville's supposed progress. By the time Louisville won the All American City Award, the open accommodations law was still not being enforced and indeed was threatened by lawsuits. The *Defender* had cause to claim that "some of the very gains over which we have swelled with pride in recent months now stand in jeopardy."[81]

From the beginning, the ordinance was met with resistance as well as praise. In the weeks immediately preceding the vote on the ordinance, authors of letters to the editor of the *Louisville Courier-Journal* decried the bill as a violation of the right to choose one's "own personal habits and associations," warned that it would be a "terrible blow" to business and would "bring racial hatred to a degree never realized" by its authors, and declared that the majority of local citizens opposed it. After it passed, other opponents added that "our neighbors in the South should know that neither our mayor nor his political stooges represent the feelings of the people of Louisville." One group sought to capitalize on that majority opinion, organizing an "independent ticket of segregationists" for governor and lieutenant governor in the next election. Some businessmen took a more direct approach and violated the letter and spirit of the new law. When the ordinance went into effect on September 12 and NAACP volunteers tested public accommodations, they found a number of establishments still refusing to serve blacks. When challenged, the proprietors referred all questions to their lawyer, Jack Lowery.[82]

Lowery represented the Louisville Tavern Operators Association in a suit in circuit court challenging the open accommodations ordinance. First, the proprietors maintained that the 120-day waiting period should not include Sundays or holidays, so when tested on September 12, they were still within their rights to discriminate. Then it was discovered that, because of a technicality—the minutes had been recorded incorrectly—the passage of the law might not have been legal. In November the aldermen repassed the law, this time with no waiting period. After some delay, the HRC filed complaints against the businesses, which asked for and got a continuance of the case in police court until January 1964. At that time, Judge William G. Colson ruled that the punitive measures of the law were unconstitutional. The city appealed to Jefferson Circuit Court and then to the Kentucky Court of Appeals. Finally, in February 1965, following the passage of the federal Civil Rights Act of 1964, the appeals court ruled that the Louisville law was constitutional and that the punitive measures could be enforced. Ironically, the reasoning of the court decision emphasized that these sorts of laws were "no longer open to debate" and were "firmly established." Louisville's "first in the South" ordinance thus was not completely enforced until such laws were adopted elsewhere and backed by federal legislation.[83]

While fighting to get their own ordinance enforced, Louisvillians were simultaneously campaigning for a civil rights bill on the state level that would end discrimination in both accommodations and employment. Within months of the passage of the Louisville open accommodations law, Frank Stanley Jr. organized a new group to lobby for a state measure, the Allied Organization for Civil Rights. Stanley hired Georgia Davis Powers to manage the office and provide the behind-the-scenes logistical support for the organization's main event, a mass march on the state capital. Powers had already engaged in Democratic Party activism, serving as a volunteer for Governor Edward Breathitt's campaign, which gave her contacts in Frankfort. Over one hundred organizations around the state became members of the Allied Organization for Civil Rights and sent delegations to the march. On March 5, 1964, a crowd estimated by organizers at ten thousand stood in the cold to hear music by Peter, Paul and Mary and speeches by Martin Luther King Jr. and Jackie Robinson. Then eight leaders of the group met with Governor Breathitt. Yet that meeting—and the weeklong vigil of younger demonstrators, some attempting a partial hunger strike, in the balcony of the statehouse—failed to sway the legislators, and the bill failed. Two years later, however, during the next General Assembly session, in the spring of 1966 and in the wake of the federal legislation, the Kentucky legislature passed a civil rights measure that outlawed discrimination by "employers of eight or more persons" and in public accommodations.[84]

By 1965, after a two-year delay, the much praised open accommodations ordinance was confirmed as law, and Louisville officially had a policy of nondiscrimination in public places. Both at the time and since then, observers have posited theories regarding how Louisvillians accomplished a victory over that manifestation of Jim Crow. The day after the vote, white establishment spokesmen began to paint a picture of a progressive city government that had taken the initiative and given African Americans their status as equal citizens. The *Louisville Courier-Journal* credited first the aldermen, then the HRC, and finally the mayor and county judge executive. Drew Pearson was more specific in his guest column, describing how "Louisville city leaders called together Negro leaders and proposed an experiment in trust and understanding," out of which had come the HRC. Then "Mayor Cowger decided that an anti-bias statute should be adopted." Outsiders helped to reinforce this version, as when Hedrick Smith of the *New York Times* wrote that the city had taken this move toward progress without "public turmoil," with the goal of stopping trouble "before it occurs."[85] The story as presented in the *Courier-Journal,* despite the paper's coverage over the past years that proved otherwise, effectively wiped out black agency and activism and gave the impression that white city fathers had taken the action on their own to solve the problem.

As might be expected, civil rights leaders and activists took exception to this portrayal of the open accommodations victory. The real agents for change, they argued, were the NAACP's court cases that had chipped away at segregation, the three efforts to get a public accommodations law passed, and, more than anything else, the young people who marched and were arrested by the hundreds. As Mervin Aubespin recalled, emphasizing the overlapping strategies employed by the steering committee, there had been "a lot of prongs going on. You had the actual demonstrations, you had others who were trying to work within the system . . . working with the mayor to get the mayor to sign on to an ordinance or to try to get him to form the type of committees where there would be some sort of dialogue." Others, such as *Louisville Defender* reporter Cecil Blye, gave primary credit to the young people, praising them for making the establishment see the "writing on the wall" and forcing change. Anne Braden, in a letter to the *Courier-Journal,* added that it was only after these demonstrations that white city officials had begun to support an ordinance. She concluded by tying direct action to the vote, saying that the real story proved that "the average citizen can make his voice heard and bring change in his community by peaceful demonstrations and political action."[86]

Though none of these versions of events are entirely accurate—all tend to abbreviate the story and render the process of accomplishing open accommodations far too easy—together they contain most of the elements that were pivotal in bringing about the official end of Jim Crow in the city. First, the most important factor in the integration of public facilities in Louisville was the constant pressure toward that end by black leaders, including the *Louisville Defender,* civil rights groups, sit-in protesters, politicians, and, near the end, the African American members of the HRC. The black community made segregation in public facilities an issue from the time the *Defender* began calling for a law and refused to settle for the "better than the Deep South" situation that had resulted from voluntary integration alone. Second, the 1961 election had direct and indirect influences on the outcome. It demonstrated the power of an organized, angry black voting bloc, which could be held over leaders' heads as a threat. More directly, it removed the old board of aldermen, which was almost uniformly—excepting Beckett—opposed and even hostile to the idea of a legislative solution. The old board had not been swayed by the region-wide movement gaining momentum for integration. It had not yielded in the face of the threat of violent racial crises like the Freedom Rides, which were taking place just as the board voted down the spring 1961 bill. The new board, however, came in with a more malleable position. It included two African American representatives, plus at least a few others who in interviews with reporters admitted to "having an open mind" or being willing to consider a law under "certain circumstances." This was progress. White leaders appropriately pointed out that the spread of support for integration itself, and then for a law mandating it, through the city's white moderates was also important. In particular, the *Louisville Courier-*

Journal's switch to supporting the open accommodations law can be credited, just as it was during the lead-up to school integration, with creating an environment in which change was seen as acceptable, even inevitable. Finally, the context of the demonstrations in Birmingham, the violence that met them, and the threat that the same could happen in Louisville helped to give the final push to the open accommodations bill. In the end, the concern that demonstrations by the black community might renew and make Louisville look like another Birmingham or Jackson pushed white leaders finally to succumb to pressure and take action to pass the public accommodations law.

The much acclaimed victory in public accommodations is remembered by local activists as part of the larger movement sweeping through the South. Young sit-in participants identified with their fellow demonstrators; the civil rights community kept in touch with and received support from activists elsewhere; and white and black leaders believed they were providing a model for other communities to follow. Louisvillians also regarded this battle as only one part of a longer and ongoing process because, as Aubespin put it, "As soon as you get through with the demonstrations on Fourth Street, public accommodations, then you got to do open housing." He was not the only one who made that connection. If, as writer Hunter S. Thompson said of his hometown, Louisville had "integrated itself right out of the South," it would now have to confront the racial problems associated with the North, as well as the resistance to further changes in the racial status quo that was spreading across that region.[87]

4

The Battle for Open Housing

In May 1963, in the heady atmosphere of optimism that accompanied the passage of Louisville's open accommodations ordinance, both Mayor William Cowger and civil rights leaders predicted the next step would be the quick adoption of a similar law on open housing. United by the assumptions that housing was the linchpin for undoing segregation in all other parts of life and that if Louisville could accomplish this victory it could be a model for how to overcome what many considered northern racial problems, civil rights advocates set out to secure such a measure. Over the next four years, the open housing issue united myriad organizations in a broad-based campaign that used persuasion, mass demonstrations, and the power of the black vote to attack residential segregation. The combination of tactics employed by this coalition of black and white activists, including many who were brought into the civil rights movement for the first time, demonstrated the flexibility of the local movement and its ability to incorporate strategies acceptable to a number of constituencies. But the prospect of an open housing law also sparked the most vocal and violent opposition to antidiscrimination measures yet seen in Louisville, both on the streets, where mobs of whites heckled and stoned civil rights demonstrators, and in city government. This resistance to integration created disillusionment within the movement and revealed the limits of acceptability of change in the racial status quo.

Years before Louisvillians addressed the issue of segregated housing, African Americans and their white allies elsewhere had begun to fight what Eleanor Roosevelt called the "number one civil rights problem in the North."[1] In 1950 the National Committee against Discrimination in Housing, a coalition of civil rights, religious, labor, civil liberties, and other organizations, formed to coordinate efforts in communities across the North and West to change public housing policies, educate white residents to accept black neighbors, help African American families find homes, and, most important, lobby city, state, and federal governments for "fair housing" laws. As a result, between 1957, when New York City passed the first such law covering private residences, and 1967, the height of Louisville's campaign, forty cities and twenty-two states adopted policies that made discrimination in housing illegal.[2]

These victories never came easily. Though civil rights advocates argued that fair housing was the "logical sequel to fair employment and fair education," government policies, assumptions by real estate and financial professionals about property values, persistent economic inequalities, and white prejudice made housing segregation a much more complex and volatile subject. Even many whites who accepted integrated schools and businesses objected to African Americans moving into their neighborhoods and to government regulation of the most private space, the home. Both opponents and advocates realized the issue was crucial because, regardless of official policies, residential segregation or integration helped determine the extent of actual mixing in schools, in public accommodations, and even in workplaces. Over time, attacks on "forced housing" and declarations of homeowners' rights to control their property not only slowed down but reversed fair housing gains.[3]

This rising wave of opposition to open housing was part of a backlash among white Americans against further racial and social change that, in combination with burgeoning black power ideology, changed the context for civil rights struggles across the nation. The passage of the Civil Rights and Voting Rights acts marked the high point of white public support outside the South for equal rights. Thereafter, perceptions that too much was changing too fast, combined with hostile reactions to the violent confrontations between African Americans and police in summer riots after 1964, emboldened whites to resist further antidiscrimination policies. At the same time, the rising black power movement, with its critique of integration and call for black dominance of the freedom struggle, created divisions within the civil rights movement, led white moderates and liberals to distance themselves, and further stoked public and political resistance. Thus Louisville civil rights advocates launched the movement for open housing, declaring it the inevitable next step after open accommodations, just as the political climate for it became more hostile.

The open housing movement in Louisville began in the spring of 1963, when the *Louisville Defender* argued that since nearby states, including Illinois, Indiana, and Ohio—common benchmarks for local African American leaders—were considering open occupancy laws, Louisville should do so as well. The call to battle against housing discrimination, however, got its first serious attention in the wake of the passage of the open accommodations ordinance. In the celebration of that major first for a southern city, activists, officials, and outside observers noted that the next step, along with employment, was housing. Maurice Rabb of the HRC's housing committee spoke out first, arguing that housing integration was needed to achieve true integration in both schools and the newly opened accommodations. Other members of the commission urged the city to take advantage of the momentum and its leadership position and tackle this next problem. Hedrick Smith of the *New York Times* invoked Louisville's position as a border city, saying that as it became more northern than southern in the wake of the public accommodations ordinance, it now had to fight northern racial problems, most notably segregated housing. Even Cowger encouraged the next steps, declaring he expected laws against discrimination in housing and employment before he left office in December 1965. In keeping with this determination, the HRC's committee on housing initiated efforts to prepare public opinion for an open occupancy statute.[4]

The open housing issue gained a sense of urgency at this time because of the impact of urban renewal projects and the reaction to blockbusting tactics in the west end. The national urban renewal program, which had roots in the Housing Act of 1949, became an established program during the Eisenhower administration. It aimed to replace "blighted" or distressed areas of inner cities with projects that would foster downtown economic growth. In practice, this often meant razing poor and minority neighborhoods and replacing them with large construction projects. The program required city governments to guarantee replacement housing for those displaced, but with relocation in the hands of local authorities who honored community segregation practices, many African Americans who lost their homes and their neighborhoods were forced into overcrowded, poor, slum conditions in increasingly segregated areas.[5] In Louisville, urban renewal focused on the older midcity and near east African American neighborhoods. When these projects destroyed housing, civil rights advocates claimed, the affected residents were steered toward—indeed, had little choice other than to relocate to—the west end of the city. This created a problem of overcrowding in an area where housing conditions were already relatively poor.[6]

As pressure grew on the housing market in the west end, the practice of blockbusting spread. "Blockbusting" could mean a range of practices, but most commonly it referred to real estate agents' facilitating the sale of properties in a formerly all-white neighborhood to African Americans and then fostering panic among whites, who would sell out rapidly and cheaply. Thus a neighborhood's racial homogeneity and character were "broken"; white homeowners fled at a loss; and the agents made profits by reselling the homes at inflated prices to African Americans. Interestingly, the first charges of this roundly condemned practice in Louisville were leveled at black realtors. They defended themselves, saying that they sold to black buyers wherever they could and that they abhorred the panic selling and resegregation that followed. They also blamed white lending institutions for making it difficult for black families to purchase homes.[7] Regardless of who started the practice locally, in the early 1960s, a change in racial composition began to roll across the west end.

One group that responded to this escalating sense of crisis was the newly formed West End Community Council (WECC). In the summer of 1963, Anne Braden, who had experience with whites' resistance to the encroachment of blacks in their neighborhood, grew increasingly concerned about the blockbusting and white flight that were slowly changing the racial character of the west end from white to black. She tried convincing area clergymen to take the lead to stop it and, after failing in that, took action on her own. She contacted Gladys Carter, who worked for the Phyllis Wheatley YWCA, and together they called a meeting of people interested in keeping the neighborhood integrated. Eighteen residents attended the meeting on May 22, 1963, mostly women but including a few men, and they decided to form WECC "to help the west end become an integrated community."[8]

Over the next two months, WECC organized and launched its campaign against neighborhood blockbusting. By August the group had approximately forty members and had elected a slate of officers.

Striving to be interracial in its membership and leadership, the group selected the Reverend Don Keller, a white minister of the Evangelical United Brethren Church, and Mildred Robinson, a black housewife, as the first cochairs. Although Anne Braden had arranged the initial meeting, continued to provide behind-the-scenes organizing, and helped to produce the newsletter, which was launched by the summer of 1964, she and her husband Carl never took leadership roles in the group. WECC set up monthly membership meetings, which were open to the public and became forums for whatever issues people wanted to raise, but conducted much of its work through volunteers who took on individual tasks. The members articulated their basic philosophy in their constitution, in their bylaws, and in printed materials they began circulating to the neighborhood and the press. The group's primary mission was to promote "true community living by bringing together residents of the west end of Louisville to study mutual problems and challenges of this area," and its underlying philosophy was a commitment to interracial cooperation. The immediate goal was to create an integrated neighborhood by welcoming black newcomers and discouraging white flight. A history of the organization emphasized that members saw housing integration as the key to better human relations in general. Moreover, framing the issue in terms of the city's border position, they argued that the west end, and all of Louisville, had an opportunity to avoid the "frightening racial problems of the North" and once again lead the South by modeling interracial community.[9]

WECC launched its campaign for housing integration by calling for legislation and working to influence attitudes on the issue. Members argued that as long as African Americans did not have the option of living elsewhere in the city, the west end would be destined to become an overcrowded, all-black ghetto. If they wanted to keep their neighborhood integrated, the whole city needed to be. Lobbying for an open housing law later became the central focus of the group, but first its members engaged in efforts to convince whites to support integration both in their neighborhood and more broadly in the city. Biracial teams of members went door-to-door in the west end to talk to homeowners about the value of an integrated neighborhood and to conduct surveys to assess white residents' potential acceptance of black neighbors. WECC also sponsored get-acquainted block meetings, neighborhood clubs, and arts events to promote a sense of community. They published a pamphlet, *Well I'm Not Moving*, which contained information about changing neighborhoods. Their literally most visible project was to distribute yard signs that declared "Not for Sale" and "I'm Not Moving" to discourage blockbusting and panic selling. Finally, WECC reached out to other groups in the community, particularly religious leaders. In a letter to the Louisville Area Council of Churches, the group called "good human relations essentially a religious question" and solicited clergymen to help by welcoming black neighbors, distributing pledge cards by which whites promised not to move, and speaking on the subject.[10]

While WECC worked to promote a positive community climate for integrated housing, in April 1964 the HRC began studying options for an ordinance to guarantee it. Almost immediately, contrary to his May 1963 declarations of support, Mayor Cowger came out strongly against any law, arguing that leadership on housing should come from other levels of government. He then softened his position, saying he would support an ordinance that did not contain enforcement or punishment provisions but instead relied on conciliation and voluntary compliance by real estate institutions and professionals. Faced with the mayor's promise of resistance to anything stronger, the HRC agreed to try his approach.[11] Later that spring, the commission drafted a statement of principles on "freedom of occupancy," and it worked through the fall and winter to convince the professional organizations involved with housing sales to adopt it. By May 1965, all of them had agreed to a "code of ethics" that pledged them to promote freedom of choice in housing, to make loans only on the basis of ability to pay, and to give no group special consideration or privileges in home sales or purchases. A freedom of residence panel, composed of members of the professional organizations plus one member of the HRC, would hear complaints about housing discrimination. Since there were no provisions for penalties, however, the panel could only negotiate solutions and had to rely on the member organizations to police themselves.[12]

Civil rights leaders opposed the code of ethics approach from the beginning. Even as the program was being put in place, officials from the local NAACP expressed their misgivings about its weakness. The Reverend W. J. Hodge commented, "The voluntary approach did not work in the case of public accommodations and I think it has even less of a chance of succeeding in housing." Over the course of the next year, the freedom of residence panel did nothing to stop blockbusting or housing discrimination, proving their doubts. In that year, few complaints were lodged, and the panel rarely met. The housing sub-committee of the HRC also reported problems in handling what few complaints did come in, for "if the accused person refuses to negotiate, there is nothing the commission can do about it." Anticipating the failure of the conciliatory approach, the NAACP and Kentucky Christian Leadership Conference (KCLC) began drafting a substitute ordinance that would contain enforcement and penalty provisions. KCLC was a relatively new organization, led by the Reverend A. D. King, Martin Luther King Jr.'s brother, who had taken over the pastorate at Zion Baptist Church in 1965. Such an ordinance, the *Louisville Defender* argued, would "give Louisville the opportunity to rise and be an example for Kentucky and the South." On a more ominous note, the paper also warned that stronger action was needed to avoid the racial violence seen in northern cities, the first of many uses of the threat of rising black militancy against inactive city officials. Mayor Kenneth Schmied, elected in November 1965 after acknowledging in his campaign that the code of ethics might need strengthening, was apparently influenced by the fear that violence might break out in the event of open housing demonstrations, and he created an advisory committee to study the effectiveness of the current plan.[13]

In September 1966, representatives from the NAACP, KCLC, and WECC presented an ordinance to the board of aldermen to outlaw housing discrimination. Specifically, the bill prohibited "discrimination because of race, color, creed or national origin in the sale, rental or financing of housing by salesmen, lenders, brokers, mortgage bankers," and others engaged in the real estate business. Penalties ranged from five hundred dollars to imprisonment for up to thirty days. This effort by black leaders to insert strong penalty provisions, however, inspired immediate opposition from the mayor and aldermen, who objected to the possibility of jail sentences. This impasse led to several months of delay in the consideration of the measure. In an appeal for compromise, the *Defender* pointed out that cities across the nation required only fines and that, if modeled on the public accommodations ordinance, the law could at least subject repeat offenders to contempt of court citations. By the beginning of 1967, it was clear that civil rights leaders would accept dropping jail terms in exchange for a broad definition of who and what types of housing would be included.[14]

In response to the delay caused by the debate over the ordinance's provisions, in the late fall of 1966, open housing advocates began to threaten demonstrations. In early November, KCLC chair King declared that, if the board of aldermen did not act soon, several groups in the community would protest. Not long after, the NAACP, KCLC, Episcopal Diocese of Kentucky, Louisville Area Council on Religion and Race (LACRR), WECC, and AME Ministerial Alliance held a prayer vigil of one hundred people at city hall. In a move reminiscent of the organization of the open accommodations steering committee, the same groups, minus the Episcopal Diocese of Kentucky, formed the Committee on Open Housing (COH) to coordinate future actions. The biracial make-up of most of these organizations hinted at the eventual character of the whole open housing movement. In the opening weeks of 1967, civil rights leaders continued to stress that they appreciated Louisville's good record in race relations and did not want to demonstrate but that African Americans would not wait forever for action on open housing.[15]

The likelihood of demonstrations increased, however, when local leaders began talking about receiving help from outsiders, in particular organizers, or "technicians" as they were sometimes called, from SCLC. SCLC had adopted open housing as its next goal in the summer of 1966 when it cooperated with local activists to launch the Chicago Freedom Movement.[16] In January, Hulbert James, who had been hired as the executive director of WECC in May 1966, confirmed that SCLC officials in Atlanta, Chicago, and New York had offered to come to Louisville to conduct workshops in preparation for a protest campaign. The Reverend E. Randall Osburn, an SCLC activist working in Alabama, visited the city and, at a mass meeting at Antioch Baptist Church, charged that it was time to "stop having tea parties" with the city administration and start acting. Declaring, "Get ready Louisville, we're coming after you," Osburn indicated that his organization had chosen Louisville as one of its focal points for the spring. In late February, when no progress had yet been made, technicians from the Chicago movement, including Golden A. Frinks, began arriving to organize support for demonstrations. The winter lull in the movement in Chicago freed up more SCLC personnel, and thirteen activists eventually joined Frinks. One of the newcomers was Robert Sims, who was soon to become a pivotal figure in the Louisville movement.[17] While preparations for demonstrations were laid, James urged city leaders to meet with the COH to "save Louisville from the turmoil of demonstrations," avoid the chaos that shook Chicago when leaders there waited too long—a substitution of that northern city for the southern negative referents used during the open accommodations struggle—and thus prevent damage to Louisville's reputation.[18]

In the midst of this organizing, the prospect of an open housing law became the topic of heated public debate, as both opponents and supporters increasingly voiced their opinions. In late December, Mayor Schmied proposed that the board of aldermen hold hearings to give the public a chance to express itself on the issue. HRC members and civil rights advocates recognized this as a delaying tactic but conceded there was no way to avoid such hearings. The first hearing was scheduled for February 2 at Southern High School, in a primarily white, working-class neighborhood. The *Louisville Courier-Journal* expressed misgivings about the constructiveness of the hearings, pointing out that they were going to focus on the original bill with the jail penalty provision, not the compromise versions that had been suggested, and worrying about potential damage to Louisville's reputation if the meeting did not go well. The editors' concerns turned out to be well founded. The first public hearing was, in the eyes of open housing advocates and both the *Courier-Journal* and the *Defender,* an unmitigated disaster. Over one thousand people showed up, many of whom had to be turned away. The crowd booed and jeered the ten people who braved public scorn by testifying in favor of the ordinance. The presiding judge several times had to "chastise the audience for its unruliness." The *Courier-Journal* immediately declared that further hearings would only heighten tensions and should be canceled. The *Defender* concurred, suspecting that the outcome had been predetermined by the choice of location and paucity of black speakers. For their part, supporters of open housing, including WECC members George Kimbrough and Sister Pauline Marie, declared that such a basic human right should not be put up for public debate and threatened to boycott future hearings.[19]

The opposition took other opportunities to express itself. Throughout the debate over open housing legislation, the Louisville Real Estate Board, despite its participation in the freedom of residence panel, consistently rejected legislation with any enforcement provisions as denying individuals the right to dispose of their property as they saw fit. In the spring of 1967, Republican candidate for governor Louis B. Nunn campaigned against "forced" housing by any means. Letters to the editor of the *Louisville Courier-Journal* on the subject reflected similar concerns. C. W. McFerran, for example, wrote, "You should have the right in a free country to select the buyer you wish." Others,

while calling for sanctions against blockbusting realtors, said an individual's freedom to sell should not be limited. The complaints of
these leaders and letter writers reflected the rhetoric of the homeowners' rights movements that were turning back open housing advances
across the nation, including in California and Michigan, by invoking
American values of private property and security from government in
one's own home. They also harkened back to the earlier position taken
by white Louisvillians in defense of Jim Crow that whites had the right
to maintain exclusion in their neighborhoods and businesses by making
private choices about their property. Not all arguments were couched
in such seemingly high-minded terms, however. There was also much
talk of safeguarding homes against unwanted "noisy" minorities and
of having worked to make nice neighborhoods and not wanting to lose
them to "outsiders." By the middle of the spring of 1967, the Concerned Citizens Committee had formed to harness such resentment and
organize the opposition. Its leader was businessman Joseph Krieger,
who became a public figure over the next several months as a result of
his debates with open housing advocates.[20]

Countering this increasingly vocal opposition, throughout the
spring of 1967, more individuals, many of them white, began expressing support for open housing and for strong legislation to guarantee
it. In letters to the editor of the *Courier-Journal,* advocates based their
support on three overlapping themes. First, they invoked Louisville's
status as an All American City and declared it was time to pass a strong
ordinance, lest that reputation crumble. Second, and more commonly,
people claimed a Christian or moral basis for their endorsement. Philip
Vernon Baker, for example, identified himself as a Christian and member of the National Council of Catholic Men and quoted Vatican II.
Others more simply declared that it was "not morally right" that white
families could live anywhere and blacks could not. Finally, in the wake
of the public hearings, several writers stressed that an issue of human
rights and dignity should not be left up to the majority opinion or be
up for debate at all. Dan Foley asked, "Does a majority have the right
to deny a helpless minority decent housing?"[21] Many of these writers lived in primarily white neighborhoods, ranging from the working-
class suburbs of the south end to the wealthy enclaves along the river
in the northeast, signaling a base of support in those communities for
the concept of open housing.

In addition to the support of individuals, by the time the strengthened ordinance was being considered by the board of aldermen, a wide variety of church and civic organizations had gone on record in favor of the bill. In January 1967, WECC compiled a list of over fifty organizations that had endorsed the measure.[22] Beyond simply voicing their support, many of these individuals and organizations took actions to promote open housing. Before the board of aldermen's hearing on the issue provided a bullhorn for the opposition, community groups were hosting their own forums in favor of integration. Indeed, the Louisville branch of the National Council of Jewish Women began hosting weekly meetings on the issue almost immediately after the passage of the open accommodations law in 1963. Over time, other sponsors held debates to promote a more reasoned discussion than had occurred at Southern High School.[23] Meanwhile, some groups went beyond discussion and persuasion. In 1964 local white realtor Dorcas Ruthenburg worked with the Kentucky Council on Human Relations, the state affiliate of the SRC, to create Housing Clearance Inc. to help African American families find housing. In 1966 west end resident Pat Allgeier organized five hundred college students to go door-to-door in the south end of the city, urging people to sign a pledge to welcome black newcomers. Those students also held twice-weekly vigils downtown. Finally, the KCLU offered its help to the movement in the form of fund-raising for bail, observers at the marches themselves, and legal aid for those arrested. By the time the movement was in full swing, WECC was encouraged by the sheer number of groups supporting open housing and the diversity of strategies in use. Rather than valuing actions as more or less important, spokesmen for the movement preferred to characterize all contributions as equally valid, emphasizing the openness of the movement to anyone who wanted to help as he or she saw fit. As William Reddin, who was both a WECC cochair and an NAACP member and, during the open housing movement, spoke for both, pointed out, "There is something everybody can do."[24]

White clergymen and clergy and lay organizations played a particularly active role in the open housing movement in Louisville. One of the most prominent groups channeling the energy of religious white men and women was the LACRR. In January 1963 the Reverend Hodge and white Episcopal bishop C. Gresham Marmion had attended the meeting in Chicago that created the National Conference on Religion and Race. A year later a group of Louisville clergy, including Rabbi Martin Perley and the Reverend Ted Hightower, one of the advocates of the open accommodations law, formed the local unit of the group. Within two years, LACRR had 140 members. Though it was officially open to anyone, the initial lists of leadership indicate that it was primarily made up of white clergy and laypeople. The goal of the members was, in broad terms, to work through the churches and synagogues to "end racial injustice." In response to the growing open housing controversy, the group released a more explicit statement linking faith to activism, saying, "Social justice and equal opportunity for all people are fundamental in the teaching of our Judeo-Christian and American Democratic heritage." The statement continued, "We cannot consistently affirm the fatherhood of God and the brotherhood of men and yet deny fellow citizens the same rights which we would affirm for ourselves."[25]

During the open housing movement, the LACRR hosted public forums, encouraged church groups to reach out to new black neighbors, and sponsored the All American Neighborhood Award. Cooperating with WECC and drawing on the praise Louisville had earned as an All American City for its open accommodations ordinance, the group gave a commendation to the neighborhood that best illustrated the values of integrated communities by having a "significant degree" of racial mixing and, just as important, strong resident involvement in civic and social activities. Then, at the height of demonstrations for an open housing ordinance, the group sponsored special rallies at the Jefferson County courthouse for religious people to make "a mass witness" for the legislation. At the first such rally, about five hundred people heard white and black ministers declare that open housing was the "number one moral issue facing" the community.[26]

White Presbyterian minister Tom Moffett organized a similar march. Moffett was a son of missionaries who grew up in Korea and in cities across the United States. He attended Princeton Theological Seminary and, in part because of a fellow student's influence, took his first job working as a missionary in West Virginia coal-mining communities. From there he moved to inner-city churches in Wheeling and then in Kansas City, Missouri. Because his church in Kansas City was in a neighborhood that was undergoing a transition from white to black, he tried to include some of the new black residents in church programs such as vacation Bible school. During his time there, from 1960 to 1966, he was also influenced by Saul Alinsky's approach to community organization and by a trip he took to Mississippi with a group of clergy to register voters. He became convinced that his calling was to lead an interracial ministry and to use his church as an agent for social change. In 1966 he discovered that the New Covenant Presbyterian Church in Louisville was looking for a pastor. The church was in a part of the west end that was shifting from majority white to black, and it already had a handful of black members. Moffett accepted the position and arrived there in the fall of 1966. He immediately contacted activist organizations in the area and became involved in WECC, seeing it as a natural vehicle for his work in the community. Through WECC he got involved in the open housing struggle and put together Clergy for Open Housing, a short-lived, issue-focused organization dedicated solely to putting together a march of white clergy and laypeople into the south end. That march, and the activities of Moffett and others like him, exemplified the role of the white church, through its socially conscious ministers and some of their flock, in the open housing campaign.[27]

One of the most important organizations in Louisville for marshaling the support of white civic groups not formerly involved in civil rights activity was the Ad Hoc Committee on Open Housing (ACOH). In the wake of the first board of aldermen public hearing, organizations that supported open housing called a meeting at Christ Church Cathedral to discuss how to react to the growing hostility in the community and in the city government and how best to lend their aid. The first meeting included representatives from the Metropolitan Action Commission of the Episcopal Diocese of Kentucky, the Kentucky Association of Colored Women's Clubs, and University of Louisville Students and Faculty for Open Housing, as well as from the NAACP, WECC, and others. This group decided to form ACOH as a separate organization from the more activist COH. They sought not to lead the movement—they left that to COH—but to support it. They requested meetings with the mayor and aldermen, issued statements endorsing demonstrations, and worked to influence downtown businesses to support open housing. The purpose of this group, then, was to unite and speak for the wide variety of organizations sympathetic to the cause.[28]

After extended debate on the provisions of the open housing ordinance, on February 14 the HRC submitted a new version to the board of aldermen. This version exempted sales by individuals—an apparent effort to head off opposition based on the denial of individual property rights—eliminated jail sentences and fines, provided for enforcement by court orders, and set up a fair housing division within the HRC to enforce the law. Reaction by black leaders to the proposal hinted at cracks in the movement that would soon split it open. Bishop Tucker immediately praised the changes, saying that the HRC could obtain cease and desist orders from the court more quickly than violators could be prosecuted. Harry McAlpin, who as a member of the HRC had helped to redraft the bill, also defended it, saying that it was workable and should be passed without delay.[29] COH and others, however, immediately attacked the new version of the bill. On the day the bill was to be introduced, Bishop Tucker's son Neville, a young attorney, declared that eliminating jail time and fines and exempting sales by owners would render the law ineffective. In a press release, COH added that the changes reduced the bill to "no more than a voluntary compliance resolution," which had proved already to be inadequate. As the debate heated up, A. D. King, speaking for COH, declared that the organization would not accept the law unless it was strengthened.[30]

In response to the weakness of the new proposal, in March 1967 the threatened demonstrations broke out. A wave of nearly daily demonstrations commenced on March 7, after Hosea Williams of SCLC led a march to a furniture store owned by Mayor Schmied. The next day, sixty-five people held a half-hour sing-in at city hall. The demonstrations escalated a few days later, when, at the Reverend W. J. Hodge's invitation, five hundred delegates from an NAACP regional conference, which was meeting in the city at the time, joined a march. After that, the local leadership of KCLC, Reverends Fred Sampson, Leo Lessor, and A. D. King, initiated a new strategy: having the crowds descend on the homes of the mayor, the aldermen, and eventually the leadership of the opposition, all of which were in securely all-white neighborhoods. The first violence came a week later, during a sit-in after a board of aldermen meeting on March 14, when police cleared out the chamber by pushing and pulling demonstrators down the stairs and into the street. Although the *Louisville Courier-Journal* initially reported only one person hurt, an SCLC activist from Chicago said he was "stomped" on by police, and at a rally the next day, two black teenage girls, a Catholic priest, and a fifty-one-year-old white woman testified that they had been abused. Through the rest of the month, the demonstrations continued, combining city hall picketing, rallies, prayer vigils, and marches into white neighborhoods.[31]

In the wake of the violence at the board of aldermen meeting, Schmied issued a statement declaring that he would "not take another step" on open housing and calling on local leaders to repudiate "outsiders." The group to whom the mayor referred were members of SCLC who had come to town to take an active role in the demonstrations. Although Louisville activists had always welcomed help from those in other cities, this was the first time officials criticized their role publicly. Over the course of the month and into the later spring, SCLC, specifically Martin Luther King, expanded its commitment to the city's movement. Almost as soon as the demonstrations began, SCLC executive director Andrew Young said that the organization would devote its resources to Louisville while the Chicago movement awaited the return of better weather. In response to the mayor's denunciation of the organization's involvement, King sent him a telegram praising the city's "reputation for pioneering in creative social progress" but expressing his disappointment over the reversal of that trend by the current administration. SCLC's commitment became even stronger when the group held its national executive board meeting in the city at the end of March, highlighted by a rally and a speech by King. After that speech, King led a march of five hundred open housing advocates to Memorial Auditorium, where opponents of open housing were having a rally. Although King had to leave for other commitments the next day, he promised to keep in "close touch" and return soon, which he did in late spring.[32]

The mayor's criticism of outsiders echoed a source of rising tension among black leaders, which, together with different positions on the provisions of the ordinance itself, threatened to pull apart the forces supporting open housing. In late December 1966, Ray Bixler, a psychology professor at the University of Louisville who had done studies about whites' attitudes regarding integration, criticized some civil rights leaders for their inaction on open housing. He singled out Bishop Tucker for his willingness, rooted in his Republican Party loyalty, to let the Schmied administration set the pace. Tucker defended his commitment to civil rights while declaring himself "unequivocally opposed to some of the ill-advised methods employed by inexperienced newcomers" and the "meddling of outside agitators." After that, moderate black leaders' criticism of outsiders—specifically members of SCLC—escalated. Tucker renewed his censure a month later, decrying the "importation of people to foment trouble." More formally, Tucker, along with Harry McAlpin, Felix Anderson, Frank Stanley Sr., and others issued a statement denouncing Golden Frinks, Robert Sims, and the

SCLC team as "itinerant rabble rousers." Blasting rumored threats by Frinks to sponsor "creative" means of demonstrating, including letting chickens loose in the streets and dumping garbage at city hall, they identified themselves with the "better thinking, more responsible elements of our community" and denounced not just these specific tactics but what they saw as demonstration for its own sake. In fact, they proposed that demonstrations were unnecessary because lines of communications were open among the HRC, movement leaders, and city government. This was the first sign of questioning the efficacy of tactics associated with the southern civil rights movement.[33]

Other supporters of open housing responded quickly to these criticisms and defended both the role of SCLC and demonstrations in general. COH released an immediate rebuttal, saying, "We are pleased to have heard from the so-called better thinking Negroes," while accusing them of "knowingly betraying" the community. Meanwhile the cochairs of WECC, while indicating their discomfort with Frinks's threatened tactics, affirmed their support for A. D. King and for SCLC's record. Member Ken Phillips, moreover, made the case for demonstrations in the organization's newsletter, saying that the authors of the Tucker-McAlpin statement were asking blacks to behave "calmly and obediently (like children) and beg for this 'gift' from the 'Great White Master.'" On the contrary, he closed, demonstrations were an "extension of free speech" and thus were endorsed by the organization. In a sign that white open housing supporters would not necessarily line up with the more moderate black leaders, ACOH also challenged Tucker and the moderates' criticism of "outsiders." At a meeting of the organization, Episcopal priest Charles Tachau secured a resolution stating the group's opposition to the implication that "people who were not born and reared in Louisville are second-class citizens, unfit for leadership," and declaring their appreciation for help from outside Louisville.[34]

Tachau was, like Tom Moffett, a white minister who became involved in open housing through WECC, in which he had gotten involved through his pastorate in a west end church. Unlike Moffett and those now being declared outside agitators, however, he was a native Louisvillian with deep family roots in the community. His mother, who was related to Supreme Court justice Louis Brandeis, was an organizer for the Kentucky Birth Control League. His father served on the board of the Red Cross Hospital for African Americans and had helped initiate the process that led to the integration of the Jefferson County Medical Society. Tachau's brother Eric had worked behind the scenes to make sure Andrew and Charlotte Wade got home insurance after their house was bombed, and he had been treasurer for the 1964 march on Frankfort. Nevertheless, Tachau recalled growing up with no questions about what he called "southern conventions" in race relations, having little sympathy for either the Bradens or the Wades, and paying little attention to the open accommodations struggle. He first trained as a lawyer and served as a juvenile court judge. But in 1960 he changed paths and attended seminary to become an Episcopal priest. After short terms in Glasgow and Bowling Green, Kentucky, in 1965 Tachau moved to Louisville to help revive St. George Church in the west end. When he arrived, the church had "a half-dozen old white ladies and perhaps twenty-five or thirty black members; most of them were children." The church, however, was a contract agency for the War on Poverty, and Tachau threw himself into that work. Through that he got to know other community organizers, including those associated with WECC. He was only beginning to become more vocal in that organization and its drive for open housing when the demonstrations broke out.[35]

As the demonstrations continued into the spring, the dispute between the groups and individuals associated with COH and its SCLC allies on the one hand and older, local black leaders, including Tucker, McAlpin, and Stanley, on the other hand continued to simmer and cause distractions. Tucker and longtime NAACP leader Lyman Johnson charged the newcomers and their local associates with circulating the "Uncle Tom" label and defended their records of militant service. In a speech at a rally, Tachau responded that, at least on open housing, the "recent arrivals in Louisville have done more in a few months than had been accomplished over the years by the established leadership," a statement to which Tucker and Stanley took vocal exception. Shortly thereafter, Tucker formed a new group, the Louisville Committee of Negro Churchmen, which consisted of older black ministers who criticized the role of clergy in the open housing demonstrations. Tucker and the new group injected a new line of attack, accusing the entire open housing movement of being influenced by "known communist followers and sympathizers." The accusation was based on WECC's role in the movement, Anne Braden's membership in WECC, and her affiliation with SCEF, which Tucker and others around the South claimed was a Communist front. This tactic did not get very far. A local radio program investigated the charges, carried a statement by A. D. King denying them, and concluded that there was no basis for them. The matter was quickly dropped. The incident revealed the rift between factions of black leaders in the community, however, and the increasing tensions of the time.[36]

Meanwhile, the opposition to any open housing ordinance at all was growing. In the first two weeks of March, the Concerned Citizens Committee geared up to fight the passage of any law, regardless of the provisions. President Joseph Krieger declared the group would fight any "forced housing ordinance here in Louisville and at the federal level in Washington" by petitions, referendums, and conferences. The committee commenced its campaign with the rally at Memorial Auditorium that was the target of the Martin Luther King–led demonstration at the end of March. Another new organization that gained less attention from the media at the time, Truth about Civil Turmoil in Kentucky, circulated a broadside linking Martin Luther King, SCLC, WECC, and various other open housing advocates to a long list of supposed Communists in Louisville and around the South. Its main theme was echoed in a flurry of letters to the editor of the *Louisville Courier-Journal* in February and March that linked the ordinance to "Hitlerism," "Socialism," and the goals of the "tyrannical few in Russia."[37]

As the temperatures of both advocates and opponents rose, the major local papers weighed in, supporting the compromise version of the ordinance in the interest of community peace. The *Courier-Journal* used the same argument it had at the time of the open accommodations law: the need to protect Louisville's good image. Pointing out that Louisville had enjoyed a good reputation nationally ever since its peaceful integration of schools in 1956, the editors warned that demonstrations would damage that good name and scare off industry. Reflecting the growing national concern with the rising black power movement, the paper also warned that inaction would cause responsible black leaders to lose their position to younger militants. The paper praised the moderate black leaders who had displayed faith in Louisville by denouncing demonstrations and called on the city to repay that faith. Failure to do so, it more ominously predicted, would leave the local movement in "the hands of those who believe progress only comes from violence and even bloodshed."[38] For its part, the *Defender* essentially echoed these themes, stressing that the compromise version of the bill was the best that could be passed at the time and that both delays and the demonstrations they provoked would hurt the city. In this the paper reflected the position of its publisher, Frank Stanley Sr., who was one of the signatories of the Tucker-McAlpin statement.[39]

While the provisions of the bill were being debated in public, open housing advocates in the movement and in city government engaged in a flurry of negotiations to try to bring about some progress. These discussions culminated on March 31 when Schmied presented the ordinance, with seven amendments, including an exemption for buildings where owners lived and removal of all apartments from coverage for the first year after they were constructed, to the aldermen. COH leaders, already opposed to the previous version of the bill as too weak, charged that the mayor's version was even worse and returned to protesting. This time, they led marches into the south end of the city, an area that was affordable for low- and moderate-income black home seekers. The first of these demonstrations was met with hecklers throwing rocks and eggs, foreshadowing more violent confrontations to come. At the same time, Martin Luther King and Dick Gregory, fresh from the Chicago campaign, pledged to make Louisville the site of "intensive" demonstrations if a "meaningful" law was not passed.[40]

On April 11, 1967, the board of aldermen voted on the open housing ordinance with the proposed amendments and, despite last minute, behind-closed-doors lobbying by the mayor and members of the HRC, defeated the measure nine to three. The three voting in support were the two African American aldermen, Louise Reynolds and Eugene Ford, and Oscar Stoll, whose district included a relatively large black constituency. In their statement accompanying the vote, the aldermen blamed the demonstrations and "widespread disorders" created by "outside agitators." They argued that to pass the ordinance at that time would be to yield to "mob rule" and pledged that they would take no action on the issue until all outsiders left the community and the demonstrations ended. The aldermen went on to take credit for recent racial progress, including the public accommodations ordinance, saying, "Our Republican administration in the last five years has been instrumental in accomplishing more in the civil rights field than had previously been attained in nearly a century." In short, Republican city officials, with the help of "responsible" local black leaders, were taking care of the problem, and outsiders, militant demonstrators, and new laws were not necessary.[41]

Open housing activists reacted immediately in anger at the outcome. After the vote, A. D. King left the aldermanic chambers and addressed the crowd of about three hundred people who were waiting for news outside city hall. He announced the result, then called for an immediate march through downtown, which became a two-hour series of parades and sit-ins through the vicinity of city hall and the police station. Approximately 250 demonstrators flooded the streets, blocked traffic, sat in protest of the arrest of SCLC's Robert Sims, and encountered growing crowds of hecklers along the sidewalks. In the course of the protest, Dick Gregory, who had arrived in town earlier that day, pledged that movement supporters would stop the Kentucky Derby if necessary, saying, "I ain't going to lay down in front of a horse myself, but there's a lot of cats that will. If it comes to closing the Derby up, we'll just have to close it up." At the same time, A. D. King of KCLC and Hulbert James of WECC made a proposal to the city. The two men, both of whom had lived in Louisville at least two years, had been singled out as "outsiders" leading the movement. They offered to leave the city temporarily if the aldermen would agree to pass the movement's version of the open housing ordinance. The aldermen rejected their offer the next day, and in response, the two men pledged to "double up" the demonstrations through the Derby.[42]

The movement made good on that promise, holding rallies and marches nearly every day for the next month, leading up to the first week of May and the Kentucky Derby. The target of the demonstrations was again the south end of the city. Marchers met at west end churches for mass meetings, then rode in buses, enclosed trucks, and private cars to gathering places near the white southern neighborhoods. Quickly, white opponents learned to anticipate the marches and gathered, sometimes hours in advance of the activists' arrival, greeting them with storms of rocks, bottles, eggs, and even firecrackers. As Ruth Bryant recalled, "They had all these Ku Klux Klan signs up across the street when we got out over there by Iroquois Park. Looked like thousands of people. And they were holding up signs and they were yelling and calling names and all of that. It was pretty scary. There were plenty of police cars out there and police wagons . . . ready to take people in. I had never seen anything like that."[43] On one early occasion, when about 150 marchers met an estimated 600 hecklers, a rock hit A. D. King in the eye, and a thrown board knocked his sixteen-year-old daughter flat.[44]

Less than a week later, A. D. King led another march. The demonstration began at Quinn Chapel, where participants heard from Louisville native and boxing champ Cassius Clay, who had recently changed his name to Muhammad Ali and was in the early stages of his draft refusal. He declared that he had come home to Louisville to support the movement after hearing of A. D. King's injury. After the rally, the marchers drove to the south end, parked their cars, and began to move. Both police and mobs of hecklers met and surrounded the group. After King offered to take the group back to their cars and Chief of Police William Bindner refused to let them walk from the scene, King and others led the group in a spontaneous sit-in. The group remained sitting on the sidewalk from ten o'clock until almost midnight as a crowd of hostile whites gathered across the street. Cherry bombs exploded over the demonstrators' heads, and police threw canisters of tear gas at the hecklers to keep them at bay but still refused to let the marchers leave. The sit-in participants were rescued when some members of the NAACP arrived and negotiated with police to allow them to drive people away from the scene. During this week of turmoil, the mayor issued a "plea for public order," admonishing people to stay at home and not get involved. His request made little difference, however, as similar scenes repeated almost nightly throughout April.[45]

The bitterness of the reaction to the demonstrations and the aldermen's rejection of the ordinance brought a wave of negative attention to the city from the national media. The story reported by various mainstream and liberal newsmagazines followed a similar outline. Writers praised Louisville's reputation, earned by its peaceful and pioneering school integration. They described the next step, echoing the myth established by the *Louisville Courier-Journal* in 1963, as a relatively easy acceptance of an open accommodations ordinance after "a few demonstrations in 1961." Although the *Nation* pointed out that a study of residential segregation listed Louisville among the worst in the country, the consensus was that white civic leaders were moving toward the inevitable next step of open housing. But using a variety of metaphors, national reporters criticized the city for refusing to cross the next line, for dropping the ball, or, in the more colorful imagery of the *Christian Century,* turning heavy footed in the third leg of the Triple Crown (the essay was written at Derby time). Instead of peaceful school integration or mild sit-ins, now the city hosted a public hearing that brought out the "Snopses"—a reference to Faulkner's benighted Mississippians—and demonstrations had been met by "mobs of snarling white youths," producing the "year's ugliest racial confrontation."

So much for Louisville the enlightened city; now it was portrayed as one of the worst.[46]

For a city that prided itself on its peaceful school desegregation and relative lack of violence during the open accommodations sit-ins—as exaggerated as the latter was—this coverage, and the hostile confrontations provoking it, was a shock. The daily papers reported on the number and character and actions of open housing opponents in detail. Police and newspaper estimates of the opposition crowds on any given night ranged from six hundred to two thousand. Reports frequently mentioned that people in the crowds carried Confederate flags and signs with George Wallace presidential campaign slogans. The papers also reported almost daily the number of people injured, including members of the national media. Over time, the police became targets too, in particular after they used tear gas and arrests to protect marchers from the worst of the violence. A cherry bomb temporarily blinded one officer when it exploded in his face. On another occasion, one thousand "jeering white hecklers" surrounded and overturned a police car and "showered the officers with bricks, bottles and rocks." Ironically, as the local press pointed out on a number of occasions, some of the mob were from out of town, including two members of the American Nazi Party who had come to join the fray from Chicago—the home of most of the SCLC "outside agitators" criticized by the aldermen. By the end of the month, the disorder and the negative publicity it provoked pressured the mayor to try to control the white mobs by proposing a curfew to keep at least the youngest hecklers off the street and threatening to charge their parents with contributing to the delinquency of minors.[47]

The police's protection of demonstrators and arrests of hecklers did not indicate any sympathy on their or the city government's part for the open housing movement, however. Indeed, throughout the month, arrests of demonstrators and legal action against open housing leaders and activists escalated. Although, during the night of the aldermen's vote, police arrested only Robert Sims, and in the first days they targeted hecklers rather than demonstrators for detention, the city quickly took steps aimed at the movement. City law director Eugene Alvey obtained a court order from Judge Marvin J. Sternberg that prohibited marches at night and during rush hour, required leaders to give police twelve hours' notice of demonstrations, and limited the number of participants to 150. COH immediately announced its intention to march anyway and to challenge the order in federal court because it denied protesters the rights of free speech and peaceable assembly. When the first group of seven leaders were arrested after violating the injunction, COH lawyer Neville Tucker was unable to get the order vacated, and they served thirty-hour jail terms for contempt of court.[48] After those arrests, the marches continued under the leadership of one black and three white clergymen—Charles Kirby of the Southern Star Baptist Church, Harold M. Warheim of the Louisville Presbyterian Theological Seminary, and Episcopal priests Charles Tachau and Ralph Leach. Meanwhile, police continued to try to prevent demonstrations by arresting leaders, confining the participants before they could move, and filming protesters in order to charge them with contempt of court.[49]

As demonstrations continued, the city upped the ante by increasing the severity of the charges against those arrested. After an April 20 incident during which protesters created diversions to avoid being stopped before they could start, police arrested 119 people and charged 42 of them with "banding together to commit a felony," which was punishable by up to a year in prison. City officials filed the most serious charge, criminal syndicalism, against Tachau on April 21. Like many antidissent laws, this one was vague and broad. Although one local professor joked to his class that "criminal syndicalism is when a preacher leads a parade," the penalty, up to twenty-one years in prison, was no laughing matter. By the end of April, the number of arrests on various charges passed 500, and police court judge William G. Colson was responsible for plowing through the growing backlog. He quickly filed away the syndicalism accusation, saying it required a conspiracy and thus one person could not be guilty of it. Then, after taking hours to judge and sentence a single defendant, he continued all the cases until May, then August and November. In late October, a U.S. district court ruled that many of the charges were unconstitutional because of their ambiguity, and the cases were dismissed. Those charged specifically with violating the injunction received a fine.[50]

While demonstrators confronted the opposition on the streets and lawyers defended their rights in the courts, other interested parties worked behind the scenes to try to bring about a resolution of the crisis. A week after the aldermen's negative vote, the Louisville Urban League sent invitations to organizations involved in open housing, "both pro and con," to meet with city officials to discuss possible solutions. About one hundred people attended the meeting, including representatives of the city, the Louisville Real Estate Board, and the Concerned Citizens Committee. At the Urban League's suggestion, they agreed on a moratorium on demonstrations while all sides met in continuous session, though COH insisted that, if progress was not made, they would return to the streets as the Derby approached. The talks broke down when Judge Colson revoked the bail of thirty-five people who returned late from a recess, costing the movement about seven thousand dollars. Then, in one last-ditch maneuver before the Derby, Alderman Chester Jennings suggested that existing laws—specifically the ordinances giving the HRC the power to punish discrimination by seeking contempt of court rulings—might be enough to take the place of a specific open housing ordinance. COH leaders were skeptical, and the HRC declared that the existing laws did not grant them enough power. An impasse thus was reached on the eve of the biggest event of the year.[51]

In the weeks leading up to the Derby, the NAACP had also tried to pressure officials by calling for a boycott. The Reverend W. J. Hodge, the president of the local branch, first suggested a boycott of both the Derby itself and downtown businesses in the week before the board of aldermen vote. He soon specified that the selective buying campaign would be aimed at Mayor Schmied's furniture store, the businesses of a few of the aldermen, downtown businesses, and their affiliates throughout the city. To encourage compliance, the organization announced that marshals would take pictures of African Americans who patronized downtown stores. Moderate black leaders, ACOH, COH, and the Interdenominational Ministerial Alliance endorsed the boycott. Local branch officers also wrote to the national headquarters to solicit aid in encouraging NAACP members from around the country not to come to the Derby. These actions signaled that the NAACP was becoming more involved in the movement. Up to this time, it had been overshadowed by the more activist KCLC and WECC, but in late April there were noticeable efforts by A. D. King and Hodge to demonstrate solidarity. Hodge joined a march and pledged to be more personally involved, and William Reddin, speaking for the NAACP, announced that the group planned to hold Saturday demonstrations to last "for the duration" until a bill was passed. The boycott lasted until mid-July, when the NAACP called it off as the focus shifted toward voter registration.[52]

As April wore on with no resolution to the crisis in sight, the inevitable and uniquely Louisvillian question arose—as it had during the open accommodations struggle in 1961—what to do about the Derby? From the day of the aldermen's vote, activists threatened and debated demonstrations at the Derby. Then, in late April, leaders began to plan strategies for disrupting the race and its associated events, and Martin Luther King and Dick Gregory pledged to return to the city in time to participate. One suggestion was a series of "drive-ins" during which people would purposely drive their cars very slowly along routes leading to Derby activities, mimicking the "stall-ins" outside the New York World's Fair in 1964. A few trial runs of this tactic occurred in the weeks leading up to the big day. Hulbert James also threatened to find ways to disrupt the television broadcast of the race, hoping CBS would pressure city officials to yield on open housing. James further claimed that the NAACP boycott and concerns about canceled events were already having an impact as local businesses reported a rash of room and transportation reservation cancellations.[53]

Not all open housing advocates agreed with plans to disrupt Louisville's main event. Moderate leader Harry McAlpin, while supporting the NAACP boycott, said that demonstrations in general were not serving a useful purpose and that those against the Derby would be particularly counterproductive. The *Louisville Defender,* reflecting Frank Stanley Sr.'s alliance with moderate black leaders, came out against demonstrations aimed at Derby events. After the first threats in early April, the paper called the proposed Derby boycott "misdirected" because Churchill Downs had a good record of complying with open accommodations and anti–job discrimination laws. Later it added that demonstrations would be "neither prudent nor helpful." It praised the decision in 1961 by open accommodations leaders to forgo such protests and credited it with winning sympathy for that cause. Reiterating McAlpin's point that Derby demonstrations would be ineffective, the paper argued that making the city look bad was shortsighted. It went further, claiming credit for working for civil rights reform for over thirty years—before many of the current young outsiders were born, implicitly resurrecting the division between older, local leaders and more militant "newcomers."[54]

The threats against the Derby began to take effect when, in the last week before the race, the city took steps to thwart protests. First, Derby festival organizers cancelled the popular Pegasus Parade, an event on the Thursday before the race that traditionally attracted up to two hundred thousand spectators, because they feared the police would be unable to maintain crowd control and safety. The NAACP offered to hold a "black and white" parade instead, which it admitted would be more of a demonstration than entertainment, but it was denied a permit. During one of the races in the days leading up to the big event, five young men, led by SCLC activist Robert Sims, managed to get onto the track and run in front of the horses. They were caught and arrested, but the incident raised fears of potentially dangerous demonstrations on the big day. In the wake of this protest, the mayor wrote to the governor, asking for increased National Guard presence at Churchill Downs. Guardsmen customarily received admission to the race so that they could be on hand in case of trouble, but the mayor was looking for an extra large contingent. He did receive an offer of support from another source. Officials of the Ku Klux Klan promised to attend in their regalia and help the police to keep order. Eventually, three hundred extra police, six hundred national guardsmen, and an air police unit provided security for the event.[55]

In the end, the bluster from both sides came to naught. The morning of the Derby, Martin Luther King announced that there would be no demonstrations, as an act of good faith and a show that protesters were not seeking disruption for its own sake. Privately, movement leaders were also worried about rumors that "racist hoodlums would start a riot." King included in his announcement, however, a pledge to redouble efforts in the coming weeks, and his lieutenant Hosea Williams declared, "We've got to change something in this town. Derby or no Derby, there's going to be some hell in Louisville until a housing bill is passed." Instead of the threatened disruptions at the race, about 140 people marched through downtown without incident. At Churchill Downs, things went more smoothly than usual, with police reporting fewer arrests than in other years. There were some problems, such as a firecracker tossed on the track and reports of bomb threats. But the worst incidents involved college students drinking beer in the infield, a Derby tradition. The *Louisville Defender* quickly praised King's "good judgement," but other open housing advocates were not so pleased. An anonymous letter "to folks" called King a "super-tom" and chastised him for not consulting with the demonstrators before making the decision. Indicating the rise of a more militant spirit and invoking new black power leaders, the letter went on to say the movement had lost momentum, and "we need Stokely badly."[56]

In the weeks after the Derby, COH acted on its promise to escalate protests after its "act of good faith" in canceling disturbances at the Derby. Members began by alternating marches to the south end and into the downtown area around city hall. Martin Luther King and his advisers also came back to town to lead a rally to reinvigorate the movement. During one of King's first marches, a rock thrown from a crowd of spectators grazed him. He had been speaking directly to hecklers to try to sway some away from the crowd. Police had just suggested that he and local black leader Reverend Leo Lesser should move to safety when the rock was thrown. At a rally that night, King used the incident to reaffirm his and his organization's commitment to the local struggle, declaring, "Upon this rock we are going to build an open city," and pledging to "create a crisis so great that this city will have to respond." Specifically, he promised that SCLC would help to lead nightly marches into the south end to pressure the city, if necessary, because "Pharaoh had to be plagued."[57]

The reaction against these nightly demonstrations became increasingly violent, creating an atmosphere local commentators feared could lead Louisville to join the list of cities experiencing the riots of the "long hot summers." Showers of rocks and eggs met nearly every march, and vandals sabotaged and smashed the windows of demonstrators' cars. In a sign that tensions were escalating, south end residents attempted to drive their cars through marches, and spectators urged them to "hit them, hit them." Protesters began to respond verbally to the crowds, singing "heckling songs at them" and taunting. Physical confrontations became more likely when groups of opponents blocked the sidewalk paths of marches and police did little to intervene. Eventually there were reports of scuffles breaking out, punches thrown, and one accusation that KCLC leader Reverend Lesser assaulted a south end woman. Former mayor and now congressman William Cowger blamed the confrontations on "agitators on the far left and from the far right" and warned that these outsiders could spark a riot. The *Louisville Defender* concurred with his fear of mass violence but argued that, if it happened, it would be the result of homegrown problems, namely the increasing concentration and resentment of blacks because of urban renewal and new highway construction and, most important, the encouragement of lawless behavior by a police force that seemed to side openly with hecklers and conspire with them to mistreat protesters.[58]

The increased visibility of the WCC and Ku Klux Klan in the opposition added to the tension. Newspaper coverage of the opponents of open housing initially portrayed them as crowds of youthful hecklers, stressing their age and disorganization and, in one case, describing the atmosphere as "carnival-like." While reporters noted Confederate flags and Wallace-for-president stickers, they conveyed the overall impression that these crowds—not yet "mobs"—were relatively harmless. As May wore on, signs appeared of more adult and organized leadership. A man who used the name John Marshall rose to prominence as a leader of the hecklers. In late May, he circulated a petition asking the city to enjoin all marches and applied for a parade permit for the same time and place as the COH's. The permit application was made in the name of the Citizens Councils of America, the Wallace for president campaign, and a new local group, "Anti–Open Housing." It turned out that "Marshall" was actually Charles Purlee, a south ender who was also an organizer for the WCC and a leader in the local Klan. The Klan more publicly made its presence known when two members in full regalia were arrested for disorderly conduct at a march on May 31. In June Purlee applied for a permit to have a mass march of robed and masked members for the purpose of recruitment and to oppose open housing through downtown Louisville. The city safety director denied the permit, saying such an event would be "reasonably likely to provoke disorder and to create disturbances." Barred from an organized protest, the Klan instead held a "mingle-in" during which groups of two and three strode through downtown.[59]

While the opposition was becoming more organized and visible, there were signs that the open housing demonstrations were weakening. Although COH and SCLC came out of Derby week promising an escalation of demonstrations, the number of marchers declined from the level in April to between forty and seventy-five on a typical night. Then Martin Luther King postponed his return to Louisville, originally anticipated to be only a "few days" after his early May visit, until June because his advisers feared too small a turnout for his visit. Meanwhile, the Reverend W. J. Hodge cancelled a midday demonstration downtown when only seventeen participants showed up because he worried such a small turnout would be "embarrassing." Just one month previously, a junior high school student, Priscilla Hancock, wrote in the *Louisville Defender* that she had been caught up in the "spirit of freedom and equality" and reported that her friends who attended the open housing demonstrations had believed the demonstrations would bring quick action. But by late May, they had become disillusioned and believed the protests were not working. In June, movement leaders began to reevaluate their strategy in a series of meetings, in part because of financial problems, which left COH seventeen hundred dollars in the red and threatened the movement's ability to make bail for those arrested.[60]

As enthusiasm for direct action began to fade, leaders turned to the tactic that in the end made the difference: the vote. In June COH announced it would limit demonstrations to one a week while launching a voter registration campaign. The *Defender* praised the decision and added that "the only way to get an open housing ordinance is to vote out the eight aldermen who voted no." At the same time, the NAACP called off its boycott of downtown merchants because it had proved ineffective and called for all interested parties to join a new voter registration coalition. The result was the All Citizens Non-partisan Voter Registration Crusade, headed by Raoul Cunningham, the former leader of the high school sit-in participants, now back in town from college. To kick off the drive, Martin Luther King returned to the city and urged eight hundred people at Green Street Baptist Church to "vote baby vote" instead of "burn baby burn." Unlike the 1961 effort, this voter registration campaign encountered resistance from some city officials. Cunningham accused Jefferson County clerk James Hallahan of "playing politics" when he allowed the Republican Party to hold a voting booth demonstration at the state fair but would not allow the open housing coalition to do the same and denied requests for extended registration hours and more locations. Nevertheless, the crusade claimed some victory, reporting 1,115 new voters concentrated in the west end.[61]

Just as the voter registration drive was drawing to a close, an open housing ordinance once again came before the board of aldermen. In the late spring, the aldermen had put forward the notion that existing laws gave the HRC the ability to enforce nondiscrimination in housing, a theory the commission had rejected. Now, in early September, the mayor reiterated that small editorial changes would make current statutes strong enough, and he introduced a new ordinance with those changes. Alderman Louise Reynolds immediately denounced the move, saying the sponsors of the new measure were "more interested in engaging in a delusory act to give the Negro the false security of being protected . . . when in fact this ordinance is weak and impotent." Most important, the mayor's measure contained neither a definition of discrimination nor penalty provisions. Nevertheless, without consulting the HRC, on September 13 the board of aldermen adopted the mayor's proposal. Safety director Alvey contended that now the city had all the power it needed to guarantee open housing. Movement leaders, much more skeptical, called it nothing but "false promises" and warned of an imminent return to "force and pressure" to secure a meaningful law.[62]

In the months leading up to the election, movement leaders could not deliver on the threat to keep up the pressure with rejuvenated demonstrations. In the wake of the vote, they promised a massive new plan of direct action, including demonstrations aimed specifically at the aldermen and visits by open housing leaders from around the country. But calls for renewed protests appear to have fallen flat. The *Louisville Defender* labeled demonstrations "old hat" and asked why, since they had not worked before, and nothing in city government had yet changed, they would work now. Moreover, there was a danger of making people feel there was never any use for demonstrations if they were employed at the wrong time. The editors concluded that the best tactic at this point was political action.[63]

Fortunately for civil rights advocates, that strategy worked. Early in the fall election season, open housing leaders opposed the current administration and declared the goal of the registration drive to be to remove them. At first the *Defender* complained that there was little difference between the two parties on the state level, noting that the Democrats had yet to take a strong stand in favor of civil rights. On the eve of the election, however, the paper changed tone, and the editors strongly endorsed the full Democratic slate, even at the risk of losing the few friendly Republicans—Reynolds, Ford, and Stoll—on the board. By that time, five of the nine Democratic candidates had pledged some sort of action on open housing. One called an enforceable law the "first order of business." Others were more vague about their position, but only two believed existing laws were enough. On election day, turnout appeared to be low, and the vote seemed close. But when the tallies were recorded, the Republican board had been defeated, with only Reynolds keeping her seat. As in the 1961 campaign, movement leaders took credit for influencing the result. This time, though, the daily papers did not dispute that notion.[64]

Also unlike the aftermath of the 1961 election, the newly elected board of aldermen did not wait a year and a half to pass demanded civil rights legislation. Immediately after the election, Democratic representative Albert B. Harris, an African American doctor just elected to the board, declared that all those of his party who were joining the board of aldermen favored an open housing ordinance. Perhaps seeing the writing on the wall, Mayor Schmied changed his position and asked the board to pass a "meaningful measure." By the end of the month, the HRC prepared a new draft ordinance to be ready for consideration as soon as the new board was sworn in. There were some threats of resistance. Joseph Krieger, head of the Concerned Citizens Committee, for example, pledged to push for a recall of the aldermen, a referendum on the law, or a state law prohibiting cities from passing such legislation. But on the first reading of the bill in early December, only a small crowd turned out, and advocates outnumbered opponents. Then, on December 13, the board passed the open housing law by a vote of nine to three, making it illegal to "sell, purchase, exchange, rent, or lease or withhold any housing accommodation from a person because of race or color." The ordinance put enforcement in the hands of the HRC and called for penalties of up to five hundred dollars per infraction. The only exceptions were for properties of four or fewer rental or rooming units where the owner or a family member of the owner lived on the premises. Louisville was not the first in the South this time, or even in the state; the Bardstown–Nelson County government in nearby rural Kentucky had already adopted a model ordinance designed by the Kentucky Commission on Human Rights. But leaders still claimed Louisville's bragging rights as the first large southern community to adopt an open housing law.[65]

A few months later, the Kentucky legislature passed its own open housing act, in part on the momentum established by Bardstown–Nelson County and Louisville. In the November election, Georgia Davis Powers, who had gotten her start in civil rights work by organizing the march on Frankfort, won a seat as the first woman and first African American in the Kentucky senate. In the first days of her term, she introduced a fair housing bill, but it was not given much chance of succeeding. Powers went to work lobbying her colleagues. She later recalled how she traded votes with Tom Garrett from Paducah, Kentucky, who was pushing a daylight saving bill and had eighteen votes lined up in favor while nineteen senators opposed it. Powers promised she would use her vote to bring the tally to a tie if Garrett could line up his supporters behind open housing. The exchange worked. Daylight saving time was adopted in Kentucky after the lieutenant governor broke the tie. And the fair housing bill passed by a vote of twenty-seven to three, with eight abstentions. Soon after, Norbert Blume and African American representatives Mae Street Kidd and Hughes McGill marshaled it through the Kentucky house, giving Kentucky the first state fair housing law in the South.[66]

Despite the seeming ease with which both the state and local laws finally passed, open housing advocates had their work cut out for them well into the next decade. The *Louisville Defender* published a series of reports of blatant housing discrimination and violence against blacks who tried to overcome it. Rock throwing and threats of worse forced a black family out of the west end neighborhood of Portland in the summer of 1968. A year later, irate neighbors harassed a white family who offered to sell its house to a black family. *Defender* reporters uncovered persistent bias in trailer park facilities, which completely barred blacks from buying and renting properties. The paper also revealed that white opposition had sabotaged a plan to build subsidized housing in a south end suburb, leading to its cancellation. Housing opportunity centers, established by the Kentucky Commission on Human Rights to help black families find homes in previously white areas, tried to bring some positive news, reporting in 1970 that most blacks who moved into white areas had positive experiences. But subsequent studies by the state commission in 1973 and 1974 showed that housing segregation in the city and county was getting worse. Indeed, a 1974 study by the Council on Municipal Performance demonstrated that "Louisville is more residentially segregated than 79 of 109 major US cities." This, according to Kentucky Commission on Human Rights head Galen Martin, compared "unfavorably with sister cities and even deep southern cities." In contrast to its earlier reputation, Louisville appeared to be leading not in progress but in stagnation.[67]

With the passage of the open housing ordinance, the long struggle in Louisville ended in victory. Yet despite the fact that housing discrimination had been made illegal, many participants in the movement did not see it as a success. At the root of the disillusionment about the open housing movement was the level of opposition to it not only in government but in the streets and neighborhoods. The marches met more violence and ugly rhetoric than had been seen at any previous time in the Louisville movement—resembling confrontations in Chicago and Birmingham more than the city's own relatively peaceful sit-ins. The organized opposition, namely the Concerned Citizens Committee, held larger and more vocal events and garnered greater attention and membership than had the Committee for Business Freedom, the relatively small center of opposition to public accommodations. Although opposition came from across the city and all socioeconomic classes, the public confrontations most often took place in the lower-income white neighborhoods in the south end of the city that were most likely to see African American families moving in if the barriers of overt discrimination broke down. In these areas, the product of white flight from the west end in the late 1950s and early 1960s, the 1963 open accommodations ordinance, and the integration of the Louisville schools had not affected most whites in their day-to-day lives. But open housing endangered these neighborhoods' isolation from the impact of civil rights legislation. This threat brought out denunciations of government intrusion into homes and calls for white majority rights against "outsiders." The national backlash, and with it increasing racial tension and resistance to further change, had come to Louisville.

In the short run, opponents did not stop the open housing ordinance. But regardless of the city's new policy of antidiscrimination, open housing advocates also did not meet their broader goals. Most important, housing in the city did not integrate. By the mid-1970s, the west end would become even more concentrated African American, a harbinger of patterns that continued into the ensuing decades, undermining school and employment integration, as predicted. As a result, the housing, economic, and even environmental conditions in the area deteriorated. At the same time, race relations in the city worsened. Whites became further emboldened to question policies for racial change, and younger African Americans turned to militancy and other expressions of frustration. Now, instead of reciting the litany of successes that made Louisville a leader for the region, local civic leaders, media, and civil rights activists invoked long lists of problems that continued to plague the city and to render it among the worst in both the North and South. And rhetoric about the community's role as a leader and its progressive history became rare and halfhearted.

Despite the technical victory, then, the wider failure of the open housing movement caused frustration and disillusionment among African Americans and many of their white allies and led activists to turn to different strategies for confronting the manifestations of racism. Young militants began to doubt the value of mass marches because they did not seem to work anymore. Frustrated by what they now saw as outmoded tactics, they turned to black power. WECC, dismayed at the prospects for integrating the entire city, focused on improving and empowering the neighborhood. Other activists turned their attention to the problem of economic inequality, including moderate black leaders who launched jobs campaigns and others who engaged in the War on Poverty. White liberals frustrated by their impotence took up the defense of radicals and militants against the political impact of the backlash and the repression it brought with it. The shift to these new concerns made the open housing movement a turning point in Louisville's struggle for racial equality. What had begun as an optimistic campaign to create an open community based on the vision and tactics of the early 1960s southern civil rights movement ran aground on the increasing resistance to further racial change. Open housing was the last of the city's mass nonviolent direct action campaigns for change through local civil rights legislation. It would be replaced by myriad strategies aimed at creating and empowering community.

5

Building Bridges, Fighting Poverty, and Empowering Citizens

In the mid-1960s, while the members of WECC were marching in support of an ordinance banning discrimination in housing, they also were organizing residents of public housing projects to demand garbage pickup and a tráffic signal; hosting weekend-long arts festivals where blacks and whites could have fellowship while enjoying music, theater, and dance; and coordinating the fight against poverty in one of the poorest sections of the city. And WECC was not alone in engaging in this broad spectrum of action. LACRR, while sponsoring vigils of laypeople and clergy for open housing, also attempted to bridge the gap between whites and blacks by hosting discussion sessions on race relations. In addition, young men who came to town with SCLC to work for open housing legislation joined Volunteers in Service to America (VISTA) and worked with WECC to organize for the empowerment of the black community. Meanwhile, the NAACP led boycotts and negotiated for equal access to jobs for blacks while campaigning for improvement of the schools. In short, in the mid-1960s, civil rights advocates in Louisville fanned out into myriad actions around the issues of race and class in the community.

Members of WECC articulated the concern underlying much of this work: the sense that Louisville and the broader civil rights movement were now at a crossroads. When it passed the open accommodations ordinance, the city had earned a victory, at least on paper, over the manifestation of racism most associated with the region: Jim Crow in public spaces. But it was now at a "perilous point" because it was developing the potentially explosive conditions that plagued the North.

The effort to overcome what was considered that region's primary race relations problem, segregation in housing, although it eventually resulted in a local ordinance against discrimination, in the meantime caused increased racial tension in the city and frustration among movement activists. The local conundrum reflected the national situation at mid-decade: despite civil rights legislation, ongoing racial inequality was creating a rise in discontent and leading to waves of violence in the "long hot summers" of 1964 and thereafter. As the end of legal Jim Crow left activists in both North and South with the task of fighting de facto segregation and institutionalized racism, the distinction between the regions' racial problems began to blur. Now the question for civil rights advocates in Louisville, as across the country, was whether the passage of civil rights laws merely highlighted remaining inequalities less amenable to legislative solution or, more hopefully, marked the beginning of a concerted effort to achieve the "beloved community." To nudge the answer toward the latter, in Louisville WECC activists and others simultaneously worked to empower west end citizens to fight the poor housing, lack of opportunity, and crumbling schools that buttressed continued inequality and to create relationships across race and class that would be the start of a truly interracial community. In language that had inspired civil rights activity in the city for at least a decade, they hoped that by doing so they would make the west end "a model for North and South."[1]

Standing at the crossroads of the mid-1960s, Louisville activists understood the need to develop new strategies to accomplish those goals. Just as this period saw a lessening of the distinction between northern and southern racial problems, it also saw a melding of different approaches to confronting them. In the popular imagination, the civil rights era is often divided into two periods, with corresponding characteristic ways of acting and regional identification: the early southern mass movement of nonviolent direct action aimed at securing the end of discrimination through legislation, followed later in the decade by northern militants' calling for community solidarity, pride, and self-determination. Historians have recently challenged this dichotomy, pointing out the overlap in the ideology, personnel, and even timing of these two supposedly separate phases of the freedom struggle. Incorporating the War on Poverty into the mix, scholars now emphasize the interconnections among these three important phenomena of the period.[2] Louisville activists' move in this period from older ideas about the nature of racial problems and tactics to new understandings and methods illustrates how such connections were made. The fight against economic discrimination became a War on Poverty, which led to the goal of empowerment of the poor and black residents of the west end. Campaigns to integrate public space inspired some Louisvillians to work to build a sense of interracial community, over time realizing that that must rest on a recognition of and respect for black culture. In short, there was not a sharp break between mass nonviolent direct action and black power militancy; instead, the activism of the mid-1960s served as a bridge between the struggles of the late and early years of the decade and thus demonstrates the links among and compatibility of different forms of action.

The most common new tool for equal rights advocates in the middle years of the decade was community organization by church, civil rights, and civic organizations in their own programs, channeled through the city and county War on Poverty. The widespread turn to community organizing not only in Louisville but in cities across the country reflects the merging of northern and southern strategies for confronting racial and economic problems in this mid-decade period. Community organizing drew on models in SNCC's work in southern rural areas but also on the work of Saul Alinsky and others in northern and midwestern industrial neighborhoods, combining them into a pattern of work that became more distinctively urban than regional. In Louisville, much of this activity was focused on the west end, the center of both the black community and poverty in the city, and the work of WECC is a microcosm of the efforts of the period. While it does not encapsulate the entirety of the freedom struggle or War on Poverty in this period, WECC's program can be used as a window to view how activists used community organizing to achieve the twin goals of overcoming segregation and building a "beloved community."

Early in the 1960s, activists used protests, boycotts, nonviolent pressure, and legislation to address a new—or rather newly rediscovered—issue: economic inequality. Pressure against employment discrimination had not gone away since the postwar campaigns for jobs in city government and industry. Throughout the 1950s and 1960s, the Louisville Urban League, although only minimally involved in open accommodations and housing, had quietly used negotiation to secure jobs for African Americans in private business. Meanwhile, the NAACP had filed lawsuits and forced investigations of discrimination by unions and management in factories with federal contracts. But neither group's efforts made significant headway or impacted very many black workers. Then, during the open accommodations struggle, the issue of jobs rose again, and civil rights leaders approached it in the same way as they did discrimination in facilities, with protest campaigns consisting of negotiation, pressure, and nonviolent direct action in the forms of demonstrations and boycotts, and then by working for a city ordinance outlawing discrimination. These actions reflected a faith in being able to use persuasion and legislation to end economic inequality.

In the late 1950s, Frank Stanley Sr. urged local African Americans to follow the lead of other cities and revive the Buy Where You Can Work campaigns of the Depression era to call for jobs in businesses in black neighborhoods.[3] A few years later, alongside mass demonstrations for open accommodations, the NAACP, CORE, and an unaffiliated group of young people organized by Andrew Wade engaged in pickets and boycotts against selected stores and companies. Attention focused first on the Algonquin Manor shopping center, located in the heart of the west end, near majority-black housing projects, and then on three targeted companies—Sears, Sealtest, and Coca-Cola. Over the next few years, the goals developed from the hiring of some black workers to what Wade called "proportional employment opportunities," a sign that African Americans would no longer accept tokenism and the celebration of individual firsts. The campaigns saw some success. When the Algonquin Manor shopping center hired thirty-five blacks, the *Louisville Defender* called it the "most integrated shopping center in the Falls City area." Sears agreed relatively quickly to hire black sales clerks, but Sealtest managers claimed that seniority issues prohibited them from making changes right away, and Coca-Cola refused to discuss the issue. By the summer of 1962, although CORE leaders insisted that the boycott was continuing, this direct action approach to employment in private business fizzled. The local CORE chapter disbanded soon thereafter, the victim of internal differences and its persistent inability to attract large numbers.[4]

While campaigning for job opportunities for blacks in private business, civil rights leaders went back to a target from the postwar era: city government jobs. Louisville had prided itself on being among "the first southern cities to have Negro fire and policemen," with the first hired in the 1920s. Yet, by the early 1960s, African Americans still could not be promoted to high ranks in either department and found themselves segregated into separate units, barred from certain activities, and excluded from the events of the professional associations. In recalling his career in the police force, Shelby Lanier said that after struggling even to get hired by the department in 1961—despite high scores on his civil service exam—he, along with all other black officers, was assigned to a walking beat in the west end. At first he could not ride in a squad car, and he was pressured not to arrest whites but to call for help if a need to do so arose. Meanwhile, in the county, black officers charged there was a "racial purge" of the department, attempting to push African Americans out. Complaints crescendoed in early 1965, when longtime NAACP leader Dr. Maurice Rabb brought fourteen specific cases of ill treatment and discrimination to the HRC for investigation. In response, the director of public safety promised to open the motorcycle unit and homicide investigations to blacks, but he continued to deny there was discrimination in the department. Of a total force of 520 officers, 32 were African American.[5]

Civil rights leaders responded to the recalcitrance within city government to equal employment for African Americans by escalating the pressure for an ordinance against job discrimination. Initially they focused on a ban on discrimination within city government itself. In 1961 the state government had set a precedent when it adopted a merit system requiring nondiscrimination in jobs within the government and in firms contracting with the state. In May 1962 the NAACP asked the Louisville city government to establish a similar "fair employment policy" but got no response. Then, in early 1963, as the new HRC was laying out its agenda, it listed equal employment along with open accommodations and open housing as its main goals. Once the open accommodations law passed and the HRC geared up on housing and jobs, it was able to accomplish jobs first. Through the spring and summer of 1964, the commission investigated employment conditions and negotiated with local business and industrial leaders to determine the shape of a potential law. After the adoption of the Civil Rights Act of 1964, HRC leaders urged the passage of a city ordinance so that local complaints would not have to go to the federal level for resolution. By the end of the year, a measure was drafted, and in February 1965, the board of aldermen adopted an ordinance banning discrimination in employment by both public and private employers, with little discussion or debate. The measure, which went into effect the same day as

the federal bill, in the summer of 1965, was expected to meet little resistance. Indeed, its passage elicited almost no notice, let alone opposition, perhaps because, with the federal law already adopted, it seemed
relatively unthreatening, or because the more contentious issue of open
housing drew attention away.[6]

The lack of overt opposition to a city equal employment ordinance
did not mean the end of job discrimination and economic inequality in
the community. Instead, the new ordinance triggered a second phase
of activism aimed at enforcement and prying open the doors to new
opportunities for African Americans. The HRC, the *Louisville Defender,* and civil rights groups continually documented and publicized
persistent problems in employment. The state and city human relations
groups charged that the new city law needed to be strengthened. Officials of the local commission admitted after one year that the number
of complaints was low but contrasted that with the two or three a week
the NAACP was receiving. The officials argued this proved that blacks
either were intimidated from coming forward or feared they would
get no satisfaction from such weak legislation. Over the next couple
of years, a variety of studies revealed the barriers blacks continued to
face. One year after the law went into effect, the HRC surveyed almost
one hundred businesses and found that nearly half of all retail stores
still had no black sales staff, and the "remainder had one or two."
Moreover, industry still confined African Americans to unskilled jobs
and "token representation" at higher levels. Within city government,
the story was no better. In summer 1967, the employment director of
the HRC found that blacks held only one-fifth of city and county jobs.
Although in 1970—the next census count—the city would be 24 percent black and the county approximately 14 percent, and thus the HRC
numbers on the surface reflected the proportion of African Americans
in the population, the report pointed out that, again, most of those jobs
were in unskilled positions. Moreover, in 1968 the U.S. Department of
Labor revealed that only 5 percent of the members of the local building
trades were black.[7]

To confront this continuing problem, members of the HRC and
others in the city administration attempted to enforce local and federal laws through negotiations and more assertive policies. The HRC
could claim a few successes. In 1967, working with the Urban League,
the Louisville Building Trades Council, and others, it convinced the
contractors responsible for the new U.S. government office building

downtown to hire black workers in compliance with federal guidelines. Buoyed by the success of negotiation in that case, the agency undertook a series of conferences with local businesses to investigate patterns of discrimination and start an education and persuasion campaign to address them. Meanwhile, Mayor Kenneth Schmied, in what the *Louisville Defender* called a "display of affirmative action leadership," issued an executive order "barring the city from doing business with firms that discriminate in hiring," a measure that might seem unnecessary, given that city law already prohibited such discrimination. That Schmied felt compelled to issue the order indicates the lack of compliance with employment legislation. Indeed, the law apparently had little impact on behavior; in 1968 a state survey revealed that only 2.7 percent of employees in skilled and white-collar positions in industry were held by nonwhites. HRC enforcement of bans on discrimination through negotiation and persuasion was for all practical purposes going nowhere, especially for working-class African Americans.[8]

In employment outside city government, civil rights organizations tried a variety of strategies to force equal opportunity. The NAACP at mid-decade focused its energies on pursuing complaints of discrimination through local and federal bureaucracies. As indicated above, the organization received complaints from local workers and helped them to file with the HRC. In addition, the branch initiated its own charges with the federal Equal Employment Opportunity Commission (EEOC) against large firms like Ford Motor Company and Olin Mathieson Chemical Corporation. While the NAACP emphasized enforcement of antidiscrimination laws, the more conservative Urban League focused on job training and placement. In 1965 the organization secured a contract with the Bureau of Apprenticeship and Training and started to recruit African American workers and to help them secure apprenticeships with trade unions. This program became the core of the Urban League's participation in the local War on Poverty when it got contracts to run the manpower training program. Whereas the NAACP's role in the War on Poverty was limited to participation on the Community Action Commission (CAC), the Urban League became a steady fixture of the local effort, using it as a channel for its traditional work in training and placing black workers in industry and making a smooth transition from antidiscrimination civil rights work to antipoverty action.

Meanwhile, other groups took a more protest-oriented approach to the continuing problem of employment discrimination. KCLC joined

SCLC's Operation Breadbasket, a campaign of protests aimed at firms that were still discriminating. Like their involvement in open housing, KCLC's and SCLC's engagement in Louisville provoked criticism from leaders such as Bishop Tucker, who resisted interference by "outsiders" and challenges to his status as leader of the local movement. But in this case, the *Louisville Defender* welcomed the organizations "into the fray." One partner in Operation Breadbasket was the Jefferson County Sunday School Association, which under Daniel Hughlett had been focused on equal employment opportunity since the early 1950s. To bring attention to the problem of employment discrimination, the JCSSA organized black religious groups to hold rallies.[9] The work of these organizations was a link between the boycott and direct action campaigns against employers in the early part of the 1960s and the focus on economic inequality by black workers' organizations in the coming decade.

While some civil rights groups worked for equal employment opportunity through nonviolent direct action and antidiscrimination legislation, others looked for new tactics to overcome racism by creating a "beloved community," a real sense of respect and sharing between whites and blacks. By this time it was apparent that antidiscrimination court orders and legislation, and desegregation in schools, accommodations, housing, and jobs, were not going to be enough. Indeed, in Louisville the struggle for open housing legislation was in the mid-1960s engendering increased racial tension and driving whites and blacks further apart. Thus some activists turned their attention to building bridges to try to reach across that gap.

When WECC formed, the members' explicit purposes were to "foster a real community spirit" and to promote integration in the neighborhood in order to model interracial community. In their own organization, the members were committed to interracial cooperation and equality, as seen in their requirement for biracial leadership and striving for a mixed membership. As they set out to keep the west end mixed by fighting white flight and securing an open housing ordinance, the members recognized the need also to generate a community atmosphere that would make both whites and blacks want to live there. In April 1965, to expand on its early get-acquainted and community-building activities, the organization formed a human relations committee under chairman George Kimbrough, a white doctor who had participated in demonstrations through the Unitarian Church and

CORE and had been in WECC since its founding. In its early meetings, the committee considered a long list of potential activities, from organizing teen discussion groups to working through parent-teacher associations and hosting social activities. The group quickly focused on sponsoring "group activities to enable west end citizens to mingle socially" and chose to sponsor a community arts festival as its first event.[10]

The WECC human relations committee decided to hold the first arts festival on the weekend of July 4 in Shawnee Park. The purposes of the event were to "build community spirit," to "showcase west end talent," and, most important, "to permit members of the community to find out what their next-door neighbor has to offer in the way of talent and friendship." The printed program of the festival expressed the spirit of the event with a declaration and invitation:

> On this most patriotic weekend it is a fitting time for all of us to give thanks for our country—and our community, the WEST END. It is because we live under a democratic system that we find so much talent among us. It is also because all WEST ENDERS *can* live in harmony that our WEST END will continue to be the best place to live and raise a family. Would you like to join us in our efforts to insure that the WEST END is a true community—a place where people work together for the betterment of all?[11]

In building the program, the organizers decided to open participation to those outside the neighborhood and invited performers from across the city. The schedule ultimately included a performance of Shakespeare's *Midsummer Night's Dream;* classical, folk, rock, and jazz music; and dance. Despite rain on the first night, approximately three hundred people attended, and the committee declared the event a success, noting in particular the "relaxed informality among all those who attended."[12]

After the success of the first festival, the event became an annual affair. Over the next three years, WECC added features such as a children's night, a literary digest, a juried art competition, and a food sale to benefit a neighborhood social service center. The goal of the festival remained remarkably the same, however. The program for the second year, titled "Living in a New World," described WECC's vision of a world in which "men have found that the barriers that have divided them—the different race, the different religion, the different economic conditions, all of these things—are not so important after all" and that "there is a common humanity that binds us all." At the same time, around the nation, racial tension increased in the wake of summer riots, and the rise of black power augured increased demands for black separatism and consciousness. WECC's festival, while acknowledging those changes, emphasized the "things we share" and the need to "demonstrate that the obstacles that block brotherhood in this city and the world shall be overcome." Indeed, in 1968, one month after a riot just blocks from the park where the annual festival was held, organizers declared, "Many of us will continue to dream (and hope) that this country will eventually undergo a personal and social renaissance involving real brotherhood."[13] The annual festivals best illustrated WECC's ongoing commitment to bringing whites and blacks together, regardless of changing circumstances, and also revealed the group's belief that art and culture could be an interracial meeting ground.

In much of its work in promoting better race relations, WECC cooperated with other organizations, particularly religion-based groups. Inspired by the growing fear of racial and class tension in the cities, in the mid-1960s, national white church bodies turned their resources to the problem of racism in American society, in particular outside the Deep South, where they had previously focused their attention.[14] Louisville clergy and laypeople got caught up in this spirit. One of WECC's main allies was LACRR, which was also its major partner in the open housing movement. In response to the tension that movement provoked, LACRR started Operation Brotherhood, a series of study sessions held in churches at which whites and blacks talked about the "biblical and theological basis for brotherhood" as well as other "contemporary issues." WECC joined as a cosponsor of this series after members were inspired by a visiting lecturer on the power of conversation groups. LACRR also sponsored panel discussions with local clergymen, including Rabbi Martin Perley, the Reverend Irvin Moxley, Louisville Presbyterian Theological Seminary professor Olaf Anderson, and the editor of the local Catholic paper, the Reverend William Zahner, speaking about the role of religious people in racial issues. The group continued to be a local leader in interracial organizing, especially through the schools, into the next decade.[15]

Another partner was the West Louisville Cooperative Ministry

(WLCM), a group of thirteen churches and religious agencies, both black and white, that formed in May 1966 to "administer to the needs of the whole man in the total community, reaching across boundaries of race, class and denomination, serving the physical as well as the spiritual, social and personal needs" of the residents of the neighborhood.[16] The rhetoric of groups like WLCM illustrated the ways in which people in this period made connections among issues and saw the solutions to them from a holistic approach. WECC and WLCM acted on these ideas when they combined forces to promote social events to pull together white and black, such as what became the annual Peace and Brotherhood Dinner. They also shared a headquarters building donated by an anonymous west end resident and used the space to cosponsor a coffeehouse for young people. This was intended as a space where art, music, and controversial speakers would provoke dialogue between white and black youth. Over the next few years, WECC continued to use the coffeehouse as a base for arts and community activities that engaged and empowered the youth of the area.[17]

The cooperative ventures of WECC, LACRR, and WLCM took place in a larger context in which church, civil rights, and even city agencies promoted the quest for better "human relations"—as interracial contact was increasingly known. Religious organizations sponsored workshops and forums on racial problems. The mayor's office initiated a "visitation day" program in which whites and blacks met in each other's homes.[18] All this activity assumed that laws desegregating public space were not enough to overcome the racial divide. At the same time, those involved believed that education, dialogue, social interaction, and the modeling of good relations would do so. These initiatives did promote a general sense of the need for better racial understanding and were well received by the *Louisville Courier-Journal*. But as some contemporary observers noted, they were limited in their effectiveness.[19] The forums and meetings included small numbers of people, often those already interested in race relations—they literally preached to the converted—and failed to touch most people's daily lives. WECC hoped its neighborhood-based approach was better but acknowledged the need to attract more middle-class blacks and lower-class whites. Despite these failings, however, the idealism inherent in these interracial programs continued to inspire WECC and faith-based human relations activists through the next decade and beyond.

In WECC's early pronouncements, the members declared not just a commitment to promoting interracial understanding but also a determination to work for the overall improvement of the neighborhood, to make it a place where whites and blacks would *want* to live together. As the second set of cochairs, white minister Dalton Love and Norma Shobe, the wife of attorney Benjamin Shobe, put it, the group wanted not only to make the neighborhood an integrated community but to make the council itself a "vehicle through which west end citizens can work together to solve many mutual problems." By 1965 the group had grown from an initial 40 members to 230 members. With an enlarged base of people engaged in its work, and with the frustration of the open housing movement turning the focus to empowering and improving the west end, WECC began to address problems in education, recreation, and the environment.[20] It started by developing committees on jobs, zoning, recreational facilities, juvenile delinquency, and school issues. Over the years, WECC would get involved in issues ranging from the physical condition of the schools to bus fare rates, pollution, and pornography sales. It would also become one of the main conduits for War on Poverty organizing in the west end. From their civil rights campaign for open housing legislation, then, WECC members moved seamlessly to working for better human relations and against the results of economic inequality in their neighborhood.[21]

In the mid-1960s, as WECC members and others turned their attention to the social, economic, and physical conditions in the west end, they adopted strategies commonly described as "community organizing." Community organizing in this period is most often associated with the student movement, War on Poverty community action projects, and the grassroots activism of SNCC. Though it had many expressions, there were common elements in its meaning. Community organizing was fundamentally about adopting a bottom-up approach to bringing about social change. It involved mobilizing poor, minority, geographically bounded—neighborhood- or community-based—groups. In community organizing, the role of the activist was to work with local people as they identified the roots of their problems—be they economic, racial, or political—tapped into their own knowledge and resources, developed their own leadership, and cooperated to overcome oppression. This process was informed by a commitment to a form of democracy that resulted when individuals had input into the day-to-day decisions that affected their lives and by a faith in the power of individuals working together to make a movement.[22]

Although much of its community organizing was eventually channeled through federal programs, WECC always maintained separate
activities. The first and most enduring focus was on improving conditions in the Southwick public housing project, a 149-acre residential
development built in 1960 as part of an urban renewal plan along the
far western edge of the city. The connection between WECC and the
residents of the Southwick project was made by Ruth Bryant. Bryant
was an African American civic leader and the wife of Dr. Roscoe Bryant. She had grown up in Detroit, the daughter of a politically active
real estate developer. As a teenager, she had read about Louisville in the
Pittsburgh Courier and had always been interested in the city. But she
was shocked and depressed by her first experience in Louisville, when
her husband moved the family there to start his practice and for fifteen
months rented a home in Little Africa, a low-income neighborhood
in the west end that in 1956 still lacked paved roads. Although the
Bryants soon bought a home in a neighborhood populated by middle-
class and professional blacks, she recalled that the experience made her
determined to help those who could not get out of the neighborhood.
She volunteered at her children's school, joined the Urban League's
women's auxiliary, and was appointed to city committees. Her interest
in housing problems and the prodding of her teenage daughters, who
participated in the street demonstrations, encouraged her to join the
open housing movement. After encountering WECC in that movement,
she joined the group because she shared its goal of keeping the west
end a desirable place to live. Then, in early 1965, while driving her
daughters to school, she noticed "a mountain of trash" on the side of
the road by the Southwick housing project. Wondering "what the hell
is going on down here," she investigated and put WECC in touch with
the members of the Southwick Improvement Club.[23]

At early meetings between the two groups, WECC heard black
women (despite official integration of public housing, Southwick was
in fact all black) talk about the need for trash pickup and the lack
of shopping and other services and amenities nearby. WECC quickly
decided to "go all the way" in "organizing people to help themselves"
while being careful to guide the residents to ensure that action went
"through the correct channels."[24] During these discussions, however,
WECC members learned about a history of organized dissent in the
project. As early as 1962, the Southwick women had begun complaining about the lack of shopping facilities that had been promised as

part of the urban renewal plan. Some residents had engaged in voter registration drives and participated in the early-1960s demonstrations for jobs and open accommodations at the nearby Algonquin Manor shopping center. And the women boasted that they had forced the local schools to provide safety patrols for their children in busy intersections. Thus what started as a middle-class initiative in reaching out to help poor residents quickly changed tone. WECC members stepped back, realizing that the women had "enough initiative" and that little guidance was needed. From then on, the relationship was more cooperative, with WECC helping the Southwick women to make contacts and acting alongside them but making sure that the latter got the credit and spoke for themselves. Although this approach was probably somewhat awkward initially for some of the middle-class members of the organization, WECC thus quickly learned a fundamental feature of community organizing—promoting grassroots leadership and initiative.[25]

WECC's cooperation with Southwick linked a grassroots community betterment project with the citywide protest movement and in doing so highlighted the relationship between neighborhood conditions in the west end and the problem of housing discrimination. In 1965 local officials announced a plan to build 152 additional apartments in the Southwick project. At the residents' request, WECC set up a committee to organize around this issue. Although the initiative came from WECC and the Southwick residents themselves, other allies joined the protest because they saw its connection to open housing. Members of the welfare and social action committee of the Southern Baptist Theological Seminary, for example, criticized it as a plan to "bulldoze" more African Americans into the "ghetto." At their urging, LACRR called for a moratorium on housing units until overall conditions in the area were improved and an open housing ordinance was passed. The city-county urban renewal office did temporarily withhold approval for the project to begin. But the leadership of WECC wrote to the secretary of the U.S. Department of Housing and Urban Development (HUD), Robert Weaver, complaining that construction had begun anyway and asking that urban renewal plans for the area be reevaluated. Meanwhile, KCLC leader A. D. King met with Mayor Schmied with the same demands. Ultimately the project was canceled, and the promise of shopping in the area was renewed. The more important result to Ruth Bryant was that what started as a complaint by community residents in Southwick had blossomed into a civic and religious movement that had both forced "officials to recognize the problems" and demonstrated that "the people are united."[26]

At the same time that WECC turned its attention to the broader social and economic problems of the west end, the federal government initiated the War on Poverty to combat some of the same issues and similarly employed community organizing as one strategy. President Lyndon Johnson began talking about making a national attack on poverty a central component of his envisioned Great Society in the spring of 1964. Louisvillians immediately took notice and joined a statewide summit meeting to hear about potential programs. After Congress passed the Economic Opportunity Act of 1964, local officials began planning how Louisville could benefit from the myriad initiatives being launched. In September 1964, the Health and Welfare Council of Louisville and Jefferson County, a nonprofit organization, submitted a proposal to the city and county governments for a system of poverty "target" areas, service centers, and neighborhood organization. It proposed that five target areas—the number was later increased to seven—be selected, choosing areas of concentrated poverty, poor housing, and other social ills. Each would have a neighborhood center in a school or other institution that would be a base for providing services and for promoting a sense of community. Echoing WECC's vision, the authors of the proposal suggested that these centers would "become the instrument for bringing strangers together to talk about their children or community problems" and thus learn to act together. Each service center, as they became called, would also hire a set of area residents to serve as "community workers" to organize the local people to help themselves. This proposal formed the basis of Louisville's War on Poverty.[27]

City and county government officials began implementing the proposal and launching local programs within months. Initially the antipoverty effort was coordinated through the Louisville and Jefferson County Youth Commission. That body had only fifteen members, however, and none of them came from the neighborhoods designated as poverty target areas. Within a year, after complaints from the NAACP and the local unit of the American Friends Service Committee (AFSC), the city and county governments created the CAC to take over direction of the local War on Poverty. The CAC originally included thirty-three representatives: nine from poverty areas and the rest from city and county agencies, as well as nongovernmental organizations interested in social welfare such as the Urban League, Health and Welfare Council, and NAACP. Inclusion of the representatives of the poverty target areas, who were initially appointed but later were elected, was an effort to achieve the federally mandated "maximum feasible participation" of the poor by involving residents in the planning and implementation of poverty programs. The CAC members received proposals from community groups and determined who would get grants to run antipoverty efforts. In addition, the CAC developed "area councils." These bodies were set up in target areas to oversee the work in those neighborhoods. They too were mandated to include representatives of the poor as well as of neighborhood institutions. By the end of 1965, the target areas, CAC, and area councils were in place and active.[28]

WECC got involved in the War on Poverty almost immediately. In December 1964, the group hosted a forum at which government leaders spoke about the program and urged local people to bring their own ideas. At the end of the meeting, WECC members decided to submit a request for a grant in order to participate. In "Community Mobilization through Neighborhood Councils," WECC proposed hiring community organizers who would work through block and neighborhood clubs—like the Southwick Improvement Club and others with which WECC already had contact—to address local needs. The language of its proposal reflected WECC's long-standing goals and vision of how change should be accomplished in the west end. Members hoped to "stimulate organizational forms through which people can take creative action in relieving problems and in developing community consciousness." More important, they hoped to show poor and mostly African American residents that "they can have a voice, that democracy will be as good as they make it, and that they should get together with their neighbors, talk over their problems, and decide how they can act in unison to deal with them." In the end, like their interracial efforts, this would "foster a real community spirit by providing an active clearing house through which people of all races and backgrounds can work jointly to meet their common problems."[29]

Within two months, federal officials had approved WECC's proposal and given the organization the responsibility for coordinating the antipoverty program in the Duvalle target area, which was centered around Duvalle Junior High School and included the Southwick and Cotter Homes housing projects. WECC members expressed some misgivings about being limited to work in one target area. Immediately after being approved and again one year later, the group wrote to local officials requesting that they be responsible for the whole west end. They were not seeking "to get power" for themselves or to "compete with other agencies" but rather were concerned that carving the west end into discrete target areas would create unnecessary divisions. They saw WECC, "an independent community organization," as best suited to unite and organize the neighborhood. The CAC denied this request, however, and thereafter WECC's work through the federal program was confined to the Duvalle section. For two years, WECC conducted a program within the structure established by the CAC, though the relationship was always contentious, as WECC pushed for more grassroots power within the antipoverty program.[30]

In late 1965, after it was clear that the organization would be given responsibility for only one poverty area, the group decided to launch an independent program. WECC members wanted to focus not only on a larger geographic area—avoiding the disuniting impact of the target area divisions—but on a broader vision. Thus, at the same time that it was working through the CAC in the Duvalle target area, it engaged in community organizing and human relations work throughout the area under the umbrella of a separate program, Operation West End. This program would both organize citizens to raise their voices and take action against poor conditions, economic inequality, and injustice in the west end and create "an atmosphere that transcends traditional barriers, most especially those of race but also religious and economic." In short, it sought to combine organizing for better human relations and organizing for community empowerment.[31]

To accomplish these goals, WECC sought funding from local and national church organizations. By this time, some local white churches and faith-based organizations had engaged in community organizing. West end Episcopalian congregations, for example, supported Head Start and other programs in the local target areas, and the Louisville AFSC had sponsored Learn More—Earn More, one of the first War on Poverty initiatives in the city. Moreover, as part of the growing interest of national denominational bodies in doing something about racism in American society, many churches had established grants for community organizations working in urban areas. These funds provided not only financial support but also connections among churches and community groups across the nation. WECC sought to tap into some of these resources by sending the proposal for Operation West End to local and national officials of the Episcopal, Methodist, and Presbyterian churches, the United Church of Christ, and the local AFSC. They also tried to raise funds from local businessmen, though with little success. Over the next several years, the organization received funding primarily from the Episcopal Church and United Church of Christ, but also from the United Church Board for Homeland Ministries and its Indiana-Kentucky conference.[32]

With money from these sources, WECC hired its first paid staff: neighborhood organizers, human relations workers, and an executive director. The neighborhood organizers were not intended to compete with the community organizers working in the Duvalle area but to supplement their work and broaden it across the community. Over time, it became clear that those hired under Operation West End were also more engaged in protest activities. In keeping with the organization's tradition of biracial cooperation, WECC first hired a white man and a black woman. Ricky Key was a white native of the west end who had attended Shawnee High School and was a student at Murray State University. Dolores White was an African American substitute teacher and drama instructor for the west end YMCA. In May 1966, WECC hired Hulbert James as its first executive director. James was born in the Virgin Islands but grew up in New York City. He attended law school first at Howard University and then at the University of Louisville. His first community job in the city was with the staff of the CAC, and he briefly worked in the Russell target area before WECC hired him to direct its new initiative. As executive director of Operation West End, he oversaw all the operations of the organization and led both its neighborhood work and involvement in the open housing movement. His job thus reflected the way WECC combined neighborhood organizing, protest, and human relations activities.[33]

While working independently through Operation West End, WECC coordinated the federal antipoverty programs in the Duvalle target area through the Duvalle Area Council, the community and resident organizers, and the Lang Social Service Center. WECC's program in the Duvalle area was a microcosm of the community action projects in Louisville. It illustrates how neighborhood activists attempted to use War on Poverty structures as a forum for empowering poor and black residents by giving them a voice in the decisions affecting their lives. The area council was the representative body that was meant to make the antipoverty program a democratic venture. The Duvalle

Area Council was organized in late fall 1965, and WECC member Ken Phillips was elected as its chair. Its primary responsibility was to receive proposals from neighborhood residents and organizations for programs and to send those it approved for further review by the CAC and ultimately by federal officials. But the area council went beyond that, and its meetings provided opportunities for people to hear about the work in the neighborhood and a sounding board for residents to vent their frustrations and ask for help on personal and community problems. At one meeting, for example, Vernice Hunter and other local women challenged officials about why more African Americans were not being hired in various programs. At another, public housing tenants complained of rising rents and convinced the council and WECC to write to Washington for relief. Over time, the meetings became occasions for protests against cuts in federal funds and for debates over the nature of demonstrations for open housing. Although there were questions from the beginning about the extent to which the CAC and higher officials were listening, which would fester and break out into major controversies later, for some residents the area council became—as its newsletter title indicated—a place where "the people speak."[34]

The key element in the community action approach to the War on Poverty, and the feature that embodied the hope for grassroots mobilization, was the community organizers. The day-to-day work of meeting with residents and mobilizing them around neighborhood problems was done by a team of one lead organizer, first Robert Douglas and later Sylvester Tutt, and resident organizers Doris Calvin and Rosa Henderson. Douglas grew up in Cotter Homes, attended local schools, and became an artist and social worker. He had been a member of the NAACP Youth Council and participant in the Brown Theatre demonstrations of 1959. Tutt was a native west ender who spent some time as a union organizer. Calvin was already familiar with WECC because she was the leader of the Southwick Improvement Club. Henderson was a resident of Cotter Homes who likewise had a history of involvement in neighborhood improvement activities. Thus the team of community organizers came to their work with a background in community and social justice activism.[35]

What community organizers did on a daily and weekly basis varied widely, from filing paperwork to organizing meetings and helping people with individual needs. One report from Calvin for October 1966 reveals the sometimes seemingly mundane nature of the job. She held a coffee hour to discuss with parents how to reorganize their parent-teacher association and to find out what programs they would like to see added to the schools. She planned the area council meeting and helped a group of mothers set up an evening English class. A few days later, she talked with a mothers' group about the need for recreational equipment in the schools. She sponsored a panel discussion by young women who had gone through the Job Corps yet had failed to get jobs, and she went door-to-door visiting people to see what other needs they might have. On occasion she expressed frustration, noting time spent in a particular neighborhood finding "not many people home" or a lack of interest. In the next month, she noted several attempts to return to the same blocks to show people "I'm still interested in their problems."[36]

Reports from Calvin and other organizers reveal they spent time meeting with parents about concerns for their children, organized residents into block clubs focused on improving conditions, and worked with individuals to make sure they had access to services. They continually struggled to balance the need to be out in the neighborhood making contacts and being in the offices of welfare agencies. The schedules of these organizers reveal both the strengths and weaknesses of the community action component of the War on Poverty. The organizers were from the neighborhood and had experience working for community improvement through existing organizations such as the Southwick Improvement Club and church groups. They were immersed in the neighborhood and could relate to the residents. But the level of demand for services, plus the rather quick cuts in federal funding for community organizing, meant these workers could spend very little time mobilizing the poor for real social change.

Over time, much of the social welfare service that was aimed at local residents was centralized in the Lang Social Service Center. As noted above, the original plan for the Louisville War on Poverty involved establishing neighborhood centers in each target area that would be both a point of delivery for social services and a place where people could come together to work toward solving their problems. In other words, the initial vision conceived them as a democratic institution for the poor. The Lang Social Service Center fulfilled the first part of its mission by housing part-time offices of the Family and Children Agency; the Youth Opportunity Center, a branch of the Kentucky Employment Service; and the Urban League. The center also hosted cooking classes and some adult education, tutoring, and cultural programs. In response to local demand, Legal Aid began assigning lawyers to hold office hours in the center. Newly created programs such as Ambition Inc., a CAC-funded effort to provide job training and activities for young black men, also found a home there.[37]

In 1968 the service center underwent some changes and became the Park Duvalle Neighborhood Service Center, a more independent, resident-operated "supermarket" for services under the pilot cities program of the federal War on Poverty. The pilot program provided funding to eleven cities across the country to develop these community-based institutions, furthering the idea that residents of poverty neighborhoods should have control over initiatives affecting them. A group of forty residents planned the center and wrote its constitution, which required that half of the governing board of thirty-two people be from the poverty area. The mayor and county judge executive had no representatives on the board, rendering it relatively independent in its decision making. Funding for programs came from four federal departments: the Office of Economic Opportunity, HUD, the Department of Labor, and the Department of Health, Education, and Welfare. The center was housed in renovated apartment buildings in the Cotter Homes public housing project.[38]

Within a year, however, there was disillusionment with the center. Although it opened and began offering services—in one year over forty-five thousand people visited, seeking one of fourteen services—residents complained that red tape, delays in Washington, and poor responsiveness meant that it was not meeting its real goal of being a democratic institution for empowering the poor. The plan for an office of juvenile court was scrapped, and the day care center was delayed a year and then accepted only sixty children. When the community was polled and a list of priorities was sent to Washington, it was several months before it was even acknowledged. The problems were blamed in part on a split between the poor and nonpoor representatives on the board and in part on bad advice from the Office of Economic Opportunity. Residents also complained that the CAC had adopted a "hands-off" policy and purposely lost or ignored the center's proposals. Though the center eventually stabilized and became an important fixture in the neighborhood, over time the original vision of a community-controlled institution was lost.[39]

One person who articulated the dissatisfaction with the center was one of its employees, Sterling Neal Jr. Neal grew up in west Louisville, hearing family stories of a great-grandfather who fought for the Union in the Civil War and a grandfather who was a Garveyite. His father, Sterling Neal Sr., was a union organizer for the FE at International Harvester during its postwar heyday. The younger Neal recalled sitting in his living room with left-wing labor activists and joining the picket lines. He also remembered that, as a result of his father's involvement in the union, FBI agents were often parked outside his home—and he and his friends threw mud and bricks at their cars. The "politically charged" atmosphere of his youth also included participating in CORE demonstrations alongside his sister Beverly. The combination of those experiences and the disrespect he received from white teachers in the newly integrated schools led him to decide to devote his life to revolution. Although he wanted to leave the country, his father convinced him to stay and attend Kentucky State College. There, and later at the University of Michigan and then the University of Louisville, he studied social work so that he could be part of a "social transformation." His career led him to positions in Louisville, including for the War on Poverty in the Duvalle target area. That work ultimately disappointed him, however. As he saw it, what started out as an experiment in "true democracy" at the Park Duvalle Neighborhood Service Center was watered down so that its purpose became "simply to give social services."[40]

The neighborhood center had trouble getting off the ground in part because it was very quickly overshadowed by an affiliated institution, the Park Duvalle Neighborhood Health Center. In the initial discussions about what they wanted, Duvalle target area residents had put access to health care high on the list. In spring 1967, the Duvalle Area Council requested that health and dental services be added to any neighborhood center plan. The local unit of the AFSC and Dr. Harvey Sloane of the U.S. Public Health Service also pushed the idea. By the end of 1967, plans for the health center were approved. It was slated to be included in the renovation of Cotter Homes. After some delays caused by rising construction costs, the health center opened its doors in early February 1968. At first it provided pediatric care for children under fourteen only, but within a year, it had expanded to a full range of medical services.[41]

The health center and its relationship to the community were criticized from the start. In January 1968, a group of middle-class black women associated with the Louisville section of the National Council of Negro Women, led by Ruth Bryant, sent complaints to the board of aldermen, saying that the center was not providing the jobs to the community that had been promised and that it was not receptive to input from the poor. They specifically raised questions about the lack of black doctors. Bryant described the tension over broken promises as a "powder keg" and urged that officials look into the situation. In an indication of a class division in the black community, members of the area council and other poor residents initially criticized the women for getting involved late and only when there were federal funds at stake. Others, including the *Louisville Defender,* however, praised their action as evidence that the middle class was joining the poor in monitoring broken promises by the local and federal War on Poverty. In defense of the health center board, Sloane responded that 70 percent of employees of the center were black—though he did not say whether that included any medical professionals—and that one-third of the seats on the board were poverty area residents.[42]

In retrospect, Sterling Neal Jr. argued that the health center overshadowed the service center and helped to hamstring its development. The professionalization of the health center put a damper on the democratic spirit of the enterprise. The health center's board was dominated by medical professionals and others from outside the neighborhood who saw it as a charitable service rather than a community institution. Indeed, this is evidenced by newspaper and retrospective accounts that give credit for the health center to wealthy local families and the AFSC and neglect the role of the Duvalle Area Council in promoting the need for health care in the first place. Though the health center succeeded in providing medical care, along with the neighborhood center it stood as an example of how a community-based institution meant to be an expression of the empowerment of the poor became part of a service-providing bureaucracy.[43] Criticisms of the center, as articulated by Neal, also demonstrate the rising expectations of community input into and even control over local institutions, and disillusionment with government- and elite-run operations.

Concerns about the lack of poor resident input in the health center were part of a more general charge about the failure of the Louisville CAC to achieve "maximum feasible participation." This in turn was seen as only one of the problems plaguing both the local and national War on Poverty. Though representatives from the poverty target areas held at least nine seats on the council—eventually raised to ten—that was still only one-third of the total, and, as observers pointed out, they could easily be outvoted in any decision. Moreover, there were criticisms about the undemocratic way they were initially chosen: appointed by the mayor and county judge executive rather than elected. The debate over the choice for a permanent executive director highlighted these problems immediately. Harold C. Yeager, an anthropology professor from the University of Louisville, held the temporary position while a committee searched for a permanent director. Yeager applied for the permanent job and offered to resign from the university. All of the representatives from the poverty areas supported him, as did activist groups in the community, including WECC. Other members of the commission opposed him, however, claiming he had poor management skills, and the vote against him was twenty-two to ten, with the ten coming from all the poverty area members. Despite a petition campaign in the community to keep him, he was replaced by Neal Bellos, who had worked in the War on Poverty in Cleveland, Ohio. Critics of the decision pointed to it as an example of poor people's lack of power in the commission and continued to hammer local government with demands for a restructuring to make the program more democratic.[44]

In response, there was some discussion in the early spring of 1966 about how to improve the CAC specifically and the poverty program more generally. A few proposals were floated to reorganize the commission to invite more participation by the poor. In the end, the decision was made to keep the proportion of target area residents the same but to have them elected by the residents of the neighborhoods instead of appointed. Then the commission organized an evaluation of the programs by poverty area residents with a series of meetings in the areas. In the Duvalle area, residents praised the recreational programs, Head Start, expanded library hours, and Learn More—Earn More, which combined adult education and job training. They criticized the lack of communication between residents and officials; the paucity of jobs in the program for area residents, especially those with minimal education; and the fact that the poorest residents did not seem to be affected. If there was more money, they wanted expanded Learn More—Earn More classes, day care, and more jobs for young people and area residents.[45]

In the evaluation procedure, local officials at least sought input about what poverty area residents wanted. Their response, however, was that there would not be money available to expand in any of the areas residents requested. One month after the evaluations were concluded, local officials were informed that there would be no federal money for new initiatives, though at that time it seemed that funding for existing programs was secure. In the fall, however, Congress began to cut back on the War on Poverty in response to both the rising costs of the war in Vietnam and political opposition to the community action initiatives. The total funding for the national program was reduced. Moreover, according to one report, Congress "made clear it wants money to go to service programs over action programs." For Louisville that meant a cut of $1.1 million from the program, plus a requirement that 45 percent of the funds be spent on Head Start, the Neighborhood Youth Corps, and neighborhood health centers.[46]

Like others across the country, local officials and activists did what they could to protest the cuts. Neal Bellos and his associate director traveled to Washington DC to try to get some of the money restored. They also encouraged local organizations to protest through letter-writing campaigns and mass meetings. WECC was already doing so. As soon as the cuts were announced, the group held an emergency meeting and launched a petition and letter-writing campaign to fight this "tragic blow" to the community, the first of what would be regular protest activities aimed at both the national and local programs. Meanwhile, the city and county governments and boards of education contributed extra money to the CAC operations and cut staff, including some organizers. As a result, they were able to maintain the programs through the summer.[47]

The controversies plaguing the local CAC, which resembled similar conflicts across the country, caught the attention of the federal Office of Economic Opportunity, charged with overseeing the national antipoverty program, and officials there ordered an audit of the local arrangements in the spring of 1967. In its report, the office praised Louisville for some aspects of its efforts. The extra funding from city and county government had demonstrated local commitment to the War on Poverty. Contrary to local activists' complaints, the federal reviewers found that the Louisville CAC had good consultation with the poor and the area councils and had succeeded in encouraging the participation of poverty area residents. Nevertheless, the evaluation also concluded that the CAC lacked precise information on the impact of its programs, which were also spread too thin. Moreover, the representatives of the poor seemed to be consulted in only a pro forma manner.

For example, the responsibility of members of the commission was limited to recommending project proposals, and often those recommendations were ignored. Federal officials suggested a reorganization of the CAC to address some of these problems.[48]

The CAC did reorganize, but the new structure was objectionable to community activists. One proposed change was that thirty social workers working through five agencies, including WECC, that held contracts for the poverty areas, would be moved under the direct authority of the CAC. The neighborhood councils would likewise report directly to the agency. WECC released a statement criticizing the move and calling for public hearings before the changes were implemented. When that did not happen, WECC members voted to pull out of the program. The heart of their complaint was that, by centralizing community organization under the authority of a government agency, the CAC would be squelching independent action by the organizers and the residents with whom they worked. WECC cochairs William Reddin and Harvey Webster, the latter a white professor from the University of Louisville, and Hulbert James listed the group's objections: the CAC had tried to discourage organizers and contract agencies from fighting for code enforcement, registering voters, and doing anything else that might "rock the boat." WECC leaders feared that under this new arrangement the poor and their organizers and representatives would be prevented from protesting or even voicing their needs. Given that situation, WECC chose to maintain its independence as a community organization and give up its contract, thus ending its official position as coordinator for the Duvalle target area.[49]

After WECC severed its relationship with the CAC, it devoted its attention to Operation West End. By the late 1960s, much of the community organizing under that program was done by young men and women working under the auspices of VISTA. This initiative, modeled on John F. Kennedy's Peace Corps, placed volunteers recruited from around the country into poverty-stricken areas to engage and mobilize the poor. Louisville began receiving young volunteers in fall 1966, with eight new workers assigned to the WECC program in the west end. Some of them were put to work in cultural programs, such as the coffeehouse for young people, and in that capacity became the heart of the human relations side of Operation West End. Others were assigned to work at the Lang Social Service Center, coordinating activities there. Indeed, the responsibility for running the center fell increasingly on the

VISTA volunteers. As they began to go door-to-door and meet with mothers' clubs, they heard complaints that the resident organizers under the area council authority were relatively inactive and that some of the community groups that had been established were "merely social clubs and [met] infrequently." The volunteers' decision to try to revitalize local organizing led them to a new, more political and confrontational approach that came to characterize the later 1960s War on Poverty and was a bridge to the more militant efforts to mobilize the black community.[50]

WECC folded the human relations side of Operation West End into its ongoing programs and focused on the arts to bring people together. In addition to sponsoring the annual arts festivals, the WECC human relations committee organized an interracial choir. Soon after starting her work with WECC as a resident organizer, Dolores White drew on her experience in drama at the west end YMCA and started the Pigeon Roost Theater. Once the VISTA volunteers were on board, the arts and cultural programming expanded. Indeed, the "program of cultural enrichment" attracted some of the VISTA volunteers who saw it as a way to use their skills, such as Richard Fine, who launched an arts and crafts program for boys. Laura Furlong, a VISTA volunteer from a local white family, likewise used her artistic training to start a series of art classes at the coffeehouse. One of the longest-running and most successful efforts was the West Side Players, founded and directed by a white volunteer from Maryland, Carroll Schempp. Schempp started the biracial youth theater group as a way to reach out to young people who had few chances to experience art in their lives. He quickly developed it into a forum for provoking interracial dialogue by performing plays that raised questions about race in American society. In this way WECC, through its VISTA volunteers, continued to use the arts and cultural programs to try to create a sense of community in the west end.[51]

While some of the VISTA volunteers spent their time on human relations work, the others assigned to community organizing got involved in protest-oriented activities. When VISTA volunteer Beverly White went door-to-door telling residents about food stamps, she also encouraged them to "take action regarding the proposed" cut in federal funding for the program. Another volunteer helped mothers who relied on Aid to Families with Dependent Children to "press their rights." White later worked with a tenants' rights organization, which picketed the housing commission and protested for better code enforcement. In February and March 1967, volunteer Judy Corse delved into explicitly political work, initiating a voter registration drive that engaged west end youth and community groups. Not everyone approved of the easy movement between the ostensible social welfare work of the War on Poverty and more overt political organizing. In fact, some local civic leaders criticized the VISTA personnel for being too concerned with the "action aspects of civil rights" and neglecting their social service duties.[52] WECC not only did not mind this turn of events but later even encouraged it when it recruited two SCLC workers—Sam Hawkins and Robert Sims—to train as VISTA volunteers and go to work organizing young black men into a militant action–oriented organization. Indeed, the work of the VISTA volunteers under WECC's control in organizing west end citizens for protest and political action reflected the organization's larger goal of empowering the community.

Under the umbrella of Operation West End, WECC saw its role as agitating on issues that affected the whole community and got to the roots of poverty and inequality. One issue that continually arose in WECC's discussions, and also in investigations into what poverty-area residents saw as important, was the state of the schools in the west end. To begin to address problems in education, WECC sponsored a February 1966 community meeting of approximately one hundred people to challenge school officials to answer questions about perceived inequalities. A few months later, the group allied with the NAACP to investigate and to propose solutions. Their starting point was that, although the city had received praise for the integration of the schools a decade before, the local system had in fact resegregated dramatically. WECC's solution was a policy of "compensatory education." Specifically, it wanted funding "distributed to schools based on need," more teachers and money spent on west end schools, a program of tutoring and teacher's aides for poverty area classrooms, higher pay for west end teachers, and early reading instruction. At a workshop in August 1966, WECC investigated a "community school" model exemplified by a program in Flint, Michigan. Then, two years later, the group opposed a proposal that would integrate the system by cutting up the west end and sending students from there to suburban white middle-class schools. Speaking for the group, Prudence Moffett, the wife of the white Presbyterian minister and open housing organizer Tom Moffett, argued that this "robs the black community, family, and schools of self-determination." Instead, WECC advocated community control of majority-black schools in the west end, citing favorably the Ocean Hill–Brownsville experiment in New York. WECC received little positive response to its protests and proposals. Indeed, school officials insisted the west end schools were already equal. But its agitation on this issue, and especially the attention it brought to the problem from the NAACP, did lay the groundwork for challenges to the continued segregation and inequality of the system in the next decade.[53]

In Operation West End, WECC members believed their role was to react to problems the residents of the whole west end brought to them, either because they did not feel the CAC could address them or because they did not have another community organization to turn to, and to help people organize to solve them. When women in Southwick complained about the lack of police protection in their area, for example, WECC helped them to organize Citizens Action for More Police (CAMP). Southwick women grew agitated on this issue after police responded slowly when a teenage girl was attacked in June 1966. What started as a localized response by African Americans in the projects to a neighborhood concern quickly grew, however. In late June, CAMP became Community Action on Metropolitan Problems, a coalition of representatives from thirty-five small neighborhood groups including area councils and block clubs. CAMP expanded its range of interests to conditions in the west end in general. The goal now was to unite to have a stronger voice for the area. CAMP was relatively short lived, however, and its main accomplishments were promises of more foot patrols and substations in the area. More important for the long term, it focused the attention of activists and the media on tense relations between the police department and residents of the poverty areas.[54]

WECC also stimulated the action of a number of organizations that were longer lived than CAMP, indeed that outlived WECC itself. For example, one VISTA volunteer devoted her time to organizing the Public Housing Tenants' Association (PHTA) and helping residents to fight oppressive policies and bad conditions in the projects. Early in Operation West End's existence, WECC had helped to protest rising public housing rents. Then, in January 1967, the group held the first meeting of the PHTA, at which residents complained of lax maintenance, long waits and charges for repairs, "erratic" garbage collection, and the lack of police protection in the area. About fifty people joined the group, representing all the public housing projects, including those outside the west end. WECC organizers worked with them to survey residents and collect over eighty specific complaints. But the official response was hostile and evasive. The director of the Municipal Housing Commission would not recognize the PHTA's right to speak for tenants and dismissed the complaints delivered by WECC as the product of outsiders misrepresenting themselves and pestering residents. Some of the women involved with the PHTA were also threatened with retaliation. When it failed to get satisfactory responses to its complaints, the PHTA demanded seats on the housing commission for residents of the project, which would allow them to voice their own demands directly and thus would give residents more control over policies affecting them. This too was denied, because the housing commission preferred to work through its own system of residents' councils.[55]

WECC organizers also helped to launch the Louisville Welfare Rights Organization (LWRO). WECC and local residents had participated in protests against cuts to and changes in antipoverty policies from the beginning, making them part of a national movement. In June 1966, WECC sponsored a local demonstration to coincide with others across the country about the problems in the welfare system. Then, in February 1967, Pat Wagner, a VISTA volunteer, attended a meeting of the National Welfare Rights Organization in Washington DC and came back with the plan for initiating such a group locally. She organized mass meetings to protest cuts in the War on Poverty generally and to criticize policies that impacted poor women specifically, such as new guidelines requiring them to work or be cut off from assistance with no provision for child care. The group eventually petitioned to have a seat on the CAC as a true representative voice of the poor. Like the PHTA, the LWRO began under the guidance of Operation West End organizers, but it went on to become an independent activist voice for the poor that outlasted its parent.[56] As such, it fulfilled one of the original goals of Operation West End: to organize citizens to "protest injustice, to act, to make their voices heard," and to influence the decisions that affected their lives.[57]

The PHTA and LWRO were also examples of the changing tone of activism in the west end and among civil rights advocates. By the late 1960s, local civil rights groups, WECC, and other west end organizations were beginning to talk about how independent black action, African American community control of institutions in the neighborhood, and a rise in black pride could address the continuing problems of economic inequality, poor living conditions, and the divide between the races, reflecting the rise of the black power movement. Although the NAACP and its allies had secured local and state laws against job discrimination and had pursued enforcement through the appropriate human relations agencies, it was obvious that equal employment opportunity remained elusive in the city. As Rosa Henderson, a former resident organizer for WECC in the Duvalle target area and now an official with the LWRO, put it in late 1967, the "meaningful jobs" on which a mother could raise a family were seemingly reserved for "the right race." West end residents demanded jobs for blacks in the poverty program itself. In the same period, African American police officers began organizing to fight discrimination against them, and black workers' organizations began to form to question the lack of opportunity in construction and continued unequal treatment in industry. All of these actions took the issues of employment and economic equality out of the realm of legislative debate and bureaucratic enforcement and put them back into the streets and into the hands of a new group of militant black men and women activists.[58]

WECC's arts programs, conducted by its own human relations committee and the VISTA volunteers, were based on the assumption that such efforts would bring whites and blacks together, create dialogue, and foster interracial community. Over time the emphasis in these programs shifted toward promoting expressions of black pride, with the aim of inspiring self-respect among blacks while encouraging whites to confront and understand black culture. For example, the original goal of the West Side Players, the theater group formed by VISTA volunteer Carroll Schempp and sponsored by WECC, was to provide exposure to the arts for young people but also to encourage dialogue between the white and black performers and their white and black audiences. Over time, elements of black consciousness emerged in the performances, such as when one actor spontaneously broke character and asked an audience at a predominantly black high school if they were "colored" or "black." Soon thereafter, the group also started inserting a reading of the Black Manifesto into their self-composed skits and performing pieces on "what it is like to be black in a nation dominated by whites."[59] Moreover, the arts festivals, while continuing to emphasize the theme of racial brotherhood, included poetry and art inspired by black consciousness. The art exhibit, for example, was organized by members of the Louisville Art Workshop, a group of African American painters influenced by the black arts movement. And the printed program began to include essays and poetry, such as Fred Bond's "The New 1966 American Ghetto" and Ken Clay's "Black Utopia," both of which expressed black nationalist ideals. WECC arts programs' inclusion of this material reflected not only members' commitment to freedom of expression but also the idea, which later reached fruition in the organization's embrace of black power, that real interracial understanding in fact required the promotion of and acceptance of black pride.[60]

Changes in the goals, tactics, and rhetoric of the community organizing by both WECC and other organizations in the west end similarly reflected a growing militancy and demand for a greater voice for the poor and black residents of the area, paving the way for ideas about black community control of local institutions. WECC started in the early 1960s with a goal of keeping the west end integrated, in part by making it a place where whites and blacks would want to live. It quickly moved into the task of trying to improve the area by addressing problems such as the lack of recreation, the conditions of the schools, and garbage dumping near the projects. Inspired in part by the War on Poverty and in part by their own expanding vision of how to bring about a truly integrated and democratic community, WECC members sought ways to give local residents, especially poor black residents, more input in the decisions that affected their lives. For them, community organizing was a way to empower the African American and poor residents of the west end. In Operation West End, WECC hoped that this empowerment would overcome the conditions that produced ghettos and reinforced separation between whites and blacks. In moving among these issues and approaches, however, WECC members considered themselves to be pursuing their original goal of creating an interracial community by bringing blacks and whites together and fighting the various manifestations of racism affecting the neighborhood. Their efforts produced forums for activism, such as the PHTA and LWRO, that contributed to a more militant, confrontational spirit among the poor and mostly black residents of the west end, manifested most clearly in their demand for a literal place at the table on the CAC and Municipal Housing Commission.

Beyond WECC and its work in Operation West End, the War on Poverty also paved the way, and indeed was a training ground, for the black power movement in the city. The language in the federal program demanded "maximum feasible participation" of the poor. Whereas to officials that often meant allocating a fixed number of seats—never a majority—to residents of poverty target areas, the poor themselves took it to mean an opportunity for them to have a significant role in determining the nature of programs affecting them. Over time, this grew to the desire for real power, expressed in proposals for increased numbers of seats on decision-making bodies, consideration of community control of the schools, and the change to resident control of the Park Duvalle Neighborhood Service Center. Moreover, individuals who worked in community organizing and in War on Poverty–funded agencies moved into more militant organizations associated with black power. Rosa Henderson, a resident organizer for the Duvalle target area, became a leader in the LWRO. Robert Douglas became active in the black arts movement. Two young men who worked as social workers for the Lang Social Service Center, Henry Owens and Sterling Neal Jr., became members of several black nationalist organizations over the next five years. VISTA volunteers Sam Hawkins, Robert Sims, and Willie Coggins cofounded one of the most important black power organizations in the city. More generally, young men and women working as VISTA volunteers, resident organizers, and in the service centers got experience in grassroots organizing, saw up close the intransigent problems confronting African Americans, made connections with other activists in the city and in national organizations, and tapped into a more confrontational spirit in the community. And they became the core of Louisville's black power movement.

Charles W. Anderson Jr. on the steps of the Kentucky capitol in Frankfort. (Courtesy of the *Louisville Defender* Collection, Special Collections, University of Louisville.)

Frank Stanley Sr., publisher of the *Louisville Defender*. (Courtesy of the *Louisville Defender* Collection, Special Collections, University of Louisville.)

Charles Eubank Tucker, bishop of the African Methodist Episcopal Zion Church and leader of the Kentucky Bureau for Negro Affairs. (Courtesy of the *Louisville Defender* Collection, Special Collections, University of Louisville.)

Andrew and Charlotte Wade and their daughter Rosemary in front of their home, which was damaged by vandals protesting the family's move into an all-white subdivision in May 1954. (Courtesy of the *Louisville Courier-Journal.*)

Carl and Anne Braden with their children, Jim and Anita, in 1954.
(Courtesy of the Anne Braden Institute for Social Justice Research,
University of Louisville.)

Students enter Male High School on the first day of integration, September 1956. (Courtesy of the *Louisville Defender* Collection, Special Collections, University of Louisville.)

High school students lead a sit-in in front of the Blue Boar Cafeteria in downtown Louisville, spring 1961. (Courtesy of the photographic archives, Special Collections, University of Louisville.)

(Above) Louisville civil rights leaders, 1963. *From left:* unidentified, Garland Offutt, Lyman Johnson, James Crumlin, and Frederick Sampson. (Courtesy of the *Louisville Defender* Collection, Special Collections, University of Louisville.) *(Below)* Frank Stanley Jr. addresses the march on Frankfort, 1964. (Courtesy of the James N. Keen Collection, Special Collections, University of Louisville.)

Open housing advocates march through a residential neighborhood, spring 1967. (Courtesy of the photographic archives, Special Collections, University of Louisville.)

Mass arrests of open housing demonstrators, spring 1967. (Courtesy of the photographic archives, Special Collections, University of Louisville.)

Leaders of black militant organizations at a Black Student Union meeting at the University of Louisville, 1969. *From left:* Ben Baker, Sterling Neal Jr., and Steve Stevenson. (Courtesy of the *Louisville Defender* Collection, Special Collections, University of Louisville.)

West End Community Council workshop, summer 1969. (Courtesy of Fred Hicks.)

Louisville Welfare Rights Organization demonstration, 1968. (Courtesy of the *Louisville Defender* Collection, Special Collections, University of Louisville.)

The Unity Slate, 1969. *Standing, from left:* Morris F. X. Jeff, Raoul Cunningham, and Darryl T. Owens. *Sitting, from left:* Irv Moxley, Neville Tucker, and D. Edward Turner. (Courtesy of the *Louisville Defender* Collection, Special Collections, University of Louisville.)

Black Workers' Coalition members picket outside McCrory Restaurant, 1973. (Courtesy of the *Louisville Defender* Collection, Special Collections, University of Louisville.)

The Reverend W. J. Hodge serving as president of the Louisville Board of Aldermen, 1978. (Courtesy of the *Louisville Defender* Collection, Special Collections, University of Louisville.)

African Liberation Day march, 1976. (Courtesy of the *Louisville Defender* Collection, Special Collections, University of Louisville.)

Antibusing demonstration, circa 1975–1976. (Courtesy of the *Louisville Defender* Collection, Special Collections, University of Louisville.)

Probusing and anti-Klan demonstration, circa 1975–1976. (Courtesy of the *Louisville Defender* Collection, Special Collections, University of Louisville.)

6

Militancy, Repression, and Resistance in the Black Power Era

By the end of the summer of 1967, many residents in the west end felt increasingly frustrated and powerless. The open housing movement was stalled. Despite residents' complaints, the urban renewal authority scheduled the building of more public housing units in an already overcrowded area. School officials refused to replace firetrap facilities. The CAC had shifted power away from community representatives. In the midst of this atmosphere of crisis, Hulbert James, WECC's forceful executive director, resigned and left the city. In response, WECC hosted a workshop to consider his replacement and determine what new directions it might take in light of its seeming inability to reach its goals.[1] Approximately fifty people (no one recorded attendance or the racial balance) attended the Citizens' Power Conference in September 1967. At the end of the all-day meeting, the group made two decisions. First, it resolved that henceforth WECC "should become a force for black power," making it the first local civil rights organization to publicly declare its support for the rising militant movement.[2] Then, seeking a strong replacement for James, the group voted to hire the white Episcopal priest Reverend Charles Tachau as the new executive director.[3] One year later, when nationalist sentiment among African Americans engendered calls for separate institutions and led to demands for black-only civil rights organizations, the new "voice for black power" in Louisville found itself at the head of a broad-based interracial coalition formed to defend six of its members accused of conspiracy that reunited the black and white partners of the open housing movement.

The seemingly contradictory elements of this story—a self-pro-

179

claimed black power organization hires a white leader and then, in response to the persecution of black militants, rallies an outpouring of interracial cooperation—suggest how examining the expressions of the black power philosophy on the local level can complicate our understanding of this part of the freedom struggle. The narrative of black power is often construed as part of a trajectory of the southern integrationist campaigns' giving way to a northern nationalist ferment. But just as the movement in Louisville had in many ways blurred the line between North and South, during the late 1960s and early 1970s, activists in the city rarely made a sharp distinction between black power organizing and other ideas and tactics in the broader movement. Integrationists in WECC embraced black consciousness. War on Poverty organizers saw their task as empowering the black community. Some signs of this interconnectedness were already evident in the demands for more black control of the War on Poverty and social services in the west end and in the promotion of African American artistic expression by VISTA, WECC, and others. In short, the story of black power in Louisville illuminates how that philosophy and movement flowed seamlessly out of earlier organizing as part of a longer search for new visions and strategies that would contribute to the ongoing project of overcoming racism.

WECC's black power program, the subsequent expressions of black power in Louisville, and the events that followed the persecution of militant activists took place in a context shaped by changes in the national freedom struggle and the response to them. Although it had deep roots, and elements of black nationalism had emerged at various times throughout the modern era, by the mid-1960s the black power philosophy had become more popular and widespread, especially among the younger generation of African American activists. As a result, by that time the struggle for racial equality had shifted in tone and adopted somewhat different goals. Younger blacks rejected integration for its own sake, questioned nonviolence and promised self-defense, and promoted black community pride and solidarity. In communities across the country, African Americans embraced African cultural expressions, called for separate organizations and institutions, and demonstrated their willingness to use armed struggle. The actions and rhetoric of these young activists at times produced divisions within the civil rights movement as people lined up to support or oppose the new direction. At the same time, and in the minds of many whites inextricably linked, a wave of urban disorders that began in Harlem in 1964 and spread in succeeding years to Watts, Cleveland, Newark, and other cities across the country heightened interracial tensions. The contrast between the "new" black power movement and the earlier integrationist campaigns, along with the specter of black violence, frightened the white public and officials and, in combination with the growing radicalism of the antiwar movement, provoked calls for "law and order" and a crackdown on activists of all kinds.[4]

In Louisville the black power philosophy manifested itself both in the work of indigenous activists like those in WECC and through local units of national organizations, such as the Black Panthers, that linked the city to a broader movement. The activities of these groups made clear that the philosophy meant different things to different people and did not always fit the stereotypical image of black power. Over time, as the black power movement grew, local activists focused on empowerment, pride, and community development and protection. Regardless of the diversity in the black power movement, however, militants shared the common aim of shifting agency into the hands of black people, who would then assert their legitimate authority in, and in the interest of, their communities. But, as local African Americans began to adopt the language of black power and promote its expression in community programs, the rising racial tension across the nation inspired fear among white city leaders about the potential for radicalism and violence, which led to repression of activists through conspiracy and other trumped-up charges. This in turn sparked a "fight back" campaign—also part of a broader national movement—that in Louisville united black power militants, white leftists, and moderate whites who saw it as a way to oppose racism. To some extent, the black power philosophy did cause divisions within the local movement, as older African American leaders criticized the tactics and rhetoric of the rising generation. But those divisions were generational, not racial. Instead, the reaction against black power and the repression that resulted provided the context for interracial organizing in the name of civil liberties and antiracism. The story of the black power era in Louisville, then, is a twofold tale of the diverse ways that local people interpreted and acted on the philosophy and how the reaction to it provided the rallying point for the civil rights forces of the city.

Just as black power had deep roots and a gradual pattern of development in general, it grew in Louisville slowly and from multiple sources. There were early expressions of some of the ideas that would be called black power in the preaching of Louisville's Nation of Islam congregation, which existed by 1963. It expressed both a desire "for the separation of Negroes and whites" and a rejection of integration as a "hypocritical notion" offered "by those who are trying to deceive the black people." While receiving mostly negative attention from the black press, after native son and hero Cassius Clay converted and became Muhammad Ali, younger activists were more admiring, although the Nation of Islam never grew to significant numbers or influence in the community. The more important root of black militancy was the rising frustration with the open housing movement and, more generally, with both legislation and the mass nonviolent direct action meant to procure it. As Blaine Hudson, a future leader of the Black Student Union (BSU), recalled, the younger activists who moved toward black power were those who recognized "the ineffectiveness of those old strategies and the fact that we were using tools that were already worn out and that needed to be discarded." Some of those young people gained experience in War on Poverty and social service agencies, where ideas about the need for more black community control were already gaining hold. Finally, by the late 1960s, some people were recognizing that to change race relations, they needed to build black self-respect and promote recognition of African American culture, as evidenced by the arts programs of WECC's VISTA volunteers.[5]

These roots of black power in Louisville were also nurtured by influences from outside the community. Robert Cunningham, who would help to launch a black workers' organization, traveled to California in the 1960s and there was introduced to the ideas of Stokely Carmichael and H. Rap Brown, which he brought back with him. He remembered the particular importance for him of the African independence movements, which inspired him to name his children for revolutionary leaders Lumumba and Kenyatta. Hudson, the student leader, credited older activists who left the city for work with SNCC and returned radicalized. Ken Clay, a staff member of the CAC, was inspired by friends in Chicago and New York to open the Corner of Jazz, a store that displayed posters of Malcolm X and Muhammad Ali, sold African clothes and art, and hosted discussions of black art and culture.[6] The experiences of these leaders, all of whom played a role in nurturing a particular organization or expression of black power in the city, demonstrate the ways that ideas traveled across space through personal encounters and connections, linking activists in different cities in a national movement.

When WECC became Louisville's first major civil rights organization to embrace black power, internal discussions and newspaper reports immediately focused on what that did and did not mean. The council presented the shift as a natural outgrowth of its goals. Members had set out to keep the west end integrated and ensure that it was a nice place to live by promoting interracial understanding and cooperation. It seemed, however, that they were failing. The west end neighborhoods had become predominantly black and relatively powerless compared to other areas. Thus members realized that speaking for the west end now meant speaking for a black community, and seeking power for the west end meant seeking black power. The goal of integration had not been abandoned, however. WECC reasoned that it could accomplish its vision of integration only if "Negroes can generate enough power and leadership to force the rest of the community to grant them equal housing, job, and educational opportunities." As Sister Rose Colley, the white supervisor of elementary education for the Catholic school board, who lived and worked in the west end, put it, "We all want integration, and if to get integration we have to move the way black power is moving, then we will have to move with black power."[7]

A number of members, including Anne Braden, at first questioned whether this meant that whites were no longer welcome in the council. The consensus was that white residents of the west end neighborhoods should still participate but that they would have to reorient their thinking about their role in the organization. As African American member and future chairman Ken Phillips declared, "It doesn't mean we are excluding whites. It means white people are going to have to reassess their relationship with Negroes" and get used to taking "something less than a leadership position."[8] Yet whites, including Tachau, did continue to share leadership in the organization. Shortly after the Citizens' Power Conference, WECC members elected a new roster of officers that reflected the class and organizational diversity of the group. Eugene Robinson, an African American community organizer, became chair. Prudence Moffett, the white wife of a Presbyterian minister, was cochair, continuing the practice of having a white and black executive team. War on Poverty community organizer Rosa Henderson became recording secretary, while a white woman, Rose Grenough, who had just returned from the Peace Corps, became the assistant recording secretary. Sister Pauline Marie, a white teacher at a west end Catholic school, was elected treasurer, while Mildred Robinson, a black member of the NAACP, became assistant treasurer.[9]

WECC's positioning of itself as a "force for black power" illustrates the flexibility of the term, which enabled community organizations to adapt it for their own ends. When held up against the Black Panthers, the US organization, and other groups that dominate the historiography of late-1960s black militancy, WECC does not look like a black power organization at all. But, while rejecting separatism and showing no interest in armed self-defense—there is no evidence the idea was ever discussed—members of WECC found something useful and appealing in the philosophy, specifically the idea of empowering a black community. WECC members and leaders saw black power as another tool for organizing for the betterment of the west end, one that was a logical extension of the work they were already doing under the rubric of community organizing. WECC's embrace of black power and action on it also belies the notion of a rigid distinction or hostility between advocates of integration and black power. Rather than getting caught up in such philosophical disputes, the group at times focused on seemingly mundane issues, such as bus fare rates, night games for the local high school teams, the need for a new swimming pool, and whatever issues neighborhood residents brought to them. Two major emphases in the black power phase of the organization were schools and jobs. WECC publicized overcrowding and deteriorating conditions in the schools and organized parents to protest. The group also pressured employers in the west end to hire blacks, securing over sixty jobs by 1969.[10] Finally, WECC assisted other west end activist organizations such as the Black Workers' Coalition (BWC), Louisville Art Workshop, and LWRO by providing a printing press and a place for meetings and by publicizing their activities.[11]

WECC's most important contribution to the black power movement in the city was the founding of the Black Unity League of Kentucky (BULK). Inspired by his experience in open housing and by James Groppi, a priest in Milwaukee, Wisconsin, who led a group of young black activists, Tachau wanted WECC to launch an organizing effort by and for black youth. In October 1967, he recruited Sam Hawkins and Robert Sims, two staff members of SCLC who first engaged in local activism in the open housing campaign, and a new VISTA worker,

Willie Coggins, to head the effort. Hawkins and Sims received VISTA training from the National Student Association at Temple University, and then the three got to work. Initially they planned to "use activist methods" to "fight discrimination on issues like police and court practices and job discrimination." Within a few months, however, the young men named the group the Black Unity League of Kentucky and reoriented it to focus on promoting black consciousness. They aimed "to teach black people to think black" and thereby to "instill identity and self-pride into Negroes." Specifically, they reached out to African American high school and college students and developed a black history curriculum to be introduced into the schools. BULK was "under the Council's sponsorship but not control." Tachau sought funds for the group, which WECC would "receive, disburse, and keep track of." But Hawkins, Sims, and Coggins made the decisions about program and activity, with advice from a board of five "older Negroes"—middle-class professional African Americans associated with WECC. Financial support for the organization came primarily from a grant from the national executive council of the Episcopal Church.[12]

In its first year, BULK promoted black consciousness through various programs. It used a donated building to establish a "Black House" headquarters where "black consciousness and pride can be symbolized and dramatized by the display of appropriate literature, visual art, music and so forth." BULK members turned their attention immediately to the preparation of a black culture curriculum, which included topics such as "the relation to society of black youth," the "need for unity among black people," and "the mechanics of the power structure," as well as readings about Malcolm X, slave revolts, and the origins of segregation. Meanwhile, they planned workshops, recruited instructors, and negotiated with the board of education to get the material into the schools. They succeeded in securing an agreement from the board, although principals of individual high schools often balked. BULK also followed the example of WECC's art fairs and in spring 1968 sponsored a "Soul Session," featuring food, music, and dancing, attended by about three hundred people, followed by the larger "Black Is Beautiful Festival," with "African inspired" arts and crafts. Members also cooperated with students at the University of Louisville, Kentucky State College, and the University of Kentucky to form black student unions.[13]

The prominent roles BULK leaders had played in the local open housing movement, and rhetoric that linked them to the national black power movement, drew attention from city authorities. Police identified Sims and Hawkins as potential troublemakers because they, especially Sims, had been prominent in some of the more controversial demonstrations for open housing around the Kentucky Derby. The first sign of this came in August 1967, when Sims and Hawkins were arrested along with three others for arson. The only evidence against them was an eyewitness who had been a block away. Moreover, other witnesses reported seeing the men in another neighborhood at the time, participating in an open housing demonstration. Nevertheless, the court set their bond so high that they would have had to pay two thousand dollars each to get out on bail, which none of them could afford. As a result, they spent two months in jail, awaiting their trial in October, when Sims, Hawkins, and one other were acquitted. Tachau took up the issue, writing a series of letters and articles condemning the Louisville justice system for keeping three innocent men in jail. He charged city officials with arresting the men and holding them on the theory that the "community would be 'better off' with these men 'out of circulation' until cool weather." Linking this to the broader problem of police mistreatment and injustice, Tachau cited another case of two west enders who were in jail for robbery despite a confession by someone else, and he warned that the poor of the neighborhood, both black and white, were losing faith in the police. Tachau's campaigning on this issue led WECC to create a legal committee to investigate and take action on police relations, court practices, bail regulations, jury selection, and inadequate legal aid.[14]

By this time, local leaders, both black and white, expressed concerns about rising racial tension and the potential for its eruption into civil disorder. Discussing the confrontations between police and young blacks in Harlem and elsewhere, Louisvillians debated whether the same could happen there. At first, despite some concerns over reported near riots, civil rights spokesmen repeatedly reassured white authorities that Louisville was safe from the conflagrations plaguing other cities. Drawing on the city's self-image as a progressive leader in civil rights, black leaders argued that the city was different from Los Angeles and other places because the "lines of communication are open" and that the only cause for worry was a few "unsophisticated individuals who do not realize the progress being made in all areas of race relations in the city." By the summer of 1967, however, the tune had changed, pri-

marily because of frustration over the failure of open housing demonstrations and the city's reaction to them. Indeed, by then Nat Tillman
of the *Louisville Defender* could argue that, especially because of housing segregation and the resulting overcrowding in neighborhoods and
schools, tinderbox conditions in the west end could lead to a riot.[15]

Then, in the spring of 1968, the arrest of two prominent African
American professionals set off a chain of events leading to a riot and
conspiracy charges against six members and associates of WECC and
BULK. The city had remained quiet after Martin Luther King Jr.'s assassination in April, although Hawkins and Sims, both former SCLC
members, released a statement saying his death left them with "bitterness in our hearts" and warning that they might abandon nonviolence.[16]
Then, on May 7, police pulled over Charles Thomas, a black school-
teacher, on suspicion of robbery. Manfred Reid, an African American
real estate agent and businessman, saw his friend Thomas with the police and, fearing he had been in an accident, stopped to see if he could
help. When he approached, police officer Michael Clifford demanded
that Reid move back and pushed him on the chest. Reid recalled that,
when he knocked the officer's hand away, "He grabbed me and started
hitting me in the face. He hit me once with his open hand and then with
his fist." Reid was arrested for breach of peace and assault and battery.
No charges were brought against Thomas.[17]

For the next three weeks, the atmosphere in the city grew increasingly hostile as African Americans and their white allies waited to see
whether action would be taken against Clifford. At first, signs from city
hall were encouraging. After an immediate uproar by black leaders,
Mayor Schmied suspended Clifford, and the police department's review
board upheld that decision. His dismissal, however, caused a backlash
in protests from the Fraternal Order of Police and the anti–open housing group the Concerned Citizens Committee, which called on the city
to reinstate Clifford. In the midst of this, on Monday, May 20, eight
hundred members of SCLC's Poor People's Campaign came through
the city. During a rally to support that campaign, the police tried to
move the crowd off the street. When some people refused to move,
there were minor confrontations, a window of a store was broken, and
tensions escalated. Later that week, on May 23, the civil service board
held a hearing at which only witnesses for Clifford appeared, and the
board overturned his suspension.[18]

That night BULK and the Southern Conference Educational

Fund called for a rally to protest Clifford's reinstatement, promising speeches by Stokely Carmichael and James Cortez of SNCC. SCEF had moved its headquarters to Louisville in 1966 and was directed by the Bradens. Although committed to integration and interracial coopera- tion, the group endorsed black power and would be one of the key allies of black militants in the city. Cortez had met Ruth Bryant when she was in Washington DC having lunch with Andrew Young and some other civil rights leaders. He introduced himself as a close associate of Carmichael's, and she invited him to come to Louisville. Cortez ar- rived in the midst of the Clifford controversy. On Sunday, May 26, Zion Baptist Church held a third anniversary celebration for A. D. King's pastorate. After the public part of the meeting, thirty-five to forty activists stayed for a discussion of the Reid and Clifford situation, which broke down into a bitter exchange between Cortez, speaking for younger militants, and Lyman Johnson, representing the established African American leadership of the community. The next morning, a delegation attempted to see the mayor to ask him what he was going to do about Clifford. The mayor's assistant, Schrader Miller, character- ized the group as "troublemakers," barred their access, treated them discourteously, and dismissed them.[19]

Beginning at about 7:30 p.m. on Monday, May 27, BULK held its rally to protest the reinstatement of Clifford at the intersection of Twenty-eighth Street and Greenwood Avenue, the location of a small number of black-owned businesses. With no public address system, speakers stood on the hood of a car to address the crowd. According to Carl Braden, "Police were parked in the alleys, not visible to people in the street, but maybe to those on rooftops." The speeches focused on "respecting black women and black power," recalled Eugene Rob- inson, "nothing any of us hadn't heard day in and day out for some time." More specifically, Cortez and Charles X of the Louisville Na- tion of Islam mosque called for unity in the black community. They and others urged African Americans to shun association with whites, to rid the neighborhood of "honkies," and to assert black control over the community. There was some hint of violence in the speeches. Sims pointed out that Mayor Schmied had a furniture store with trucks in the area and declared, "I ain't preaching no violence, so don't quote me. If it was me I'd turn it over, I'd turn it over!" Hawkins added that although he "used to be nonviolent" and had marched with King, times had changed. Cortez caused a "ripple" in the crowd when he claimed that Carmichael was in a plane circling the city and white officials were refusing to let it land. He asked the crowd to listen to the radio to find out when the SNCC leader would arrive and then return.[20]

As the speeches wound down and the crowd began to disperse, the sound of a broken bottle, the screeching arrival of a police cruiser, and the general confusion of the crowd combined to trigger an expanding wave of looting, confrontations with police, and riotous violence that lasted throughout the week. At 8:15 p.m., a bus rode through the intersection, and some witnesses recalled that someone, most likely teenagers on the roofs of the buildings, threw bottles and rocks at it. Then, just as the speeches were ending, a few more bottles rained down. Witnesses recalled that the crowd shouted "Cool it" and continued to disperse. Just then, a lone police car came into the intersection with lights and sirens on. The officer jumped out of the car with his gun drawn. People who were near the intersection later disagreed as to whether the cruiser arrived before or after the bottles were thrown, though the consensus was that the events were close enough in time to be simultaneous, and thus the cause and effect were ambiguous. Then suddenly "bottles were hurtling everywhere," the people began to rush away from the intersection, and, according to Manfred Reid, "the police were chasing people into lots to make arrests." It all happened quickly. By 8:34 the police had called for reinforcements, and a few minutes later, there was a call for all available cars to go to the intersection to quell a civil disturbance.[21]

In the next couple of hours, the riot spread across several blocks and spilled into the downtown shopping district. Police reported sniper fire. Rioters set a police car and civilian vehicle on fire. A short while later, a business was firebombed and looting began. Because looters hit pawnshops first, police feared guns would circulate. Within forty-five minutes of the outbreak of violence, the mayor contacted the governor, who ordered the Kentucky National Guard into the city. By the next afternoon, the guardsmen patrolled the streets. According to some observers, this heightened tensions and caused a renewal of violence. By later that day, there were widespread reports of confrontations between African Americans and guardsmen, including taunting, stoning, and near shootings. A black reporter recalled, "The guardsmen would shake their guns at me and say 'you're next.'" Ken Clay found himself face-to-face with a guardsman's rifle when a rock thrown by a teenager landed at his feet. The situation calmed somewhat on Wednesday, but there was a burst of new violence and arrests on Thursday. By the weekend, the disturbance had diminished and the riot was declared over. There had been $250,000 in property damage, 119 fires set, 472 people arrested, 52 people injured, and 2 people killed.[22]

The most serious results of the riot were the fatal shootings of James Groves and Matthias Washington Browder during the night of May 29–30. Fannie Groves recalled asking her children not to go out because "you could just be standing and watching and you'd get hurt." Nevertheless, fourteen-year-old James went to a nearby gas station to get a soda from a vending machine. Police reports stated that Officer Charles Noe shot Groves when he caught him and other boys looting. Other witnesses reported that, as James walked on the street, a group of boys running out of a store went past him. Medical evidence released later showed that he had been hit in the stomach and thus could not have been running away. Neighbors told Fannie Groves her son had been hit and taken away in a paddy wagon. He was pronounced dead on arrival at the hospital.[23] The same night, liquor store owner W. J. Berger shot and killed Browder, a nineteen-year-old African American. Berger's store had been looted, and he had gotten a gun to defend the property. He reported that he had seen someone about to enter and had shot the person, killing Browder instantly. Police initially charged Berger with manslaughter, but Judge William Colsen said he was "justified in firing his weapon to protect his property and was legally excused from the killing." Charles Tachau, writing a legal opinion on the case, later pointed out that there was no evidence that Browder was in fact entering the building but seemed to have been "just a passerby."[24]

During the week, black community leaders tried to quell the unrest and respond to police violence. Late on Monday night, WAVE-TV ran a special broadcast with Neville Tucker, James Cortez, and the Reverends W. J. Hodge and A. D. King, urging people off the street for their own protection. On Tuesday King held a press conference calling on the mayor to visit the west end, with no reply. During the day on Wednesday, members of KCLC, including the Reverends Leo Lesser and King, successfully negotiated with city hall an agreement to pull back the National Guard and the police and let a group of young black marshals keep order. King announced the agreement at a "cool-it" rally organized by WECC chair Eugene Robinson, urging people to show calm now that blacks were "patrolling the area." Other speakers at the rally showed less interest in soothing tempers, however. Hawkins accused the mayor of being "afraid of black people," and Sims declared that he hoped "the frustration is still inside of you. I hope you'll tell the white man that you won't accept any more crumbs. . . . I won't tell you to stop rioting. I tell you to do whatever is necessary."[25] Meanwhile, a group of white Louisvillians organized to support the black community. On Monday a small group went to the jails to observe the treatment of those arrested in the disturbance. On Tuesday about eighty white citizens, led by two ministers, went to city hall to try to meet with the mayor. They were turned away and met only with new HRC executive director Rabbi Martin Perley. Not discouraged, the group met again on Thursday and formed the White Emergency Support Team (WEST) to begin to investigate the causes and events of the riot and to provide whatever assistance they could to black victims.[26]

WEST's activity soon became part of a larger movement, which included WECC, BULK, SCEF, and others, to support victims of the riot while defending those accused of conspiring to cause it. They focused their attention first on a drive to secure charges in the murders of Groves and Browder. During the riot, Fannie Groves had called for the firing of Noe. Shortly after the disturbance subsided, she met with the mayor to complain about the treatment she had received on the night of her son's death and to demand an investigation into the killing. She also sought an FBI inquiry into the incident. By the end of June, unhappy with the city's response, she asked BULK, the NAACP, SCEF, and WECC for help "to determine the best methods for demanding justice for her son and disciplinary action against the police." These organizations took up the case, and WEST began circulating petitions calling for the firing of Noe, eventually collecting five hundred names. At this point the Browder case got folded in, as the civil rights groups called for the review of Judge Colson's dismissal of charges against Berger in that shooting. In response to this pressure, the mayor passed the buck. He claimed he had no jurisdiction over Noe and that the matter was in the hands of the police court or county coroner. Neither of those offices took any action on the case.[27]

While black militants and their white allies sought justice for victims of police violence during the riots, city officials developed their own plans for investigating and punishing the causes of the disorder itself. The federal and local governments had attempted to squelch civil rights agitation as long as there had been a black freedom struggle, but the late 1960s saw an increase in repression as white fears of militancy and disorder grew and as white leaders felt the control of the pace of change slip from their grasp. The rise of the black power philosophy and of agitation by its adherents provoked intense government harassment at all levels. Nationally, this was led by the FBI's counterintelligence program, which included infiltration of activist groups, provocation, and outright violence. Around the country, meanwhile, the determination to silence activists led to a series of conspiracy trials of both black and antiwar activists, including the Chicago Eight, Wilmington Ten, and Charlotte Three. This climate of repression included a revival of anticommunism and of state machinery to search out and punish signs of "subversion."[28]

In Louisville the first significant signs of this repression came in response to the riot. At first there were hints that police suspected BULK and its allies of starting the trouble. Carl Braden heard on the radio that police chief Colonel Hyde had accused him of instigating the riot. Some police detectives testified later that the fact that the young boys on the roofs of nearby buildings had brought bottles and light bulbs to the rally was evidence of planning of violence. On May 31, the city-county crime commission ordered an investigation into various people and groups associated with the black community, activism, and the War on Poverty. The same day, police arrested Cortez and held him overnight. On the morning of June 1, police and FBI agents claimed Cortez had confessed to a conspiracy to blow up the oil refineries in the west end. They also arrested Sims and Hawkins, and, after a hasty court of inquiry, with no witnesses for the defense or opportunity for cross-examination of the prosecution's witnesses, Judge Colson ordered the three held on security warrants and charged Cortez with "common law nuisance." Sims and Hawkins were placed under $50,000 bonds and Cortez under a $75,000 bond. Within a few days, Mayor Schmied announced he would form a biracial panel to investigate the cause of the disturbance, though he remarked, "I think it [the rioting] was planned and set. When a known outside agitator, looter, and rioter comes to town, that's the cause of all the trouble."[29]

Cortez's role in the conspiracy charges raised suspicions in the black community. Nancy Pennick Pollock, who at age fourteen had been in the open accommodations demonstrations before going to Atlanta to join SNCC, recalled contacting friends in the organization to ask about Cortez and learning they had no idea who he was. He was rumored to have been an FBI informant, and at times he admitted that was true, though he insisted he was acting as a "double agent" for SNCC. The autobiography of FBI agent William C. Sullivan contains inconclusive confirmation of the stories about Cortez. Sullivan describes working with an agent, Peter Cardoza, who had infiltrated SNCC to report on Stokely Carmichael. Cardoza went to Louisville "without telling anyone at the bureau" and "had been part of a group that started a riot in which two men were killed. When the Louisville police arrested him, Cardoza told them that he had been acting under the instructions of the FBI." Sullivan continues that, because of the "sticky situation," the FBI "cut our ties with him, and he ended up in jail." Though the name is different, this scenario matches precisely the story of what transpired with Cortez. The activist community in Louisville was not aware of this information or anything about the background of Cortez at the time, but suspicions and rumors made rallying support for him more difficult over time than it was for the others who had been charged along with him.[30]

Civil rights advocates immediately criticized the conspiracy charges against Sims, Hawkins, and Cortez and mobilized to get them out of jail. Moderate civic leaders such as the editors of the *Louisville Courier-Journal* criticized what looked like a "scapegoat hunt" and the "dangerous manipulation of bail power," saying that the city seemed to be "making a concerted effort to have it appear that a few agitators are the root of all of Louisville's racial troubles." The KCLU criticized the use of excessive bail to "restrain Hawkins and Sims, who had not yet been accused of any crime." Meanwhile, as during the open accommodations and open housing campaigns, the many organizations involved in the response to the riot and the accusations against black militants came together in a coordinating committee. In this case BULK, WECC, SCEF, WEST, the LWRO, and a group of Southern Baptist Theological Seminary students initiated an ad hoc coalition to coordinate the defense. The coalition's first action was to host a rally on June 8. A diverse slate of speakers—including Terry Davis, a white Presbyterian minister representing WEST; Charles X of the Louisville Nation of Islam mosque; Hulbert James, now a National Welfare Rights Organization staff member in New York, who had returned to support his former colleagues; and William Kunstler, a white attorney—addressed the crowd of 350 people, about one-third of whom were white. Over the next two days, local leaders met with representatives from various national organizations, forging links between the actors in the Louisville case and those fighting the repression of militant activists across the country.[31]

Meanwhile, the case against the three men ground extremely slowly through the justice system. Although there were still no official charges against them, they remained in jail on their security warrants and with high bail while officials investigated accusations that they had conspired to dynamite the oil refineries. In mid-June, Hawkins and Sims succeeded in getting their bonds reduced to $5,000 each and were able to get out of jail, but Cortez remained imprisoned on a $15,000 bond. In July officials added charges of carrying a gun across state lines and cashing worthless money orders against him. Court officials continually postponed his trial on these charges in what WECC claimed was a strategy designed to keep militants in jail. In early October, after repeated protests from the three men, their attorneys, and supporters, the conspiracy charges were dropped because the grand jury had failed to bring an indictment. This brought little relief, however, as Cortez remained imprisoned on the other charges, and local officials promised an investigation by the next grand jury.[32]

By the end of the month, a new grand jury had met and had, with relative speed, indicted Hawkins, Sims, Cortez, and three other local African Americans for conspiracy to destroy private property. The authorities charged them with conspiring to damage a taxi company, dry cleaners, and the oil refineries. In addition to the original three, the "Black Six" included Manfred Reid, Walter "Pete" Cosby, and Ruth Bryant. Reid's confrontation with Officer Clifford had been the trigger of the controversy leading to the rally and linked him to the cause of the trouble. The indictment asserted that an African American police detective saw Cosby riding around in a car with Cortez, "pointing at places to dynamite." Bryant's relationship with WECC and BULK brought her under suspicion. She had donated money to WECC to pay for Hawkins's and Sims's VISTA training and thus indirectly supported their leadership of BULK. She had also donated money to WECC to pay for Cortez's trip to Louisville. Moreover, he had stayed at her home during part of the week of the riot. Finally, police asserted that they had had her home under surveillance and had evidence that a bombing conspiracy had been discussed there. The theory behind the charges was that this group had conspired to cause the riot and the violence that followed and had planned even greater damage in a plot to blow up the refineries.[33]

An uproar against the charges began immediately in the west end and among the African American community and white supporters of the black freedom struggle. White Presbyterian minister Thomas Moffett characterized the conspiracy as a stretch, saying, "The only clear fact linking these six people is that they are all black and have openly spoken and acted to stop injustices and to promote justice." Civil rights lawyers pointed out that the charges against them were "almost identical to those used against the open housing demonstrators" and were so vague as to be unconstitutional. WECC released a statement addressed to "members and friends" calling the charges ridiculous but warning that "the indictment of these six" was a "foreshadowing of the total suppression of free speech in America." Indeed, from the start, the case was seen as an attack on black militants, an attempt to scare moderate and middle-class blacks—such as Cosby, Reid, and Bryant—away from their cause, and part of the broader national repression of dissent. The affected individuals denied and dismissed the accusations against them. Cosby maintained that he had never met Cortez until their first pretrial hearing. Bryant had perhaps the clearest defense. She later pointed out that her daughter's birthday was during the riot and the refinery was at the end of her street. "They accused me of wanting to blow up the refinery," she recalled. "Why would you blow up your home, yourself, your children, on your daughter's birthday?"[34]

After the indictments, a coalition of black and white, black power, New Left, civil rights, religious, and community organizations formed around the defense of the Black Six. WECC led the way. It felt the heat from the conspiracy charges because local media quickly pointed out that it held BULK's purse strings, and BULK had paid to bring Cortez to town.[35] Moreover, most of those accused had some direct or indirect link with the organization. Thus WECC was mobilizing support for friends and members as well as defending the broader principle of the right to dissent. Within weeks of the indictments, the organization produced a plan to defend the Black Six that included fund-raising for legal expenses, hosting forums to publicize the issues in the case, writing letters to the editor, visiting and delivering petitions to city officials, and calling for a U.S. Department of Justice investigation. To fulfill the last goal, the group filed a complaint stating that the "constitutional rights" of the six had been violated because the law under which they were charged was "so broad that it violates" the rights of "free speech and peaceful assembly."[36]

The forums held by WECC to inform Louisvillians about the Black Six spawned an interracial coalition effort not only to defend these accused but to oppose government repression of dissent in general. In early November 1968, the group hosted meetings in the south and east ends of the city specifically to attract white interest in the case. In the east end, approximately 200 white residents attended, and the next day 150 of them formed the Ad Hoc Committee for Justice. Spokesman John Filiatreau reported, "Our members are mostly white people who have been wondering what they could do to combat racism—and now they are acting on their convictions." The new group formed committees to contact officials, spread information, and, most important, raise bail money for Cortez. The statements of the group revealed that the primary consideration was the "violations of Constitutional rights in the handling of the case," specifically the "denial of the right to reasonable bail, speedy trail, and free speech," though members also spoke of the need to combat the "unjust conditions" that caused the riot rather than search for a scapegoat in black activists. Although black participants were welcome, Filiatreau stressed that members believed it was important for whites "to protest this kind of injustice against black people." Thus the Ad Hoc Committee for Justice joined WEST in representing white Louisville in a coalition with SCEF, WECC, the LWRO, KCLC, and BULK, among others, to defend black militants.[37]

While these groups raised money, held rallies, circulated petitions, and organized protests, the legal maneuvering around the case began. The first priority was to get Cortez out of jail on bail. The other five "conspirators" had successfully made bail and were at liberty until the trial. The additional charges against Cortez complicated his situation, however. His attorney, Louisvillian Dan Taylor, filed a motion in federal court to have some of the bond reduced under the federal Bail Reform Act of 1966, which was designed to keep people from being held in jail because of poverty alone. In February 1969, Judge J. Miles Pound filed away the money order charges, leaving Cortez to face the shotgun and conspiracy issues. Cortez argued that he had never seen the gun before, that no witnesses saw him with it, and that the whole thing was a "frame up" by the FBI. Nevertheless, although the only evidence against him was police officers' testimony that they had found the gun in his room, in late April the court convicted him and sentenced him to five years.[38]

Meanwhile, lawyers for the other five fought trial postponements and a change of venue in the conspiracy case. Focusing on the latter, Charles Tachau urged lawyers Neville Tucker, Dan Taylor, and Bob Delahanty to stop removal of the case because any venue "outside of Jefferson County would be a disaster." As feared, however, in January 1969, assistant commonwealth's attorney Edward Schoering asked for and received a change of venue to Hart County, citing pretrial publicity about the case. Supporters of the Black Six decried the decision, citing the "southern" character of the rural county; in the words of one observer, "Them poor people is Alabammy bound. Hart County and Mumfordville is George Wallace country." The decision was not popular with the people of Hart County either. While claiming that the area "always had good relations between the two races," the local county attorney argued that most people believed the case should stay in Louisville and that the people of Hart County should not have to deal with the city's problems. They got what they wanted. A year later, in January 1970, after many delays having to do with Cortez's other charges, changes in lawyers, and other issues, Judge Charles R. Richardson ordered the case "bounced back to Louisville."[39]

The Black Six conspiracy trial finally began in late June 1970. As the jury was being selected, demonstrators gathered outside the court house chanting "Free the Black Six." Prosecutors offered a last-minute deal: a fifty-dollar fine and a reduced charge of disorderly conduct against Hawkins, Sims, and Cortez in exchange for dropping the charges on the others. The six defendants rejected the deal. In their opening statements, prosecutors promised to prove that "the riots were not spontaneous; they were planned and executed by the defendants." Twenty-two witnesses testified over two weeks of the trial. The most damning evidence was a report that, at a meeting with the mayor, Cortez had promised "trouble" if Officer Clifford was not fired. But the commonwealth's attorney was never able to provide evidence of the six defendants meeting, let alone planning a conspiracy, and some witnesses asserted that the violence of the riot had begun only in response to police intervention at the rally. After the prosecution rested its case, on July 7 Judge S. Rush Nicholson ordered a directed verdict of not guilty because of insufficient evidence of the charges. While the Black Six and their supporters celebrated this much delayed victory, they also criticized the whole affair as manufactured by a commonwealth's attorney seeking reelection and pointed out that the real causes of the riots—poverty, police misconduct, unemployment—remained unaddressed.[40]

During the years when the case of the Black Six "conspirators" wound its way through the legal system, WECC, SCEF, and others who mobilized for their defense also attacked the repression of black militants and their white sympathizers in other ways. In March 1968, the Kentucky legislature created the Joint Legislative Committee on Un-American Activities, commonly referred to as the Kentucky Un-American Activities Committee (KUAC), and the governor promised to work with it to force subversive organizations out of the state. In June the committee began its work, with its first order of business being an investigation into potential subversion in the causes of the riot in Louisville. Simultaneously, Anne and Carl Braden rallied civil rights, peace, and student organizations to file suit to stop the committee from operating. They charged that it was designed, like other such state committees, to deny people their rights of speech and assembly and to maintain segregation. When KUAC hinted that WECC might be a target for investigation, the group refused to cooperate with any hearings. Meanwhile, WECC sponsored educational forums through various civic and church groups to teach people how to oppose KUAC's investigative strategy, which the *Louisville Defender* argued "smells like old McCarthy tactics."[41] Although a judge dismissed the suit, the coalition kept up the attack with demonstrations at the state capital and humorous propaganda playing on the sound of the name—"quack." After holding two hearings in 1968—in addition to the racial disorder in Louisville, the committee investigated charges of sedition in the antipoverty movement in eastern Kentucky—KUAC lost its funding. Braden gave credit to the movement against it, concluding, "We laughed it out of existence."[42]

The demise of KUAC did not stop the attempted repression of activists of all kinds in Louisville or the state, nor the campaign to resist it. In January 1970, the Kentucky chapter of the Southern Committee against Repression worked with several local groups to hold a "mock trial" of local and state officials for "conspiracy to deprive people of their rights." The Southern Committee against Repression had been formed by SCEF and the Southern Student Organizing Committee, a white group that acted as "a complement" to SNCC, to focus on the harassment of antiwar and antiracism activists. Because she was active in all three groups, Anne Braden helped to focus the attention of the Southern Committee against Repression on Louisville. The event pulled together a coalition of white and black civil libertarian, peace, New Left, and militant organizations. Zion Baptist Church, a leader in the integrationist civil rights struggle, hosted the trial, which was cosponsored by WECC and the Black Liberation Front, a small, radical black power organization. Although the intended focus was the Black Six case, the "interrogators"—black students from the University of Louisville—also criticized the Groves murder during the riot, the "police beating of an east end woman," derogatory remarks about the poor and African Americans by the governor, and the effort to merge the city-county governments, which if successful would disempower black urban residents.[43]

The defense of the Black Six, anti-KUAC campaign, and mock trial were the start of what Anne Braden called the fight-back movement against government repression of black militants, antiwar demonstrators, and activists of all kinds. The fight-back campaign opposed the effort to harass and silence activists and the revival of anti-Communist rhetoric and machinery to do so. It united black power militants, antiwar and leftist organizations, civil rights groups, civil libertarians, and whites looking for a way to oppose racism, particularly those living in the west end and those inspired to action by the open housing movement. The new movement was related through the Bradens and SCEF to a region-wide effort that included the Southern Committee against Repression and the defense of others accused in conspiracy trials. But it was also rooted in Louisville's history of interracial coalition building across the political spectrum and in the civil libertarian involvement in civil rights dating back to the postwar era and the Wade-Braden case. At a time when the main legislative goals of the local movement had been accomplished, when people were beginning to question the efficacy of that approach, when it was unclear what strategies would work in the continuing struggle against inequality, the fight-back campaign was one way people could express their opposition to racism. Moreover, the cooperation around the Black Six and government harassment kept the lines of communication open among different groups in the city and sustained relationships among activists through a period when the combination of repression and divisions within civil rights forces had the potential to weaken the movement.

By the end of the 1960s, the hostility against black power and its influence expressed by older, longtime civil rights leaders had begun to cause some of those divisions in Louisville. A few leaders, including Frank Stanley Sr. of the *Louisville Defender,* had criticized black power since the term came into general use. Now, in the wake of the riot and in the midst of the Black Six controversy, moderate leaders increased their attacks on the militants and their defense of older approaches. In December 1968, Bishop Tucker declared that black power leaders—or, in his words, "wild-eyed radicals"—"are dangerous to the welfare of the United States in general and to the Negro race in particular." In the spring of 1969, longtime NAACP leader Lyman Johnson wrote that the new generation needed to recognize that people of his generation had been fighting racism since "long before some of these present 'leaders' were born." The *Defender* editor likewise called on Louisville's African Americans to defend their leaders against charges of "Uncle Tomism" and continue to work for integration. Yet, while the paper continually criticized militants, associated them with youth violence and vandalism, and declared their leadership bad for the community, it also routinely covered the activities of black power–oriented organizations, and it came to endorse some aspects of political and economic independence.[44] Moreover, these criticisms did not keep older leaders from cooperating with militants on issues of unequal justice and repression. And the antagonism that burst out occasionally between "moderates" and "militants" did not stop either group from organizing in its own way on its own issues. In short, these divisions were often mainly rhetorical and did not greatly impact the groups' ability to work together on problems of mutual concern.

The more serious result of the repression of and division within the movement was the death of one of the most active grassroots organizations, WECC. Because it was in the thick of the campaign for the Black Six and was associated with BULK, it began to lose its financial support. Almost immediately after the riot, members of churches that funded the group started to raise questions, though at first the Episcopal Church reaffirmed its grants. By the end of 1969, however, all WECC's external funding had dried up, forcing the group to let its paid executive director go and rely on volunteer leadership. At the same time that financial troubles were brewing, divisions widened among the members over the direction the group should take. When Tachau had stepped down in late 1968, the new executive director, the Reverend Leo Lesser, formerly of KCLC, shifted the rhetoric to a more "black-oriented" emphasis. At first, to a great extent, the group continued to fight crowded housing, dilapidated schools, and the rising problem of pollution, and some people, including Manfred Reid, urged it to stay focused on "non-controversial issues." But there were signs of discontent with that agenda among black members. One member was quoted anonymously saying, "We were never able to overcome the feeling among some blacks that the council was too conservative and the feeling among some whites that it was too radical." The emotional strain increased after a group of black militants "invited all the whites to get out." Unlike other civil rights groups, most notably SNCC and CORE, in this case the majority voted to reject that suggestion. Nevertheless, according to news coverage of the group's demise, the whites "just didn't feel comfortable after that."[45]

In spring 1970, WECC faced a precipitous decline in participation: fewer than twenty-five people were regularly attending meetings, although in 1968 the group had had four hundred members on its mailing list. The remaining WECC loyalists decided to disband their organization and donate their paltry remaining resources to other organizations. New chairman James Kiphart, who replaced Eugene Robinson when the latter got a job with the HRC, blamed lack of funds and poor media coverage and the resulting misunderstanding of the council's program in the community. Carl Braden, looking for the silver lining, pointed out that they were not needed as much because other groups were working on most of WECC's issues. The BWC was conducting an economic campaign; the KCLU and NAACP were initiating suits regarding the schools; and a new organization, the West End Task Force, had picked up the antipollution issue. The impacts of internal tensions over direction and racial divisions cannot be denied, however. In particular, the meaning and desirability of integration were at issue. Braden optimistically stated that "integration has become so commonplace that people don't want to work for it anymore." By 1970 legal integration was indeed "commonplace," explaining in part the difficulty of inspiring mass white and black enthusiasm for campaigning for it. But, as his wife Anne put it more pessimistically, "I think the Council finally had to die because it was built on a dream that no longer has validity in the minds of many people. That dream was integration." She believed that WECC had tried and sometimes succeeded in promoting interracial understanding within itself but that the white racism that was "entrenched in our society" had doomed its larger goal of accomplishing true and meaningful integration in the broader community.[46]

While WECC members had embraced black power and given it their own distinctive spin of community empowerment and, through BULK, promoted black consciousness, other small and short-lived groups formed in the community to act on their own interpretations of the philosophy. The intellectual center of the black power movement in Louisville involved a group of young men and women who, while the Black Six and their supporters focused on the conspiracy trial and efforts to repress dissent, created a stir on the University of Louisville campus. By the late 1960s, the larger movement to reshape higher education and reform its relationship to the community, which had its roots at the University of California at Berkeley in 1964, had influenced African American students at both mixed and historically black colleges. They began to seek courses reflective of their own experience and history and to make their education relevant to their community.[47]

The BSU at the University of Louisville began in fall 1967 when a handful of African American student leaders reached out to others through social events and informal organizing. One of the early leaders of the group was Blaine Hudson. A lifelong Louisvillian, Hudson was the son of a pharmacist and the grandson of an educator. Though he grew up surrounded by middle-class professionals, his father died when Hudson was young, and thereafter he was raised by his mother, who worked in management at a public housing project. He recalls that his relatives taught him two lessons: that education would help you get ahead and was the path to overcoming racism and that, when that did not work, you had to stand up for yourself. Although too young himself for the open accommodations demonstrations, he admired his cousins who participated. Later, when his mother was in WECC and he was a high school senior, he participated to a small extent in the open housing movement. Fresh from that experience, he entered the University of Louisville, having been personally recruited by President Woodrow Strickler because he was a National Merit semifinalist. He soon got involved in the social activities sponsored by the BSU.[48]

In the spring of 1968, in reaction to the Martin Luther King assassination, the BSU adopted a more political focus. In addition to Hudson, early leaders were undergraduate Bobby Martin, social work student Sterling Neal Jr., and his brother Gerald Neal, who was in law school. Initially the BSU focused on producing a newsletter and starting a tutoring program. It had some early success in June 1968, when it convinced the university to have a summer school course on the "civilizations and cultures of Africa" and the "Negro in American culture." In the fall, the students grew more militant, and the BSU became more structured. In October the newsletter carried a formal list of "purposes and aims," which included "to instill black consciousness within our group," "to unlearn the white mind," and to "create black loyalty." While maintaining a social program by sponsoring dances and mixers, the group spent more time studying the black consciousness philosophy. At the end of their first year, they called on their fellow students to "bring the Black Revolution to the academic community" by resisting the myth of the "integrating power of education" and the "deceitful instruction" they received at the hands of racist professors.[49]

In March 1969, the BSU acted on these general ideas by submitting an extensive "recruiting proposal" to university administrators. The group collaborated with community black power organizations Our Black Thing and Black United Brothers under an umbrella organization, the Black Coalition Association, but throughout the ensuing controversy, it was clear that the university students were the leaders of the effort. The problem as they saw it was that the university focused on training whites, ignoring black students and failing to prepare them for leadership positions in the community. As a solution, they proposed a multipronged effort to recruit students and faculty, enhance the curriculum, involve black students in the machinery of the university, and serve the community. As a number of observers pointed out, the University of Louisville BSU proposal combined elements from similar demands being made by black students across the country. Indeed, student leader Blaine Hudson recalled, "We felt we were part of this nationwide or worldwide movement." Specifically, the proposal called for enhanced efforts in recruiting black faculty and students, the latter through two hundred Martin Luther King scholarships. The BSU also wanted additional courses at both the graduate and undergraduate levels on African and African American history and culture, working toward the establishment of a department of African studies. To help black students succeed, tutoring programs would be established, with paid black students as staff. To create a stream of potential applicants as well as serve the community more generally, the BSU wanted to run an outreach program. Finally, the proposal demanded that the university employ graduate- and undergraduate-level coordinators to manage these programs and that the BSU and its allies in the community have a voice in who was hired.[50]

University officials initially responded moderately favorably to the proposal. BSU leaders met on March 4, 1969, with university president Strickler in his office, and after they read the proposal, he expressed some sympathy with their goals. He cautioned them, however, that the price tag would be high and that he would have to discuss the issues with the board of trustees and others. Two days later, the group invited him to attend an upcoming rally. He declined and warned the students against violence, which might have surprised them, since to that point there had been no militant rhetoric or threats. After the rally on March 8, Strickler agreed with the proposal "in principle" and promised to begin implementing it. But he had unilaterally changed the proposal to a "compromise" version and was working on a watered-down list that included only twenty scholarships, one director, and no African studies department. Still, the students promised to work with the university as long as it was moving forward "in good faith." Meanwhile, the HRC and the *Louisville Defender* praised the BSU for the reasonableness of its approach and its apparent restraint.[51]

By the end of the next month, however, negotiations were off, and relations between the university and the BSU had soured dramatically. The sticking point was the issue of who would be hired as director of the recruiting program. The BSU's own Sterling Neal was the group's first choice, with Morris Jeff, the director of the Plymouth Community Center, a community organization in the African American neighborhoods just south and east of downtown, as an alternate. Hudson recalled submitting a third name, Hanford Stafford, somewhat reluctantly. Strickler informed the group that he had heard Neal was "emotionally unstable," though he could not name his source and eventually admitted the opinion came from within the state government in Frankfort. To press for their choice as well as the right of the BSU and black community to have a say in the hire, the group collected letters and petitions supporting Neal. When they delivered them, however, Strickler abruptly reversed course, cut off negotiations, and declared there was no money for the implementation of the program. In response the BSU released a statement calling for one more meeting and promising "should the results of today's meeting prove unacceptable, it would be impossible for us to justify dealing through the channels of an institution whose main concern with black people is lack of concern."[52]

A week later, the BSU carried out its implied threat to cease working through "channels" and take direct action. On April 30, fifteen members attempted to meet with Strickler. When they arrived at his office and found he was not there, they seized the room, launching a sit-in in the administration building. They remained for three hours, until the Reverends Leo Lesser and Fred G. Sampson, as well as Morris Jeff, arrived and served as mediators. They secured a promise from Strickler that he would have a short conversation with them and would impose no penalties on the protestors. After the confrontation was over, however, Strickler warned that any repeat performance would result in expulsions. According to Blaine Hudson, the BSU was already planning an escalation of actions, including the seizure of the student activities building. It organized support from allies in the community. On the day of the action, May 1, however, police picked up many of their nonstudent supporters on a variety of charges, leading Hudson and others to suspect that they had been tipped off by an infiltrator. Instead, a smaller number of students took over the arts and sciences administration building. White students from Young Americans for Freedom, wearing George Wallace stickers, gathered outside the building and tried to rush the doors, but black athletes—a group that had kept its distance from the BSU until then—formed a barricade and prevented them. Although the university later charged property damage and there were some efforts to frame the students on the more serious charge of kidnapping, the BSU maintained that the only problems were a few windows broken and one of their own members who lost her cool. The situation came to an end when police in riot gear stormed the building and, as white students cheered them on, removed the protesters.[53]

With the end of the takeover, BSU leaders found themselves facing arrest and expulsion. The students spent the night in jail, and the next morning, after a hasty hearing, Judge Colson fined each of the leaders one hundred dollars and sentenced them to three days in jail on charges of violating the state's antiriot law and disorderly conduct. The students appealed, and almost a year later, a jury found they had been neither disorderly nor rioting and overturned the conviction. Meanwhile, the university expelled eight of the leaders. Three were allowed back in on probation. The BSU concluded, "In other words, the 'good niggers' were separated from the bad, at least as UL would have the community believe." The others appealed the decision to the university's student conduct and appeals committee. Hudson recalled that the hearing took on the characteristics of a "star chamber." A former attorney general of Kentucky acted as the "prosecuting attorney." Faculty members were selected for the committee by the administration rather than elected. The students had no time to prepare a defense, and the proceedings lasted until 4:30 a.m. At the start of the hearing, it was announced that the committee did not have the power to reinstate the students. The result was a foregone conclusion: the expulsion of the five leaders. After a year of appeals to various university committees, all the students were readmitted.[54] In an ironic twist, Hudson, the ringleader in many ways of the takeover of the administration building, reentered it over thirty years later when he became dean of the university's College of Arts and Sciences.

The takeover, arrests, and expulsions brought a mixed response from the black community and civil rights activists. The *Louisville Defender*'s coverage of the events was initially tinged with disapproval. Reporting the "man on the street" opinion, the paper endorsed the goals of the BSU but criticized its methods, characterizing the takeover as unwise, disorganized, and violent—although the protest had been no more violent than the sit-ins that the paper had enthusiastically supported a few years earlier. Bishop Tucker, who by this time saw himself as a "voice crying in the wilderness" for law and order, echoed these sentiments, saying he agreed with the students' objectives but not "with the disrupting of school business." On the other hand, WECC condemned the interference in university affairs by outside forces—political and economic pressure from city and state powers—and likened the punishment of the students to the "suppression of the black community in general." Meanwhile, SCEF worked to rally white support for the BSU. Although white allies of black militants focused most of their attention on the Black Six case at this time, the Ad Hoc Committee for Justice added the students' predicament to its agenda, collected petitions supporting their readmission to the university, and met with Strickler. Compared to the groundswell of activity in support of the Black Six, however, the attention given to the students was relatively small and short lived.[55] While the precise reasons are unclear, the relative lightness of the legal penalties, the swiftness of the university's reversal, and the fact that activists' energy was consumed with the conspiracy trial may have contributed to this seeming lack of concern.

In the wake of the takeover and controversy, the university began to take steps to implement parts of the BSU proposal. In late May 1969, as it was expelling the leaders of the group, the board of trustees voted to accept some of their demands. Hanford Stafford became the interim coordinator of the Office of Black Affairs and began building a program over the summer. In July the program launched elementary school tutoring efforts in the five War on Poverty target areas. Also in keeping with the community outreach vision of the BSU, the university sponsored an arts festival in Shawnee Park and a junior high summer theater school. At the same time, two representatives from the black community, Margaret Harris of the Russell Area Council and Ken Phillips of both WECC and the NAACP, joined a committee to screen African American student applications. By September this early success encouraged the *Louisville Defender* to call the program a "model for the Southeast," touting the six courses, fourteen faculty members, and twelve tutors that had been secured for the fall. A year later, the school offered financial aid to one hundred black students and promised to teach "black awareness, black culture, and history" as part of an "attempt to develop racial pride and black identity." In 1973 the efforts initiated by the BSU were formally organized as a program, which later became the Department of Pan-African Studies.[56]

Meanwhile, the BSU, even with many of its leaders first fighting for readmission and then on probation, continued to agitate for its goals. The group participated in service projects in the War on Poverty target areas separately from the Office of Black Affairs. The BSU also hosted its own arts festivals. Most important, the students continued to press for the full implementation of their proposal. In their view, Stafford and the Office of Black Affairs were being used to "placate the black community" and had succeeded in impressing middle-class blacks. Indeed, Tucker and the *Louisville Defender* exemplified this, declaring the problems on campus solved and praising the program. The BSU and other black students organized in Blacks Getting Together felt otherwise. Continuing problems with the shortage of black faculty and staff, insensitivity to black students, and the lack of a black-oriented newspaper led to renewed demonstrations and even a sit-in in the administration building in 1971. In the early 1970s, black students at the university joined with those at nearby Bellarmine College and Jefferson Community College to form the Black Students Coalition of Louisville and called for "self-determination" for black students on area campuses.[57]

As the new decade dawned, the black power philosophy continued to inspire a number of small nationalist organizations with overlapping memberships and agendas. The members tended to be primarily men under thirty-five associated with the university or War on Poverty and community development projects in the west end. Regulars included Robert—now Kuyu—Sims, Blaine Hudson, and Sterling Neal, who took leadership roles and helped to found organizations or did behind-the-scenes intellectual, communications, and public relations work. George Owsley, who founded Black United Brothers, Morris Jeff of the Plymouth Community Center, and Walter Stephenson of BULK also affiliated frequently. These young men considered themselves part of a broader national and even international movement, as evidenced by the Our Black Thing pamphlet that pictured local men alongside national revolutionaries. Indeed, Neal considered joining the Algerian freedom fight. Their organizations were linked to groups in other cities. The Louisville Junta of Militant Organizations (JOMO) grew out of a national group founded in Florida, for example, and maintained ties to leaders there. Neal also recalled visits by members of the Republic of New Africa, who inspired some of his activity. None of these groups were particularly large; Hudson commented, "You couldn't really say that they represented legitimate organizations." And some of them appeared only sporadically in lists of sponsors of rallies and festivals. But taken together, they represented a community of militants who shared an outlook, goals, and strategies and who regarded themselves as part of a worldwide revolution of people of color against racism.[58]

Three themes dominated the work of these militant organizations: unity, cultural pride, and protection of the community in the form of resistance to the influx of drugs. The local branch of JOMO made unity its main goal. JOMO was founded in May 1968 by Joe Waller of St. Petersburg, Florida. The organization claimed a Marxist-Leninist position, describing Western whites as the bourgeoisie and nonwhites as a worldwide proletariat. Its official list of positions emphasized the colonial nature of the black community, rejected all "white" law, and called on blacks to be ready to "build our own nation and separate from this brutal racist nation." Local leader Henri Williams Jr. argued that, to prepare for that time, Louisville blacks needed to unify. Although there was a range of black organizations "from conservative to revolutionary" in the community, JOMO saw no coalition fighting to protect the colonized. In the interest of promoting that unity, JOMO first established the Institute of Black Unity in October 1970, housed in the offices of SCEF, and then organized Black Solidarity Week, during which speakers from a variety of organizations were featured, in the spring of 1971. JOMO made a strong beginning in the city, even winning an indirect endorsement from the *Defender,* which published several articles about its ideology and goals. It never succeeded in developing a large following, however, and according to Hudson it remained a "fringe" group.[59]

A second major emphasis in the later black power years was the need for racial consciousness and pride. In the late 1960s, several organizations, including the BSU, WECC, city agencies, and the university, sponsored programs to promote African American arts and culture. Black nationalist organizations joined in the 1970s with their own events. One leader in this area was Our Black Thing, formed by Blaine Hudson, Sterling Neal, and others as an arm of the BSU in the community. Neal recalled that members of the group obtained permission from Reynolds Metal Company to use a house it owned in the west end as a base of operations. They moved in, called it the Black House—the same name BULK used for its headquarters—and painted it accordingly. From there it launched a number of outreach programs with the goal of stirring "up the awareness and the consciousness of the people about the oppression that we saw." Though the group provided some social services, they became most known for the cultural events they sponsored, including a production of theater, poetry, and music for young people and a performance and workshop by a Kent State University African culture group. Through its jazz exhibitions, rap sessions, and theater they could relate to, Our Black Thing aimed to recruit young people into the revolution.[60] It was one of the longer lived and better received of the black nationalist organizations. After it faded from the scene, groups such as Burning Spear, the Kentucky branch of the World Black and African Festival, and others maintained the cultural emphasis with periodic arts and cultural festivals.[61]

The third common agenda for the various black power organizations in the city was a campaign to stem the flood of drugs into the African American community and to confront drugs' effects. Black power groups across the country made community defense a central feature of their agenda, at times forming armed neighborhood patrols to monitor the police. Few of the organizations in Louisville emphasized armed self-defense, but several prioritized protecting the community from what was seen as a state-sponsored attempt to undermine it. By the early 1970s, a coalition of such groups began to fight the tide of drugs sweeping into black communities. For some this was part of community empowerment and protection in a general sense, though for others it grew out of the theory, as Sterling Neal put it, that "dope is a way to keep blacks 'stupefied' and fighting each other" and that "the government, starting in 1960 had begun pumping drugs into the black community as a way of smoldering the social agitation that was going on at the time." In late 1971, the Black Committee for Self-Defense formed to educate blacks against heroin through leaflets, movies, rap sessions, and a hotline. And a coalition of civil rights and militant organizations worked together to urge theaters to refuse to show "black exploitation films" that "condone dope, free sex, and bad race relations," demonstrating how older leaders and the new generation continued to cooperate on some issues despite their differences. In 1969 Neal and sixteen other black men incorporated as Enterprise Unlimited to do community development work and launched an initiative called Stop Dope Now to run a methadone clinic, lecture series, and radio show. In the mid-1970s, Stop Dope Now became part of River Region Eight, a government-funded complex of anti–drug and alcohol programs. That success left Neal a little uneasy, however. He believed antidrug programs for the black community needed to be in the hands of African Americans and not dependent on the government, which he saw as the source of the problem, for funding. Nevertheless, the work of Stop Dope Now illustrated the potential for overlap and cooperation between the community self-determination and strengthening projects of black power advocates and government social service programs.[62]

Louisville did later have a unit of the most famous black power organization of the time, the Black Panther Party. Local organizers aborted an effort to organize a Black Panther group in the city in 1969 when national party officers insisted someone go to California for training and to pick up the charter, and no one could afford to go. As a consequence, the Black Panthers were late in arriving to the city, not getting well established until 1972. At that time, they emphasized community survival and social programs. Nancy Pennick Pollock, a former sit-in participant and SNCC activist who had in the late 1960s joined the Black Panthers first in Cincinnati and then in Chicago, remembered her activity with the Louisville group: "If a person didn't have food we got the food, we went and [bought] it, took the food. If they needed something, clothes, even if they needed a pack of cigarettes or whatever, we helped them get it, or if they needed to get on social security we took them to the social security office. We were trying to serve the black community." The group set up a sickle-cell anemia testing clinic, provided transportation to area medical offices, ran a shuttle bus to the state prisons for family members to visit inmates, and sponsored a local version of the Black Panthers' well-known free breakfast program. Black Panthers also joined other black power organizations in their own version of the war on drugs.[63]

The Black Panthers became the target of police repression in 1972 when, the night before the Kentucky Derby, police arrested five members and two associates for armed robbery. Authorities alleged that the group had crashed a Derby party at Laird's Tourist Home and "forced a large group of people to undress and stole $8,200 in cash and jewelry." During the arrest, police confiscated lists of "revolutionary readings" and of "dope pushers marked for assassination." In a scenario familiar by now in the black militant community, Judge S. Rush Nicholson ordered high bonds—$67,500 for each of the men and $7,500 for the woman. He also bypassed a public hearing and instead ordered a secret grand jury for the case. Although most of the alleged thieves made bail, three of the group remained in jail. Similarities to the Black Six case were obvious. Although the charges against them came quickly, by late September the Louisville Seven had still not seen the evidence against them, even up to the week before the trial was to take place. Moreover, jail authorities transferred the three in custody to a maximum security facility without notifying their lawyers. When the trial began, the judge immediately released five of the group for lack of evidence because no witness could identify them as having been present at the party. When an all-white jury tried the remaining two men, Ben Simmons, who was the local leader of the Black Panthers, and William "Darryl" Blakemore, Simmons was acquitted, but because one witness now claimed to have seen Blakemore at the party, he was convicted. Police added charges of carrying a sawed-off shotgun—the same charge laid against Cortez—that guaranteed him extra jail time.[64]

Just as in the Black Six case, a defense effort sprang up around the Louisville Seven. The Black Panthers called the charges against their members part of a national pattern of political harassment of the party and of a local police conspiracy to "bust" those who were fighting the drug problem. They pointed out the irony that they, who had a public position against drug pushers, were accused of robbing a known "dope house." Moreover, their supporters argued that the excessive bonds were part of the "annual summer cleanup of militants" designed to divert energy from organizing and to keep the Black Panthers off the street. An ad hoc group dubbed the Louisville Seven Defense Fund Committee coordinated a coalition of black power, New Left, and antirepression organizations in an effort to get the charges dropped and then aid Blakemore. SCEF played the role WECC had performed in the Black Six case, reaching out to the white community and publicizing the case. Sims and his African Liberation Committee brought in the black nationalists. A new organization, the Kentucky Committee to Smash Repression, reached out to the broader national effort to fight official persecution of activists. But the defense effort also again rallied more moderate local activists. The KCLU protested Judge Nicholson's behavior, and Suzy Post, a white Jewish woman who was both a member of the KCLU and a representative of a group seeking a civilian review board of the police, criticized law enforcement's "frame up" of the Black Panthers. Finally, a black minister, Joseph Bell, lent his prestige at the rallies, praising the Black Panthers for their antidrug campaign and their efforts to "administer to the sick." The defense effort had mixed success. The coalition celebrated the dropped charges and acquittal of most of the seven but continued to challenge Blakemore's conviction. The enduring result was the formation of the Kentucky Political Prisoners' Committee, an interracial organization that was formed to work on Blakemore's case and more generally "to support brothers and sisters in prison and fight police brutality."[65]

In the early part of the decade, the Kentucky Political Prisoners' Committee hosted rallies to bring attention to the trials of African Americans they felt were unfairly accused in the city. The organization's major event was a rally held in July 1973 with a long list of sponsors, including Black Six defendant Ruth Bryant, Sterling Neal, Anne and Carl Braden, and Suzy Post. The group reestablished connections with the national antirepression movement, bringing representatives of the National Alliance of Postal and Federal Employees and the National Alliance against Racist and Political Repression to the city as cosponsors and featuring Ben Chavis of the Wilmington Ten as the key speaker. By this point, the far left was openly represented and embraced, with participation by the Communist Party USA, Socialist Women's Caucus, and Young Workers' Liberation League. The rally focused on the case of Cedric Wilson, a young man who was accused of killing a Kroger grocery store security guard during a robbery and held on a one hundred thousand–dollar bond, despite his sister's insistence that he was at her home at the time. Wilson was acquitted for lack of evidence.[66]

A more enduring local organization that arose out of the antire-pression efforts of the early 1970s was the Kentucky Alliance against Racist and Political Repression. During this period Anne and Carl Braden led an SCEF campaign against the persecution of activists not just in Louisville but across the South and the nation. In 1970 California officials charged Communist Party member Angela Davis with conspiracy, murder, and kidnapping. Her case interested the Bradens, who knew what it meant to have their politics held against them in a criminal trial, and they became active supporters. Thus, when Davis was acquitted in 1972, Carl joined a small group who worked with her to found a new organization devoted to defending political prisoners. Indeed, Anne recalled that Carl suggested the long name: the National Alliance against Racist and Political Repression. Between 1973 and 1975, the informal coalitions that had formed around celebrated local cases such as the Louisville Seven coalesced into a Kentucky branch of the organization, located in Louisville and known commonly as the Kentucky Alliance. Over time the Kentucky Alliance would become one of the main organizations in the community working against both police brutality and repression.[67]

Although the campaign to defend the Black Panthers spawned a local movement to defend black militants and fight police repression more generally, indirectly it also revealed the declining significance of the black power movement in the city. When the Black Panthers were arrested, their white and black allies organized to stand up for them, but as their lawyer Bill Allison recalled, the broader community, white and black, failed to show much interest in the outcome. As he put it, "There wasn't the kind of filling up of the courtroom" that had been seen in the case of the Black Six. He attributed this to the change in atmosphere in the new decade: "By this time, the repression had set in, the war had divided people, the economy was turning down." The Black Panthers never recovered from the setback of having to devote their energy to the case, and no strong black power organization arose to take their place. Moreover, although individuals like Sterling Neal and Kuyu Sims showed up on lists of sponsors of events, white left-wing organizations and the Kentucky Alliance directed further anti-repression efforts. Meanwhile, civil rights and civil libertarian groups working for a civilian review board took the lead against police brutality. The Black Panthers and other, small nationalist organizations did not completely disappear, however. They resurfaced in the community-wide controversy over school integration in 1975, taking their place alongside moderate civil rights groups and interracial organizations in the resistance to antibusing forces.[68]

In the public imagination and in much of what has been traditionally taught about the black freedom struggle, the mid-1960s saw a turn from the "heroic" southern integrationist campaigns led by Martin Luther King to the nihilistic, destructive path of the black power militants of northern and western cities. The story of the latter is dominated by images of angry, gun-toting Black Panthers, separatists kicking whites out of SNCC and CORE, and the less violent—but as confusing to whites—blacks in Afros and dashikis rejecting their slave names and embracing their African heritage. The story continues with how these radicals' efforts ostensibly led to division, antagonism, and repression and thus to the end of the civil rights movement. In recent years, scholars have thoroughly debunked almost every part of this narrative, from its "beginning" in 1966 to its nature and impact. We now know that the roots of black power reach back into a period of nationalist organizing earlier in the century and that, to a great extent, the modern black power movement grew contemporaneously with the civil rights struggle.[69]

The story of the Louisville black power era contributes to this rethinking of black power. Put most simply, black power meant different things to different activists and organizations. For some it was another tool to bring about community empowerment by getting black voices heard. WECC members who saw it this way acted on their interpretation by organizing black residents of the west end to protest poor housing and school conditions and to demand black input into War on Poverty institutions. Most black power advocates in the city put their central focus on promoting black consciousness and pride. Indeed, the arts and culture programs of BULK, the BSU, and others stood as the most visible, consistent, and popular expression of black power in the city. Finally, black power meant community self-improvement and solidarity, whether that took the form of a specific program such as stemming the influx of drugs or a more ambiguous call for unity.

This black power activity, however, was not separate from other forms of activism in some false dichotomy between it and the civil rights and antipoverty, or even antiwar, movements of the time. Integrationists in WECC embraced black power as a means to achieving interracial understanding. White leftists, antiwar activists, and civil libertarians rallied around black militants to face the common enemy of the repression of dissent. Individuals like Sterling Neal, who worked in War on Poverty agencies and later in social service agencies, demonstrate how community organizing could overlap with community empowerment. Finally, although there was some discord between older civil rights leaders and the new generation, even they were able to cooperate and respect each other in the fight against drugs. In short, in the interests of fighting racism and resisting common enemies, a wide variety of activists—from liberal whites new to the cause to black moderate traditional leaders to the rising generation of militants—could overcome differences and cooperate in shifting alliances that made up a larger movement. Seeing black power and the black power era in the context of this set of connections across issue, race, and generation highlights both the multiple meanings and expressions of African American militancy in the late 1960s and the lack of rigid regional, chronological, and ideological breaks in the larger struggle against racism.

7

Making Civil Rights Gains Real

In 1969 the *Louisville Courier-Journal* and *Louisville Times* enlisted Roper Research Associates to conduct an in-depth study of the living conditions and attitudes about race relations of white and black residents of Louisville. The resulting report documented the stark differences in whites' and blacks' living conditions, the "dismal" state of the latter, and the "frightening" lack of awareness and concern of the white community about both. The divergence on particular points was striking. Close to half of African Americans reported a shortage of housing or problems with landlords, while only 3 percent of whites considered access to good housing a problem at all. When asked whether blacks had equal opportunity when applying for employment, 72 percent of blacks said no. But only 25 percent of whites agreed that those of their race would have a better chance at a job than an equally qualified African American. When asked if policemen disrespected or treated blacks unequally, 68 percent of blacks said yes, but only 30 percent of whites did so. More generally, the researchers found that African American residents felt alienated from and underserved by their local government. And, perhaps most troubling to a community that had long prided itself on its racial progress, white Louisvillians overwhelmingly believed blacks were better off in the city than elsewhere and that government was doing enough to guarantee equality, while blacks disagreed on both scores. The authors' stark conclusion was that in 1969, despite purported gains in civil rights over the last decade, in Louisville whites and blacks continued to live in two separate and unequal worlds.[1]

Most narratives of the fight for racial equality begin to wind down after 1968, describing movement forces dissipating or collapsing from internal differences, or tales of government repression forcing activists into quiescence. Yet the Roper study's findings and the persistence of racial tension around the country revealed that, as the new decade began, the work of the movement was far from over. Moreover, in the experience of civil rights activists, the freedom struggle stretched on into succeeding decades as they continued to fight to realize the equality that was promised in the legislation of the 1960s. The question in the 1970s for activists around the country was how to translate that promise into real social, economic, and political change. In Louisville, the answer was to combine the enforcement of existing laws by human relations agencies with persistent pressure by African Americans and their white allies working both inside and outside government. Although other issues arose, civil rights advocates focused on campaigns for African Americans' rights to equal treatment by and within law enforcement, economic opportunity, and the just rewards of black political participation. The primacy of these issues, which call to mind places like Oakland, Philadelphia, and Gary, in a border city and self-proclaimed leader of the South, demonstrates the blurring of differences between racial problems and the action to overcome them in northern and southern urban areas by the later years of the civil rights era.[2]

The story of these three at times overlapping issues in the early 1970s highlights the ongoing interconnectedness of the struggle for racial equality as it moved into a time when it was considered to be dead or dying. In the post-King and, at least locally, post–black power era, the work of equal rights advocates became more sporadic, with less mass mobilizing and much more of the action confined to bureaucratic channels and negotiating chambers. Civil rights activists at this time operated in a changing political context, with an emboldened resistance reinforced by a conservative turn in state and national politics. This made the efforts of those who continued to press for further change appear less like a movement. But the connections that had undergirded activism for racial equality in the city did not go away. Activists continued to identify the links between issues such as jobs and police behavior, and political strength and antipoverty funding. And people of varying philosophies, races, and classes continued to find themselves working together, at times in coalitions of strange bedfellows. Moreover, they persisted in combining tactics, including attempted revivals of nonviolent direct action, enforcement through new human relations agencies, and political pressure. Just as racial inequality persisted in the city, as demonstrated by the Roper study, so too did the movement seeking to end it.

By the late 1960s, the race riots in American cities had brought to a head the long-standing tensions between African Americans and white police and made those relations one of the most literally explosive issues of the time. Specific incidents of rough arrests and brutality had sparked some of the major disorders of the decade. In Louisville, the 1968 civil unrest had followed a protest against police misconduct. White fears inflamed by these riots fueled the conservative political movement calling for "law and order" and increased public approval for police crackdowns and extreme measures, specifically against activists but also, more generally, against perceived disorder. At the same time, black citizens, emboldened by the civil rights movement and the examples of such groups as the Black Panthers, began to stand up and resist the misuse of authority by local law enforcement. Criticism of unequal treatment by the police was not new in Louisville. In the wake of the arrests of Robert Sims and Sam Hawkins for arson during the open housing movement, WECC had organized its justice committee to monitor the actions of law enforcement in majority black neighborhoods. Over the next few years, however, reports of abuse, ranging from harassment and beatings to shooting deaths, became a drumbeat in the black press and a central organizing issue for the activist community.[3]

One of the first incidents in the post-riot period between the black community and the police occurred in August 1969, when a police officer beat a black mother after her sons were arrested for inciting others to riot. The trouble started when three white men drove past a black church in the Jackson area, southeast of downtown, and fired gunshots into it, wounding a young black teenager, Willie Roberson, in the neck. Though police arrested the men quickly, a large crowd of black residents gathered and barricaded the street, throwing rocks and bottles at passing cars carrying white passengers. When the police arrived—according to witnesses, as many as twenty-five cars with shotguns aimed out the windows—officers began dispersing the crowd. Helen Wickliffe claimed that police beat her sons with billy clubs, leaving sixteen-year-old Ellis unconscious on the ground. When she tried to stop them, "They told me I talked too much and knocked me into the police car.

They sat a straddle me and choked and beat me, calling me all kind of bitches." Police reported she had assaulted them and arrested her and her sons for inciting a riot. The incident raised fears of another riot in the city and contributed to a demand, not only by the black community but by white civil rights leaders, that the use of force by the police against black residents be restrained.[4]

The conflict between black residents and the police was not, as the Wickliffe case demonstrated, confined to the west end. At the end of the year, a shoot-out during a robbery led to more incidents in the Smoketown area, a black neighborhood in the central city. In December 1969, an attempted robbery at Greenwell Market resulted in two police officers being killed. The black men accused with robbery and assault were found guilty, and despite the efforts of some activists, their fate drew little attention. Over the next two years, however, African Americans and some of their white allies noted an increase in abuse of Smoketown residents by the police. In June 1971, for example, two white medical students tried to intervene when they witnessed police beating three black youths. Concurrent with the trial of the two men accused of shooting the officers, the *Louisville Defender* conducted a survey that revealed that the black community believed "white policemen . . . have elected to take the law into their own hands." Around the same time, a community watch group called the Equal Justice Committee held a panel discussion of young people and a local high school principal to tell their stories about abuse in the area. The committee concluded that white police were "seeking reprisals" for the deaths of their colleagues.[5]

Black activists blamed the "oppressing that white police officers were putting on black people at that time" for an incident that became one of the most controversial of the early 1970s. In May 1971 two white police officers, Wilbur Hayes and John Schaefer, were found dead, having been shot several times each in a small street southeast of downtown. Within a week, officers arrested brothers William and Narvel Tinsley of Smoketown and charged them with the murders. At the trial, a witness reported that the brothers were having "shooting practice" when the police approached them and asked them for identification. The Tinsleys dropped the guns in the grass. According to the brothers and their supporters, Narvel was handcuffed and beaten, and in defense William grabbed a gun and shot the police. Local activists later recalled that the defense tried to introduce the record of the officers' brutality in the area as a mitigating circumstance. The *Louisville Courier-Journal* reported that Hayes had fatally wounded an eighteen-year-old during an investigation of a break-in in April. But the judge did not allow that line of argument. Moreover, during the trial, the Tinsleys' attorney, Dan Taylor, the former lawyer for the Black Six and other activists, was cited for contempt repeatedly by Judge John P. Hayes in what civil rights advocates saw as retaliation against him for his work on behalf of black militants. An all-white jury convicted the brothers, and the judge gave them death sentences. Both decisions were appealed. Although the appeals failed, the Kentucky legislature outlawed the death penalty, and the sentences were commuted to jail time.[6] The case was important not only because it demonstrated the tensions between black youth and the police but because it became one of a number of incidents that rallied an interracial alliance against police misconduct.

As the number of reports climbed and the incidents of police brutality grew more serious, civil rights advocates began demanding a response from the city. The HRC had first launched an effort to address the "worsened feelings" between law enforcement and the community in the summer of 1968. In August, Rabbi Martin Perley, the executive director, proposed a "community relations training program" for the police and city employees. Perley, who described his theology by saying, "My concept of religion is to pursue justice," had been chair of LACRR and was involved in the open housing campaign. He had become head of the HRC after the controversial firing of J. Mansir Tydings for being too outspoken. White police officers overwhelmingly rejected what they called "sensitivity training" sessions—73 percent expressed disapproval in a wrap-up survey—because they were imposed on them by the "outsiders" of the HRC. Meanwhile, conservative groups led by the anti–open housing Concerned Citizens Committee called it brainwashing, an attempt to undermine law and order, and a plan "designed by communist infiltrators out to destroy democracy." This hinted at the spread of the backlash against integration in housing to a more general resistance to further change in the status quo, especially change that was perceived to stem from government interference, and contributed to the more conservative and more difficult climate for civil rights action.[7]

A year later, Perley tried again to get the city to take some action, arguing that acts of violence against black citizens by the police, especially shootings, fueled racial tension and riots. Under his guidance the commission called for clear regulations limiting the use of firearms by police to situations in which there "is a clear threat to life or body." Moreover, the commission requested that complaints about police behavior be investigated quickly, that the complainant have the right to a lawyer and to cross-examine witnesses, and that the results be communicated to all those concerned. Mayor Kenneth Schmied immediately dismissed these demands, telling Perley "to run his department and let others run theirs." There was also internal dissension, as a number of members of the commission worried that these policies would "weaken the police" and "alienate whites." The police department took no action on the proposals.[8]

Meanwhile, groups of west end citizens and civil rights organizations began organizing on their own against police abuse. At first much of this activity took the form of sporadic, short-lived protests inspired by particular events, with ad hoc groups of citizens calling for better treatment, investigations, and communication.[9] Then, in spring 1972, a number of community groups came together in a coalition of what one leader called "strange bedfellows" to press for a civilian review board to hear complaints of police brutality. The idea was not completely new; Philadelphia had been the first major city to establish such a body in 1958. In 1969 the *Defender* had argued that other communities had such a system and that the Louisville authorities should consider it. The review board that was eventually considered in Louisville was modeled on one suggested by the National Advisory Commission on Civil Disorders. If adopted, it would include nine members selected by "interested" community organizations, with the requirement that one person come from each of the seven poverty target areas. The supporters of civilian review included the Urban League, NAACP, CAC, and, according to longtime civil libertarian Suzy Post, both the Black Panther Party and the Junior League. Women in the latter joined, Post recalled, because "at that time, white kids with long hair in the east end were being hassled by the cops. And the parents, who weren't used to having problems with police, were very up in arms." Eventually over thirty organizations signed on to help run a hotline for complaints, circulate flyers, and press for an ordinance.[10]

The proposed ordinance creating a civilian review board immediately ran into sharp opposition in both the police department and city government. First, the Fraternal Order of Police threatened that "police officers would resign en masse if such a board" were established. This response mirrored opposition by law enforcement to similar measures across the country. Spokesmen for the Fraternal Order of Police labeled the proposal the work of "wild-eyed idealists and extremist groups," including "radicals" who wanted to undermine the police and sow chaos in the community. Putting it bluntly, Fraternal Order of Police president Tom Denton said to the voters of Louisville, "If you want to continue to have a police department," defeat this bill.[11] When Lois Morris introduced the civilian review measure to the board of aldermen in June 1972, it met expeditious and almost complete opposition. The day the aldermen first considered the bill, city law director James E. Thornberry announced his legal opinion that the measure was unconstitutional because it singled out the police for extra review and because the measure designated certain community groups—the poverty area councils—to have representation. The bill was referred to the safety committee of the board of aldermen, which decided within a week to bring it to a vote without a public hearing. After some parliamentary moves by Morris and attempts to forestall the inevitable, the board of aldermen voted down the measure by eight to two. Supporters of the measure promised to keep it alive, and the debate over a civilian review procedure was periodically revisited, but it would not come to fruition for nearly thirty years.[12]

In the wake of the defeat of the civilian review board, the *Louisville Defender* reported yet more complaints of police brutality and harassment, and more local civil rights organizations began devoting their energy to the issue.[13] In spring 1974, after white officers shot seventeen-year-old Roland James in the back, the Urban League's new director of housing and urban affairs, Louis Coleman, took on the issue for the normally conservative organization. Coleman was born in the black working-class neighborhood of Smoketown and moved to the west end as a teenager, giving him experience in both local African American communities. He dreamed of being a baseball player, but when that did not happen, he attended Kentucky State College, then the University of Louisville, and finally the Louisville Presbyterian Theological Seminary, from which he earned a divinity degree in 1974. Fresh out of Kentucky State, he was recruited by local Urban League officials to be in charge of their "New Thrust" program, a national initiative aimed at getting the organization more involved with the grassroots black community. His office was next door to that of the

Reverend W. J. Hodge, whom the NAACP had hired to reenergize its community-level work. The two of them, Coleman recalled, set out to "shake some trees."[14]

Soon after starting in his Urban League position, Coleman focused his attention on police-community relations. He set up a program to collect complaints and help people navigate the police department's review procedure and organized workshops to allow residents to testify about their experiences in the presence of police department and city officials. Eventually the group cooperated with the HRC to circulate a monthly police report card listing complaints and their outcome. During the same period, the Louisville Black Police Officers Organization (LBPOO), a group formed by African American police who were fighting discrimination on the job and what they saw as racism in white police behavior in general, held a series of hearings in different neighborhoods to give victims a chance to tell their stories and thus publicize the problem. These events, which lasted until 1976 and were cosponsored by the Urban League, documented police officers driving at high speeds through residential streets, brandishing weapons, kicking open doors, and endangering children by pulling cars onto the front lawns of people's homes.[15]

In response to this organizing in the community, by the mid-1970s local government made some attempts, however small and aborted, to respond to the evidence of police misconduct. More reports of police violence led to investigations and disciplinary measures. For example, in 1974, the county police suspended an officer and prohibited police from using mace after one teenager was hurt. But investigations were still slow, and complainants still had trouble finding out results. Moreover, officers under investigation continued in their patrol duties, often in the same neighborhoods. In April 1976, the HRC asked the board of aldermen to hold public hearings to look into the internal affairs division of the police department. The department made some moves in the summer of 1976, when the assistant chief of police organized a task force on police conduct and promised to include citizens in its work. But that effort appeared to go nowhere, and within six months the board of aldermen's promised investigation was also postponed.[16] By this time, police behavior had become entangled in a broader community crisis—the conflict over school desegregation and the rise of extremist violence that accompanied it—and the problem of brutality against the black community moved out of the spotlight.

Throughout the debate over police brutality and what to do about it, one solution often proposed was the hiring of more black officers. This in turn reopened the debate over discrimination against African Americans in hiring by the county and city police forces as well as in treatment and promotions once they were on the job. Despite charges and investigations by the HRC in the mid-1960s and declarations by city officials, including the directors of the civil service commission and the department of public safety, that they wanted to hire more blacks to improve police relations in the west end, in September 1970 the city police force included only 27 black officers out of a total of 624, and the county had just 1 black officer on a force of 290. This clear imbalance sparked a campaign by several local civil rights groups to force the department to hire more African Americans.[17]

In the spring of 1970, both the HRC and the NAACP Ministerial Coalition began asking questions about city police hiring practices, but for the next several years the Urban League, under the direction of Louis Coleman, took the lead on this issue, as it had on police brutality. Initially the organization limited its involvement to sponsoring recruiting campaigns and a summer intern program aimed at preparing African Americans to apply for jobs, reflecting its traditional role identifying candidates for positions and working to open doors to individuals. In 1973 a study done by the group revealed that, despite promises and some effort by local officials, the recruitment class for that year was all white, and blacks still made up only 5.2 percent of the force. At that point, the Urban League became more assertive. It sought outside funding to launch a major recruiting drive but also requested that it be permitted to open a "police career center" to work with black job candidates and that more African Americans have roles in the police department's recruiting and hiring procedures.[18]

When Harvey Sloane was inaugurated as mayor in 1974, he promised to hire more black police. In response, John Arnold, the project director for the Urban League minority police recruitment drive, pressed the mayor to promise that 25 percent of the department's officers would be black by the end of his term, to match the proportion of African Americans in the city. That could be accomplished, Arnold pointed out, by taking the African Americans on the eligibility list and creating a recruitment class from them. Sloane balked at the idea of an all-black recruit class, saying it "would be discriminating against whites," but agreed to look into ways to expand recruitment. Nevertheless, by late 1974, very little progress had been made; indeed, the percentage of the force that was African American had not changed at all.[19]

In response to the lack of progress, in 1974 the LBPOO filed a lawsuit in federal district court, accusing the police department of discriminating in its hiring and promotion practices and asking the court to order a remedy to end the unequal treatment. Like black law enforcement organizations in cities such as Chicago, San Francisco, and Philadelphia, the LBPOO was formed to engage in issues in the black community and to protect black officers' own rights on the force. The lawsuit reflected precedents established by other groups that had won court-ordered solutions for discrimination in police departments. In its suit, the LBPOO specifically requested that the court order the Louisville department to hire only African Americans until their proportion on the force matched the local black population and that all blacks with twelve or more years of service be promoted until the number of blacks at higher ranks was likewise proportional. In addition, the suit asked that the qualifying test be invalidated and that other measures that were used to screen out blacks be dropped.[20]

The LBPOO lawsuit reflected the fact that hiring was not the only problem; black police were also discriminated against in myriad ways once they were on the force. Throughout the history of black involvement in the Louisville police force, African American officers had suffered limits on their authority to make arrests, humiliation by white officers, and restriction to low-level duties and black community–only patrols. The *Louisville Courier-Journal* published a series of stories in the early 1970s in which black police officers aired their concerns about "persistent, subtle" discrimination, unequal discipline, and lack of promotions. In addition, in 1970 a survey of all police officers showed that a majority did not believe the department would benefit from hiring more minorities. Repeated accusations that police chief Hyde was a "nigger lover" also indicated the level of white racial hostility on the force. After the suit was filed, harassment of black officers increased as tensions in the department worsened.[21]

The experience of Shelby Lanier, who was the founder and president of the LBPOO and the victim of repeated disciplinary actions, highlighted the disparate treatment and harassment of black officers. Lanier was born and raised in the Limerick neighborhood, just south of downtown, and graduated from Central High School in 1954, before integration. He attended Central State College in Ohio and then played baseball briefly in the Negro American League. When he doubted that he had a future as an athlete, he joined the air force. The training he received there did not help him get a job in Louisville when he returned, however. He was turned away for skilled positions at GE and IBM and was on unemployment when he decided to try the police force. Despite scoring high on the required exams, he was repeatedly turned down for a job there as well. He eventually gained admission to the police academy only after a personal recommendation, and he finally joined the force in 1961. Though he was confronted with restrictions on his authority, over time Lanier broke some of the barriers, becoming the first black officer on the motorcycle and homicide squads.[22]

Despite some successes in his own career, however, Lanier knew that the problem of discrimination against blacks in the force and ill treatment of black citizens by white officers persisted. By the early 1970s, he had become one of what has been called the "new breed of African-American police officer," who, inspired by the broader militancy in the black community, "spoke out against racism in the police department" and faced the consequences.[23] In 1972 he wrote a letter to the mayor on behalf of the LBPOO, asking him both to rescind orders that allowed police "to function as judge and executioner" and to involve blacks in the investigation of brutality complaints. For doing so, he was charged with violating regulations against making political statements without the approval of his superior. A court order stopped his punishment, but seven months later, his supervisors transferred him from his job as a police-school liaison officer to a less desirable position. In response to what many in the black community saw as racially motivated attacks on Lanier and others, King Solomon Baptist Church initiated a fund-raising drive to pay for salary loss whenever a black police officer was suspended.[24]

In late 1974, as the LBPOO suit moved through the courts, the pressure on the Louisville police department increased when the EEOC district office in Memphis initiated action against the department and the civil service board. Responding to a complaint filed by Lanier and fellow officer James N. Brown that black police were discriminated against in hiring and promotion and were subject to more severe discipline and retaliation when they complained, the EEOC concluded there was "reasonable cause to believe" them and ordered conciliation.[25] The process of conciliation at first focused on the eligibility exam. Nationally, civil rights groups had criticized screening tests for being biased toward whites in their content and for including questions not relevant to the job. In *Griggs v. Duke Power* in 1971, the Supreme Court had ruled that non-job-related tests with adverse impacts on minority groups were considered evidence of discrimination and were thus illegal. This opened the door to challenges to such tests in both private industry and public employment.[26] In Louisville, in response to the LBPOO complaint and EEOC conciliation, the civil service board changed the test to include only questions about police work and, within a year, dropped the oral portion and adopted a standardized exam used by other communities. By the end of 1975, fifteen of the top thirty-five scores were achieved by blacks, and eleven of the top twenty-two people on the eligibility list were black.[27]

One year later, however, the LBPOO and Louis Coleman complained to the HRC that, despite the changes made under conciliation, the 1976 recruit class was again all white, an indication that "there has been no perceptible progress made." Coleman asked the HRC to review the goals and timetables that had been established under the EEOC conciliation and determine what further changes were required to "enhance affirmative action" in the police department. In response, the HRC initiated action against the City of Louisville, the civil service board, and the police department. In response, in early 1977, the city ordered a hiring freeze until problems could be addressed and then initiated a recruiting effort among African Americans. The civil service board also started providing study guides for the tests and giving candidates two weeks to study. The director of the board consistently resisted one major demand by rights activists, however: that he keep separate eligibility lists for whites and blacks and alternate in accepting candidates from each. Proponents argued this would more quickly get blacks on the force, but opponents said it was unfair to the whites already on the list.[28]

The lawsuit by the LBPOO yielded court orders that gradually affected the police department's policies. After small changes made in 1977 did not bring about enough results, in 1979 Judge Charles Allen issued a consent decree that ordered that, for the next five years, the department had to use two separate eligibility lists to admit candidates to the recruiting class. Under the order, for every two white officers hired, one black person had to be added to the department until the force was 15 percent black. In addition, the court ordered the promotion of black officers until the leadership ranks were also 15 percent black, giving the city until 1987 to accomplish that goal. In 1987, after both consent decrees had expired, the recruiting class still did not meet the proportion goal. Nevertheless, in the succeeding years, responding to national trends away from affirmative action and decisions against "reverse discrimination," the department dropped efforts to maintain even a "voluntary quota" in the police department.[29] Although neither equality nor even proportional representation had been reached in the department, the more conservative political climate of the 1980s and the accompanying limits on federal policies and agencies' support for change dampened the chances for further action on the issue.

The police department was not the only contested area of employment in the early 1970s. Indeed, during that period, both locally and nationally, equal employment opportunity became a central focus of civil rights activists as they worked to enforce the city, state, and federal laws against discrimination that had been passed in the previous decade. African Americans sought to tear down institutional barriers to equal employment and began to argue for going beyond merely eliminating overt "disparate treatment" and toward ending "disparate results." In the early 1970s, they had allies in federal government policy-making bodies who were beginning to call for specific "affirmative action" toward ending discrimination.[30] Much, though certainly not all, of this activity moved out of the streets and into the halls of the courts and government agencies charged with such enforcement, and thus it seemed less like a movement than had the mass campaigns of the previous years. Nevertheless, it was the second wave of activism that was necessary to make real the promises of equality brought by demonstrations and agitation.

In Louisville there were three main leaders in the effort to open economic opportunity to African Americans: the HRC; the NAACP, which was being revived by Hodge after a period of relative quiet; and a new grassroots organization, the Black Workers' Coalition (BWC). Though the members of these three groups did not always get along, and they represented very different elements of the civil rights movement—a government bureaucracy, a "moderate mainstream" national organization, and a black power–influenced "militant" grassroots group—they often cooperated, demonstrating the extent to which equal employment opportunity was a unifying goal in this period.

The HRC, which, because of changes in its enabling legislation, had expanded its jurisdiction to include Jefferson County, held the responsibility for enforcing local civil rights laws, including those on employment. Under executive director Martin Perley, the HRC investigated business practices to monitor and encourage compliance. In the summer of 1968, the commission surveyed fifty of the largest local firms that had high turnover and thus did a lot of hiring, with the goal of finding three thousand new jobs for African Americans. Then, in January 1969, the HRC received a grant from the EEOC to do more specific research, investigating the twenty-five top firms in the community for "hidden" forms of discrimination. At about the same time, the agency took on the job of ensuring that local businesses followed an executive order from the mayor that all firms doing work under city contract follow equal employment guidelines. Generally in this period, Perley tried to take what he saw as a positive, nonadversarial position, working with companies to help them comply rather than focusing on punishment.[31]

While the local HRC worked on a proactive approach to enforcement, the Kentucky Commission on Human Rights began receiving, investigating, and mediating complaints of discrimination under federal and state law. The first employment case to work through the system was a charge that Louisville and Nashville Railroad Company, headquartered in Louisville, confined blacks to a separate seniority roster that prohibited them from transferring to better jobs. The railroad and the machinist union said that employees could not transfer from one roster to another without losing seniority but that this was not meant to perpetuate racial segregation. The Kentucky Commission on Human Rights argued that, although there might not be intent to discriminate, the effect was discriminatory, and it wanted the two lists merged. Despite a federal district court order in another case that blacks be allowed to transfer to other rosters without losing seniority, it took nearly five years for all the issues to be worked out in a conciliation order signed by both the state commission and L&N, which gave black employees back pay and established a number of requirements for moving them into higher-level positions.[32] Not all state commission cases took as long as this one. While the L&N case was working its way through conciliation, the Kentucky Commission on Human Rights secured changes in the hiring and promotion policies at the Philip Morris factory and at area restaurants, theaters, and hotels.[33] Nevertheless, it remained true that the complaint investigation and conciliation processes were slow and thus had little short-term impact on the African American community.

To affect a larger number of black workers, the HRC decided to take on the discriminatory practices of the building trade unions and from there to secure positions for African Americans in construction. The local agency joined an effort sweeping across northern and midwestern cities to gain access to what at the time was an overwhelmingly white line of work. In Detroit, Cleveland, and other cities, but most famously in Philadelphia, black workers and their allies butted up against the exclusionary apprenticeship and membership policies of the building trades. They pushed hard enough to get federal attention and, eventually, the development of federal affirmative action policies. After years of protests and negotiations, including a failed effort under the Johnson administration, in 1969 Richard Nixon initiated the Philadelphia Plan, which, according to historian Nancy MacLean, "promised to bypass all-white hiring halls and put non-union minority craftsmen on city jobs." The plan established goals and timetables for the inclusion of minority workers in each of the crafts contracted in a publicly funded construction project and charged contractors with hiring to meet those goals. This plan became a model for other cities as they began to formulate their own programs for opening the construction industry.[34]

Following these models, in the summer of 1968 the HRC began a campaign to "get minorities into construction jobs and training programs," which resulted in the Louisville Plan. The commission's efforts hit a snag, however, when they became embroiled in a controversy over discrimination in construction of a new housing project in the west end. The Village West housing project was funded by HUD and directed by Action Now and its subsidiary Housing Now. The latter were groups of white, liberal, "influential businessmen" who were seeking to create both jobs and low-income housing. In early April 1970, however, an ad hoc coalition of fifteen African American groups complained that the project, though it was in a primarily black neighborhood and likely to attract mainly black tenants, was not hiring sufficient African American workers. The group formed the Committee of United Blacks and issued demands for affirmative action to guarantee the inclusion of black contractors and training programs to help minorities enter the construction field. Shortly thereafter, it added demands for representation on the board of Action Now, for blacks' inclusion in all levels of project development, and for African American management of the completed housing project. Finally, the committee wanted blacks to be able to skip apprenticeships and be accepted directly into unions, bypassing the means by which they had been excluded in the past. The protests of the Committee of United Blacks revealed not only the potential for community action around the issue of construction jobs but the rejection of what black leaders called a white paternalistic approach to development in the west end.[35]

The HRC initially agreed to put its negotiations for the Louisville Plan on hold to allow the Committee of United Blacks to take the lead, but when no progress was made for several weeks, the agency restarted its own efforts. By late fall, it was clear that its negotiations with unions were likewise bogging down, leading to the conclusion by the end of the year that "virtually no progress" was being made on the plan. It was not until over a year later, in January 1972, that civil rights groups, the HRC, and representatives of the General Contractors' Association of Louisville, Builders' Exchange of Louisville, and Construction Trades Council signed the plan. Under the plan, an administrative committee composed of representatives from business, labor, and civil rights groups would oversee the incorporation of minority workers into apprenticeship and other training programs, with a goal of hiring seventy-five additional workers in the building trades by the end of the year.[36]

As the controversy with the Committee of United Blacks indicates, while the HRC pursued its campaign to encourage equal job opportunity, civil rights organizations from the moderate to the militant also engaged in campaigns toward the same goal. During this period, the NAACP spearheaded enforcement of antidiscrimination legislation by filing complaints and lawsuits. For example, in 1968, longtime NAACP attorney James Crumlin, with backing from the national organization's Legal Defense Fund, filed suit on behalf of seven black employees against E. I. du Pont de Nemours and Company for maintaining separate seniority and bidding systems that discriminated against African Americans. District court judge Henry Brooks ruled in July 1969 in favor of the plaintiffs, ordering the company to allow blacks to transfer to other divisions and keep their seniority and by doing so to stop perpetuating "the results of past discrimination." Over the next few years, the local branch of the NAACP, often with the help of the Legal Defense Fund, filed lawsuits and HRC and EEOC complaints against Philip Morris and the Tobacco Workers International Union, the University of Louisville School of Medicine, and the

Olin Mathieson Chemical Corporation at the Indiana Army Ammunition Plant, among others, taking advantage of precedents that favored complainants. As with the case of government enforcement agencies, however, this strategy of filing case-by-case suits was slow and cumbersome, and while it did build up precedents, it affected relatively few people at a time.[37]

The NAACP also combined direct actions such as pickets and boycotts with negotiations to try to secure opportunities for blacks in grocery store chains, a source of employment both embedded physically in the black community and, at least in some locations, dependent on it for its income. The local branch's first target was the A&P chain. After an attempt at negotiation with area managers, the NAACP reported that, between 1969 and 1972, the percentage of blacks in the chain's workforce had dropped from 8 to 6 percent. There were no black employees at all in certain areas of the store. Accusing the chain of "cheating the black community," in May 1972 the organization called on blacks and "fair minded whites" to boycott the business. The goals of the nonbuying campaign were to increase total black employment until it made up 35 percent of the salary budget, to raise part-time employees to full-time, and to improve the quality of products in black neighborhoods. At the end of the summer, the organization negotiated a settlement with A&P officials that included some but not all of the demands, and it subsequently called off the boycott. Three months later, however, in anger over not only the failure of A&P managers to "live up to its commitments" but also apparent efforts to provide "falsified" data to make it seem that they had, the NAACP threatened to submit a complaint to the EEOC. There was a short break in the conflict as the organization focused its energies elsewhere, but continued bad faith on the part of the grocery store chain and a persistent problem of unequal treatment, particularly of black women, led the NAACP finally to file an EEOC complaint in January 1975.[38]

Meanwhile, the organization turned its attention to a competing chain, the Kroger Company. In 1969 the NAACP and Kroger managers had agreed that the company would "provide an atmosphere . . . conducive to equal opportunity" and recruit from black high schools with the aim of hiring African Americans while upgrading current employees to management positions. But a survey in 1971 showed the company still failed to hire and promote minorities, with only about 6 percent black employees. A year later, after the NAACP gave the company more time, the statistics showed no improvement. In response, the NAACP started the new year with a boycott of Kroger stores, asking blacks in both Louisville and southern Indiana to refuse to shop there. Concurrently, leaders organized picketing of the chain's stores by church groups, black Greek organizations, and the poverty area councils, the latter two representing very different class constituencies in the African American community. Kroger came back with an offer of a moderate affirmative action plan, but James Coleman, the head of the labor and industry committee of the NAACP, said it was not enough; it did not make up for previous broken promises. Coleman called for local blacks to continue to boycott.[39]

At this point, the Kentucky Commission on Human Rights interceded and complicated the conflict. In response to complaints elsewhere in the state against Kroger, the commission ordered the company to hire blacks to bring their proportion of the workforce to 13 percent. Louisville activists cried foul, however, because the order let the company off too easily by not specifying whether positions be full- or part-time or at managerial levels. The dispute got so heated that the NAACP filed a complaint with the federal EEOC against the Kentucky Commission on Human Rights for "aiding and abetting the perpetuation of racial discrimination." Not only did the state commission's order short-circuit the NAACP campaign against Kroger, causing managers to cease to negotiate with the civil rights organization and leading to a loss of support for the ongoing boycott, but the controversy over it illustrated the frustration of local community groups with the pace and moderation of state enforcement agencies.[40]

The NAACP—a moderate establishment organization—was joined in using this combination of negotiations and community pressure by a grassroots group that in some ways invoked the black power philosophy, the BWC. In the late 1960s, the ideology of black power had given rise around the country to black workers' organizations, sometimes formed explicitly as unions and sometimes as grassroots community groups, to focus on jobs. The founders and leaders of the BWC, such as Moscoe Rapier, who worked at Lorillard Tobacco Company, and Roosevelt Roberts, a Ford employee, were mostly young people who had experienced discrimination on the job and, influenced by the black power movement, were "gaining a political conscience, a black conscience, and wanted to do something about it," recalled member Robert Cunningham. The group had approximately fifteen active participants but attracted as many as fifty people, primarily blacks but also some radical whites, to their meetings. Although they were influenced by some of the black power philosophy, the organization did not identify itself as a nationalist group. Moreover, although it was labeled a militant organization, its tactics were not so dissimilar from those of the NAACP and other ad hoc community coalitions, and indeed it often worked side by side with both the NAACP and the HRC.[41]

Early in its history, the BWC focused on one campaign at a time, and in its first several years, it organized small actions at a number of local firms. In November 1970, the group organized a one-day walkout of black employees at Ford as "an act of solidarity" meant to "dramatize that we will no long accept bias." Roberts called it a "warning" for future action if Ford did not change its employment practices. A year later the group led a similar action at International Harvester. On what they called Black Friday, black employees took the day off to protest the unequal discipline and treatment there. Although these actions did not make an immediate or visible impact—problems at Ford, for example, dragged on for years and later involved the HRC—the group was more successful with other campaigns. In 1972, when the Brown-Forman Corporation fired fifteen black janitors, some of whom had worked for the company for twenty years, with thirty minutes' notice in order to hire an outside contractor, the BWC launched a round of pickets and other protests. One of the janitors later pointed out that the men had asked both the NAACP and the HRC for help and gotten no response. But after the BWC protests, the workers were rehired with back pay and benefits. In another case, the organization objected to the firing of a black woman from McCrory's five and ten cent store in the Algonquin Manor shopping center after she allegedly refused "personal advances" from her boss, and it forced the firing and replacement of the offending manager.[42]

The BWC's most dramatic protest and its outcome revealed the extent of cooperation among black community and civil rights groups around African American workers' rights and the participation of whites in that cause. In August 1973, the group decided to focus on jobs and conditions for black workers at Lorillard Tobacco Company. Although the company was in a primarily black neighborhood, the number of black workers had not risen in decades; indeed, some evidence showed it had declined. Moreover, black workers were confined to the hardest, dirtiest jobs and were treated disrespectfully by supervisors, who insisted on using "boy" and "girl" to refer to them. To protest these facts, the BWC organized a work stoppage. Six black employees locked themselves on the fourth floor of the building and ceased working. Organizer Robert Cunningham recalled, "So they closed off this upstairs, locked the doors, and had a work stoppage. Because without these guys the whole plant had to shut down, nobody could work. Oh God, the plant went crazy; I mean, the bigwigs who run the plant, they called the police, and the police with all you would have thought that the whole west end was being seized by police."[43] When the police cleared the building, witnesses claimed they used brutality to do so. One man was hit on the head and choked by police. BWC leader Moscoe Rapier reported an officer "stuck a gun under his chin, into his back, and called him a 'black M.F.'" Others reported the "police charged the crowd with shot guns and billies." A total of ten black men were arrested, four workers for "not working," as Cunningham put it, and six bystanders.[44]

The perceived overreaction by the company and police, by tapping into concurrent resentment over police behavior in the black community, transformed a workers' protest into a broader issue and, in the process, illustrated the extent to which a wide variety of organizations—black and white, moderate and militant—could contribute to a campaign in their own ways. In the wake of the arrests, the BWC organized a meeting between officials of the company and representatives of the Urban League, NAACP, KCLC, and Sisters of Charity, an order with sisters who lived in the west end and served its schools. Coming out of that meeting, the Urban League promised to help Lorillard Tobacco Company recruit black employees to meet the 23 percent of the workforce demanded by civil rights groups. The NAACP launched its own investigation and, when it validated the charges of discrimination made by the black workers, filed a complaint with the EEOC. The organization also offered legal help to those arrested and to anyone who engaged in work stoppages at the company in the future. The HRC also got involved, launching its own investigation and public hearing at Rapier's request. Finally, the BWC continued to lead pickets outside the company and other protests. It called for a boycott of the tobacco products of the firm, which was endorsed by a wide range of groups, including the Catholic Archdiocese of Louisville. In the end, Lorillard dropped the charges against employees arrested inside the plant, though it did not reinstate them, and the bystanders arrested outside received suspended sentences for disorderly conduct.[45] But the more important outcome for the local movement was that the incident helped sustain a relationship among a range of groups that, though they did not always agree on tactics, could cooperate in times of crisis.

This was not the only example of the BWC's working with other mainstream, governmental, community, and interracial organizations. In its first year, it worked closely with the activist and grassroots black community in WECC to support workers in a grievance against Louisville Gas and Electric. Indeed, the close overlap between the organizations on the issue of employment opportunity was one of the reasons that, when WECC folded, the members chose to donate their remaining funds to the BWC. On the other end of the spectrum, in January 1972, the BWC entered negotiations with the HRC to change the way the latter worked to make it more responsive to the community. The BWC accused the HRC of being too slow and demanded that it be "reconstructed to replace industry people with representatives of grassroots blacks." HRC commissioners, for their part, objected to the way the BWC raised funds in the community, specifically its practice of "demanding" contributions from area businesses for community work. Nevertheless, the HRC did agree it could use more input and help in its investigations of discrimination and agreed to allow representatives of the BWC to accompany staff in their work, demonstrating a willingness to look beyond ideology and to cooperate.[46]

Sporadic actions by the BWC and other community groups against specific cases of job discrimination continued into the late 1970s. Over time, however, the focus of attention shifted to enacting a city affirmative action policy that would have broader reach than case-by-case complaints. The city equal employment ordinance already outlawed discrimination in city government, and there was a precedent in Mayor Schmied's 1968 executive order mandating that firms doing business with the city follow all equal employment laws for a proactive city government approach to making equal opportunity real. The city's first affirmative action plan was written in 1976, under the Sloane administration. Cheri Hamilton, a former open housing demonstrator and the daughter of Black Six member Ruth Bryant, recalled that, as an assistant in the city law department, she helped two other women to draft the first plan. Mayor Sloane met some resistance from the HRC because he had ignored it in the preparation of the plan and bypassed it in the monitoring mechanism. But after accepting some suggestions for improvements, in October Sloane forwarded the plan to the board of aldermen for their consideration. Once the plan was approved, the city established an affirmative action monitor and equal opportunity coordinator.[47]

Within two years, however, civil rights advocates inside and outside city government were pressing for a more sweeping approach to enforcement. In 1977 the Reverend W. J. Hodge of the NAACP wrote to HUD about problems he saw in the city's employment practices, including in the police department and on projects subcontracted to private businesses. HUD reviewed the city's practices and concurred that there were serious deficiencies in its affirmative action plans. Ten government agencies were in noncompliance with HUD orders, and goals and timetables were not being met. Warning that the city could lose federal dollars, Hodge invited the NAACP, Urban League, Kentucky Minority Businessmen's Association, Kentucky Commission on Human Rights, and HRC to join the newly formed Louisville Affirmative Action Coalition to push for a stronger approach by the city and to monitor its efforts in the future.[48]

Though Hodge had hoped that the report would inspire newly elected mayor William Stansbury to take positive action, a stronger affirmative action policy got caught up in a conflict between the board of aldermen and the mayor and faced resistance even as it was being passed. By early 1978, Hodge was not only on the board of aldermen but had been elected its president, chosen as a compromise candidate after a fight between two other Democrats. He helped to steer the black and liberal coalition on the board toward passing an ordinance to require companies seeking contracts with the city to file their affirmative action plans with the HRC for review. When this ordinance was adopted in early July 1978, however, Stansbury vetoed it. He argued that it gave the HRC too much power; he wanted an executive branch department to provide enforcement. Coincidentally, this veto was reported on the same day as the Supreme Court decision in *Regents of the University of California v. Bakke*, and black leaders saw in the combination an indication of what would happen to affirmative action and equal economic opportunity in the new, conservative climate.[49]

Undaunted, the board of aldermen amended the measure and passed it again. They kept the enforcement in the hands of the HRC, arguing that a relatively independent body needed to monitor the city's actions, but limited the law to cover companies of over ten people seeking to do more than ten thousand dollars' worth of business with the city. In the month the aldermen took to make these amendments, the mayor caused controversy when he reported that he had gone to Atlanta to consult with officials there about affirmative action, when in reality he had gone on a social trip to New Orleans with a female companion. His relations with the black community now strained not only by his initial veto but by the sense that he had used them as cover for an unethical trip, Stansbury was pushed into signing the new measure though he continued to oppose it. The law, which went into effect on January 1, 1979, required all the businesses covered to demonstrate their commitment to equal opportunity for minorities and women and gave the HRC the chance to review companies before they could get contracts.[50]

The new affirmative action ordinance met criticism and resistance immediately, confirming black leaders' fears of the conservative turn in the political climate. Less than a month after the bill was signed, the state attorney general's office released an opinion stating that the original veto had been correct because the HRC did not have the power to preapprove contracts and because the local law was more restrictive than the state equivalent. Moreover, within months of the bill's going into effect, the *Louisville Courier-Journal* reported overt resistance to the law. When the HRC associate director sent seven thousand letters to firms doing business with the city, asking for reports on their compliance with equal opportunity law, only eleven hundred responded. Some businesses made it clear they had no intention of complying with the new procedure and would simply stop seeking contracts with the city. Some political leaders expressed concern that the city might not be able to secure the goods and services it required. There was little evidence of that outcome by the spring of 1979, however, and as African American alderman Porter Hatcher responded, "If businesses really object to equal employment then the city shouldn't buy from them anyway." Other officials predicted that the glitches would work themselves out as people adjusted to the procedure.[51] Regardless, with this plan in place, and with the enforcement mechanism built into the HRC, for a short while economic opportunity issues moved out of the realm of movement action.

The adoption of the affirmative action plan, and the support by the board of aldermen and belated and reluctant endorsement by the mayor, reflected changing politics in the city, which resulted at least in part from the assertion of the black political voice in local government and the Democratic Party. Throughout the civil rights era, African Americans and their white allies in Louisville had used the power of the vote to pressure administrations to address civil rights issues, most notably in the aldermanic elections of 1961 and 1967. At the same time, African American officials had been elected into local and even state offices representing majority black districts. From those positions, they had been able to keep black grievances on the table and, by the late 1960s, to translate that into legislative success. As the 1970s began, African American communities in the South were testing the results of the Voting Rights Act and pressing for political gains. Meanwhile, those across the urban North and West were demanding more return for their vote and a political version of black power. Because Louisville had always had a more "northern" approach to black political participation, the story of the local black community's engagement in politics in this period more closely resembles that of northern and midwestern cities: more black political officeholders, demands for more power within the city and within the Democratic Party, and efforts to take the pinnacle of urban power—the office of mayor. The extent of successes and failures in these regards, however, reveals the limitations of black political power despite the access to voting rights.

African Americans had been running for and being elected to office in Louisville since Charles W. Anderson won a seat in the Kentucky General Assembly in 1935. Throughout the 1960s, the number of candidates seeking office had steadily increased, but in the 1970s, the rate jumped dramatically. In the five-year span from 1969 to 1974, the *Louisville Defender,* always an ardent champion of black political action, repeatedly carried stories touting the record number of black candidates and officeholders. And the offices being sought became more diverse. Blacks no longer confined themselves to aldermanic seats from majority black wards and the state assembly seat held by Anderson. Now they began to challenge white officeholders in mixed districts. The most groundbreaking was Georgia Powers, who, as we have seen, in 1968 became a double pioneer as the first African American and first woman elected to the Kentucky senate. A different Charles Anderson—no relation to the early legislator—a year later sought and won the office of third district magistrate, in an area that was almost equally divided between whites and blacks and included part of the county outside the city boundary. Moreover, black candidates began running for positions such as county sheriff and coroner and for judicial posts, especially in police court, reflecting the extent to which law enforcement had become a major concern for the community. This enthusiasm for seeking office did not translate to victory as often as black leaders, not to mention the candidates themselves, hoped. Many of the aspirants were defeated at the primary stage, and it remained true that the securest chances were positions representing the west end. Nevertheless, although the slow progress did not fulfill the sense of what was owed to the community, there was a steady increase in electoral positions.[52]

One particular campaign to elect blacks to new positions taught potential African American political leaders a lesson about what it would take to move into power in Louisville. In early 1969, a group of five black Democrats announced that they would run in the primaries as a slate to try to get the party's nomination for "traditional white" offices. Neville Tucker, Darryl Owens, and D. Edward Turner ran for police court judge, third district magistrate, and twelfth ward alderman, respectively, while Raoul Cunningham—the former student sit-in leader—sought the county clerk position, and the Reverend Irvin Moxley ran for county commissioner. Influenced by black power, around the country African Americans advocated independent political action and even formed separate political parties. But the members of the Unity Slate, as they called themselves, expressly disavowed an affiliation with the black power movement. They insisted they were not separatists but were merely trying to win recognition for blacks within the Democratic Party and thus to reform it. In announcing their candidacy, their campaign manager, Morris Jeff, said that they were concerned about problems affecting specifically the black community but also wanted to boost the Democratic Party in that community and help it to defeat the Republicans. Their biggest challenge to the system was that they were running for offices not typically sought by blacks and for which the party had never supported a black candidate.[53]

While parts of the black community rallied to support the Unity Slate, differences over strategy weakened it from the beginning, leading to a split and its failure. Community clubs held fund-raisers for the group, and WECC both gave it prominent coverage in its newsletter and sponsored forums for the candidates to advertise their views. But a month before the spring primary, Neville Tucker pulled out to run for the same office, police court judge, on the slate of Democratic mayoral candidate Frank Burke. Tucker sought support from Burke, and the others objected because they had agreed not to endorse a mayoral candidate without a consensus. As he left the group, Tucker argued that he was joining an integrated slate that, if it won, would result in "an unprecedented number of Negroes being elected." The other men maintained that Burke represented "the old pattern of whites choosing our leaders." They charged that "Tucker is just a pawn being used to divide the political strength of the black community." One month later, the remaining members of the slate voted to endorse Jim Thornberry for the Democratic nomination.[54]

In the primary, Burke won the Democratic nomination—and would go on to be elected mayor—and Tucker won the nomination for police court judge. The rest of the Unity Slate lost their primaries. They promised to rally behind Tucker, however, in his quest to be the "first elected black police court judge in Kentucky." He too won in November. According to the *Louisville Defender*, the Unity Slate challenge involved the question of whether "black candidates win by appealing to black votes or forming black-white coalitions" and concluded, "So far this indicates the latter." While that oversimplified the situation and misrepresented the position of the Unity Slate to put the *Defender*'s own anti–black power spin on the outcome, it did accurately reflect the larger pattern in Louisville: black candidates succeeded more often when they worked alongside liberal elements in the Democratic Party.[55]

Indeed, to a great extent, blacks' political gains in this period grew out of their increasing role in the local party. In the postwar period, black Louisvillians had been divided almost evenly between the two major parties. In the 1960s, swings between parties at strategic moments had led to important political and legislative outcomes: the 1961 election of a Republican board that eventually adopted the open accommodations ordinance and the 1967 return to power of the Democrats, who immediately passed the open housing law. By the end of the decade, changes in the parties—the national organizations solidified as conservative (Republican) and liberal (Democrat), especially on race issues—impacted the local scene. A few local black leaders held out for consideration within the Republican Party. Prior to the 1968 national convention, local activists criticized the all-white makeup of the Kentucky Republican delegation, contrasting it with the Democrats' delegation, which included seven black representatives and three black alternates. A year later, longtime local black Republicans Charles

Lunderman and Bishop Tucker criticized the executive committee for failing to nominate James Crumlin for circuit court judge, calling it a "fatal error" that indicated a disregard for African Americans. In the election that fall, as a way of protesting, black precinct captains promised to "put out minimal effort to get out the vote" to demonstrate the importance of black participation for the party. This threat was a last-ditch effort to try to change the apparent fact that "the party has written off the west end."[56]

Meanwhile, reflecting the changes on the national level, the Democratic Party in Louisville was opening its doors to more black involvement, both in party structures and in city government, over which the Democrats had uninterrupted control beginning in 1969, when Republican Kenneth Schmied left office. Following the lead of the national party, the Louisville and Kentucky organizations began sending more African American delegates to the national conventions in 1968. More important, the party opened decision-making and organizing positions to black participation. For example, Charlotte McGill, whose family had been involved in Democratic politics for at least a generation, served as both the vice chair of the Jefferson County Democratic Executive Committee and a member of the state executive committee in 1971. Moreover, through the early 1970s, there developed a coterie of influential African Americans who worked within and alongside the party on election campaigns and thus had a connection to the winners. These included businessmen Joe Hammond and Leonard Gray and former sit-in demonstrator Bill Gatewood, among others. Cheri Hamilton recalled being introduced by this group to campaigning and working with them as the NAACP political action chair. Eventually, according to Hamilton, these leaders started insisting that blacks be given paid positions on election staffs, and she herself earned a job on the gubernatorial campaign of John Y. Brown.[57]

Parallel to their increasing voice within the Democratic Party, blacks began to hold more appointed positions in city government, including those at higher ranks of power. When Frank Burke was elected mayor in 1969, he began a process that continued through successive administrations of incorporating African Americans into city government through appointive staff positions, reflecting their growing importance in the Democratic Party and political clout in general. As noted above, he welcomed Neville Tucker onto his slate for a judicial position not held before by an African American. Though he was criticized by the Unity Slate at the time for dividing the black vote, once he and his slate won, the prominence of Tucker and others in the administration healed that rift. Most significant, Burke appointed William Summers IV to be his administrative assistant, the highest position in the mayor's office held by an African American to that date and a precedent followed by later mayors.[58]

Early in his term, Burke promised to "depolarize" the races in Louisville and bring "all into the decision-making process." Similar rhetoric had infused statements by Louisville mayors at least back to the administrations of Charles Farnsley and Andrew Broaddus, though those men followed through with varying amounts of commitment. But at the end of Burke's term in office, the *Defender* concluded that the promise had been partly met and that his had been a "more progressive and productive administration" than the city had seen in decades, making Louisville once again a "beacon of progressive liberalism." The editor pointed out that, together with the liberal head of the board of aldermen, the city administration had secured $15 million in federal funds for programs in the black community. Moreover, during Burke's term, blacks made gains in city government positions. In one case, reflecting the prominence of police relations issues at the time, Burke appointed longtime black officer Colonel A. Wilson Edwards as director of public safety.[59]

Mayor Harvey Sloane, who served two terms, 1973–1977 and 1982–1985, followed the precedent established by Burke of appointing blacks to positions in city government. Sloane already had a positive reputation in the black community because of his work in cofounding the Park Duvalle Neighborhood Health Center. One of his first acts as mayor was to appoint three African Americans to the committee to help him choose a new police chief. He also named former sit-in participant and Democratic Party activist Bill Gatewood as "special assistant to the mayor" and charged him with being a liaison with the HRC, CAC, and department of human resources. Within six months, Gatewood had succeeded in securing $1.2 million in federal funds for programs aimed at combating poverty in the west end and had convinced the board of aldermen to establish an economic development office to continue that kind of work. It was also under Sloane's administration that Cheri Hamilton worked in the city law department to help to write the city's first affirmative action policy.[60] Thus, at least indirectly, the increasing roles of black voters in the Democratic Party and city government impacted issues of economic development and job opportunity for the African American community.

William Stansbury had a tenser relationship with black political leaders surrounding his veto of the city affirmative action ordinance and the way he handled himself at that time, but his term in office, sandwiched between Sloane's terms, is remembered as a high point of black political influence in the city. He continued the tradition of hiring a black assistant by appointing Charles Roberts as the first black deputy mayor. In addition, shortly after Stansbury was inaugurated, the Reverend W. J. Hodge became the first black president of the board of aldermen, which gave him influence over the progress of legislation. According to Aubrey Williams, who served as NAACP president at the time and was himself elected to a number of offices, during the Stansbury years, "you had key blacks in key places in the city administration" who pushed city hall to provide more benefits to the community. And this, together with the atmosphere created nationally by the Jimmy Carter administration, provided hope for more progress.[61]

Of course, to reach the pinnacle of power in the city, African Americans aspired not only to serve as assistant to the mayor but to win that office itself. Some of the most important political stories of the period were the elections of the first black mayors in major American cities, beginning with Carl Stokes of Cleveland and Richard Hatcher of Gary, Indiana, in 1967 and followed not long after by the first black mayor in a major southern city, Maynard Jackson in Atlanta in 1973. Closer to home, Louisvillians had the example of Luska J. Twyman, who was appointed as mayor of Glasgow, Kentucky, after the sitting mayor resigned in 1968, and who won election on his own to that office in 1973. Twice during this period, prominent local African Americans attempted to secure the Democratic Party nomination for mayor of Louisville. Both went down to defeat, however, revealing the glass ceiling on black political power in the city.

In 1973 the Reverend Leo Lesser announced he would seek the nomination and the office to "remove the coldness from government" and to focus attention on the problems of "housing, education, unemployment," and poverty. Lesser had begun his career in Louisville with KCLC during the open housing crisis and had then become a militant community activist during his brief tenure as head of WECC. His campaign chances were hurt when Carroll Witten joined the race as a write-in candidate. Witten, a white doctor who was president of the board of aldermen, had earned a strong reputation among blacks and, in the months leading up to the primary, seemed to be leading in the black community. Lesser compensated by picking up the support of some white liberals, but in the primary, he came in third behind Witten and the eventual victor, Harvey Sloane. Although the *Louisville Defender* praised Lesser's campaign and said it benefitted the community by providing lessons for future black candidates, the editor also expressed great frustration that "in this border city, generally described as neither southern nor northern in its racial attitudes—somewhere in between the extremes of racism and liberalism"—a well-qualified black candidate could not get enough support. More pointedly, the paper blamed black voters, who, "having never had to fight for the ballot, have stubbornly and ignorantly refused to register to even one half of their full potential." Seeking a silver lining, the paper concluded that perhaps this would teach the community to rise to its potential the next time, in 1977.[62]

Indeed, in 1977 Louisville voters had another chance to select a black candidate for mayor in the Democratic primary. In 1975 Lois Morris, who had lost her seat on the board of aldermen after Sloane did not include her on his Democrats for Progress Slate, announced that she would run for mayor in 1977. She initially cast her plans as an attack on Sloane, but in the course of her campaign, she argued that it was time for Louisville to join other cities in having a black mayor. Then, in the fall of 1976, Milburn Maupin, who at that time was an official with the newly merged Jefferson County Public Schools and thus was at the center of the controversy over busing and desegregation, announced that he too would run for mayor. This led to a debate in the community as black activists tried to encourage one of them to back down to avoid dividing the vote in the primary. Morris insisted that she was better qualified because of her experience on the board of aldermen and attendance at national meetings of the U.S. Conference of Mayors. Moreover, she added, Maupin's duties in the school system would prevent him from campaigning adequately. Maupin did eventually withdraw from the race, leaving Morris facing white candidates William Stansbury and Creighton Mershon in the May 1977 primary.[63]

As the primary election approached, black political activists and civic leaders lined up behind either Mershon or Stansbury, and Morris's race was all but ignored. She did win some support: Shelby Lanier and the LBPOO endorsed her, as did Anne Braden, indicating militant black and white support. But Morris was never able to secure much attention from the local media—which she blamed for the failure of her campaign—or the black community. The *Louisville Defender* faulted Morris, saying she "could have been the best and most qualified candidate," but she held back and refused to campaign on issues or say anything controversial. The paper also hypothesized that black political activists supported candidates who were more likely to win in an effort to make them "obligated to recognize the needs of the black community" as payment for their votes. Charles Roberts and Bill Gatewood, who had both worked for Sloane, led the support for Mershon, while businessmen Lenny Lyles and Joe Hammond and longtime party activist Maude Benboe campaigned for Stansbury. Just before the election, a new group, the Urban Political Caucus, threw its support behind Stansbury as a break from the Sloane administration, with which Mershon was closely identified. In the primary, Stansbury defeated his opponents, with Morris getting only 2,200 votes and coming in a distant third, and he went on to win office in November. With African Americans making up only a quarter of the population of the city, it may have been unrealistic for blacks to anticipate winning the mayoral race. But the very low number of votes recorded for Morris revealed that many black voters chose to cast their lot with white leaders in black-white liberal coalitions.[64]

By the late 1970s, then, Louisville's African American community could celebrate gains in the diversity of offices held by blacks, the authority they had within city government, and the influence such positions had over policy while decrying the limits on and threats to that power. While Morris went down to defeat, Carl Hines defeated Norbert Blume for the Democratic nomination for the forty-third district representative to the General Assembly. This district was majority black, and African American political leaders, while appreciating Blume's service as a reliable liberal in Frankfort, had long wanted the seat held by one of their own. NAACP leader Aubrey Williams joined Hines in the capital and became the first black legislative committee chair not long after. And in the Stansbury administration, increasing numbers of black activists held positions of authority and helped to make policy, assisted by Hodge as leader of the board of aldermen, as well as by white liberal allies.[65]

But the political clout of the black community seemed to have reached a plateau, and there was a looming threat to further gains on the horizon. In 1976 the Kentucky Commission on Human Rights reported that, statewide, the number of black elected officials had fallen behind that in other states. Locally, besides not being able to secure the top position, African Americans still "held no sizeable number of elective offices." Moreover, as black civic leaders and political observers repeatedly pointed out, west end and black majority districts showed relatively low levels of voter registration and participation, which seemed to doom future races. The *Louisville Courier-Journal* reported after the 1977 primary, for example, that although the forty-first, forty-second, and forty-third legislative districts contained 32,000 registered voters, only approximately 4,000 people had gone to the polls. There were also fears beginning to circulate that in the near future the political power of blacks might be diluted. In her campaign literature, for example, Lois Morris declared she was the last chance for Louisville to have a black mayor because of the impending merger of city and county government, which would greatly reduce the black proportion of the voting population.[66] Though that merger would not take place for another two decades, that she raised it as a threat demonstrates the insecurity the black community felt in their political power based on their numbers by the late 1970s.

In the decade after the assassination of Martin Luther King, the task for the black community and its white allies was how to make real the gains promised by the legislation of the 1960s. Those laws had resulted from the pressure created by demonstrations and policy makers' response. That pressure was direct, in the form of black votes and boycotts, but also indirect, in the forms of concern about the city's image and ability to attract investment and the desire of middle-of-the-road white voters for calm. Once the crisis passed and the demonstrators were off the streets, the question was how to make sure that government and private business officials made good on their promises. In Louisville the answer was a combination of working within and outside the legal and political systems. The enforcement agency in Louisville, the HRC, staffed by liberal whites and increasingly by black activists, took a relatively proactive approach to seeking compliance with civil rights laws. The work of the HRC does not look like movement activity, but it led to compliance by employers with equal employment laws and to the small steps taken by the Louisville Plan to ease black entry into the construction industry. Working both in cooperation with and parallel to the HRC, the NAACP used the legal machinery established by 1960s legislation to pursue complaints and win agreements from employers. And African Americans worked within the system by seeking election to office and working for both the Democratic Party and city government to gain a voice in policy making.

But in the 1970s, Louisvillians also continued to work outside the system to bring about social change. The NAACP, BWC, and a number of smaller organizations used protests and boycotts to put pressure on business and government on issues of police brutality and jobs. This strategy went hand in hand with the work of enforcement bureaucracies because it was the activists' use of external pressure that created the climate in which officials negotiated and responded with concessions; thus they were parts of an inseparable effort. Repeated complaints of police brutality inspired the HRC to seek civilian review of the department, and protests against racism within the police department led to the board of aldermen's interest in the issue. These approaches also more literally went hand in hand as the staffs of the enforcement bureaucracy and the members of militant grassroots protest organizations, like the BWC, worked together on particular issues and as activists moved into government.

This combination of strategies resulted in some progress in the three arenas—law enforcement, employment, and government—that were the focus of civil rights activists in this period. More employers, though often grudgingly, agreed to equal employment policies; the hiring policies of the police force changed under conciliation agreements with the EEOC; blacks moved into positions of authority in city government. In each case, a statement of gains could and should be followed by a disclaimer. Though the issue gained less attention in the short term, police misconduct continued to be a major concern for the black community in the coming decades. Indeed, in the 1970s, this issue produced the next generation of local civil rights leaders, including Louis Coleman, and one of the most significant new civil rights organizations, the Kentucky Alliance. Moreover, legislative efforts to create a review procedure to rein in police behavior would not succeed until the next century. Though the HRC established the Louisville Plan and took the responsibility under new legislation for monitoring affirmative action progress in firms under contract with the city, the disparity between black and white employment persisted, and a new, conservative political atmosphere made it harder to attack. Finally, although more blacks were in positions of authority, their numbers fell below their proportion of the population, and the top level of government remained closed to them.

In each of these three stories—the fight against racism in law enforcement, the drive for equal employment, and the effort to earn real political power—the late 1970s marked a turning point, making those years the end of one story and, to some extent, the beginning of a different one. In part, changes in the political climate, specifically increased conservatism in federal government and in the local community, set limits that were obstacles to further change. The campaign for a civilian review board or aldermanic review of police conduct hit a dead end. The EEOC-mandated conciliation agreement in the police force ran out. The city adopted an affirmative action policy that moved that issue out of the realm of protest. And the political power of African Americans seemed to hit a plateau. In each case, a new set of characters emerged that would continue the struggle for racial equality. But another factor ended, or at least interrupted, these stories in the mid-1970s. They were all overshadowed by a crisis in race relations that came to dominate community life in the city: the conflict over busing and school desegregation.

8

The Busing Crisis

For two decades, the question of equal educational opportunity in the public schools had become a back-burner issue in Louisville. The city prided itself on having resolved that problem when it integrated the schools to great national acclaim in 1956. Yet in the mid-1970s, conflict over school desegregation sparked Louisville's worst race relations crisis of the postwar era. When, in September 1975, court-ordered busing began bringing black and white students together on a large scale in the newly merged city and county system, white opponents of integration launched a school boycott and mass demonstrations, the latter devolving into vandalism and rioting that required the intervention of the National Guard and earned the city condemnation from the national press. The local antibusing movement—the largest, most organized, and most vocal opposition seen during the civil rights era in Louisville—revealed the extent of resistance to further change in the racial status quo, particularly among whites in the newly developed suburban subdivisions just outside the city. Moreover, the rhetoric of the antibusers linked them to the rising New Right and tide of antigovernment conservatism that contributed to the hostile climate for progressive social activism.[1]

The crisis created by the antibusing movement, however, also produced an outburst of prointegration and antiracist activity on the part of traditional civil rights leaders, African American parents, and faith-based and secular human relations advocates. Some people and groups cared most about black access to good education and equal treatment in the schools. Many others focused on the interrelatedness of segregation in housing and schools. More important, the constituent parts of this coalition responded to what they saw as a rising, and frightening, level of open racism in the community. But just as the antibusing movement revealed the limits of the acceptance of integration by large segments of the local population, the experience of these prointegration activists over the next year raised questions about the efficacy of the traditional civil rights tactics of demonstrations, boycotts, public persuasion, and politics. Thus, during the busing crisis, a wide variety of groups and individuals rallied in an increasingly hostile climate to try to overcome not only the opposition to school integration but the persistent problem of racism, searching as they did so for a new combination of tactics that could be effective against an old enemy.

In the decade and a half after Louisville received fulsome praise for the peaceful integration of its public schools, evidence mounted that the job was not done after all. Throughout the early 1960s, school officials reported steady progress in the number of black teachers on previously all-white faculties and the rising percentage of students who attended "mixed" schools. Observers noted, however, that often that mixture included only "one or two [students] of the minority race." After the Civil Rights Act of 1964 threatened to cut federal funding for segregated schools, token integration and the continued existence of single-race schools drew increasing attention. In a study conducted in response to the law, the Kentucky Board of Education declared four schools in the city in danger of losing their support. Not long after, the HRC criticized the "limited integration of teachers, and administrative and supervising personnel" in the system. The most sweeping and damning indictment, however, came in the 1971 Kentucky Commission on Human Rights report *Louisville School System Retreats to Segregation,* which concluded that, over the preceding decade, the city schools had become racially isolated—when at least 90 percent of the student body was of one race—and in fact the polarization of the schools was worse than at any time since 1956. The report charged bluntly that "the Louisville school system has failed—either by design or by lack of effort—to deliver on the promise of full student and faculty desegregation."[2]

In response to this growing body of evidence, the NAACP began to push local officials to integrate remaining single-race facilities and to expand numbers beyond tokenism. After the Supreme Court ruled against "freedom of choice" plans in *Green v. County School Board of*

New Kent County in 1968, African Americans threatened legal action if the city did not drop the transfer option. The local NAACP received guidance from the national organization, which was devoting more energy to the school issue in anticipation of the impending ten-year deadline for desegregation established by the Civil Rights Act. In 1969 the NAACP national education director urged the Louisville group to call on the U.S. Department of Health, Education, and Welfare (HEW), which had been charged with enforcing the education component of the Civil Rights Act, for help. Two months later, the NAACP filed a complaint with HEW accusing the city of using discriminatory zoning, pupil placement, and the transfer plan to reinforce racial isolation in the schools. While the complaint was being investigated, the superintendent of schools, Samuel Noe, retired, and the system hired a young reformer named Newman Walker, formerly of Paducah, Kentucky. Walker agreed with the NAACP and promised to work with it and HEW to improve integration in the system.[3]

Meanwhile, persistent segregation and a board of education that refused to do anything about it plagued the county school system. The percentage of students attending school with those of another race had always lagged behind that in the city system. Teacher integration, too, remained a problem in the early 1960s; in the county elementary schools, not a single white student was taught by a black instructor. Moreover, assignment policies and busing bolstered student segregation.[4] After the Supreme Court's ruling in *Swann v. Charlotte-Mecklenburg Board of Education* that busing children was a legitimate and constitutional means to erase the racial identification of schools, HEW ordered Jefferson County to desegregate the all-black Newburg Elementary School by fall 1971. The county school board drew up a number of plans to do so, each of which put the burden of busing completely on black children. When HEW rejected all of the proposals, the county school board voted to ignore the integration deadline, at the risk of losing $4 million in federal funds, and seemingly invited a lawsuit.[5] Almost immediately, the KCLU obliged the board with a suit to force the integration of the school.[6]

Having launched that suit, the KCLU turned its attention to the city system and, after some debate over the appropriate remedy to seek, in June 1972 joined the NAACP in suing for the desegregation of the Louisville schools through annexation of white students who lived in the contiguous suburbs. Almost immediately, because its staff believed annexation would not be enough, the Kentucky Commission on Human Rights filed an intervention in the case, asking the court to order the merger of local school districts instead. Judge James F. Gordon of the western district court of Kentucky quickly declared that he could not order either merger or annexation. Then, after hearing arguments on the consolidated city and county suits, in March 1973 Gordon ruled that the systems were not segregated and that they were in compliance with constitutional requirements under previous school desegregation rulings. School officials were elated and relieved.[7]

Civil rights advocates, of course, had a different response. Disappointed but not deterred, they vowed to appeal the decision to the U.S. Court of Appeals for the Sixth Circuit in Cincinnati. Six months later, a three-judge panel at the appeals court heard evidence that 83 percent of city schools were "racially identifiable." Their decision, announced on December 28, 1973, was almost diametrically opposed to Gordon's. They ruled that both the city and county violated previous court rulings because they had failed to "eliminate all vestiges of state imposed segregation." Moreover, the court ordered Gordon to hold hearings on plans for desegregating the schools by the start of the new school year in September 1974. The options proposed at the time for doing so included merging the system, cross-district busing, and integrating each system separately.[8] Thus in the spring of 1974, with a notable lack of enthusiasm, the school boards of the city and county began to formulate plans for integration.

As the school boards met to produce the plan, rumors of the extent of busing they were considering ignited the first mass white opposition. Over the next several years, myriad grassroots antibusing organizations formed behind a number of outspoken leaders. Some were relatively large and enduring, including Concerned Parents under Susan Connor, which at one time claimed sixteen thousand members, and Citizens against Busing behind William Kellerman. Others lasted for only one demonstration or were mentioned fleetingly in the press and then disappeared from view. The first major antibusing organization was Save Our Community Schools (SOCS), led by Joyce Spond. It began in 1971 as a small group of women in Shively who were concerned that busing might happen in Jefferson County. By that time, transportation of some students was commonplace, but the founders of SOCS were responding to the controversy over Newburg Elementary School and the threat of busing being used for the purpose of integration.

The organization incorporated in 1972 and eventually had a newsletter mailing list of three thousand people. Spond came from nearby Nelson County, and she and her husband, a business agent for Teamsters Local 89, owned farms in Hardin and Meade counties, though they lived in Jefferson County. Their children attended Butler High School, which because of its racial balance was not likely to be affected by busing. But that did not stop Spond from getting involved in the issue. SOCS and Spond herself would remain influential, though relatively moderate, leaders of the antibusing crusade through the mid-1970s.[9]

As the prospect of busing became more real, SOCS focused its attention on a resolution introduced to the General Assembly by Representative Dottie Priddy that called for an antibusing amendment to the Kentucky constitution. Spond claimed to have petitions with twenty thousand signatures supporting the amendment. She added that some African Americans had signed, though that was not verified, and insisted that her organization was against busing, not against integration, a refrain repeated by antibusing organizations throughout the ensuing crisis. Within a two-week period, SOCS leaders and others sponsored a rally of seven hundred people on one occasion and a thousand people on another and led a group of two hundred to Frankfort to support Priddy's measure. The General Assembly rejected the proposed amendment but did pass a resolution calling for the federal government to enact such an amendment. Meanwhile, antibusing sentiment spread in the county among white students and their parents. In late February, white students boycotted class at Fairdale High School and walked out briefly from Pleasure Ridge Park High School, Southern High School, and Lassiter Middle School to express their opposition to busing. And on the eve of the official announcement of the plan, angry white parents took two hours to berate the county board for considering busing their children to city schools.[10]

Less dramatically and with less public attention, during this period an interracial coalition of individuals and civic groups began to organize support for busing and countywide desegregation. The lawsuits that culminated in the court order had originated from cooperation between civil rights groups—chiefly the NAACP—and the predominantly white KCLU, thus grounding the issue in biracial cooperation. In 1972 the Ad Hoc Committee for School Integration formed to educate the public about the need for integration in general and busing in particular. Then, in early 1974, a number of other organizations endorsed the court order and hosted programs to smooth the way for its implementation. The list of these organizations overlapped strikingly with those who had worked for open housing; moreover, their goal of creating a positive community climate for integration hearkened back to the efforts of community groups and school administrators in 1956. The HRC, for example, held meetings with white suburban organizations to help find ways to make busing work, and the local units of the National Council of Jewish Women and League of Women Voters once again sought, as they had with open housing beginning in 1963, to foster productive discussion by hosting public forums.[11]

Participants in this fledgling probusing movement demonstrated their willingness to speak out against the growing local and national backlash against court-ordered integration at a county board of education meeting shortly after the plan was announced. In contrast to rallies across the county denouncing the prospect of busing, in this case a group of about 150 people "turned out to congratulate the board." Sally Baker, speaking for Citizens for Affirmative Integration, argued that quality education required integration and promised to work with any other like-minded organization toward promoting acceptance of the plan. Tom Jones, a Jefferson County resident representing an unnamed, unorganized group of what he claimed were hundreds of black and white concerned citizens, spoke up, calling the fears of his white neighbors about school integration "hogwash." The Eastern Area Council submitted a list of suggestions for how the school board might prepare teachers, students, and the community.[12]

Meanwhile, a court case initiated in Detroit caused a legal snag that postponed implementation of the order. In late July, the Supreme Court ruled in *Milliken v. Bradley* against cross-district busing to achieve integration and remanded the Louisville and Jefferson County case to the court of appeals for reconsideration. With school desegregation ruled out for the fall of 1974, civil rights leaders and their lawyers returned to court to argue that the reasoning and conditions in *Milliken* did not apply to the local case. They asserted that the Supreme Court had declared cross-district busing acceptable if both districts had been found to be in constitutional violation, as both Louisville and Jefferson County had been. Moreover, they pointed out that district lines had been crossed historically for the purposes of maintaining segregation, and thus those lines should not be used as an impediment to correcting segregation now. In December 1974 the appeals court upheld its decision of the year before. Ruling that, in this case, district lines could be crossed for the purposes of desegregation, it reopened the door for countywide busing.[13]

In the middle of this legal battle, the Louisville school system began the process that led to the merger of the school systems, making any challenge to cross-district busing moot. The possibility of merging the two systems had come up periodically since the 1950s, but consideration of the move repeatedly bogged down in questions of money and concerned parties' potential benefits and losses.[14] But after the original circuit court decision in December 1973, and with fiscal problems threatening the shutdown of facilities in the city system, the Louisville board began to push to bring the two districts together. At first, county officials expressed willingness to consider the idea, and within a month, the state legislature passed a law sponsored by Louisville representative Norbert Blume to enable it. But negotiations about how to accomplish it, which occurred simultaneously with and were intricately connected to those regarding a desegregation plan, got held up by "philosophical differences, personalities, and old resentments." General distrust, as well as concerns about how to integrate the two boards, protect black representation, and coordinate different approaches to education, hampered any agreement. It was not until the implication of the appeals court ruling sank in—busing could occur regardless of whether the districts remained separate—that county opposition softened. After a few more months spent working out the details of representation on a combined board, the two systems finally merged in April 1975. This established a unified district charged with finding ways to integrate its schools.[15]

After the circuit court ruling and the merger of the systems, planning for desegregation began again, though it was still hampered by divisions over implementation and relied on pressure from the courts to move it along. When the parties still could not agree on a plan in July 1975, the circuit court grew impatient and ordered Gordon to come up with one. A few weeks later he did so, and in early August, he announced the busing plan that would assign students to schools one month later. Under Gordon's plan, all schools had between 12 and 35 percent black student bodies. To accomplish this, white students were bused to school during one or two academic years, whereas black students traveled every school day for as many as nine years. One black school and a number of white schools were joined in a cluster, and students moved among them alphabetically by their last names. The plan exempted any schools with ratios that fell into the prescribed range, rewarding already integrated schools, as well as all seniors and first graders for the first year. Gordon charged the schools with assigning students and working out the logistics before school started on September 4.[16]

In the summer of 1975, as the courts deliberated and school officials developed the final student assignments, the opposition to busing grew increasingly vocal. The editorial pages of the papers carried nearly daily letters from citizens expressing their views on the issue, overwhelmingly in the negative. The uniformity in the arguments against the busing plan, which called it a dictatorial action by Judge Gordon against the rights of the majority, was striking. Explicit references to race were rare, although some writers hinted that the civil rights movement had gone too far, and anticommunism arose again. When leaders of various antibusing organizations spoke at hearings of the U.S. Commission on Civil Rights a year later, their remarks confirmed the importance of these themes. Writers of letters to the *Louisville Times* declared, "We are not against desegregation or integration" but for "quality education for all." They considered busing to be "discrimination in reverse," however. More emphatically, they insisted that "forced busing reduces our basic freedom" and was a "communist-inspired" act of judicial tyranny that had taken the rights of the parents and made their children the property of the state.[17]

The sentiment in these letters and pronouncements reflected the rise of a New Right ideology, which viewed the social movements of the 1960s as having gone too far and leading to overweening federal government power. This rhetoric resembled that of the anti–open housing movement—indeed, the language of "forced housing" easily transformed to "forced busing"—in the emphasis on the loss of majority rights rather than on a defense of segregation. It is worth noting that, based on the addresses listed with the letters, many of the authors resided in the same southern Louisville neighborhoods that had so vocally opposed open housing or in the contiguous southern and southwestern parts of the county. That the two most concerted opposition movements of the civil rights era were grounded in the same rhetoric and location was no coincidence. The connections between the oppositions to open housing and to school desegregation through busing demonstrate that, in arenas where there was potential for more extensive "mixing"—in neighborhoods and schools, where children and families met—resistance to integration was strongest, especially when it was perceived as happening over private wishes and at the hands of government. The same men and women who might work with African Americans on the plant floor regarded their personal control of their children, homes, neighborhoods, and schools as a hard-won privilege not to be yielded to outside authorities in the name of integration. This belief became the mainspring of resistance to busing that animated a large segment of the community for the next several years.[18]

The geographic and class makeup of the opposition became clearer when labor organizations representing the white working class of the county started to speak out. At a public meeting in early August about the impending change in the school system, labor leaders told city and county officials that their rank-and-file members resolutely opposed busing. Delbert J. Melcher, secretary of the Kentucky State Building and Construction Trades Council, went further, saying not only would he "not endorse a program [that is] an outrageous miscarriage of justice," but he also would not advise his members to be peaceful or abide by the law. In the next few weeks, union locals began publishing advertisements in and sending letters to the papers announcing their resolutions against busing. In late August, United Electrical Workers Local 761, at the GE plant, one of the largest and strongest unions in the area, joined with two antibusing organizations—Parents for Freedom and Citizens against Busing—for a demonstration of about seven hundred people downtown. Local 761 executive board member James Luckett called for workers to show their opposition to busing by staying home from work, saying, "A general strike is the only answer to busing." Thereafter, organized in United Labor against Busing (ULAB), union opponents to busing began calling for a boycott of the schools and work stoppages during the first day of classes.[19] This blue-collar component of the antibusing movement reflected in part the defensive insecurity of working-class Americans, who felt squeezed between the economic downturn of the time and their perception that the federal government was helping others at their expense. It also recalled the lack of support for unionists Carl Braden and Andrew Wade by the local rank and file during the 1950s crisis, conflating housing and school desegregation.

The tension around busing rose dramatically when it attracted the first major appearance of the Ku Klux Klan in the community. With the exception of some extremist elements in the anti–open housing crowds, Louisville had not experienced much agitation by regional or national segregationist organizations in the civil rights era. When a few segregationist organizers like Millard Grubbs tried to rally whites to join the Klan or the WCC, they had little luck. But in mid-July 1975, a new organization, the Kentucky Tax Payers' Association, which described itself as "a coalition of conservative and right-wing philosophies," invited the Klan to a rally at a local Holiday Inn, which was attended by approximately four hundred people. An induction ceremony for new members and a series of rallies around the country followed over the next months. At these gatherings, regional and local leaders of the organization promised not just to protect community schools but to stop integration. Busing was part of "an assault on white people since 1963," they insisted, and, invoking the fear of miscegenation seen in the massive resistance to an earlier round of school integration, it was a step in the NAACP's plan for producing a "coffee colored race." These remarks not only alarmed African Americans and their white allies in the prointegration cause but also contradicted the claim of local antibusing leaders that they did not oppose integration per se.[20]

The increasingly vocal opposition to busing sparked a series of last-minute efforts to rally support for it and for integration. The ad hoc prointegration civic groups that had formed around the time of the lawsuits had begun this work, but in the last month there was a wider burst of activity. The school administration cosponsored workshops with the Urban League at which representatives of thirty churches heard suggestions for how to promote peaceful implementation of the busing system. New community organizations also sprang up. The predominantly black Council of Parents for Quality Education, organized by BWC member Robert Cunningham, called for integration as the best way to get their children into the schools where the best resources were. A group of media professionals sponsored CALM—Concerned about Louisville's Mood—which posted advertisements asking people to keep their cool. Black and white religious leaders also urged their congregants to abide by the law. Perhaps unsurprisingly, the majority-black Louisville Area Baptist Ministers and Deacons deplored unlawful and disruptive opposition to the desegregation plan. But the Fern Creek Ministerial Association, located in the heart of the predominantly white southwestern corner of the county, also encouraged peace and acceptance. Finally, on the eve of the new school year, a student organization published a list of dos and don'ts for their parents, admonishing them in biblical language: "Thou shalt obey the desegregation law."[21]

In addition to this support for school integration, the appearance of the Klan and smaller extremist groups over the summer provoked an alliance of left-wing, antiwar, and black power organizations to confront the rising visibility of racism in the community. The reaction started with a few public pronouncements condemning the Klan's arrival in the area and criticizing it for being the enemy not only of African Americans but also of the working-class whites who were rallying against busing. Then, as the opening day of school neared and people started fearing potential violence by the opposition, a coalition of groups called People United, which included, among others, the Black Panther Party, SCEF, the Council of Parents for Quality Education, and the International Socialists, sponsored a rally and march to show concern for the students and opposition to the "racist boycott movement." Rally speakers demanded that the buses receive protection, that demonstrations be banned near the schools, and that the schools themselves be improved and teach black history. After this initial event, the group promised to conduct more actions on the first day of school, and it sponsored small demonstrations downtown, but then it faded from the scene. In the members' rhetoric and their focus on fighting the Klan, however, they highlighted the connection between the issue of the schools and the larger fight against right-wing and racist reaction to change.[22]

With all the agitation both against and in favor of busing and integration, the atmosphere in the local area became increasingly tense. Just before the opening day of school, black parents held meetings at which they expressed their fears for the mental and physical well-being of their children. At the same time, a biracial group of young people based in school-sponsored human relations clubs expressed their own trepidation about what the antibusing forces might do in their frustration. City officials acknowledged this level of anxiety by promising to uphold the law and do their best to make sure Louisville did not become the next Boston—one of many references during this period to the turmoil that had rocked the northern city the previous September. To demonstrate their commitment to enforcing the court order, city and school officials, with the support of Judge Gordon, set up rules limiting demonstrations and forbidding obstruction of the buses. Moreover, city police chief John Nevin took elaborate precautions to prepare his officers, devoting half the department to a busing task force, training them in mob control, and establishing a tight chain of command for emergency situations.[23]

Amid all this growing tension, the relative quiet of the first day of school on September 4 allowed officials and civic leaders to breathe a sigh of relief. Although, the night before the schools opened, a mass rally of between ten and fifteen thousand people at the Kentucky State Fairgrounds once again revealed the extent of antibusing feeling in the community, and two thousand labor and Klan protestors marched downtown, the schools themselves were quiet, and demonstrations were for the most part confined to the protest zones designated by Gordon. The relatively low student turnout on opening day may have helped. The boycott organized by Concerned Parents and the fear of what might happen at the schools led many white and a few black parents to keep their children at home. In one hopeful sign that morning, white football players at Fairdale High School met the black students at the bus, welcomed them, and escorted them into the building. By the end of the day, the local and national media pronounced the first day of school a success and concluded it was "evidence of a community's good sense."[24]

Unfortunately, the events of the next twenty-four hours quickly disproved that verdict. Over the course of the second day of school and that evening, violence broke out around four county high schools, leading to vandalism, arson, rioting, and ultimately the arrival of the Kentucky National Guard. Despite the promise of the first morning, by the end of the second day, about 150 protesters gathered at Fairdale High School and began attacking school buses. Belying the claim that opposition to busing was based in concern about the loss of majority rights and not in racial antagonism, signs in the crowd and chants included phrases such as "Keep the niggers out of our school" and "Do away with the nigs and pigs." Later in the evening, the crowd grew and set a bonfire in the center of the road, blocking traffic. At first, county police officers stationed nearby allowed the fire to burn, saying it was in the street and not threatening damage. But after gunshots at a nearby furniture store—the owner was reportedly defending his property against demonstrators—police began to try to disperse the crowd. Confrontations lasted until three in the morning. A similar situation occurred at Pleasure Ridge Park High School, where, around 8 p.m., protestors lit a fire and blocked traffic. Earlier in the day, protesters had jeered and taunted blacks on the buses as they left the school; in this case the crowd was led in a chant of "white power" by young men wearing Nazi symbols. The nighttime demonstration quieted for a few hours during a school football game. But when the game was over and school security officers tried to direct the crowd away, a fight broke out between the county and state police and the demonstrators.[25]

These skirmishes paled in comparison to the violence at Southern and Valley high schools. In the afternoon of September 5, along Dixie Highway near Valley High School, protesters began gathering and slowing traffic by blocking lanes with debris. When a county police officer tried to clear the road and threatened to arrest one man, a crowd began throwing things at him. About thirty officers were able to clear the mob. But within a few hours, a larger one had reformed, reaching approximately ten thousand people by late in the evening. Protesters milled about, waved signs, yelled at passing cars, and lit a bonfire in the road. The mood became tenser when they began throwing bricks and debris at police. One officer was hit in the eye with a lead fishing weight. Also injured were two children, presumably white since the newspapers reported no African Americans on the scene. Glass from a broken window hit a three-year-old girl, and an eleven-year-old boy was inexplicitly beaten. At around 10 p.m., when fifty to seventy-five police officers in helmets moved in to clear the crowd and the road, more fighting broke out. Police arrested just under two hundred demonstrators, and, according to the county chief of police, Russell McDaniel, at least twenty officers sustained injuries.[26]

The worst of the violence was at Southern High School, where a mob of two thousand burned buses, set fires, broke windows in local businesses, and attacked police well into the early hours of the next morning. During the day on September 5, about two hundred marchers had mingled outside the school and along Preston Highway nearby. Although local Klan leader Walter Groves was present and Concerned Parents petitions circulated, people in the crowd claimed no organization was behind the gathering. Indeed, one woman insisted it was just "plain every day people" who opposed the judge's actions; the crowd, she said, "makes you proud of this damned neighborhood." Later in the day, the protestors began stopping traffic and, according to news reports, what started out "peacefully around 9 pm turned nasty about 10." When the crowd started breaking windows, about forty officers who had been working near Valley High School were dispatched to dispel it. When the protestors refused to move, the police used tear gas and moved into the crowd. The demonstrators fought back, and a battle broke out as the line between crowd and police edged back and forth. One officer noted later, "Never would I have dreamed that these people would treat us like they did tonight." Officers were not above reproach, however; some beat demonstrators or dragged them from the scene. Meanwhile, crowds blocked firefighting equipment from the area. County police struggled to clear the streets and establish calm, finally doing so around 2:30 a.m. and going home, leaving newly arrived state police to patrol in case of further outbreaks. By the end of the night, county police had made 192 arrests, mostly for disorderly conduct and resisting arrest but also for assault and battery and more serious charges.[27]

Ironically, at a joint press conference early in the evening of September 5, Mayor Harvey Sloane and County Judge Executive Todd Hollenbach had praised the order and calm in the schools. Also in the midevening, Governor Julian Carroll had said he did not think the National Guard would be necessary in Jefferson County. Within hours all three officials changed their tune. Carroll initially sent one hundred state officers to aid the county police. By the next morning, he ordered in three hundred more and, in response to a request for help from Hollenbach, called up eight hundred members of the National Guard, who patrolled the county in riot gear and with small arms. Meanwhile, although the city was unscarred overnight, Sloane issued an order banning all demonstrations until further notice to prevent more trouble. The following day, Judge Gordon issued an order abolishing the protest areas and banning any assembly on school property or along bus routes while buses were operating.[28]

With the exception of an illegal march Saturday morning, the clampdown on protests and the presence of the National Guard helped restore order to the city. In violation of Sloane's overnight order against demonstrations within the city limits, a group of protesters gathered downtown. In response, a phalanx of five hundred officers arrested or dispersed anyone who even appeared to be protesting. After that, demonstrations near the schools dropped, leaving the protest zones nearly abandoned. National guardsmen rode the buses to protect the students, and that further discouraged confrontations on the bus routes and outside the schools. Early the next week, school attendance was down, reflecting parents' understandable fears. By Friday, however,

numbers climbed above 75 percent and in some places up to capacity, although antibusing leaders disputed those numbers and insisted
more students were still boycotting. Within a week, Sloane revoked
his order against demonstrations, and local leaders again began to feel
that things were returning to normal. The quick return of relative calm
impressed outside observers such as *New York Times* reporter William
K. Stevens, who covered Louisville and Jefferson County's school desegregation case. He praised the local community for its acceptance of
integration and invoked Louisville's history of racial moderation and
tolerance, based in its border city position, as the cause of the rapid
end of the crisis.[29]

These declarations that the crisis was over were premature. The
same day Stevens lauded the city's moderation in the *New York Times,*
the Louisville papers reported a rally at a Catholic church followed by
a motorcade through the west end of one hundred cars organized by a
short-lived—this was its only demonstration—coalition of antibusing
groups called the Spirit of '76. During the rally, William Kellerman of
Citizens against Busing accused officials of violating protesters' constitutional rights and promised to revive and expand opposition activity.
Two weeks later, police had to use tear gas to break up a mob of four
hundred outside a county high school, and in reaction the next day,
eight thousand antibusing demonstrators marched through downtown
in a protest hastily organized by Concerned Parents. Prointegration
activists compiled a list of over a dozen such demonstrations and rallies
in September alone, ranging in size from ten people to six thousand. By
late fall, these gatherings were getting more menacing. In early December, while hundreds of busing opponents marched again downtown,
people in the crowd shouted insults at black pedestrians. In one incident a crowd chanting "Kill these niggers, kill these niggers" surrounded an African American man, Daryl Spain. A black police officer
pulled him to safety but then suffered punishment from his superiors
because he had brandished a gun when doing so. Antibusing leader
Kellerman admitted the "tone of the marches is getting rougher" but
blamed frustration and obstruction by officials for bringing out the
worst in people.[30]

Throughout the fall of 1975, ULAB sponsored many of the large-
scale demonstrations, indicating the importance of union members
in the opposition to integration. Throughout September union locals
continued to publish advertisements announcing their opposition to

busing. Meanwhile, rank-and-file members expressed their anger by unofficially striking—that is, staying home from work in organized sick days. Absenteeism got so high at the Ford and GE plants that production was curtailed, and Ford closed for a day. In late October, ULAB sponsored a road trip of union members to Washington DC to lobby for federal intervention against busing. It solicited the support of antibusers across the country, especially in the labor movement, mirroring the tradition of Louisville civil rights forces seeking common cause with like-minded people elsewhere. Meanwhile, the group sponsored, or cosponsored with other organizations, a series of late fall rallies and demonstrations. On November 22, a mass march downtown led to violence once again. Roving demonstrators smashed windows at the offices of the *Louisville Courier-Journal,* chanted racial slurs, and attacked a black man who was walking down the street with a white woman. The city suggested that ULAB pay for some of the property damage, but the organization refused, saying the violence was the work of outsiders and not its own members. Officials did not press the matter.[31]

In reaction to the antibusing riots and the growing tension in the community, a group of white and black activists formed Progress in Education (PIE), which became the leading probusing and prointegration organization in the city. On September 9, approximately ninety people representing "church, labor, civic, and political groups" gathered at the First Unitarian Church to express their "outrage over the racist intimidation and violence" aimed at parents and students during the first days of school and to condemn the actions of the rioters of the previous Friday night. At that meeting, they agreed to form PIE to support school desegregation and "busing as a means to achieve" it. But more broadly, the group pledged to oppose the rising racism in the community by taking positive action for integration and against the antibusing movement. Those present set up committees to help businesses resist intimidation, convince unions to eschew racial division, promote expressions of positive support, and monitor the school board and public officials. Anne Braden and Suzy Post, who in addition to her work with the KCLU was one of the plaintiffs in the suit against the city schools, were instrumental in arranging the opening meeting. Jackie Garrett, a white mother of two who had previously not been involved in civil rights activity, became the head of the new organization.[32]

For its first action, PIE organized a mass rally and march on October 11 to "make a gigantic public witness to sanity and justice and good will" and pay tribute to the students, teachers, and bus drivers who had stood up to intimidation. Over one hundred well-known and respected black and white leaders, including Alderwoman Lois Morris, Suzy Post, Episcopal bishop C. Gresham Marmion, and representatives of labor and civil rights groups, endorsed the event. The rally started with music by Pete Seeger, a friend of Braden's who came because, in her invitation, Braden linked Louisville to Boston and depicted the local crisis as "a major testing ground for new racist offensives." His participation exemplified the prointegration movement's connection to a national network against the backlash to civil rights in the 1970s. After Seeger performed, labor and religious figures spoke, as did parents, who described some of the problems their children had confronted on the buses. When the mass meeting ended, five hundred to eight hundred people marched downtown, "singing songs made popular during the civil rights movement of the 1950s," according to former activist Mervin Aubespin, now a journalist. Garrett described the march as the beginning of "turning the tide against racism in this community" and hoped it would lead to more white people's speaking out.[33] In these comments, observers and participants made clear that they saw their actions as part of a larger antiracism movement.

While PIE tried to promote calm, busing opponents kept up their fight. Though they still hit the streets, they began to use other strategies to express their opposition and to pressure officials to change policy. In the initial months of the school year, antibusing leaders threatened and to some extent orchestrated a boycott of businesses that seemed to support the busing policy and those that would not overtly oppose it. All through September, antibusing leaders called for people to use their economic power by boycotting all businesses "except for medicine, groceries, and gas from stations refusing to service the buses," referring to white service station owners who were trying to force the end of busing by refusing to provide fuel. In addition to leading nonbuying campaigns, antibusing leaders organized a work stoppage for October 1, forcing some businesses to shut down. After antibusing signs were distributed to south end and county establishments, those that did not post them were boycotted, forcing some, such as the A&P grocery chain, to agree to close for a day and to withdraw their support from a community pledge to uphold the law. After that, small businesses in the area reported receiving threatening calls that their property might be damaged for not posting the signs, showing how quickly a nonviolent strategy—a boycott—could become entangled with the threat of violence. The boycott of businesses appears never to have caught on with the broader public, however; moreover, it was aimed at individuals and entities that had little power to change busing policy.[34]

Another form of boycott—keeping children out of the public schools—continued throughout the school year as busing opponents sought ways to escape the local system. In the initial days of school, as noted above, news sources reported first a dramatic drop in attendance and then a slow increase to normal. But some parents persisted in keeping their children home and trying to find alternative education for them. The local media reported that seventy-seven Louisville and Jefferson County families had moved to Floyd and Clark counties in southern Indiana in the summer of 1975. Some families sent children eligible for busing to live with relatives in other counties or "camped out" in mobile homes outside the Jefferson County border. Nearby districts tried to prevent these maneuvers by announcing they would not be "havens" and making their rules regarding which students they would accept more stringent. Likewise, the Catholic archdiocese adopted strict procedures limiting new enrollment to siblings of those already in the schools and families with a connection to the parish.[35] A more collective reaction, and one that reflected trends elsewhere in the South, was the opening of a spate of private, often church-affiliated, schools. After a slow start, which antibusing leaders attributed to the short time between the final court decree and the start of classes and a wish by most parents to retake control of the neighborhood schools, by October forty churches had initiated plans for independent Christian schools. Many of these survived only a short time, victims of the state accreditation process and the loss of enthusiasm or lack of money from parents. But, at the same time, the existing private schools saw an increased enrollment of seven hundred, or 22 percent of their former numbers. And, despite efforts to limit the rush to their doors, the student bodies of the Catholic schools also increased.[36]

Some of the attention of the antibusing forces focused on the upcoming November election and a concerted effort to unseat local officials or, in the words of one common slogan, "vote the ins out." Authors of letters to the editor, rally speakers, and leaders of antibusing organizations voiced general anti-incumbent sentiment, blaming elected and appointed officials for not preventing busing and calling for the election of those who would stand up for the "wishes of the majority." To get this message across, antibusing organizers provided bumper stickers, held campaign rallies, and sponsored voter registration drives. In one case, over three thousand voter registration forms were picked up during an antibusing demonstration downtown, and one report held that over seven thousand new voters had registered by late September. As the election neared, one new antibusing group circulated "not wanted" posters listing Hollenbach, Sloane, and Gordon, as well as the city and county police chiefs and the city attorney, and offering voters advice about how to remove them from office. Sue Connor's group, Concerned Parents, also published a detailed voter recommendation guide. With all this energy poured into the campaign, local candidates could not help but take notice, and they scrambled to prove themselves the most opposed to busing. At the same time, local Democrats who were vehemently antibusing, such as state legislator Dottie Priddy, who was arrested for participating in the disturbances on the second day of school, worried that the anti-incumbent and anti-Democratic tide could hurt the antibusing movement's allies in the county.[37]

Ironically, most of the men listed as "not wanted" or targeted for ouster in letters to the editor were not even on the ballot in the fall of 1975. Neither Hollenbach nor Sloane was up for reelection, and appointed officials such as Judge Gordon and police chief Nevin could not be removed by the ballot. Moreover, none of those who were running for office were in any position to overturn the court's order. The focus of attention thus became Julian Carroll's reelection campaign for governor, and the question became whether he was sufficiently opposed to busing. Throughout the fall, Carroll, a Democrat, tried to prove his bona fides as an opponent of busing by testifying at U.S. Senate hearings and offering to work for a constitutional amendment against it. Regardless of how much he criticized busing, however, the leaders of opposition groups repeatedly accused him of not doing enough. Yet on election day, despite predictions that antibusing sentiment would lead to an anti-incumbent and anti-Democratic sweep, Carroll won the governor's race by a large margin. He even won Jefferson County, the first Democratic candidate for governor to do so since 1955, though just barely. Meanwhile, almost the entire Democratic slate sailed into office with him, with only two Republicans from Jefferson County picking up seats in the state legislature. Despite two months of noisy threats and heated emotion, the antibusing forces failed to translate their anger into sufficient votes to affect their only target who was up for election. Whether it was because people believed Carroll had done all he could, voted on other issues, or realized local officials could not really affect the policy is impossible to know.[38]

When political activity and other strategies did not accomplish the antibusing forces' goals, or provided a haven for only a small number of students escaping the system, some people became attracted to more extreme organizations, rhetoric, and tactics. The main source of the extremism in the antibusing movement was the Klan, whose national and regional leaders saw a ripe opportunity for growth in the local area during the fall of 1975 because of what they characterized as the "helplessness and frustration" of the antibusing forces. At one point, leaders claimed that local membership had doubled in one month and included 18 city and county policemen. In November a public ceremony inducted 132 local people into the local Klan unit, and throughout the school year, there was a rise in threats against parents who sent their children to the schools in violation of the boycott and gas stations that served the buses.[39] At gatherings around the county, often in McNeely Lake Park in south Jefferson County, speakers used racial epithets and called for white supremacy while stirring up anticommunism and anti-Semitism. The rhetoric at these rallies also hinted at the possibility of violence. On one occasion, Phillip Chopper, Grand Dragon of the local Klan, called for the lynching of Judge Gordon, for which he was investigated by the FBI, leading to his arrest on an outstanding warrant in another state. On another occasion, an Indiana leader declared, "By God if the ballots don't work, you better damn well believe we got the bullets, baby." Meanwhile, Klansman Walter Groves, though in one breath claiming to be nonviolent, in another promised to "string" to the "nearest telephone pole" any African American who came near his home "causing trouble." Although their numbers were disputed by officials and their significance was magnified by extensive coverage in the daily papers, the mere presence of Klan organizations contributed to a sense of crisis in the community because the name inspired fears of racism and conflict.[40]

Though the Klan was the best known, other extremist organizations used the busing crisis to push their agendas. In fall 1975, the Reverend Lowell Hughes of Parents for Freedom started a unit of

Posse Comitatus, an antitax, anti–gun control group, which founded Constitution Farm in Bullitt County, just south of Jefferson County, as a "training center for the defense and protection of white Christian America." In October a new organization, the National Association to Restore and Preserve Our Freedom, formed to "unite all freedom loving Americans" by liberating "the children who's [sic] safety, moral and educational standard is threatened by this monster called forced busing." The newsletter of the group carried essays linking busing with other concerns of contemporary right-wing political movements. Not only did writers regularly associate busing with a Communist plan to stir up racial hostility, but they also raised the moral issues associated with the Religious Right, including opposition to sex education and the purported moral decline in the schools. Although these groups were never large in number and did not represent the majority of busing opponents, their rhetoric illustrated the ideological connections made between the opposition to integration through busing and the resistance to federal government authority, which animated the right wing of the rising conservative movement.[41]

A wave of violence aimed at black residents of predominantly white areas soon spread across the county. The fate of the Colemans, an African American family in Okolona, received the most attention. In 1974 Alfis Coleman moved his family into a home in a white subdivision near McNeely Lake. They encountered little hostility until busing started and the Klan began using McNeely Lake Park for its rallies. Then, on September 10, 1975, rocks came through the children's bedroom windows with notes saying, "Niggers go back where you came from—Africa" and "Get out of Jefferson County, We don't want your trouble." Later that evening, the family received a call from someone threatening to burn the house, and Coleman found a bottle of diesel fuel in the yard. In November three cars pulled in front of the house and the passengers shot into it, damaging the Colemans' car and the fence. Coleman gave the shot casings to the FBI but never heard anything in response. When he started missing work to stay home to protect his family, he lost his job. Then, in March, dynamite was thrown in their driveway, and the explosion broke their windows. Though officials prosecuted no one in any of these incidents and thus the motivation cannot be proven, prointegration activists understandably saw in it a pattern of terrorism aimed at discouraging the housing integration that might contribute to school integration, and an expression of the racism that the antibusing movement had unleashed. Indeed, it must have brought back memories of the bombing of the Wade family home in the white suburbs in conjunction with the earlier wave of school desegregation.[42]

In the weeks following its opening rally and march, PIE focused much of its attention on organizing support and protection for the Coleman family because members saw the attacks against the family as one of the most overt expressions of the racism stirred up by the antibusing movement. The connection was hard to miss; shortly after the busing program started, a black family in a predominantly white section of the county, an area at the heart of much of the antibusing organizing and near the site of the Klan rallies, was attacked. After the second act of violence against the family on October 11, the same day as the first PIE rally, PIE members began staying with the family to help guard the house, much as members of the left and labor coalition of the postwar period had come to the aid of Andrew Wade. Over the next six months, PIE pressed the county police to provide better protection and do a better job seeking the perpetrators, criticizing both the "half hearted investigations" and the hints by one detective that PIE might have planted the bomb that damaged the house. The organization also reached out to others to broaden the coalition supporting the family and succeeded in getting help from other organizations, perhaps most important from the white south end Okolona Ministerial Association, which called for protection for the Coleman home. Eventually, PIE galvanized a collection of forty-six church, labor, and community organizations to protest the lack of justice for the family. Making explicit the connection between the busing crisis and broader issues of equal rights, PIE regarded its support for the Colemans as not just a statement against racism but also a chance to "affirm now the right of black people to live wherever" they chose. Despite the violence against them, by late spring the Colemans remained determined to stay in their home. Thereafter, their predicament fell out of public and media attention.[43]

PIE's criticism of county police in the Coleman case was one example of how the group monitored the actions of local officials in the busing crisis and pressed them to act in the interests of integration and fighting racism. The group considered Mayor Harvey Sloane, a liberal Democrat with a record of working with African American and civil rights communities, relatively better on the issue and more open to PIE's viewpoint. Although he opposed busing, in early September he stated that Louisville had an opportunity to demonstrate how to uphold a law even if one does not agree with it. He took steps such as establishing a police task force and working with traffic engineers to plan safe and efficient bus routes. His inaction in other areas and some of his comments did, however, cause complaint. He allowed the city police to display antibusing stickers on their vehicles, for example, stirring up complaints of racism among white officers again, and he gave a speech blaming the court's "late" decision for the crisis. But in late October, as Sloane prepared to go to Washington DC to testify before a Senate hearing on busing, he met with PIE members. Afterward, member Tom Moffett remarked, in a somewhat less than ringing endorsement, that at least Sloane had "been less negative than 95 percent of the other politicians."[44]

PIE's opinion of County Judge Executive Todd Hollenbach was less forgiving, for good reason. Hollenbach also began September with a pledge to uphold the court order, and he likewise arranged for special emergency measures on the first days of school. But within a month, it was clear that he was using his influence and county money to support the antibusing movement. He printed and circulated antibusing petitions, which he planned to take with him to the Senate hearing. He defended the move by saying he was representing the wishes of his constituents. Going beyond the duties of his office, he reached out to antibusing organizations in Boston and filed a friend of the court brief in a lawsuit on their behalf. He regularly met with leaders of the antibusing movement while refusing to meet with PIE representatives. For several weeks in the fall, PIE tried to force a meeting with the county judge executive and to organize a lawsuit challenging his use of tax money for his antibusing activities. Hollenbach eventually conceded to one meeting with PIE and other organizations, but he demonstrated no real interest in hearing their concerns or changing his behavior.[45]

In a move that led to a heated exchange between him and PIE, in November 1975 Hollenbach began sponsoring hearings to discuss alternatives to busing. At these meetings, speakers proposed potentially viable programs that would lead to further integration, such as magnet schools and improvements in the inner-city schools to make them attractive to voluntary transfers. Galen Martin of the Kentucky Commission on Human Rights and other integrationists used the opportunity to suggest that policies that led to integrated housing would make busing unnecessary. But, after a few sessions, the crowds began to get unruly. In southwest Jefferson County, antibusing protestors forced the shutdown of the hearing after pushing a white Korean War veteran, Edward N. Kleitz, of the southwest neighborhood Valley Station, from the podium after he linked housing desegregation to the issue. The fifteen-year-old daughter of Anne Braden was likewise silenced by crowds shouting "Nigger-lover," "Get out of here," and "Never, never" until she sat down. On another occasion, in Fairdale, a 350-person mob began screaming and slamming chairs when a PIE representative tried to speak. Afterward, Hollenbach blamed PIE, saying "any reasonable person" could have predicted the reaction to their presence. PIE members fired back that their organization had not caused the trouble, saying, "We do not burn crosses. . . . We do not break windows. . . . We do not terrorize black citizens living in white neighborhoods." Tensions between PIE and the county judge executive continued, as did Hollenbach's efforts to coordinate alternatives to the busing system.[46]

In their effort to confront the hostility evidenced in these meetings, PIE members and others reached out for help from those undergoing similar trials elsewhere, particularly cultivating a relationship with Boston's antiracist forces. The cooperation across distance illustrated not only how local activists made connections to a national movement but how the busing issue was linked to problems in race relations in general. As noted above, even before the 1975 school year started, some local civil rights advocates regularly made references to Boston to warn local officials to act to avoid the violence that had happened there. Louisvillians had long compared themselves to Birmingham and other benighted southern cities and congratulated themselves for emulating northern, supposedly more progressive locales, but local leaders now were horrified that Louisville might be the next Boston. The first signs of cooperation between civil rights activists in the two cities came in November 1974, when visitors from Massachusetts urged those attending a mass meeting at the Unitarian church to join them in Boston to rally for the protection of black students. Then, after Louisville's own crisis began, representatives from the Student Coalition against Racism, a "national anti-racist coalition," formed a Louisville branch and hosted a teach-in with speakers from Boston. Thereafter, Louisvillians became more involved in the student coalition, attending national conventions and reporting on the local situation. At these meetings, members linked busing to problems of police brutality and affirmative action and promoted joint efforts because "racism does not develop in

each city and town separately and spontaneously."[47] This sense of being in the fight together led PIE and other groups to recruit help from
their national allies for their events throughout the mid-1970s.

While the determination to fight the racism of the antibusing
movement continued to animate PIE members and others, by the
middle of fall 1975, the mistreatment of black young people became
the primary issue for the local freedom struggle.[48] On the first day of
school, though the ride in the morning went smoothly across the county, in the afternoon, protesters who gathered during the day launched
attacks against the buses. In the days and weeks after the riots, the
national guardsmen who rode along with the students reported incidents of sniper fire against them. But, while frightening, these incidents
were relatively isolated. Black parents complained more about the poor
treatment their children received from drivers and the overcrowded
conditions on the transportation. Bus routes going through the west
end ran behind schedule and carried numbers far over the capacity
of the vehicles. At times, the lack of transportation left as many as
150 students waiting at their stops. As a result, black students missed
classes and risked failing.[49]

Once they arrived at the schools, the students continued to encounter hostility. Sometimes the violence of antibusing protesters
spilled over into the buildings, as when two black women at Valley
High School were threatened with a gun and knife by protesters who
shouted, "There are those niggers, we're going to get them." But, just
as often, the problems were between students. The principal at Shawnee High School reported that black students complained to him that
they had to put up with whites calling them names and harassing them
all day. And sometimes that escalated to physical violence. At Iroquois
High School, after a fire drill, four white students in a car almost hit a
black youth, then jumped out of the vehicle and began hitting him with
a crowbar, setting off a wider melee. Black students also fought back,
alone and in groups, so that through the fall there were a number of
reported racial brawls around the county.[50]

Black students also suffered from the uneven application of discipline. They complained that their white peers went unpunished for
insults and harassment, but any incident involving a black person was
"blown out of proportion." The rising number of suspensions, and
the disproportionately high number of suspensions of black students
who were bused into formerly white schools, caused the most concern.

In the first week, the principal of Ballard High School, which was in the white east end suburbs, suspended twenty new black pupils. By October the rate of suspension was 40 percent above that of the previous year, and by December it was 82 percent higher. Officials usually cited as the reasons smoking, cutting classes, disruptive behavior, and lateness, although the Ballard principal added, "Some of the students are apparently not used to going to classes." Parents complained that officials suspended their children for wearing hats, carrying certain kinds of pens, being late when it was the bus's fault, and responding when coaxed into a fight. Moreover, the students added, authorities did not always follow proper procedures, such as warning them before suspending them. Responding to the rising numbers and complaints, Judge Gordon ordered an investigation into the matter in the spring of 1976. The report exonerated school officials of overt racism and documented that many of the suspensions were technically appropriate. But it warned that the lack of proper procedure and the unequal use of suspensions gave the impression of racist treatment of black students and thus created tension in the community.[51]

The problems inside the schools prompted a response from black community leaders and civil rights organizations. In October the Reverend Charles Elliott of King Solomon Baptist Church held a mass meeting, which ended in a plan to hold a march on city hall, the fiscal court of the county government, and the governor's office in Frankfort. Elliott said that officials listened to the antibusing movement because it was vocal and in the streets, so the black community needed to demonstrate its support for quality education, for busing as the current best way to achieve it, and for better treatment for its young people. Shelby Lanier, the controversial black police officer, endorsed the demonstration, arguing that black students needed better protection from law enforcement. He and other advocates for equality within the police department linked the two issues and used the perceived police sympathy for the antibusers as evidence of racism in the department. The march included 250 African Americans who visited Hollenbach's and Carroll's local offices and briefly rallied against the west end Coca-Cola plant, the only neighborhood business to yield to pressure from antibusing forces to close on the October 1 work stoppage day. A caravan then traveled to Frankfort for a rally on the capitol steps. A second probusing march by a coalition of black churches and organizations was planned for late November, with the goal of organizing the "forces opposing the rise of racism in Louisville and Jefferson County," but the restrictiveness of the permit and a blast of cold weather caused the plan to "fizzle."[52]

Civil rights organizations also sought to put economic pressure on perceived enemies of school integration. In response to Coca-Cola's seeming endorsement of the antibusing movement by giving its workers the day off on October 1, KCLC leader Reverend Charles Elliott called for a boycott of the company. He saw a massive nonbuying campaign of the company's products as a way to galvanize the black community, giving people something they could do to represent their opposition to the antibusing movement. The boycott did not catch on, however. The BWC tried a year later to revive the idea because, it said, the company had ignored the wishes of black workers. This attempt, too, was unsuccessful, and mention of the boycott in the media disappeared. The muted response to KCLC and others' chosen strategies indicated that, by the mid-1970s, the characteristic civil rights era tactics of demonstrations and boycotts were less able to rally people, perhaps because the black community had tired of those strategies, which were earning a bad name in light of their use by antibusing groups and their association with violence.[53]

Much of the day-to-day effort of putting pressure on the school system to protect black children came from a group made up primarily of working-class black women, the United Black Protective Parents (UBPP). The leader and frequent spokeswoman for the group was Benitha Ellis, a resident of the Park Duvalle neighborhood who had three children in the public schools. She had never engaged in civil rights activism before, though her brother took part in the open housing demonstrations. She gained experience in grassroots mobilization, however, when she worked as a neighborhood organizer in the War on Poverty. She recalled that, after a meeting to discuss the problems on the buses and in the schools, about ten women from Park Duvalle stood around talking about what they could do to protect their children who were being bused out to unknown and unfriendly institutions. Realizing they would get little help from school officials, they looked for support from other sources. They tried to get traditional black leaders in the NAACP and the churches to take a more overt role, but, failing that, they decided to act on their own. In a formal statement of purpose, they declared, "We believe deep in our hearts that it is essential that the children have someone out there every day protecting them in some way." To do that, they began following the buses, watching as children got off and went into the school buildings, and monitoring the antibusing crowds to make sure no one got hurt. They also began attending school board meetings, pressing lists of demands for improvement in the busing system on officials, and writing to the court of appeals and the Justice Department for help.[54]

In October 1975, UBPP cosponsored a trip to Washington to testify at the U.S. Senate hearings considering an antibusing constitutional amendment, the same hearing before which Sloane and Hollenbach appeared. A long list of black, white, and interracial antiracist organizations cooperated in putting together the trip, including the KCLU, KCLC, NAACP, West End and East End ministerial alliances, Kentucky Alliance, and LBPOO. UBPP raised funds through churches and public events to send ten people on the trip to represent black parents and call for better protection for the students. The group filled a bus, although only one person spoke at the hearing. When they returned, they joined these other organizations in a press conference to celebrate the interracial cooperation among such diverse groups and affirm the "absolute necessity of a united effort against the forces of racism."[55]

Alongside these more activist organizations, a parallel movement of faith-based and secular civic organizations, acting on their own or in newly formed coalitions around school issues, mobilized to support integration and quality education while emphasizing the need for dialogue and reconciliation in the community. The Task Force for Peaceful Desegregation, for example, formed in spring 1975 to work for the smooth implementation of the court order; after classes started, it refocused on countering the antibusing movement with a more positive, prointegration message. It included representatives of church, civic, and civil rights organizations such as the NAACP, the local Quaker meeting, the Methodist group Church Women United, the Sisters of Charity, the KCLU, and the Urban League. Led by Samuel Robinson, an African American west end resident and educator, the group commended bus drivers, teachers, and parents for resisting the violence; supported businesses who were refusing to hang antibusing signs; and held a contest to honor individuals who worked to achieve peaceful integration. Members of the task force also circulated petitions to have the board of education change meeting times to accommodate parents and monitored school-related legislation in Frankfort. They published a newsletter to increase awareness of probusing activity and worked closely with the HRC to run a rumor control center and investigate federal programs that could help in the schools.[56]

Like the early efforts to prepare for peaceful implementation of the court order, this task force included many of the same individuals and organizations as the open housing movement, offering whites who had entered civil rights activity during that campaign an outlet to express their concern about the crisis in race relations and their support for integration. And, like earlier coalitions of moderate human relations advocates, this group focused on community education and persuasion and creating a climate conducive to integration. Although its own members, such as Suzy Post, expressed frustration that the group did not do more to impact the crisis, cochair Lois Cronholm, a white professor at the University of Louisville, believed their role was to express a voice for peace and better human relations.[57]

As it had in the campaign for open housing, the religious community provided much of the white support for peaceful school desegregation and work for healing the divisions in the community. LACRR, one of the leaders of the campaign against Jim Crow in housing, responded to the violence of the antibusing movement by organizing Project Connections, which produced literature and programming aimed at schoolchildren, such as workbooks and calendars that explained the history of school segregation and used humor to demystify the buses. Ministers who had been involved with open housing and other earlier civil rights struggles, such as the Reverend Charles Tachau and Monsignor Alfred Horrigan, lent their names and prestige to try to garner white support for desegregation. And various faith organizations, including the students and faculty of the Louisville Presbyterian Theological Seminary and an ad hoc group of southern and southwestern Jefferson County ministers, issued statements calling for peace and an end to intimidation. Much of this activity was channeled through the Interfaith Task Force on School Integration, which hoped to be "the primary vehicle through which the local religious community could work cooperatively on the problems and opportunities brought about by the court order." Before the start of school, the group had sponsored a speakers' bureau and workshops to help religious leaders prepare their congregations. After the violent reaction, the task force began holding smaller gatherings, which brought together members of congregations from the southern part of the county with those in the west end.[58]

Despite this multipronged approach to promoting integration, busing, and community peace, the crisis continued into the spring and summer of 1976 as frustrated antibusing forces sought ways to continue their fight. Demonstrations by ULAB and other antibusing organizations continued through the spring and recurred in conjunction with the start of school over the next several years. In February 1976, there were large rallies and marches downtown. ULAB spent the spring trying to get permission to march on Derby Day, but authorities refused to grant it a permit. Other antibusing leaders, including state representative Dottie Priddy, vowed to stop the Derby itself if the busing plan was not overturned—an ironic and surely unintended echo of the threatened tactics of the open housing movement of 1967. At the start of the new school year in 1976, three hundred people marched on Preston Highway in Okolona, and eleven hundred demonstrated in the same area on another occasion. Police had to use tear gas against another gathering of one thousand protestors near Valley High School after they blocked traffic and threw rocks and bottles at the police. Then, in September 1977, on the anniversary of the riots at the start of the busing program, approximately three hundred demonstrators on Dixie Highway threw rocks and bricks at cars driven by African Americans, injuring a nine-year-old black girl, and fought back against the police who tried to restrain them. Despite these dramatic exceptions, however, the size and intensity of demonstrations did dissipate over time. There continued to be occasional rallies as late as 1978, but they attracted as few as one hundred people.[59]

There were also continued signs of extremist activity and violence or planned violence. In January 1976, the HRC received reports of Klan harassment of a black family in southeastern Louisville. Over the next year, vandals threw rocks in the windows of a black family's home in Shively, and arsonists burned down the houses of a black family in Okolona and an Indian family in Fairdale.[60] After paying little attention to these and other attacks, in the summer of 1976 local police began undercover investigations that reportedly uncovered plans by extremist organizations to use even greater violence. In one case, just before the start of the new school year, officials found a stash of dynamite, grenades, and ammunition at a farm the FBI said was connected to Posse Comitatus.[61] Attacks and intimidation were also aimed at white probusing activists. On September 26, 1976, vandals burned a car used by Anne Braden and Ilene Carver. Braden and authorities believed the incident was connected to "an unusually rabid rally" of the National

States' Rights Party at which she was mentioned as an "arch enemy" and which was followed by a number of threatening phone calls. Four other cars went up in flames in the west end the same night. Later in the year, Nancy Gall-Clayton, who had written a letter to the editor of the *Louisville Courier-Journal* criticizing the attacks on black county residents, woke up to find a cross burning on her lawn.[62]

In the late spring and summer of 1976, with extremist groups more active in the community and the new school year approaching, civic leaders made efforts to coordinate a collective expression of opposition to racism and violence and to promote dialogue that might lead to eliminating tension. In April, Sloane and Hollenbach somewhat belatedly sponsored a campaign to garner signatures on a "Declaration of Independence from Bigotry." The statement cited concerns that some of the opposition to busing involved both anti-Semitism and racism, and it invoked Louisville's positive self-image by calling on community leaders to "reassert the principles of tolerance and moderation which have been part of this community's history." Over one hundred representatives of civic, labor, and religious groups attended the launch of the campaign. The HRC circulated the statement to collect signatures, while churches devoted their services on the weekend of June 26–27 to messages against "the evils of bigotry." By the end of June, the *Courier-Journal* reported, over three thousand people and ninety-five organizations had signed. Although it was important that local government leaders originated such a statement against extremism and heartening that people rushed to sign it, given the pronounced tension in the community, PIE pointed out that the declaration itself did not go very far. When, at the press conference, officials referred to ending this extremist ideology, which was "not yet a danger," before it spread, PIE pointed out that homes had already been bombed. Moreover, like most such pledges and resolutions, a signature to it did not go beyond "just empty words" to a "reality that is lived in our homes, in our neighborhoods, and in our schools."[63] In the eyes of prointegration activists, this effort by officials was too little, too late.

Just before the start of classes in 1976, forty-two representatives of pro- and antibusing organizations met in the spirit of promoting dialogue and preventing the return of violence. The response to these gatherings by antibusing forces demonstrated the ineffectiveness of these efforts to use community persuasion to soothe the crisis. Joyce Spond of SOCS and Bob Deprez of the National Association to Restore and

Preserve Our Freedom attended the meeting, as did Lyman Johnson for the NAACP, the Reverend Elliott of KCLC, and members of the League of Women Voters and the Urban League. But rank-and-file antibusing forces made clear their opposition to even talking to the other side when approximately one hundred protestors demonstrated outside, saying the only answer to the crisis was the end of busing. After that, a fissure opened as some groups criticized Deprez and Spond for participating, and antibusing groups debated whether the movement opposed integration per se or just busing to achieve it. Meanwhile, the attempt to promote dialogue resulted only in a statement calling for "the better understanding of the diverse wishes and needs of the community."[64] The limited result, and the hostile reaction to the attempt by the antibusing forces, indicated that, on the eve of the second year of busing, the opposition to it was still too strongly felt to be ameliorated through dialogue. Months of activism by the prointegration and antiracism coalition had failed to dampen this resistance or to curtail the more general backlash against civil rights of which it was a part.

In the face of the continued hostility to busing, in the spring of 1976, PIE shifted attention away from confronting the racism in the community and toward a grassroots effort to monitor the treatment of black students and promote equality within the schools, joining forces with UBPP to do so. The groups helped to sponsor a small gathering in March at which "national and academic" leaders gave an overview of federal policies on student rights regarding suspensions, due process, and confidentiality. Then they spent the next two months planning their first major collaboration, the People's Workshop on the Schools, a workshop for parents, teachers, students, and the general public, funded in part by the HRC. One hundred seventy-five people of widely disparate views attended, but, much to the pleasure of the organizers, the discussion never descended into a simple "pro/con debate." Subjects discussed included suspensions, book shortages, the lack of black history in the curriculum, and parents' sense of "powerlessness." The success of this workshop led the two organizations to cooperate annually in a series of meetings focusing on how to influence policy makers, learn from other communities' experiences, and protect students.[65]

As the first year of busing came to an end and another was about to get under way, local leaders assessed the situation. The editorial page of the *Courier-Journal,* as was its tradition in matters of race relations in Louisville, tried to put a positive spin on the crisis that had consumed the community for much of the preceding twelve months. In an editorial titled "From the Trauma of Busing, an Opportunity for Change," the paper praised "the capacity of people to adjust to the inevitable" and noted that the "steam seemed to go out of the anti-busing movement." Leaders in the civil rights community were not so sure. The Reverend Charles Kirby noted that the board of education had done nothing to protect students or even to listen to their concerns. Meanwhile, "though no one was killed or seriously" injured, school officials had suspended black children and denied them the chance to learn. Moreover, as a letter to the editor pointed out at the start of the new school year, "racism [still] riddles the community," and the Klan continued to march and receive support from area businesses and officials. As the reaction to the attempt at dialogue in August displayed, some elements in the antibusing movement remained unwilling to yield at all. In the schools themselves, the story was likewise mixed. The fall semester saw little of the violence and turmoil that had accompanied the first week of classes the year before, but after a few months, black parents told officials that school staff continued to mistreat and discriminate against their children.[66]

PIE and UBPP continued to organize around grievances in the schools, and the unequal treatment of black students and the black community, through the next several years. In preparation for the second year of busing, PIE drew up a list of plans that included monitoring school funding, getting students involved in activism around their rights, and building bridges to grassroots black community organizations. The organization's students' rights committee wrote a handbook for pupils and convinced Legal Aid attorneys to attend suspension hearings. Meanwhile, UBPP established an office to hear parents' complaints and to help them get basic information about the buses. During the school year, UBPP and the BWC held meetings for disgruntled parents and organized them to take action. When school officials announced that, because of budget constraints, four elementary schools in inner-city neighborhoods would be closed, PIE and others circulated petitions and launched a grassroots campaign to keep at least one of them open.[67]

By the late 1970s, few of these activities of PIE and other equal rights advocates resembled the tactics of the prointegration mobilizations of the 1960s. Demonstrations ceased to bring out large numbers; even the antibusing forces' enthusiasm for them eventually dwindled. Likewise, neither side's boycotts ever caught on with the broad public. Political avenues of change brought mixed results. Antibusing forces tried to use the ballot to defeat those they blamed for busing, but Carroll won in 1975. And when Hollenbach lost in the county in 1977, by then the fervor of the antibusing movement had subsided, and the loss was to a young Republican named Mitch McConnell, largely on the basis of charges of corruption in Hollenbach's administration and accusations that he had become too arrogant.[68] Moreover, although PIE monitored the actions of local officials and confronted them when needed, neither it nor other probusing, prointegration activists engaged in concerted political activity. Unlike efforts in previous confrontations over civil rights, there was no effort to rally black and sympathetic white voters to accomplish a goal through the ballot. In large part, this was because the sought-for policy, the integration of the schools, was already officially in place and because Harvey Sloane was considered relatively sympathetic. Finally, the tactic preferred by moderate interracialists in the earlier school integration, open accommodations, and open housing battles—education and dialogue aimed at promoting a favorable climate for change—while providing a welcome voice for peace, failed to convince large segments of the community of the value of busing for integration.

Traditional civil rights tactics were now replaced by a new set of weapons. PIE, UBPP, and their partners at times staged rallies and marches, both in support of integration and against the racism of the antibusing movement. But by late in the decade, they more often organized people to attend school board meetings and disciplinary hearings, monitored budget and tax negotiations, held workshops to educate parents and students about their rights, and worked with the school system to promote human rights and equality inside the facilities. This day-to-day attention to problems in the schools was less dramatic and was not recognizably movement activity. But in the eyes of the participants, it was an extension of the freedom struggle because it shared the fundamental goal of furthering equality and involved black and white citizens committed to an ongoing fight against racism in its many manifestations.[69]

Conclusion

Where Does the Story End?

What is, after all, a beginning? . . . Is there, after all, a truly appropriate *incipit* for a story? Or isn't there always—latent but always there—a beginning before the beginning?

—Amos Oz

The lawsuit was the beginning of a struggle that continues to this day. The struggle has been to try and get for black kids in the public schools an equitable educational opportunity. . . . [But], even though we desegregated the buildings in 1975, we really did not do anything to dismantle racism. So no, I never thought the civil rights movement was dead.

—Suzy Post

In pondering where to begin a story, Amos Oz raises a fundamental problem in any historical narrative, including histories of popular struggles such as the civil rights movement. Just as we can always push back the birthing moment by looking at deeper roots or links to earlier precedents, we can extend the story until it meets the present. Indeed, when I asked movement participants a modified version of Oz's question—Where does the story of the local struggle end?—the majority of answers echoed Post's assertion that it never did. Cheri Hamilton noted in 1999, "We're coming to the end of the millennium and we've been in this struggle forever, always the struggle continues. . . . I don't know when you can end it." Or, as Woodford Porter put it, "The civil rights movement as far as legalizing everything is just about over, but now the fight to keep your civil rights, to exercise your civil rights will never end. . . . Let's don't kid ourselves. Human beings won't ever let it end."[1] For my immediate concern, deciding when I could stop writing, such answers were not helpful. But if the connection these participants see between the movement in the past and ongoing battles against racism today complicates the question of how to tell the end of the story, it also raises the more interesting issues of what the movement meant and continues to mean to people, and how they experienced it. Focusing on what participants saw as the problems to be addressed, what they did about them, and how such concerns continue to direct their lives and shape their community in turn illuminates the interconnections across time, people, and issues and strategies in the civil rights struggle.

Post's blunt assertion—"I never thought the civil rights movement was dead"—speaks directly to the experiences of many of the people who participated in the Louisville movement. They reject the idea that the movement has ended or that its narrative has a conclusion, insisting that it persists, even if it takes different forms. Some activists reflect this sense of ongoing struggle in the stories they tell, linking postwar campaigns to the more recent past and current debates. Others merge the story of the black freedom struggle with antiwar, women's rights, and anti–death penalty campaigns, portraying it as part of a larger, broader, and ongoing movement for social justice. Thus Dolores Delahanty, the wife of one of the lawyers who represented the Black Six, suggested the story continues at least through the 1990s in the work of the local progressive community. For white west end resident and open housing supporter Fred Hicks, labor and Central American solidarity campaigns represent later chapters of social justice protests. Others insist that, although much of the energy of the black freedom struggle has dissipated, the movement continues as long as there is a vanguard that raises issues and demonstrates. For example, Louis Coleman, whom the local media often disparaged as someone who couldn't let go of the 1960s, praised the coterie of dedicated activists he could count on to carry on the struggle.[2]

Indeed, many of the men and women, black and white, who joined the struggle against racism in earlier decades remain engaged in actions that reflect their ongoing commitment. Sit-in leader Raoul Cunningham, after a career working for Democratic senators and governors, returned to Louisville and has served as the director of NAACP voter registration projects and the president of the local branch. Tom Moffett, the white minister who joined WECC and the open housing campaign, left his parish and devoted himself to working with the Kentucky Alliance against police brutality and other expressions of social injustice. Suzy Post joined the KCLU after the Wade-Braden case, served as a plaintiff in the 1970s school desegregation lawsuits, headed the Metropolitan Housing Coalition for years, and continues to address the link between housing and school segregation. Until his death in 2006, black nationalist Sterling Neal Jr. served the poor Park Duvalle community through his jobs in neighborhood social service agencies. Likewise, until the end of her life in 2006, Anne Braden fought for gay rights and against environmental racism and police brutality. And Coleman, after serving as the Urban League's point person in its campaign against police abuse of black residents in the 1970s, founded the Justice Resource Center and became one of the community's leading activists on employment issues and west end pollution. In the personal experience of these activists, then, the movement did not end.

In many cases, these Louisvillians still find themselves struggling against problems similar to those that brought them into the movement and on which they expended much energy in earlier decades. Raoul Cunningham learned important lessons as a young man about the effectiveness of marshaling the black vote to secure antidiscrimination legislation. In 2000 he and other black leaders fought unsuccessfully to preserve the power of the black electorate by opposing the merger of city and county government. The resulting loss of black political influence—African Americans fell from 33 percent of the old city population to 15 percent of the metro area population, and from one-third of the old board of aldermen to less than a quarter of the new city council—has sparked his renewed efforts to increase black voter registration and participation.[3] Coleman, who helped to make police brutality a prominent issue in the 1970s by sponsoring Urban League forums at which victims could tell their stories, continued into the new century to publicize cases of police shootings of black victims. Likewise, Post, who as a leader of the KCLU worked in both the open housing movement of the 1960s and for the system-wide desegregation plan in the 1970s, began to agitate again in 2007 to protect diversity in the schools after the U.S. Supreme Court in *Meredith v. Jefferson County Public Schools* ruled against the schools' voluntary integration plan.

Why, then, does this study end with the denouement of the busing crisis? The activist careers of these and many other individuals, and the persistence of problems rooted in earlier decades, reveal the indeterminacy of the movement's end. As Galen Martin, longtime director of the Kentucky Commission on Human Rights, notes, any concluding date "is artificial. . . . You're just grabbing something out of the air."[4] Thus any narrative of the Louisville movement or of any activist community will be an incomplete snapshot that focuses on one era in a longer struggle. The story presented here began in the postwar era with an upsurge of activity on the part of left-wing, labor, church, and civil rights organizations. The coalitions these activists formed used the wartime rhetoric of democracy to challenge discrimination by tax-supported entities. The decision to attack segregation per se and to mobilize grassroots action rather than to rely on negotiations by elites marked a significant break with pre–World War II activism and signaled the beginning of a new era in the movement.[5] This era ended, I argue, after the reenergizing of the local civil rights community in response to the antibusing movement. The campaign for local school integration and against the rise of overt bigotry confronted a deeply hostile reaction in defense of the racial status quo. National trends, including the rise of the New Right and the retreat of the federal government from civil rights enforcement and oversight, reinforced the local backlash. Moreover, the traditional tactics of persuasion, demonstrations, and even political action had little impact on the antibusing movement and its allies in government. The campaign technically succeeded, because antibusing forces were not able at the time to stop the system-wide desegregation of the schools. But it was a Pyrrhic victory. Race relations in the community worsened, and unequal treatment of black children persisted. The concurrent lack of progress against police brutality, the turn against affirmative action, and a growing sense that the black community had reached a plateau of political power exacerbated activists' sense of failure. The end of the 1970s, then, marked the end of an era characterized by mass coalition building in campaigns that utilized the political and legal systems. Activism against racism continued into the new century, and various organizations led sporadic demonstrations, protests, and boycotts or utilized quieter organizing methods like those developed by PIE in the wake of busing. But they did so without sustained, broad-based participation and in a different political and cultural climate. The struggle thus moved into a new era with its own distinct story.

Nonetheless, the voices of local activists who see their ongoing work as part of a longer movement cannot and should not be ignored.

In addition to complicating the question of where the story ends, they highlight the importance of connections within the movement across time and among people, issues, and strategies. Louisville's position on the border, its resulting combination of northern and southern problems and socioeconomic and political characteristics, and activists' consequent embrace of a variety of strategies underscore the significance of these relationships. Activists' recurring linkage of past and contemporary events reveals the continuities across time in the movement. The local struggle consisted of an overlap of campaigns, strategies, and issues that blurred distinctions among various phases.[6] Organizing against economic discrimination in city jobs began in the 1950s and persisted through the 1960s and into the early 1970s, even if it at times drew less attention. Interracial faith-based and secular organizations sought improved human relations and racial cooperation from the 1940s to the aftermath of busing, in the latter years working alongside the black power movement and at times involving the same people. Consistent strategies—voter registration drives, campaigning for legislative office, and using the franchise to pressure political leaders—undergirded activism throughout the period. The traditional narrative of the civil rights movement sees it as a march from NAACP legal action in the pre-*Brown* era to early-1960s nonviolent direct action in the South, shifting in the late 1960s to black community empowerment and in the 1970s to bureaucratic enforcement centered in the North. The Louisville struggle, in contrast, reveals the movement to be a series of overlapping campaigns, distinguished by multifaceted organizing and punctuated by times of dramatic mass mobilization.

In the Louisville struggle, people and organizations committed to the pursuit of racial equality repeatedly and habitually forged collaborative relationships and partnerships across racial and ideological lines. Such interracial coalition building began early. In the postwar era, left-wing unions and political organizations worked with the NAACP and church-based organizations to attack job discrimination in local industry and segregation in the parks. In the 1960s, cooperation coalesced around the open accommodations steering committee, the Committee on Open Housing, and the Black Six defense. Later, many of the same constituencies that first worked together in these campaigns came together again in the reaction against the antibusing movement. At times personality clashes, political loyalties, and disagreements over tactics caused conflict, as when older leaders such as Tucker, McAlpin, and

Johnson criticized outsiders and young militants. But more often, even groups with dissimilar philosophies and approaches found ways to work together on common goals, as when the BWC and the HRC cooperated to enforce equal employment opportunity. The city's diverse population and the range of people and organizations participating in civil rights work, products of its border geography, made it difficult for any one leader or organization to dominate the local movement. Indeed, few participants in the Louisville movement identified with a single organization. Instead, in their narratives, they portray themselves as part of an undifferentiated struggle, able and willing to work within a variety of organizations and coalitions to accomplish their goals.

Individual activists' stories also reveal that the larger movement spanned not only time but space. Participants in Louisville's movement maintained connections with those in both northern and southern communities and with national and regional organizations. National leaders of the Negro Labor Council helped spark the 1950s GE protests. Representatives from the NAACP and Urban League made regular visits to the city, as did leaders of campaigns in Montgomery, Birmingham, and elsewhere. The young people who led the sit-ins recall growing up hearing such speakers and feeling immersed in a wider movement. Moreover, they were inspired to act by others of their generation demonstrating in Nashville and other cities. More concretely, they benefitted from workshops given by CORE leaders and James Farmer. These ties increased over time, with visits from SCLC organizers to Louisville and of local activists to places such as Selma. When the backlash and the repression it brought began in the late 1960s, Louisvillians worked with regional and national organizations to coordinate their response. During the busing crisis, local people drew on their connections to organizations in Boston and elsewhere to confront rising racism. The members of PIE who led the struggle practiced mutual aid with their counterparts in many cities facing similar problems, because they believed that racism anywhere threatened all communities equally.

People who willingly cooperated with others locally or nationally showed an equal flexibility in their embrace of different strategies. As William Reddin put it, speaking specifically of the open housing campaign, there was "something everyone can do." Other campaigns demonstrated a comparable inclusiveness concerning tactics and people, and most activists made little distinction among approaches. Locals made no hard and fast divisions among legal tactics, nonviolent direct action, political work, and community organizing. The "southern" strategy of mass demonstrations coincided with "northern" community empowerment and bloc voting because activists believed they were complementary weapons. In the effort to integrate the state's hospitals, for example, participants organized mass rallies, pressured politicians to pass legislation, and threatened lawsuits. Both the open accommodations and open housing campaigns combined mass nonviolent demonstrations, boycotts, negotiations, public persuasion, and the vote. In the late 1960s, WECC and its allies engaged in arts and cultural activities aimed at improving human relations, community organizing meant to empower poor blacks, and occasional protests and legislative petitions, all in their effort to address racial and economic inequalities in the west end. Even as the "typical" civil rights tactics of boycotts and demonstrations lost their appeal and effectiveness in the mid-1970s, activists worked to develop a new arsenal that combined grassroots organizing, monitoring of public officials, and the use of bureaucratic enforcement mechanisms to effect continued change. The customary use of a "multipronged approach"—to use Mervin Aubespin's description of the open accommodations campaign—enabled people and organizations of different philosophies and temperaments to participate. The embrace of diverse strategies also contributed to the overlap between ostensibly distinct movements such as black power and antipoverty. In fact, such efforts drew on many of the same strategies and people, and thus activists experienced them as different facets of the same struggle.

Local people's willingness to work alongside each other despite differences, and to employ a variety of strategies in doing so, lay ultimately in their shared goals. At base, they saw themselves attacking the same fundamental problem. In this work I have used the terms "civil rights movement," "freedom struggle," "the struggle for racial equality and democracy," and "the struggle against racism" interchangeably because the activists, both then and now, employed such phrases without discriminating between them. Movement participants also claimed to be fighting discrimination, prejudice, and white supremacy. Just as they saw little difference in these labels, they drew few distinctions between specific issues, seeing them instead as part of a whole. The FE fought discrimination in the workplace and in the parks. The sit-in participants sought jobs and access to facilities. The LBPOO saw racism in law enforcement expressed as both police brutality and job discrimination. West end residents linked deteriorating conditions in their neighborhood to housing discrimination, poverty, and mistreatment by city government. They believed the solutions were better human relations, engendering respect for black culture, and political power. For open housing advocates, the answer to inequality in the schools was the desegregation of housing, which itself depended on acquiring political and economic power. At the time, media observers and an occasional civil rights activist referred to racial problems as being either "southern"—meaning discrimination in facilities and schools—or "northern," referring to housing segregation and "ghettoization." Louisville's story and position on the border demonstrate the inextricable link between problems that plagued northern and southern communities. Indeed, Louisville activists cooperated despite personal, political, and philosophical differences because they perceived a common enemy that transcended specific issues or places. They believed that they were part of a larger struggle against the enemy of racism.

In recent years, numerous scholars have challenged the narrative of the civil rights movement that runs from Montgomery to Memphis and follows the rise of mass nonviolent direct action seeking legislation against discrimination, the conflict of the black power years, and subsequent declension. A new periodization came first, with histories of the roots of the movement in the 1930s and 1940s Popular Front and, more recently, with community studies that push the story into the 1970s and beyond. Attention to the Popular Front, and to the poor people's movements of later years, sparked awareness that activists saw little difference between civil rights and economic justice. Similarly, scholars such as Timothy B. Tyson and Rhonda K. Williams have demonstrated the overlap between what have heretofore been considered separate and even hostile movements: civil rights, black power, and antipoverty movements. The effect of this research has been to complicate what Tyson, Peter Lau, and Brian Ward in different places have described and critiqued as the triumphal narrative of the movement—the march toward freedom through mass action and national legislation—and to demonstrate that the story cannot be broken into false dichotomies around period, strategy, or ideology.[7]

This examination of the Louisville movement seeks to extend this reconsideration of the nature of the movement. As a border city, Louisville was a place where northern and southern characteristics and racial problems overlapped and mixed. Here, things "ran together." As such, Louisville enables scholars to see more clearly the characteristics shared by communities across the nation. The story of its struggle for racial equality illustrates the insights of current scholarship, but more important, the Louisville movement reveals the persistent relationships across time and among people, issues, and strategies. Participants in the movement recognized the links among issues, drew solace and support from their connections to other activists locally and across the nation, and moved easily from one campaign to another, utilizing whatever combination of strategies worked. Most important, they remember their work as part of a larger and longer, indeed ongoing, struggle against an indivisible and pervasive foe—racism in all its manifestations. When scholars focus their attention on such connections, on the type of mixing that happened in Louisville, other local movements will appear in a new light as well. Instead of consisting of division, dichotomy, or declension, the civil rights struggle can be seen as an example of cooperation, consistency, and compatibility of action. With this new way of viewing the movement, we can start to construct a narrative of the struggle that reflects how people understood and experienced it.

Notes

Introduction

1. Wilson Wyatt, interview by John Egerton, July 12, 1990, Southern Oral History Collection, Southern Historical Collection, Wilson Library, University of North Carolina, Chapel Hill (hereafter cited as SOHC); Louis C. Kesselman, "Kentucky Negro Suffrage Fact-Finding Project," September 1956, reel 10, folder 15, Southern Regional Council Papers, Robert W. Woodruff Library Archives, Atlanta University Center, Atlanta (microfilm edition, University of North Carolina, Chapel Hill; hereafter cited as SRC Papers); J. Harvey Kerns, *A Survey of the Economic and Cultural Conditions of the Negro Population of Louisville, Kentucky* (n.p.: Department of Research and Community Projects, National Urban League, 1948), 175.

2. Mark Ethridge to Virginius Dabney, June 8, 1939, box 1, file 5, Mark F. Ethridge Papers, Wilson Library, University of North Carolina, Chapel Hill; "Urban League Told Life Not So Bright for Negroes," *Louisville Courier-Journal,* April 13, 1948; "Speaker Hails Cooperation of Races Here," *Louisville Courier-Journal,* April 1, 1952; "Council on Interracial Cooperation Formed to Aid Negroes in Kentucky," *Louisville Courier-Journal,* February 15, 1941.

3. Lyman Johnson, interview by John Egerton, July 12, 1990, SOHC; J. C. Olden, "Militant Church," *Louisville Defender,* November 19, 1953; Frank L. Stanley, People, Places and Problems, *Louisville Defender,* March 18, 1954.

4. Kim Gruenwald, "Space and Place on the Early American Frontier: The Ohio Valley as a Region, 1790–1850," *Ohio Valley History* 4 (Fall 2004): 31; Robert Bruce Symon, "'Child of the North': Louisville's Transition to a Southern City, 1879–1885" (master's thesis, University of Louisville, 2005), 17–27; Allen J. Share, *Cities in the Commonwealth: Two Centuries of Urban Life in Kentucky* (Lexington: University Press of Kentucky, 1981), 89. On Louisville during the Civil War, see Lowell H. Harrison and James C. Klotter, *New History of Kentucky* (Lexington: University Press of Kentucky, 1997), 188–92.

5. Omer Carmichael and Weldon James, *The Louisville Story* (New York: Simon and Schuster, 1957), 12–13; Share, *Cities in the Commonwealth,* 68–93. Share gives the population of African Americans in the city as 6,810 in 1860, 14,956 in 1870, and 39,139 in 1900. On the economic causes of the shift to

southernness, see Symon, "'Child of the North'"; for a more cultural approach, see Anne Elizabeth Marshall, "'A Strange Conclusion to a Triumphant War': Memory, Identity and the Creation of a Confederate Kentucky, 1865–1925" (PhD diss., University of Georgia, 2004).

6. On the development of segregation in Louisville, see George C. Wright, *Life behind a Veil: Blacks in Louisville, Kentucky, 1865–1930* (Baton Rouge: Louisiana State University Press, 1985), 52–65; Share, *Cities in the Commonwealth*, 93–97.

7. Wright, *Life behind a Veil*, 100–122; E. Franklin Frazier, *Negro Youth at the Crossways: Their Personality Development in the Middle States* (New York: Schocken Books, 1967), 15–18.

8. Wright, *Life behind a Veil*, 78–101, 214–28; U.S. Department of Commerce, Bureau of the Census, *Population and Housing Statistics for Census Tracts, Louisville, Ky., and Adjacent Area* (Washington, DC, 1942).

9. "Louisville: A Blend of Almost Everywhere," *Business Week,* May 7, 1955; Scott Cummings and Michael Price, "Race Relations in Louisville: Southern Racial Traditions and Northern Class Dynamics" (Policy Paper Series, Urban Research Institute, University of Louisville, Louisville, KY, June 1990), 13; Richard Bernier, "World War II," in *Encyclopedia of Louisville,* ed. John E. Kleber (Lexington: University Press of Kentucky, 2001), 954–57.

10. On Catholics in Louisville, see Clyde F. Crews, *An American Holy Land: A History of the Archdiocese of Louisville* (Wilmington, DE: Glazier, 1987). On the Jewish community in Louisville, see Lee Shai Weissbach, "Jews," in Kleber, *Encyclopedia of Louisville,* 446–48, and Herman Landau, *Adath Louisville: The Story of a Jewish Community* (Louisville, KY: Landau, 1981). On the Southern Baptist Theological Seminary, see Henry U. Warnock, "Prophets of Change: Some Southern Baptist Leaders and the Problem of Race, 1920–1921," *Baptist History and Heritage* 7 (1972), and Tracy Elaine K'Meyer, *Interracialism and Christian Community in the Postwar South: The Story of Koinonia Farm* (Charlottesville: University of Virginia Press, 1997), 21–24, 29.

11. Murray Walls, interview by Dwayne Cox, July 27, 1977, Oral History Collection, Ekstrom Library, University of Louisville, Louisville, KY (hereafter cited as OHC); Anne Braden, *The Wall Between* (Knoxville: University of Tennessee Press, 1999), 42–43; Kerns, *Survey of the Economic and Cultural Conditions,* 184.

12. See U.S. Department of Commerce, Bureau of the Census, *Census of Population, 1950,* vol. 2, *Characteristics of the Population, Kentucky* (Washington, DC, 1952).

13. *Kentucky's Black Heritage: The Role of the Black People in the History of Kentucky from Pioneer Days to the Present* (Frankfort: Kentucky Commission on Human Rights, 1971), 45–46, 87; Wright, *Life behind a Veil,* 247–52, 271–73.

14. On the history of blacks' voting behavior, see Ernest Collins, "The Po-

litical Behavior of the Negroes in Cincinnati, Ohio, and Louisville, Kentucky" (PhD diss., University of Kentucky, 1950), and Louis C. Kesselman, "Negro Voting in a Border Community: Louisville, Kentucky," *Journal of Negro Education* 26 (Summer 1957).

15. For information on struggles for black equality and their results before 1930, see Wright, *Life behind a Veil*, 262–74.

16. Andor Skotnes, "The Black Freedom Movement and the Workers' Movement in Baltimore, 1930–1939" (PhD diss., Rutgers University, 1991), 59; David Taft Terry, "'Tramping for Justice': The Dismantling of Jim Crow in Baltimore, 1942–1954" (PhD diss., Howard University, 2002), 387. On these cities, see also Kenneth D. Durr, *Behind the Backlash: White Working-Class Politics in Baltimore, 1940–1980* (Chapel Hill: University of North Carolina Press, 2003); Michael Flug, "Organized Labor and the Civil Rights Movement in the 1960s: The Case of the Maryland Freedom Union," *Labor History* 31 (1990): 322–46; Mary Kimbrough and Margaret W. Dagen, *Victory without Violence: The First Ten Years of the St. Louis Committee of Racial Equality, 1947–1957* (Columbia: University of Missouri Press, 2000); Patricia L. Adams, "Fighting for Democracy in St. Louis: Civil Rights during World War II," *Missouri Historical Review* 80 (1985); Clarence E. Lang, "Community and Resistance in the Gateway City: Black National Consciousness, Working Class Formation, and Social Movements in St. Louis, Missouri, 1941–1964" (PhD diss., University of Illinois, Urbana-Champagne, 2004); Kenneth S. Jolly, *Black Liberation in the Midwest: The Struggle in St. Louis, Missouri, 1964–1970* (New York: Routledge, 2006); and Henry Louis Taylor Jr., ed., *Race and the City: Work, Community and Protest in Cincinnati, 1820–1970* (Chicago: University of Illinois Press, 1993).

17. On postwar labor and civil rights, see Robert Rodgers Korstad, *Civil Rights Unionism: Tobacco Workers and the Struggle for Democracy in the Mid-Twentieth-Century South* (Chapel Hill: University of North Carolina Press, 2003), and John Egerton, *Speak Now against the Day: The Generation before the Civil Rights Movement in the South* (Chapel Hill: University of North Carolina Press, 1994). On later union opposition to civil rights, see Dennis A. Deslippe, "'Do Whites Have Rights?' White Detroit Policemen and 'Reverse Discrimination' Protests in the 1970s," *Journal of American History* 91 (2004); Nancy A. Banks, "'The Last Bastion of Discrimination': The New York City Building Trades and the Struggle over Affirmative Action, 1961–1976" (PhD diss., Columbia University, 2006); Thomas J. Sugrue, "Affirmative Action from Below: Civil Rights, the Building Trades, and the Politics of Racial Equality in the Urban North, 1945–1969," *Journal of American History* 91 (2004); and Stacy Kinlock Sewell, "Left on the Construction Bench: The New York Construction Trades and Racial Integration, 1960–1972," *New York History* 83 (2002). For a detailed account of union labor's opposition to school desegregation in Louisville and Jefferson County, see Timothy J. Minchin, *From Rights to Economics: The Ongoing*

Struggle for Black Equality in the U.S. South (Gainesville: University Press of Florida, 2007), 134–50.

18. Elizabeth Jacoway and David R. Colburn, eds., *Southern Businessmen and Desegregation* (Baton Rouge: Louisiana State University Press, 1982), especially George C. Wright, "Desegregation of Public Accommodations in Louisville: The Long and Difficult Struggle in a 'Liberal Border City,'" in ibid., 191–210; David L. Chappell, *Inside Agitators: White Southerners in the Civil Rights Movement* (Baltimore: Johns Hopkins University Press, 1994); Michael B. Friedland, *Lift Up Your Voice Like a Trumpet: White Clergy and the Civil Rights and Antiwar Movements, 1954–1973* (Chapel Hill: University of North Carolina Press, 1998); Morton Sosna, *In Search of the Silent South: Southern Liberals and the Race Issue* (New York: Columbia University Press, 1977); Anthony Lake Newberry, "Without Urgency or Ardor: The South's Middle of the Road Liberals and Civil Rights, 1945–1960" (PhD diss., Ohio University, 1982); Irwin Klibaner, *Conscience of a Troubled South: The Southern Conference Educational Fund, 1946–1966* (Brooklyn, NY: Carlson, 1989); Cynthia Stokes Brown, *Refusing Racism: White Allies and the Struggle for Civil Rights* (New York: Teachers College Press, 2002). One work that takes the story of white antiracism into the more recent period is Becky Thompson, *A Promise and a Way of Life: White Antiracist Activism* (Minneapolis: University of Minnesota Press, 2001).

19. The literature on nonsouthern movements is growing rapidly. For an introduction, see Jeanne F. Theoharis and Komozi Woodard, eds., *Freedom North: Black Freedom Struggles outside the South, 1940–1980* (New York: Palgrave Macmillan, 2003); Robert O. Self, *American Babylon: Race and the Struggle for Postwar Oakland* (Princeton, NJ: Princeton University Press, 2003); and Matthew J. Countryman, *Up South: Civil Rights and Black Power in Philadelphia* (Philadelphia: University of Pennsylvania Press, 2006).

20. A monograph that weaves political strategies into the story of the movement is Gretchen Cassel Eick, *Dissent in Wichita: The Civil Rights Movement in the Midwest, 1954–1972* (Chicago: University of Illinois Press, 2001). For a study of blacks in northern politics, see William J. Grimshaw, *Bitter Fruit: Black Politics and the Chicago Machine, 1931–1991* (Chicago: University of Chicago Press, 1992).

21. My deepest gratitude goes to Kathryn Nasstrom, who in reading my chapters helped me to conceive of this image.

1. Postwar Campaigns for Citizens' Rights

1. News release, September 10, 1950, box 50, file 9, Anne and Carl Braden Papers, State Historical Society of Wisconsin, Madison; Anne Braden to the editor, *Louisville Defender*, February 3, 1951; "Hospital Movement Group Differs with Hardinsburg Rotary on Hospital Bias," *Louisville Defender*, March 10, 1951.

2. Anne Braden, interview by the author, March 22, 2001, OHC.

3. On the activities of the Louisville NAACP, see Patrick S. McElhone, "The Civil Rights Activities of the Louisville Branch of the National Association for the Advancement of Colored Persons: 1914–1960" (master's thesis, University of Louisville, 1976).

4. For a description of the Louisville left, see Braden, *Wall Between*, 33–34; Anne Braden, interview, March 22, 2001; Chris Gaslinger, interview by the author, February 7, 2000, OHC. For a full history of the FE at the International Harvester plant in Louisville, see Toni Gilpin, "Left by Themselves: A History of the United Farm Equipment and Metal Workers Union, 1938–1955" (PhD diss., Yale University, 1992). For a brief description of local postwar civil rights organizations, including the MCM and NLC, see radio script, February 14, 1954, box 54, file 4, Braden Papers.

5. "Women Take Lead in Louisville Peace Activities," [1950], box 54, file 6, Braden Papers.

6. For descriptions of the postwar window of opportunity, see Robert Korstad and Nelson Lichtenstein, "Opportunities Lost and Found: Labor, Radicals, and the Early Civil Rights Movement," *Journal of American History* 75 (1988); Korstad, *Civil Rights Unionism*; Egerton, *Speak Now against the Day*; and Patricia Sullivan, *Days of Hope: Race and Democracy in the New Deal Era* (Chapel Hill: University of North Carolina Press, 1996). Some scholars have more recently argued that this "lost opportunity" was not much of an opportunity and that reading it as such is overly optimistic and overlooks divisions between the union rank and file and the limited power of the marginalized whites in these coalitions. See, for example, Glenn Feldman, prologue to *Before "Brown": Civil Rights and White Backlash in the Modern South*, ed. Glenn Feldman (Tuscaloosa: University of Alabama Press, 2004).

7. Bud James, interview, n.d., box 53, file 17, Braden Papers; "Progressive Party—Local Adversary of US—Is Merely a Handful of Militant Reformers," *Louisville Times*, June 3, 1952, clipping, box 6, file 12, Braden Papers. See also Braden, *Wall Between,* 51, chap. 2.

8. J. M. Tydings to Guy B. Johnson, December 4, 1945, February 18, 1946, reel 1, folder 1990, SRC Papers; Edward McDowell to Guy B. Johnson, January 9, 1946, reel 1, folder 1990, SRC Papers; J. M. Tydings, "Report to the Kentucky Commission on Interracial Cooperation," 1947, reel 1, folder 1990, SRC Papers; J. M. Tydings to Barry Bingham, September 21, 1948, reel 1, folder 548, SRC Papers; J. M. Tydings to G. S. Mitchell, January 31, 1949, reel 1, folder 548, SRC Papers.

9. "Youths of Varied Faiths Plan Forum," *Louisville Defender,* December 16, 1945; "Youth in Action Eager to Boost Democracy," *Louisville Courier-Journal,* January 27, 1946.

10. I discuss this subculture and its impact on local theologian Clarence Jordan in *Interracialism and Christian Community*. For the impact of this subculture on the women's movement, see Sara Evans, *Personal Politics: The*

Roots of Women's Liberation in the Civil Rights Movement and the New Left (New York: Vintage Books, 1979).

11. "Racial Relations Meeting Sunday," *Louisville Leader,* January 12, 1946; "Fellowship Hour," *Louisville Leader,* October 12, 1946; "Urge Racial Equality; Hold City Interracial Clinic," *Louisville Leader,* November 16, 1946; "Young People's Group to Sponsor Interracial Meeting Here Sunday," *Louisville Courier-Journal,* April 16, 1948; "Teachers Are Urged to Aid in Fight on Racial Prejudice," *Louisville Courier-Journal,* April 29, 1948.

12. Mrs. E. H. Menart et al., statement, February 17, 1950, reel 1, folder 1686, SRC Papers.

13. Kerns, *Survey of the Economic and Cultural Conditions,* 29.

14. "R. C. Black Heads Unit to Plan FEPC Here," *Louisville Courier-Journal,* January 30, 1945; "FEPC Discussed at Interracial Forum," *Louisville Courier-Journal,* March 19, 1945; William Warley, "Crowd Hears Doyle and Wilson at FEPC Rally," *Louisville Leader,* February 2, 1946; "Scores Filibuster: Riling Closing FEPC Speaker," *Louisville Leader,* February 9, 1946; "Board to Continue Local Campaign for FEPC Bill," *Louisville Courier-Journal,* February 24, 1946. For the history of the first FEPC, see Merl E. Reed, *Seedtime for the Modern Civil Rights Movement: The President's Committee on Fair Employment Practice, 1941–1946* (Baton Rouge: Louisiana State University Press, 1991).

15. "Names Sought on Plea for Fair Employment," *Louisville Courier-Journal,* March 14, 1952; "3000 Here Sign Plea for FEPC Legislation," *Louisville Courier-Journal,* April 8, 1952; "3000 Signatures for FEPC," *Louisville Defender,* April 9, 1952; "Why Signing the FEPC Petition Is an Important Factor," *Cub* (FE local 286 newsletter), June 6, 1952.

16. "Aldermen Will Hear Petition for City FEP Ordinance," *Louisville Defender,* July 2, 1952; "Aldermen Questioned about FEPC Ordinance," *Louisville Defender,* July 16, 1952; "For a Healthy and Prosperous Community—Pass FEPC Now," n.d., box 54, file 4, Braden Papers; H. A. I. Rosenberg, radio address, October 18, 1952, box 54, file 4, Braden Papers; "Aldermen Will Introduce City Fair Employment Practice Law," *Louisville Defender,* October 29, 1952.

17. "Racial Discrimination to Be Outlawed in GE Jobs," *Louisville Defender,* July 28, 1951; "GE Charged with Bias in Employment," *Louisville Defender,* December 24, 1952; "GE's Stand on Race Employment Remains Secret," *Louisville Defender,* March 1, 1952; "Discrimination Charges Hurled at New GE Plant," *Louisville Defender,* March 4, 1953; "National Negro Labor Council Plans Fight for Jobs," *Cub,* November 19, 1951; "GE Hiring Policy Discussed with Plant Officials," *Louisville Defender,* May 14, 1952; "National Labor Group Endorses Fight Here on GE's Biased Hiring," *Louisville Defender,* April 9, 1953.

18. "Better Group Relations Seen for GE Plant Workers after NLRB vote," *Louisville Defender,* August 27, 1953; "Government Takes NLC GE Protest,"

Louisville Defender, February 17, 1955; "Government Probes Job Bias Charge at GE," *Louisville Defender,* May 26, 1955.

19. "'White Only' Ad Shocking," *Louisville Defender,* April 7, 1951; "Aldermen Advise Civil Service Board to Stop Race Discrimination in Selection of City Employees," *Louisville Defender,* May 5, 1951; "Civil Service Board Feels Change in City Job Policy Would 'Upset Things,'" *Louisville Defender,* May 26, 1951; "NAACP Considers Board Decision 'Challenging,'" *Louisville Defender,* May 26, 1951; "Members of NAACP Protest City's Decision," *Louisville Defender,* June 23, 1951; Mr. I-Xposit, "Being Serious after the Election as Well," *Louisville Defender,* September 17, 1953; "Department Heads Are Not Surprised," *Louisville Defender,* February 4, 1954; "Colored Clerk Employed in City Hall for First Time," *Louisville Defender,* July 16, 1952; George C. Wright, *A History of Blacks in Kentucky,* vol. 2, *In Pursuit of Equality, 1890–1980* (Frankfort: Kentucky Historical Society, 1992), 195; "City Police Now Picked without Regard for Race," *Louisville Defender,* July 7, 1955; "3 Eligible Applicants Minus Jobs Because of Bias in City Parks," *Louisville Defender,* April 15, 1954.

20. "Ministers Urge Transit Co to Change Employment Policy," *Louisville Defender,* January 21, 1953; L. E. Woodard, "Millions Spent, Still Decent Job Not Open for Negroes Who Qualify," *Louisville Defender,* September 3, 1953.

21. Alice Allison Dunnigan, *The Fascinating Story of Black Kentuckians: Their Heritage and Traditions* (Washington, DC: Association for the Study of Afro-American Life and History, 1982), 282.

22. "Hiring Phone Operators Here 'against Public Policy,'" *Louisville Defender,* September 16, 1954; "Pennies for Jobs," *Louisville Defender,* November 25, 1954; "Telephone Company Accepts Negro Applicants; Will Hire upon Qualifications," *Louisville Defender,* March 1, 1956; "Sou. Bell Interviews All but Hires Only Whites," *Louisville Defender,* June 7, 1956.

23. "Chain-Store Employment," *Louisville Defender,* May 14, 1952; L. E. Woodard, "$70 Million Market Scorned by Merchants Who Won't Hire Negroes," *Louisville Defender,* August 13, 1953; Frank L. Stanley, Being Frank About, *Louisville Defender,* March 15, 1956.

24. *Kentucky's Black Heritage,* 99; Wright, *History of Blacks in Kentucky,* 54–56. My thanks to Angela Calloway, who helped to organize the Anne and Carl Braden Papers at the University of Louisville and is writing a dissertation on the desegregation of Louisville's hospital facilities at the University of Louisville, for information on hospital segregation in Louisville.

25. Anne Braden, interview, March 22, 2001; news release, September 10, 1950, box 50, file 9, Braden Papers; Anne Braden to Caesar Bell, October 24, 1950, box 50, file 9, Braden Papers; Anne Braden to Clayton, October 24, 1950, box 50, file 9, Braden Papers; IHM, news release, November 27, 1950, box 50, file 9, Braden Papers; IHM, news release, January 20, 1951, file 26, Louisville: Campaign for Louisville Interracial Hospitals, Social Action Files, State Historical Society of Wisconsin.

26. "Hazelwood Sanatorium Opens Doors," *Louisville Defender*, February 17, 1951; "Hospital Movement Group Believes Some Progress Has Been Made," *Louisville Defender*, April 21, 1951; Carl Braden to Charles Steele, June 13, 1951, box 50, file 9, Braden Papers; Reverend J. C. Olden, "Lack of Coordination," *Louisville Defender*, May 2, 1951; "State Hospital Licensing Act Would Ban Race Discrimination," *Louisville Defender*, February 16, 1952; Reverend J. C. Olden, "Lest We Forget," *Louisville Defender*, March 1, 1952.

27. IHM, statement, January 1951, box 50, file 9, Braden Papers; IHM, news release, February 1951, box 50, file 9, Braden Papers; Anne Braden to Reverend J. W. Adams, [1951], box 50, file 9, Braden Papers.

28. Dunnigan, *Fascinating Story of Black Kentuckians*, 151; Wright, *Life behind a Veil*, 259–60. See below for Tucker's political differences with the NAACP. "Organization Formed to Protect Negroes," *Louisville Courier-Journal*, November 24, 1940; Bob Winlock, statement in radio script for Louisville NLC broadcast, February 14, 1954, box 54, file 4, Braden Papers; "County Asked to End Restroom Segregation," *Louisville Courier-Journal*, February 4, 1953; "Bias Signs Removed from Courthouse," *Louisville Defender*, March 4, 1953.

29. "Picketing Halted by Results Gotten," *Louisville Leader*, June 8, 1946; Alfred M. Carroll to Gloster B. Current, December 2, 1946, box C66, file "Louisville, KY, 1945–1949," group 2, National Association for the Advancement of Colored People Papers, Manuscript Division, Library of Congress, Washington, DC (hereafter cited as NAACP Papers); "Teachers Hit Segregation at Concerts," *Louisville Courier-Journal*, September 30, 1947; "Segregation at Concerts Is Upheld," *Louisville Courier-Journal*, September 23, 1947; Frank L. Stanley, People, Places and Problems, *Louisville Defender*, February 10, 1951.

30. For a detailed treatment of the desegregation of the parks as an example of the use of multiple strategies, see Jonathan M. Free, "Life, Liberty, and Recreation: Louisville Park Desegregation, 1947–1955" (honors thesis, University of Louisville, 2007).

31. Youth in Action to the editor, *Louisville Courier-Journal*, July 29, 1946; I. Willis Cole to the editor, *Louisville Courier-Journal*, July 29, 1946; Joseph McMillan, interview by the author, September 23, 1999, OHC; "Farnsley Promises to Poll Louisvillians on Segregation in Parks," *Louisville Courier-Journal*, May 25, 1948; "Student Fine Upheld by Jury," *Louisville Leader*, December 4, 1948; "Negro-White Picnic Set to Test Park Segregation," *Louisville Courier-Journal*, September 10, 1948; "A Thinly Transparent Wallaceite Device," *Louisville Courier-Journal*, September 11, 1948; "Civil Rights Group Votes to Postpone Interracial Picnic," *Louisville Courier-Journal*, September 30, 1948; "McCandless Charges Reds Plan to Incite Race Riot at Picnic Here," *Louisville Courier-Journal*, September 28, 1948.

32. "Suit Filed for Park Rights," *Louisville Leader*, July 5, 1947; Fletcher

Martin, "Shelbourne Inclined to Open City Public Golf Courses to All People," *Louisville Defender,* August 11, 1951; "Judge to Try 2 Phases of Antisegregation Suit," *Louisville Courier-Journal,* March 11, 1950.

33. "Don't Think City Park Suit Is Understood," *Louisville Leader,* August 30, 1947; "Park Judgement This Week," *Louisville Defender,* September 29, 1951.

34. Benjamin Shobe, interview by the author, August 27, 1999, OHC.

35. Youth in Action to the editor, *Louisville Courier-Journal,* July 29, 1946; "Civil Rights Group Votes to Postpone Interracial Picnic," *Louisville Courier-Journal,* September 30, 1948; "McCandless Charges Reds Plan to Incite Race Riot at Picnic Here," *Louisville Courier-Journal,* September 29, 1948; "Negro's Suit to Open Parks and Amphitheaters Put Off," *Louisville Courier-Journal,* July 30, 1947; Fletcher Martin, "Shelbourne Inclined to Open City Public Golf Courses to All People," *Louisville Defender,* August 11, 1951. On the use of a progressive image to thwart civil rights progress, see William H. Chafe, *Civilities and Civil Rights: Greensboro, North Carolina, and the Black Struggle for Freedom* (New York: Oxford University Press, 1980).

36. I. Willis Cole to the editor, *Louisville Courier-Journal,* July 29, 1946; "Farnsley Promises to Poll Louisvillians on Segregation in Parks," *Louisville Courier-Journal,* May 25, 1948; "Unfinished Business," *Louisville Defender,* January 20, 1951; Reverend J. C. Olden, "T. Byrne Morgan—His Record," *Louisville Defender,* February 9, 1952; "Judge Shelbourne's Decision," *Louisville Defender,* September 22, 1951.

37. "Texas Golf Argument Similar in Principle," *Louisville Defender,* December 22, 1951; "City Integrates Golf Courses; Other Inequalities Studied," *Louisville Defender,* January 26, 1952.

38. "NAACP Plans Appeal of Federal Suit on Outdoor Show Issue," *Louisville Defender,* February 23, 1952; "Amphitheater Racial Bars Are Lifted," *Louisville Courier-Journal,* March 11, 1954; "The Natural Thing Rules at Amphitheater," *Louisville Courier-Journal,* March 12, 1954; Frank L. Stanley, People, Places and Problems, *Louisville Defender,* March 18, 1954.

39. "City to Amend Regulation on Iroquois Segregation," *Louisville Courier-Journal,* June 9, 1953; "Suit Filed against City for Segregation in Parks," *Louisville Defender,* June 18, 1953; "City Right to Segregate Races in Parks Upheld," *Louisville Courier-Journal,* July 25, 1953; "Suit Seeks to Prevent City Building Segregated Pools," *Louisville Courier-Journal,* April 20, 1954; "White Team Embarrassed; Can't Play at Chickasaw," *Louisville Defender,* May 13, 1954; "Judge Drops Wade's Suit against Pools," *Louisville Courier-Journal,* January 11, 1955; "Suit Seeks to Nullify Park Bias," *Louisville Defender,* May 5, 1955.

40. "Supreme Court Rulings Ban Segregation in Public Parks, Playgrounds, Golf Courses," *Louisville Courier-Journal,* November 8, 1955; "Rulings May End Park, Pool Segregation Here," *Louisville Courier-Journal,* November 8, 1955; "Ban on Mixing Races at Parks in State Upset," *Louisville Courier-*

Journal, December 17, 1955; "5491 Bathers Open Season at 5 City Pools," *Louisville Courier-Journal,* May 31, 1956; "Now We Play Together Again," *Louisville Defender,* June 7, 1956; "Fighting Whites Stop Mixed Game," *Louisville Defender,* June 28, 1956.

41. "What Will You Do Now Mr. Morgan?" *Louisville Defender,* May 20, 1954; "Court Rules against Park Discrimination," *Louisville Defender,* March 24, 1955; "Ohio Court Bans Jim Crow in Cincinnati Park," *Louisville Defender,* August 19, 1954.

42. National Bar Association, Louisville, KY, news release, February 26, 1944, part 3, series B, reel 12, frames 588–91, NAACP Papers (microfilm); "A Glaring Inequality of Opportunity," *Louisville Courier-Journal,* February 10, 1944.

43. C. W. Anderson Jr. to Milton R. Kovitz, March 2, 1944, part 3, series B, reel 12, frame 585, NAACP Papers (microfilm); Charles W. Anderson to Roy and Thurgood, March 16, 1944, part 3, series B, reel 12, frame 595, NAACP Papers (microfilm); "Anderson's Bill Would Save State $1,000,000; At Terrific Cost to Colored Youth," *Louisville News,* March 11, 1944, clipping, part 3, series B, reel 12, frames 577–78, NAACP Papers (microfilm); "Straining at a Gnat and Swallowing the Old Camel," *Louisville News,* March 11, 1944, clipping, part 3, series B, reel 12, frame 580, NAACP Papers (microfilm); Karelen Isom, "Kentucky Senate Defeats Bill to Admit Negro Students to White Colleges," news release, March 16, 1944, part 3, series B, reel 12, frames 596–97, NAACP Papers (microfilm); John A. Hardin, *Fifty Years of Segregation: Black Higher Education in Kentucky, 1904–1954* (Lexington: University Press of Kentucky, 1997), 75–76.

44. J. M. Tydings to W. H. Perry Jr., April 10, 1946, reel 1, folder 1990, SRC Papers; "Open Letter from 3rd District Negro Democratic Organization to Governor et al.," *Louisville Leader,* April 3, 1948; "NAACP to Fight for Admission of Negroes to Kentucky Schools," *Louisville Courier-Journal,* January 15, 1948.

45. Johnson, interview; Dunnigan, *Fascinating Story of Black Kentuckians,* 226. Also see Wade H. Hall, *The Rest of the Dream: The Black Odyssey of Lyman Johnson* (Lexington: University Press of Kentucky, 1988).

46. "Subsidy of Prejudice Is a Slow Process," *Louisville Courier-Journal,* April 7, 1949; Hardin, *Fifty Years,* 90–97.

47. "Students for Repeal of Day Law," *Louisville Leader,* March 8, 1947; Hardin, *Fifty Years,* 99; James A. Crumlin to Thurgood Marshall, October 1, 1949, part 3, series B, reel 12, frame 623, NAACP Papers (microfilm); Wyatt, interview.

48. Dwayne D. Cox and William J. Morison, *University of Louisville* (Lexington: University Press of Kentucky, 2000), 115; Hardin, *Fifty Years,* 98–102; "NAACP Seeks to Avoid UL Suit," *Louisville Courier-Journal,* November 8, 1949; "Union Chiefs Ask UL to End Ban for Negroes," *Louisville Courier-Journal,* October 13, 1949; "Decisions on Education Again Dent Segrega-

tion Line," *Louisville Courier-Journal*, September 5, 1959; "Legal Barriers Removed, Seminary Admits Negroes," *Louisville Defender*, March 24, 1951; Henlee Barnett, interview by Linda White, March 28, 1984, OHC.

49. For a history of Louisville Municipal College, see James Blaine Hudson, "The History of Louisville Municipal College: Events Leading to the Desegregation of the University of Louisville" (EdD diss., University of Kentucky, 1981); Hardin, *Fifty Years*, 102–3; Fletcher Martin, "Muni College Faculty Hopping Mad about Snub Given Them by UofL," *Louisville Defender*, January 6, 1951; "Dismissed Faculty Has Cause for Legal Action," *Louisville Defender*, January 13, 1951; J. C. Olden, "Material Loss," *Louisville Defender*, January 6, 1951; "Municipal Teachers' Jobs," *Louisville Defender*, January 20, 1951; "Muni Students Believe Some Teachers Should Be Employed on Belknap Campus," *Louisville Defender*, March 10, 1951.

50. In the late 1940s and early 1950s, Louisvillians participated in a number of suits against the bus and rail companies because of discrimination encountered outside the city. Moreover, local attorneys and organizations took measures to make sure that the state followed federal court decisions on travel. See, for example, "Negro Testifies Changing Bus Seat Impaired Health," *Louisville Courier-Journal*, October 16, 1946; "Negro, Forced off Bus, Files Suit for $7500," *Louisville Courier-Journal*, February 17, 1948; "Railroad Battle Begins," *Louisville Defender*, March 8, 1952; "NAACP Plans Legal Steps to Force End to Train Segregation," *Louisville Defender*, November 26, 1952; "ICC Asked to Stop Train Segregation Here," *Louisville Defender*, December 31, 1953.

51. G. W. Sims, news release, [June 1951], box 55, file 12, Braden Papers; "Ministers to Resist Segregation," *Louisville Defender*, July 2, 1952; "Bus Patrons Here Told to Ignore Segregated Station," *Louisville Defender*, January 28, 1953; "Segregation in Railroad, Bus Terminals Won't Be Enforced by City Policy," *Louisville Defender*, December 10, 1953; "All Goes Peacefully as Negroes Use Main Waiting Room at Bus Depot," *Louisville Courier-Journal*, December 13, 1953; "Bus Station Continues Segregation Practice," *Louisville Defender*, December 17, 1953.

52. "May Sue Bus Station for Dining Room Bias," *Louisville Defender*, January 27, 1955; "How Not to Attract," *Louisville Defender*, May 19, 1955; Dot Griggs, "Some Citizens Still Use Old 'Jim Crow' Room," *Louisville Defender*, January 19, 1956.

53. "Refused Sandwich at Air Field, Woman Plans Suit," *Louisville Defender*, November 4, 1954; "Heustis Reaffirms Policy; Police Won't Enforce Private Segregation," *Louisville Defender*, November 18, 1954; "Move to Stop Standiford Bias," *Louisville Defender*, January 20, 1955; "Food Service Refused 3 at Standiford Field," *Louisville Defender*, April 28, 1955; "New Lease Includes Clause Barring Racial Discrimination," *Louisville Defender*, May 31, 1956.

54. Frank L. Stanley, People, Places and Problems, *Louisville Defender*, March 18, 1954.

55. Dunnigan, *Fascinating Story of Black Kentuckians*, 356–57; Louis C. Kesselman, "Louisville Negro Voting Fact-Finding Project" (report to SRC, October 3, 1956), reel 10, folder 15, SRC Papers. In a study of black voting behavior in 1958, the SRC surveyed voter registration numbers by state and county in seven southern states and found that nowhere did the percentage of blacks registered to vote exceed that in Louisville. Margaret Price, *The Negro and the Ballot in the South* (Atlanta: Southern Regional Council, 1959).

56. Kesselman, "Louisville Negro Voting Fact-Finding Project"; Shobe, interview; "GOP Leaders Open Quarters," *Louisville Leader*, October 5, 1946; "GOP Personnel Committee Named," *Louisville Leader*, January 5, 1946; "Democrats Name Campaign Heads," *Louisville Leader*, October 19, 1946.

57. "Anderson Breaks with GOP over Method of Delegate Selection," *Louisville Defender*, April 9, 1942; "Ol' Handkerchief Head Is Dead," *Louisville Defender*, April 16, 1952.

58. David Smith to the editor, *Louisville Leader*, September 28, 1946; "Concern Is Shown over City Hall Job Policy," *Louisville Defender*, April 14, 1951; "Mayor Fails to Name Negro," *Louisville Leader*, May 17, 1947; "FDR Independent Voters League Neutral on Childress and Henderson," *Louisville Leader*, November 1, 1947.

59. Anne Braden, interview, March 22, 2001; Gaslinger, interview; McMillan, interview; "Progressive Party—Local Adversary of US—Is Merely a Handful of Militant Reformers," *Louisville Times*, June 3, 1952.

60. "Truman Civil Rights Group to Hear Restrictive Deed Row," *Louisville Courier-Journal*, September 26, 1948. One study of black votes in the 1948 election showed that in heavily African American wards, Truman received 35.71 percent, Dewey 63.14, and Wallace only 1.15 percent of the vote. Collins, "Political Behavior of the Negroes," 101.

61. "Robsion Says He'd Appoint Negro Aide," *Louisville Courier-Journal*, September 15, 1952; "Congressional Candidates Meet at NAACP Forum," *Louisville Defender*, September 16, 1952; "Political Parties Start Fall Campaigns," *Louisville Defender*, October 8, 1953.

62. "Republicans Endorse Four," *Louisville Defender*, May 28, 1953; "Negroes May Gain More Offices at Polls Tuesday," *Louisville Defender*, October 29, 1953; "Shobe Urged to Enter Race for Legislature," *Louisville Defender*, January 13, 1955; "Five Negroes Filed for Primary," *Louisville Defender*, June 30, 1955; "Reverend Anderson Says: We Don't Advertize What We Do," *Louisville Defender*, September 29, 1955; Kesselman, "Louisville Negro Voting Fact-Finding Project."

63. "Lawyer Quits NAACP Office," *Louisville Defender*, October 29, 1952; J. Earl Dearing to NAACP, May 14, 1953, box C67, file "Louisville, KY, 1950–1955," group 2, NAACP Papers; "Crumlin Disgusted at Democratic Negligence," *Louisville Defender*, December 31, 1952; "Attorney Tucker Calls NAACP 'Partisan,'" *Louisville Defender*, January 21, 1953; "Organization Formed to Protect Negroes," *Louisville Courier-Journal*, November 24, 1940;

radio script, February 14, 1954, box 54, file 4, Braden Papers; "Negro Attorney Declares NAACP Fails to Meet People's Needs," *Louisville Courier-Journal,* January 25, 1953; "Tucker's Charges of 'Partisan' NAACP Just a Publicity Stunt," *Louisville Defender,* January 28, 1953; "McAlpin to Bolt Democratic Party," *Louisville Defender,* October 15, 1953.

64. "Negroes Active in Louisville Municipal Government," *American City,* April 1945, 86; "Nine Deputies Sworn In," *Louisville Defender,* January 7, 1954; "Anderson Gets Post," *Louisville Leader,* April 13, 1946; "Interest Is Hot in State Attorney's Race," *Louisville Defender,* September 15, 1951; Fletcher P. Martin, "Harry McAlpin Quits Law Firm," *Louisville Defender,* January 12, 1952; "Shobe Gets Commonwealth Appointment," *Louisville Defender,* October 4, 1956; Goldie Winstead Beckett, interview by Kenneth Chumbley, September 12, 1978, OHC; "New Director of Safety Says He's Not Biased," *Louisville Defender,* December 17, 1953.

65. "Defender Honor Roll," *Louisville Defender,* January 12, 1952; "14 Named to Defender 1952 Honor Roll," *Louisville Defender,* January 14, 1953; "Eleven Named Defender 1954 Honor Roll," *Louisville Defender,* January 6, 1955; L. E. Woodard, "Progress Noted in City's Race Relations in '52," *Louisville Defender,* December 31, 1952.

66. "Urban League Told Life Not So Bright for Negroes," *Louisville Courier-Journal,* April 13, 1948; "Speaker Hails Cooperation of Races Here," *Louisville Courier-Journal,* April 1, 1952; "Race Relations Apathy Dangerous League Told," *Louisville Courier-Journal,* February 15, 1952; "Town's Attitude on Race Is 'Sobering' NCCJ Believes," *Louisville Defender,* January 20, 1951; John Walls, interview by Patrick McElhone, July 31, 1973, OHC; "Race Relations to Be Studied by Police Here," *Louisville Courier-Journal,* August 3, 1948.

67. "Robinson Beats Louisville in Montreal," *Louisville Leader,* October 5, 1946; J. C. Olden, "Militant Church," *Louisville Defender,* November 19, 1953; Frank L. Stanley, People, Places and Problems, *Louisville Defender,* March 25, 1954; Charles T. Steele to John T. Kenna, December 19, 1951, and Charles T. Steele to Julius A. Thomas, January 31, 1953, both in box 13, file 8, Charles H. Parrish Papers, Ekstrom Library, University of Louisville, Louisville, KY.

68. Kerns, *Survey of the Economic and Cultural Conditions,* 180; "Our Challenge," *Louisville Defender,* May 10, 1956; Braden, *Wall Between,* 45–46; Edith M. Taylor to Lester Granger, February 24, 1956, box 105, folder "Louisville, KY, 1956," National Urban League Papers, vol. 1, 1910–1960, Manuscript Division, Library of Congress, Washington, DC.

2. Confronting School and Residential Segregation during the Cold War

1. MCM, news release, August 5, 1953, box 48, file 11, Braden Papers; "Bill Introduced to Ban Segregation in Schools," *Louisville Defender,* January

14, 1954; M. M. Perdue, statement before Joint Constitutional Amendments Committee, n.d., box 48, file 11, Braden Papers; Anne Braden to Jim [Dombrowski], February 27, 1954, box 48, file 11, Braden Papers.

2. "No Action Seen on School Bias Bill," *Louisville Defender,* March 4, 1954; "Reverend Anderson Seeks to Amend School Bias Law," *Louisville Defender,* January 21, 1954; Governor Lawrence W. Wetherby to Anne Braden, March 9, 1954, box 48, file 11, Braden Papers; "Railroad Plan, Segregation Bill Die in Senate," *Louisville Courier-Journal,* March 20, 1954; Daniel Hughlett and Lillian Elder to members of Citizens Committee for Democratic Schools in Kentucky, April 16, 1954, box 48, file 11, Braden Papers.

3. Robert J. Cottrol, Raymond J. Diamond, and Lelande B. Wave, *"Brown v. Board of Education": Caste, Culture, and the Constitution* (Lawrence: University Press of Kansas, 2003), 191; Michael J. Klarman, "Why Massive Resistance," in *Massive Resistance: Southern Opposition to the Second Reconstruction,* ed. Clive Webb (New York: Oxford University Press, 2005), 21; James T. Patterson, *"Brown v. Board of Education": A Civil Rights Milestone and Its Troubled Legacy* (New York: Oxford University Press, 2001), 72–73. For a quick survey of broader regional reaction to *Brown* in the first months, see Numan V. Bartley, *The Rise of Massive Resistance: Race and Politics in the South during the 1950s* (Baton Rouge: Louisiana State University Press, 1969), 67–81.

4. Hugh Morris, "Decision Voids State's Day Law," *Louisville Courier-Journal,* May 18, 1954; Carmichael and James, *Louisville Story,* 46.

5. "What Louisvillians Think of the Supreme Court Decision," *Louisville Defender,* May 20, 1954; "City, County Are Planning Integration," *Louisville Courier-Journal,* May 18, 1954.

6. Allan M. Trout, "Desegregation Delayed in State," *Louisville Courier-Journal,* June 18, 1954; "'We Should Not Lose Our Heads,'" *Louisville Defender,* June 24, 1954; "City Schools to Continue Segregation This Autumn," *Louisville Courier-Journal,* July 27, 1954; "Louisville Schools Await State Ruling," *Louisville Defender,* July 29, 1954; "Wetherby to Pick Group to Study Racial Integration," *Louisville Courier-Journal,* July 1, 1954; "Integration Is Legal Now," *Louisville Defender,* February 17, 1955; "State Won't Prosecute under Day Law, Aide," *Louisville Defender,* April 14, 1955.

7. Frank L. Stanley, Being Frank about People, Places and Problems, *Louisville Defender,* June 17, 1954; "Will Kentucky Be Last?" *Louisville Defender,* June 17, 1954; Frank L. Stanley, Being Frank About, *Louisville Defender,* October 7, 1954; Patterson, *Civil Rights Milestone,* 75–77; Gerald W. Heaney and Susan Uchitelle, *Unending Struggle: The Long Road to an Equal Education in St. Louis* (St. Louis: Reedy Press, 2004), 71–74; Paul Lutz, "Desegregation: A Crisis without Drama," *Journal of the West Virginia Historical Association* 10, no. 1 (1986): 16–18, 32–33.

8. Frank L. Stanley, Being Frank About, *Louisville Defender,* August 19, 1954; "Desegregation Group Meets," *Louisville Defender,* August 26, 1954;

"Preliminary Integration Steps Urged," *Louisville Courier-Journal*, December 17, 1954; NAACP, news release, July 16, 1955, box A227, file "Desegregation: Schools: Branch Action, 1955," group 2, NAACP Papers; "20 Demand Integration Here Now," *Louisville Courier-Journal*, July 22, 1955.

9. Carmichael and James, *Louisville Story*, 151, 161, 50–51; "Desegregation Study Asked by Carmichael," *Louisville Courier-Journal*, November 2, 1954; Frank L. Stanley, People, Places and Problems, *Louisville Defender*, November 25, 1954; "School Desegregation Held Needing Five Years," *Louisville Courier-Journal*, February 14, 1955; Allan M. Trout, "No Comment Is Available in Frankfort," *Louisville Courier-Journal*, June 1, 1955; Jean Howerton, "September '56 Is Still Integration Target Here," *Louisville Courier-Journal*, June 1, 1955; "Local Schools to Go Slow with Desegregation," *Louisville Defender*, June 9, 1955; "Board to Begin Planning Now for Desegregation," *Louisville Courier-Journal*, June 7, 1955.

10. Carmichael and James, *Louisville Story*, 84–86; "Desegregation Plan for City Provides for Restricting 'without Regard to Race,'" *Louisville Courier-Journal*, November 22, 1955; "Redistricting Plan Would Mix Races to Varying Extent at 46 City Schools," *Louisville Courier-Journal*, January 17, 1956; "Integration Set for All City's High Schools," *Louisville Courier-Journal*, April 24, 1956; "Pupil-Transfer Plan Criticized, Defended," *Louisville Courier-Journal*, November 23, 1955.

11. Patterson, *Civil Rights Milestone*, 85, 100–102; John A. Kirk, "Massive Resistance and Minimum Compliance: The Origins of the 1957 Little Rock School Crisis and the Failure of School Desegregation in the South," in Webb, *Massive Resistance*, 82; James H. Hershman Jr., "Massive Resistance Meets Its Match: The Emergence of a Pro–Public School Majority," in *The Moderates' Dilemma: Massive Resistance to School Desegregation in Virginia*, ed. Matthew D. Lassiter and Andrew B. Lewis (Charlottesville: University Press of Virginia, 1998), 128–30.

12. "Pupil-Transfer Plan Criticized, Defended," *Louisville Courier-Journal*, November 23, 1955; "Citizens' Views on Carmichael Desegregation Plan," *Louisville Defender*, December 1, 1955; Carmichael and James, *Louisville Story*, 85–86; "'Will Accept City School Board's Desegregation Plan'—Religious Group," *Louisville Defender*, March 15, 1956.

13. Milburn Maupin, interview by Darlene Eakin, October 2, 1978, OHC; Marion Porter, "'Climate of Approval' Is Called Key to School Desegregation," *Louisville Courier-Journal*, January 30, 1955; "County Group Publishes Data on Integration," *Louisville Courier-Journal*, April 3, 1955; "Planning Held Needed in Solving Race Issues," *Louisville Courier-Journal*, February 18, 1955; "Davidson Says Integration Can Be Calm," *Louisville Courier-Journal*, February 21, 1955; Margaret Yeager, interview by Darlene Eakin, July 1, 1973, OHC; Ora Spaid, "Many Clergymen Quietly Using Influence to Smooth Integration," *Louisville Courier-Journal*, September 10, 1956.

14. Carmichael and James, *Louisville Story*, 95, 56; Yeager, interview; Ev-

elyn Jackson, interview by Darlene Eakin, n.d., OHC; "Three School Faculties to Meet at California," *Louisville Courier-Journal*, February 14, 1956; "Desegregating Teachers Associations," *Louisville Defender*, September 29, 1955; "PTA Councils Vote to Integrate Groups Here," *Louisville Courier-Journal*, July 11, 1956; "High Schools Scheduled for Summer Integration," *Louisville Defender*, April 26, 1956; "Things Go Smoothly as First Negroes Enroll in Manual Summer School," *Louisville Courier-Journal*, June 12, 1956; "Race Integration in Schools Here Is Expected to Go Smoothly," *Louisville Courier-Journal*, August 1, 1956.

15. For more on massive resistance, see Bartley, *Rise of Massive Resistance*, and Tony Badger, "*Brown* and Backlash," in Webb, *Massive Resistance*, 39–55.

16. Wright, *History of Blacks in Kentucky*, 199–201.

17. Ibid., 201–3; *Kentucky's Black Heritage*, 106–7. On the day when the *Louisville Defender* covered the opening of Louisville's integrated public schools, the majority of front-page articles concerned conflicts in Sturgis.

18. "Questions on Integration Fired by White Parents," *Louisville Courier-Journal*, April 27, 1955; Carmichael and James, *Louisville Story*, 52–53; "Integration to Be Less than Slated," *Louisville Courier-Journal*, April 3, 1956.

19. For a review of the concept of private schools as an expression of parents' rights, see Kevin M. Kruse, "The Fight for 'Freedom of Association': Segregationist Rights and Resistance in Atlanta," in Webb, *Massive Resistance*, 105–9.

20. "Citizens Council Organized Here," *Louisville Defender*, April 28, 1956; "Millard Grubbs—September 8, 1956," and Federated news release, September 9, 1956, box 53, file 16, Braden Papers; "Citizen Council Files Suit against City's Board of Ed," *Louisville Defender*, August 23, 1956; William Patterson, interview by Darlene Eakin, n.d., OHC; Maupin, interview.

21. "Estimates Seem Awry on Integrated Classes," *Louisville Courier-Journal*, September 6, 1956; "Cross Found Burning at Barrett School," *Louisville Courier-Journal*, September 10, 1956; "Test Suit Is Possible on Picketing at Male," *Louisville Courier-Journal*, September 8, 1956; "1st Regular Term Integration Begins," *Louisville Courier-Journal*, September 11, 1956.

22. Carmichael and James, *Louisville Story*, 97–99.

23. Benjamin Fine, "Segregation End Here a Landmark," *New York Times*, reprinted in *Louisville Courier-Journal*, September 11, 1956.

24. "Ike Lauds City's Desegregation," *Louisville Courier-Journal*, September 12, 1956; Robert L. Riggs, "Carmichael Is Kept Overtime by President," *Louisville Courier-Journal*, September 21, 1956; "School Integration Success Has Put Louisville on Map, South African Says," *Louisville Courier-Journal*, November 20, 1956; "City's Integration Will Be Filmed," *Louisville Courier-Journal*, April 19, 1957; Roy Wilkins to the editor, *New York Times*, September 21, 1956, box A102, file "Desegregation, Schools, KY, 1956–1962," group 3, NAACP Papers; "NAACP Kentucky Unit Draws Praise," *Louisville*

Courier-Journal, June 28, 1957; Jean Howerton, "'Quiet Heard around the World'—School Integration in Louisville," *Louisville Courier-Journal,* January 28, 1957, clipping, box 10, file 1, Braden Papers.

25. "73.6 Percent of City Pupils Integrated," *Louisville Courier-Journal,* October 23, 1956; "Desegregation Increases in City, County," *Louisville Defender,* October 10, 1957; "Officials Say Integration Has Gone Smoothly," *Louisville Defender,* November 8, 1956; "Estimates Seem Awry on Integrated Classes," *Louisville Courier-Journal,* September 6, 1956; Anne Braden, "In Kentucky Racial Integration Is Steady If Not Speedy," *Southern Patriot,* November 1956; "Louisville Undergoes Changes in Education," *Louisville Defender,* September 6, 1956; "What about the Negro Teacher, Mr. Carmichael," *Louisville Defender,* April 26, 1956; Anne Braden, "Draft Report on School Desegregation in Kentucky," [1956], box 53, file 12, Braden Papers.

26. "City School Officials to Rule Today on Admitting Foe of Integration," *Louisville Courier-Journal,* November 29, 1956; "Carmichael's Move Was Timely," *Louisville Defender,* December 13, 1956; "Denied Admission to Male, Segregationist Sues Board," *Louisville Courier-Journal,* December 23, 1956; "Segregationist Gains Admission to Male," *Louisville Defender,* January 10, 1957; Philip Harsham, "Segregationist Seized Trying to Oust Chief," *Louisville Courier-Journal,* January 17, 1957; "School Integration Progress Made While Incidents Are at a Minimum," *Louisville Defender,* February 13, 1958.

27. "Kasper, Grubbs, Branham Harangue Fifty Persons," *Louisville Defender,* December 20, 1956; "Clinton Case Segregationist Offers Aid to Citizens' Council," *Louisville Courier-Journal,* December 13, 1956; "Kasper Says Louisville May Be Next Step," *Louisville Defender,* March 14, 1957; "Branham Continues Bias Stand as Juvenile Court Investigates," *Louisville Defender,* January 24, 1957; "Branham to Have Hearing in Juvenile Court Today," *Louisville Courier-Journal,* January 18, 1957; "Group Calls for Death of Top Court Members," *Louisville Courier-Journal,* August 4, 1957.

28. "13 Negroes Keep Citizens' Council from Meeting—Until They Leave," *Louisville Courier-Journal,* October 4, 1957; "Minister Indicted in Riot at Klan Rally Speaks Here," *Louisville Courier-Journal,* February 2, 1958; Clarence L. Matthews, "Defender Newsmen Interview the KKK's Imperial Wizard," *Louisville Defender,* June 25, 1959; "Klan Resorts to Mails in Members' Drive" *Louisville Defender,* July 16, 1969.

29. "Van Hoose's Proposals Due Study," *Louisville Courier-Journal,* January 24, 1956; "Pupils in Integrated Schools Gain Here," *Louisville Courier-Journal,* October 2, 1957; "Majority of County Pupils Now Integrated," *Louisville Courier-Journal,* September 28, 1958.

30. For a review of the literature on the impact of *Brown* on black teachers and school officials, see Adam Fairclough, "The Costs of *Brown:* Black Teachers and School Integration," *Journal of American History* 91 (2004).

31. "NAACP Will Ask City to End Park Segregation," *Louisville Cou-*

rier-Journal, May 19, 1954; "Butler Says Difficult Problem Raised by Integration of Negro Teachers," *Louisville Courier-Journal,* May 19, 1954; "Schools Will Keep Their Negro Teachers," *Louisville Courier-Journal,* June 2, 1955; "What about the Negro Teacher, Mr. Carmichael," *Louisville Defender,* April 26, 1956; "NAACP to 'Wait and See' on Negro Teacher Hirings," *Louisville Courier-Journal,* June 17, 1956.

32. "School Chief Foresees Negroes' Improvement," *Louisville Courier-Journal,* October 2, 1956; Carmichael and James, *Louisville Story,* 127–28; "Carmichael Says No Ridicule Intended," *Louisville Courier-Journal,* October 31, 1956; "Carmichael Reaffirms Beliefs," *Louisville Defender,* November 1, 1956.

33. "Integrate Teachers Here, NAACP Urges Board," *Louisville Courier-Journal,* July 11, 1957; Lyman Johnson to the editor, *Louisville Defender,* March 27, 1958; "Carmichael Says White People Not Ready," *Louisville Defender,* July 10, 1958; "Whites Not Opposed to Negro Teachers," *Louisville Defender,* July 31, 1958; "White Educators Would Work with Negro Teachers," *Louisville Defender,* August 7, 1958; "Members of School Board Expect Eventual Teacher Desegregation," *Louisville Defender,* July 24, 1958; minutes of KCLU board of directors meeting, May 21, 1959, June 18, 1959, box 1, file "Minutes, 1956–1961," Kentucky Civil Liberties Union Papers, Ekstrom Library, University of Louisville, Louisville, KY (hereafter cited as KCLU Papers); "Ministers Seek Desegregation of Teachers," *Louisville Defender,* June 11, 1959.

34. "City to Start Integrating School Staffs," *Louisville Courier-Journal,* August 2, 1959; "Board Votes to Integrate Teachers in Fall," *Louisville Defender,* August 6, 1959; "Faculty Integration Causing No Problem," *Louisville Courier-Journal,* October 7, 1959; "School Board Takes Next Logical Step," *Louisville Defender,* August 6, 1959; Lucy Larke, "Your NAACP," *Louisville Defender,* September 8, 1960.

35. On residential segregation, see Stephen Grant Meyer, *As Long as They Don't Move Next Door: Segregation and Racial Conflict in American Neighborhoods* (Lanham, MD: Rowan and Littlefield, 2000), and Kenneth T. Jackson, *Crabgrass Frontier: The Suburbanization of the United States* (New York: Oxford University Press, 1985).

36. Meyer, *As Long as They Don't,* 98–114.

37. "75 Pct. of Land Here Covered by Restrictions," *Louisville Courier-Journal,* May 4, 1948; "Woman Told Negroes May Live Anywhere," *Louisville Courier-Journal,* November 23, 1948; Grady Clay, "Deed Restrictions Block Many Property Transfers Here," *Louisville Courier-Journal,* January 18, 1950.

38. "Home Financing Is Big Problem for Negroes—but Can Be Licked," *Louisville Defender,* August 26, 1954; Catherine Fosl, *Subversive Southerner: Anne Braden and the Struggle for Racial Justice in the Cold War South* (New York: Palgrave Macmillan, 2002), 138–39.

39. Grady Clay, "Neighbors Buy House to Keep It from Negroes," *Louisville Courier-Journal*, May 14, 1950; Fosl, *Subversive Southerner*, 138; "'Klan Cross' Burned at Upper Grand Ave Home," *Louisville Defender*, July 23, 1953; "House Offer to Negroes Causes Stir," *Louisville Courier-Journal*, February 8, 1954; "House for Sale Alarms Neighbors," *Louisville Defender*, February 11, 1954; "West End Racial Flare-up Settles Down to Simmer," *Louisville Courier-Journal*, September 27, 1954; "Angry Neighbors Gather When Negro Couple Inspects House," *Louisville Defender*, September 20, 1954.

40. Braden, *Wall Between*, 6–10; Fosl, *Subversive Southerner*, 136–37; "Police Judge Cates Reminded That Police Can Be Told What Law Says," *Louisville Defender*, April 14, 1951; "Plaintiff Asks to Drop Pool Suit," *Louisville Courier-Journal*, April 22, 1954.

41. Andrew Wade, interview by Catherine Fosl, November 8, 1989, in the author's possession; Fosl, *Subversive Southerner*, 136–37; Braden, *Wall Between*, 10–11; "Every Man Has Right to Live Where He Wants To," *Louisville Defender*, May 20, 1954; Braden, *Wall Between*, 1–5.

42. For biographical information on Anne and Carl Braden, see Fosl, *Subversive Southerner*, and Braden, *Wall Between*, 1–5.

43. Fosl, *Subversive Southerner*, 140–41; Braden, *Wall Between*, 52–58; "Whites, Negroes Have Lived Together Happily in Shively for Years," *Louisville Defender*, May 27, 1954.

44. Fosl, *Subversive Southerner*, 140–41, 152; Braden, *Wall Between*, 58–61; "Whites, Negroes Have Lived Together Happily in Shively for Years," *Louisville Defender*, May 27, 1954; Leon Almon, "Protest Follows Negro's Move to Area," *Shively (KY) Newsweek*, May 20, 1954, clipping, box 10, file 2, Braden Papers; "Urban League Approves Insurance Firm for Wade," *Shively (KY) Newsweek*, June 3, 1954, clipping, box 10, file 2, Braden Papers; "Wade's Eviction Sought by Foreclosure Lawsuit," *Louisville Defender*, June 24, 1954.

45. Braden, *Wall Between*, 72–75; Joseph A. Newman to *Shively (KY) Newsweek*, May 20, 1954, box 10, file 2, Braden Papers; Braden, *Wall Between*, 76.

46. Braden, *Wall Between*, 79–81.

47. "The Test of Democracy," *Louisville Defender*, May 20, 1954; Nathaniel McKenzie to the editor, *Louisville Courier-Journal*, July 20, 1954; George T. Cordery, "Squarely behind Wade's Right," letter to the editor, *Louisville Courier-Journal*, May 19, 1954; Lillian Elder to the editor, *Louisville Courier-Journal*, May 25, 1954; I. O. Ford to the editor, *Louisville Courier-Journal*, May 25, 1954.

48. Fosl, *Subversive Southerner*, 148–49; Carl Braden, "Andrew Wade's House," n.d., box 7, file 3, Braden Papers; WDC, "Statement of Principles and Objectives," n.d., box 7, file 3, Braden Papers; minutes of WDC meeting, June 8, 1954, box 7, file 3, Braden Papers; Committee to Plan A. E. Wade Day, report, July 8, 1954, box 9, file 6, Braden Papers; "Sunday July 18 Is A E Wade Day," *Louisville Defender*, July 15, 1954; "Defenders of Wade Postpone Complaint to Grand Jury," *Louisville Courier-Journal*, July 2, 1954.

49. John Y. Hitt, "Has the Wade's [*sic*] Shively 'Dream Home' Turned Out to Be a Nightmare," *Shively (KY) Newsweek,* May 20, 1954, clipping, box 10, file 2, Braden Papers; "Data on Grubbs," June 9, 1954, box 7, file 3, Braden Papers; "New 'Anti' Paper Makes Debut Here," *Louisville Defender,* February 25, 1953; news release, June 16, 1954, box 9, file 6, Braden Papers; Braden, "Andrew Wade's House," n.d., box 7, file 3, Braden Papers.

50. Mary L. Dudziak, "Desegregation as a Cold War Imperative," *Stanford Law Review* 41, no. 1 (1988): 81, 113; J. M. Tydings, "Report to the Kentucky Commission on Interracial Cooperation," 1947, reel 1, folder 1990, SRC Papers; "Prejudice in U.S. Growing Worse, Human Relations Institute Here Told," *Louisville Courier-Journal,* November 17, 1950; "Nation Must Be Strong through Faith in Our Beliefs, Urban League Is Told," *Louisville Courier-Journal,* February 9, 1951. For surveys of the impact of the cold war on the civil rights movement, see Mary L. Dudziak, *Cold War Civil Rights: Race and the Image of American Democracy* (Princeton, NJ: Princeton University Press, 2000); Thomas Borstelmann, *The Cold War and the Color Line: American Race Relations in the Global Arena* (Cambridge, MA: Harvard University Press, 2001); and Brenda Gayle Plummer, *Rising Wind: Black Americans and U.S. Foreign Affairs, 1935–1960* (Chapel Hill: University of North Carolina Press, 1996). For surveys of the southern red scare, see Jeff Woods, *Black Struggle, Red Scare: Segregation and Anti-communism in the South, 1948–1968* (Baton Rouge: Louisiana State University Press, 2004), and George Lewis, *The White South and the Red Menace: Segregationists, Anti-communism, and Massive Resistance, 1945–1965* (Gainesville: University of Florida Press, 2004).

51. For examples of the impact of anticommunism on liberal and civil rights organizations, see Frank T. Adams, *Unearthing Seeds of Fire: The Idea of Highlander* (Winston-Salem, NC: Blair, 1975); Thomas A. Krueger, *And Promises to Keep: The Southern Conference for Human Welfare* (Nashville, TN: Vanderbilt University Press, 1967); Klibaner, *Conscience of a Troubled South;* John A. Salmond, "'The Great Southern Commie Hunt': Aubrey Williams, the Southern Conference Educational Fund, and the Internal Security Subcommittee," *South Atlantic Quarterly* 77 (1978); Sarah Hart Brown, "Congressional Anti-communism and the Segregationist South: From New Orleans to Atlanta, 1954–1958," *Georgia Historical Quarterly* 80 (1996); Michael Honey, "Operation Dixie: Labor and Civil Rights in the Postwar South," *Mississippi Quarterly* 45 (1992); Michael Goldfield, "Race and the CIO: The Possibilities for Racial Egalitarianism during the 1930s and '40s," *International Labor and Working-Class History* 44 (1993).

52. Grover G. Sales and Robert W. Zollinger to the editor, *Louisville Defender,* May 5, 1952; Louisville NLC, news release, May 19, 1952, box 6, file 12, Braden Papers; "Red Scare Results in 2nd Man Being Fired from Job in Jeff'ville," *Louisville Defender,* May 21, 1952; Louisville NLC, news release, May 26, 1952, box 54, file 4, Braden Papers; M. M. D. Perdue to the editor, *Louisville Defender,* June 4, 1952; "Q.M. Depot Suspends Barnett Again,"

Louisville Defender, July 30, 1952; "Walter Barnett to Appeal Risk Case before US Loyalty Board," *Louisville Defender*, January 28, 1953.

53. Gaslinger, interview; "Higgins to Sue for False Arrest," *Louisville Defender*, October 15, 1952; "Progressive Party Worker Fined $2," *Louisville Defender*, November 12, 1952.

54. "Grand Jury Will Hear the Wade Bombing Case," *Louisville Defender*, September 9, 1954; WDC, news release, September 13, 1954, box 9, file 6, Braden Papers; "Wade Case Rages," *Louisville Defender*, September 23, 1954; Fosl, *Subversive Southerner*, 160.

55. "Wade Case Rages," *Louisville Defender*, September 23, 1954; "Still Probing Wade's House Bombing Case," *Louisville Defender*, September 30, 1954; "Grand Jury Indicts Six in Wade House Bombing," *Louisville Defender*, October 7, 1954; Emergency Civil Liberties Committee, "The Louisville Seven," February 1, 1955, box 8, file 7, Braden Papers. For detailed descriptions of the grand jury hearing, see Braden, *Wall Between*, 168–82, and Fosl, *Subversive Southerner*, 155–62.

56. Braden, *Wall Between*, 244–53; "Reds Stir Up Race Hate, Ex-Communists Declare," *Louisville Defender*, December 9, 1954; "Braden Guilty; Jury Gives 15 Years, $5000 Fine," *Louisville Defender*, December 16, 1954.

57. "ACLU Will Aid Braden Appeal," *Louisville Defender*, January 20, 1955; Fosl, *Subversive Southerner*, 163; "Braden Says 'No Ill Feelings,'" *Louisville Defender*, July 21, 1955; "Braden Files 330 Pg Brief in Appeal," *Louisville Defender*, December 15, 1955; "Supreme Court Decision Rules Out Sedition Laws," *Louisville Defender*, April 5, 1956; "Ten Page Reply Brief for Braden Holds That Nelson Decision Not Understood," *Louisville Defender*, May 24, 1956; Fosl, *Subversive Southerner*, 193–95.

58. Fosl, *Subversive Southerner*, 194–95.

59. Braden, *Wall Between*, 317–19.

60. Ibid., 232–33; Barry Bingham to Carl Braden, June 26, 1956, box 9, file 3, Braden Papers; Fosl, *Subversive Southerner*, 199, 202, 228–37.

61. "Wade Renews Efforts to Insure Home," *Louisville Defender*, May 5, 1955; "Wade Foreclosure Suit Will Resume Hearing December 2," *Louisville Defender*, November 10, 1955; "Payment Order Suggested on Loan for Wade Home," *Louisville Courier-Journal*, February 9, 1957; "Wades Gain Clear Title to Shively House," *Louisville Defender*, May 9, 1957; WDC, news release, November 18, 1957, box 9, file 9, Braden Papers; Fosl, *Subversive Southerner*, 198.

62. "Wade Group Asks Arrests of Cross-Burners," *Louisville Defender*, February 17, 1955; "Police Have Suspect in Wade Bombing," *Louisville Defender*, February 16, 1956; resolution of Louisville and vicinity ministers and deacons meeting, April 2, 1956, box 9, file 4, Braden Papers.

63. "Rap Prosecutor's Office for Suggesting Might Be Another Wade Case If Negro Buys," *Louisville Defender*, June 16, 1955; "Jury Denies Medic in Property Suit," *Louisville Defender*, May 24, 1956; "City Real Estate Board

Charged with Aiding Housing Discrimination," *Louisville Courier-Journal,* July 7, 1955.

64. "Jury Hasn't Indicted Right Person—Tucker," *Louisville Defender,* October 7, 1954; "Braden Jailed to Protect Racists, Says Negro Group," *Daily Worker,* January 31, 1955, clipping, box 10, file 3, Braden Papers; WDC, statement, fall 1954, box 9, file 6, Braden Papers; "Labor Council Denies Red Tag," *Louisville Defender,* March 31, 1955; James L. Wright to the editor, [1954], clipping, box 9, file 6, Braden Papers; "The Rightist and the Fascist Threat," *Louisville Defender,* January 6, 1955; Jack Chancellor, "Let Me Rave," *Louisville Defender,* January 13, 1955; "Louisville Charges Yet to Be Proved," *Louisville Defender,* January 20, 1955.

65. "Red Scare Won't Stop Equality Campaign Here," *Louisville Defender,* October 7, 1954; James A. Streeter, "Local NAACP Sees Red; Asks Loyalty Oath," *Louisville Defender,* October 14, 1954; George Cordery to Gloster Current, October 8, 1954, box C67, file "Louisville Branch, 1950–55," group 2, NAACP Papers.

66. Roy Wilkins to Myrtle Moore, January 10, 1956, box A91, file "Carl Braden, 1956," group 3, NAACP Papers; Gloster B. Current to George Cordery, March 14, 1958, box C50, file "Louisville Branch, 1956–61," group 3, NAACP Papers. For a more detailed analysis of how local civil rights organizations responded to the red scare, see Tracy E. K'Meyer, "The Louisville Civil Rights Movement's Response to the Southern Red Scare," *Register of the Kentucky Historical Society* 104, no. 2 (2006).

67. "American Civil Liberties Union Opens Campaign to Form Kentucky Chapter," May 23, 1955, clipping, box 1, folder "FBI Files," KCLU Papers; Lee Thomas, interview by the author, April 10, 2000, OHC; Fosl, *Subversive Southerner,* 202.

68. Louis Redding, "Louisville Travesty" (Emergency Civil Liberties Committee, April 1955), box A91, file "Carl Braden, 1956," group 3, NAACP Papers; Fosl, *Subversive Southerner,* 184–85; "Group Asks Court of Appeals to Accept Brief from NY," *Louisville Defender,* November 3, 1955; "$1500 Given to Lubka, Braden's Legal Defense," *Louisville Defender,* January 13, 1955; "Additional Comments on the Louisville Bombing Frameup," n.d., clipping, box 9, file 4, Braden Papers.

69. "Call Gradulists [*sic*] 'Uncle Toms' in Race Issues," *Louisville Defender,* April 12, 1956; Louisville ex-defendants to friends in Brooklyn, December 15, 1956, box 9, file 7, Braden Papers. Braden made much the same argument in her memoir. Braden, *Wall Between,* 291.

3. Open Accommodations in the All American City

1. "Louisville Takes a Historic Stride in Race Relations," *Louisville Courier-Journal,* May 16, 1963; Chester Morrison, "The City That Integrated without Strife," *Look,* August 13, 1963, 41–44.

2. "City Hotels May Soon Take All Reservations," *Louisville Defender,* December 23, 1954; Frank L. Stanley, Being Frank About, *Louisville Defender,* November 11, 1956; "Henry Clay Hotel Policy Is to Bar Individual Negroes," *Louisville Defender,* July 3, 1957; Nat Tillman, "Rumors False on Policy at Seelbach Hotel," *Louisville Defender,* September 26, 1957; "Manager Says Sears Has No Bias Policy," *Louisville Defender,* February 6, 1958; "L&N Sets Integration on Interstate Riders," *Louisville Courier-Journal,* January 7, 1956; "Theater Managers Give Excuses for Jim Crow Ban," *Louisville Defender,* April 1, 1954; Nat Tillman, "Taylor Stores Serve Negroes—for a Day," *Louisville Defender,* January 22, 1959; Nat Tillman, "Public Accommodations Present Confusing Picture," *Louisville Defender,* January 8, 1959.

3. "How Not to Attract," *Louisville Defender,* May 19, 1955; Clarence L. Matthews, "Louisville Public Places Present Dismal Picture of Discrimination," *Louisville Defender,* November 29, 1956; "A Wave of Indignation Is Needed," *Louisville Defender,* December 24, 1958; "Our Challenge," *Louisville Defender,* May 10, 1956.

4. Runette Robinson, interview by the author, September 9, 2000, OHC; Arminta Poignard, interview by Gwen Potts, [1996], in the author's possession.

5. "Urban League Chief Hits Hysteria by Either Side over Integration," *Louisville Courier-Journal,* February 22, 1956; "NAACP Members Campaign Starts," *Louisville Defender,* September 24, 1959; "Local NAACP Mass Meeting Here October 16," *Louisville Defender,* October 13, 1955; confidential office memorandum, [April 1956], box 1, folder "FBI Files," KCLU Papers; "Rev. Fred L. Shuttlesworth Will Speak at Civil Liberties Rally Here May 22," *Louisville Defender,* April 9, 1959; "Speaker Hits at Attackers of Integrationists," *Louisville Defender,* May 28, 1959.

6. Raoul Cunningham, interview by the author, June 19, 1996, OHC.

7. "We Need to Follow Other Cities' Examples," *Louisville Defender,* January 15, 1959.

8. Frank L. Stanley, People, Places and Problems, *Louisville Defender,* March 18, 1954.

9. "Civil Rights Ordinance Proposed for City," *Louisville Defender,* August 29, 1957; "Progress in Accommodations Suffered during Past Year," *Louisville Defender,* February 13, 1958; "Suggested Law May Require State Action," *Louisville Courier-Journal,* August 25, 1957; "Louisvillian Introduces 3 Anti-Segregation Bills," *Louisville Courier-Journal,* February 21, 1958.

10. Clarence L. Matthews, "Frontiers Quiz Candidates on 'Rights' Bill," *Louisville Defender,* October 24, 1957; "Negro Ministers Query Candidates," *Louisville Courier-Journal,* October 15, 1957; Frank L. Stanley, Being Frank About, *Louisville Defender,* October 31, 1957; "Pressure Ill Placed for the Negro Cause," *Louisville Courier-Journal,* October 31, 1957; "Pressure Necessary for Progress," *Louisville Defender,* November 7, 1957.

11. "Anderson's Civil Rights Bills Are a Must," *Louisville Defender,* Feb-

ruary 27, 1958; minutes of mayor's advisory committee on human relations meeting, January 21, 1959, box 13, file 7, Parrish Papers; Frank L. Stanley, People, Places and Problems, *Louisville Defender*, October 22, 1959; Nat Tillman, "Mayor Opposes Enforced Desegregation," *Louisville Defender*, February 12, 1959.

12. "NAACP Youth Council to Fight Dime Store Bias," *Louisville Defender*, September 22, 1955; Raoul Cunningham, interview; "NAACP Youth Council Needs Support of Citizens," *Louisville Defender*, November 12, 1959; Aldon D. Morris, *The Origins of the Civil Rights Movement: Black Communities Organizing for Change* (New York: Free Press, 1986), 124–25.

13. Hall, *Rest of the Dream*, 134–36; Nat Tillman, "Walgreen Snubs Jamaican Mayor," *Louisville Defender*, December 4, 1958; Nat Tillman, "Taylor Stores Serve Negroes—for a Day," *Louisville Defender*, January 22, 1959; Nat Tillman, "Taylor's Serve, Refuse within Two Blocks," *Louisville Defender*, January 29, 1959; Nat Tillman, "NAACP Youth Council Wages Bias Fight," *Louisville Defender*, February 26, 1959; Nat Tillman, "St. Louis Students Begin Boycott; No Support Given in Louisville," *Louisville Defender*, March 19, 1959.

14. Raoul Cunningham, interview; "NAACP Pickets Brown Theater; Drive to Spread," *Louisville Defender*, December 31, 1959; Kenton Atwood, interview by the author, November 6, 1996, in the author's possession; "Interracial Group Views Porgy and Bess," *Louisville Defender*, February 4, 1960.

15. "An Editorial," *Louisville Defender*, January 7, 1960; "Mayor Refuses Stand in Accommodations Issue," *Louisville Defender*, January 7, 1960; Frank L. Stanley, Being Frank About, *Louisville Defender*, February 25, 1960; "Voluntary Hotel, Café, Theater Integration Sought," *Louisville Courier-Journal*, February 12, 1960.

16. "NAACP Readies Bill to Bar Bias in Privately Owned Places," *Louisville Courier-Journal*, January 9, 1960; "City NAACP Readies Proposed Civil Rights Bill for City, State," *Louisville Defender*, January 28, 1960; "Beckett Introduces 'Accommodations' Law," *Louisville Defender*, February 11, 1960; minutes of board of aldermen meeting, February 23, 1960, project B, series II, reel 4, Louisville City Records, Louisville Metro Government Archives, Louisville, KY. For a discussion of the Kilpatrick quote, which came in response to the Birmingham crisis and the call for a national civil rights law, see Nancy MacLean, *Freedom Is Not Enough: The Opening of the American Work Place* (Cambridge, MA: Harvard University Press, 2006), 63.

17. "Louisville's Great Decision of 1960," *Louisville Defender*, February 18, 1960; "Community Supports Beckett," *Louisville Defender*, February 18, 1960; "Leaders Disappointed in Aldermen's Action," *Louisville Defender*, March 3, 1960.

18. "Atty. General Rules City Can Pass Rights Ordinance," *Louisville Defender*, March 10, 1960; minutes of board of aldermen meetings, March 8, 1960, March 18, 1960, project B, series II, reel 4, Louisville City Records;

"Voting Is Delayed on Trespassing Amendment," *Louisville Defender,* April 28, 1960; "Mayor States He Was against Trespassing Law," *Louisville Defender,* May 5, 1960.

19. "It Can Happen Here," *Louisville Defender,* March 10, 1960; Raoul Cunningham, interview; "State NAACP Resolves a 'Fight for Rights,'" *Louisville Defender,* May 5, 1960.

20. Anne Braden to Marvin Rich, February 28, 1960, reel 20, file 38, Congress of Racial Equality Papers, State Historical Society of Wisconsin, Madison (microfilm edition, University of Louisville, Louisville, KY; hereafter cited as CORE Papers); "Passive Demonstrations Are Presently Unwise," *Louisville Defender,* March 3, 1960.

21. "Group Protesting Race Bias Here Plans Sit-in Demonstrator School," *Louisville Courier-Journal,* April 30, 1960; "Citizens Rally to Hear CORE Leader," *Louisville Defender,* April 28, 1960.

22. "'Sit-in' Test Is Conducted at Tearoom," *Louisville Courier-Journal,* May 1, 1960; "'Will Open Tea Room When Right,' Kaufman," *Louisville Defender,* May 5, 1960; "Youths Picket Kaufman-Strauss," *Louisville Defender,* June 2, 1960; "Three Groups Urge Kaufman Boycott," *Louisville Defender,* May 19, 1960.

23. Anne Braden to Marvin Rich, February 28, 1960, reel 20, file 38, CORE Papers; application for affiliation, n.d., reel 20, file 38, CORE Papers; "Stand-In Held at Kaufman's," *Louisville Defender,* July 28, 1960; "Pickets Stage Second Stand-In before Kaufman-Strauss Tearoom," *Louisville Defender,* August 4, 1960; Charles R. Oldham to Marvin Rich, August 25, 1960, reel 20, file 38, CORE Papers.

24. "Committee to Organize Negro Voting Drive," *Louisville Defender,* July 21, 1960; Woodford Porter, interview by the author, September 9, 1999, OHC; "Support the Movement; Register to Vote," *Louisville Defender,* July 28, 1960; Mervin Aubespin, interview by the author, September 14, 1999, OHC; "Non-Partisan Committee Registers 22,000 Voters," *Louisville Defender,* September 15, 1960. On the SNCC debate over voter registration versus direct action, see Clayborne Carson, *In Struggle: SNCC and the Black Awakening of the 1960s* (Cambridge, MA: Harvard University Press, 1981), 31, 39–42.

25. "Bowlers Again Denied Service at New Center," *Louisville Defender,* September 1, 1960; "Shopping Center Is Hit by Pickets; Talks Set," *Louisville Defender,* September 8, 1960; "Shopping Center Pickets Are Attacked; Youth Hurt," *Louisville Defender,* September 15, 1960; "Algonquin Shopping Center Pickets Will Resume on Weekend as Negotiations Fail," *Louisville Defender,* October 6, 1960; "Group Continues Boycott at Shopping Center," *Louisville Defender,* January 12, 1961.

26. Beverly Neal to Joseph P. Perkins, December 6, 1960, reel 20, file 38, CORE Papers; Lynn Pfuhl to Marvin Rich, December 7, 1960, reel 20, file 38, CORE Papers; minutes of CORE steering committee meeting, January 19,

1961, reel 20, file 38, CORE Papers; "Stewart's Dry Goods Hit by CORE Demonstrations," *Louisville Defender*, November 17, 1960.

27. Lynn Pfuhl to Marvin Rich, December 7, 1960, reel 20, file 38, CORE Papers; Birdie McHugh to Sirs, January 19, 1961, reel 20, file 38, CORE Papers; minutes of CORE meeting, January 21, 1961, reel 20, file 38, CORE Papers; Johnson quoted in Wright, "Desegregation of Public Accommodations in Louisville," 199; August Meier and Elliott Rudwick, *CORE: A Study in the Civil Rights Movement, 1942–1968* (New York: Oxford University Press, 1973), 120.

28. Philip Hodge (son of W. J. Hodge), interview by the author, February 8, 2001, OHC; W. J. Hodge, interview by Chuck Staiger, December 14, 1977, OHC.

29. Raoul Cunningham, interview.

30. "Stand-Ins Close Restaurants," *Louisville Defender*, February 9, 1961; "Stand-Ins Continue at Kaufman's and Stewart's," *Louisville Defender*, February 16, 1961; "Five Arrested for Stand-In," *Louisville Courier-Journal*, February 21, 1961; "Stewart's Has CORE-NAACP Members Arrested," *Louisville Defender*, February 23, 1961; "58 Demonstrators Arrested on Fourth," *Louisville Courier-Journal*, February 25, 1961.

31. Runette Robinson, interview; Raoul Cunningham, interview; Deanna Shobe Tinsley, interview by the author, July 16, 1996, in the author's possession.

32. Raoul Cunningham, interview; "Statement Is Presented by Negro Unit," *Louisville Courier-Journal*, March 10, 1961.

33. Gerald White, interview by the author, August 29, 2000, OHC; Hank Messick, "Integration in Downtown Seems Near," *Louisville Courier-Journal*, February 26, 1961; "Stores to Integrate by April 1," *Louisville Defender*, March 2, 1961; advertisements, *Louisville Defender*, March 2, 1961 (Bob Brady's Furniture), March 9, 1961 (Comer's Pharmacy), March 16, 1961 (Louisville Apothecary); minutes of CORE meeting, February 11, 1961, reel 20, file 38, CORE Papers; "Stand-Ins Continue at Kaufman's and Stewart's," *Louisville Defender*, February 16, 1961; "Negroes Demonstrate Here: 14 Arrested," *Louisville Courier-Journal*, February 24, 1961; "Ministers Back CORE, NAACP 'Non-buying,'" *Louisville Defender*, March 2, 1961; "Community Backs NAACP Non-buying," *Louisville Defender*, March 9, 1961; "Non-buying Extended to after Easter," *Louisville Defender*, March 30, 1961; "Non-buying Campaign Ended—Leaders to Seek Jobs," *Louisville Defender*, May 11, 1961.

34. White, interview; "21 Negroes Are Arrested in Picketing," *Louisville Courier-Journal*, April 22, 1961; Runette Robinson, interview.

35. "Stewart's Has CORE-NAACP Members Arrested," *Louisville Defender*, February 23, 1961; "58 Demonstrators Arrested on Fourth," *Louisville Courier-Journal*, February 25, 1961.

36. "149 Seized, Including 9 Adults, in Eating Place Demonstrations,"

Louisville Courier-Journal, April 21, 1961; "162 Demonstrators Arrested as 'Sit and Squat' Tactic Used," *Louisville Courier-Journal*, April 25, 1961; "Biased Policy Breeds Trouble," *Louisville Defender*, April 27, 1961; White, interview.

37. "Negroes Demonstrate Here; 14 Arrested," *Louisville Courier-Journal*, February 24, 1961; "58 Demonstrators Arrested on Fourth," *Louisville Courier-Journal*, February 25, 1961; "Police Arrest 72 Pickets," *Louisville Defender*, March 2, 1961; "177 Negroes Are Arrested in Biggest Demonstrations at Theaters, Restaurants," *Louisville Courier-Journal*, March 15, 1961; "Police Brutality, Racial Violence Now Very Evident," *Louisville Defender*, April 27, 1961.

38. "58 Demonstrators Arrested on Fourth," *Louisville Courier-Journal*, February 25, 1961; "Police Arrest 72 Pickets," *Louisville Defender*, March 2, 1961.

39. Gloster B. Current to Jesse Devere, February 28, 1961, box C50, file "Louisville Branch, 1956–61," group 3, NAACP Papers; "Police Arrest 72 Pickets," *Louisville Defender*, March 2, 1961; George Gill, "26 Negro Youths Arrested in New Demonstrations against Segregated Shows," *Louisville Courier-Journal*, March 12, 1961; "Negro March Turnout Short of Expectations," *Louisville Courier-Journal*, March 16, 1961; "Judge Finds 11 Guilty of Disorderly Conduct," *Louisville Courier-Journal*, April 12, 1961; "39 Negro Students Arrested in Sit-In at Kupie Restaurant," *Louisville Courier-Journal*, April 19, 1961; "Juvenile Case Dismissed; 49 Pending in Policy Court," *Louisville Defender*, June 8, 1961.

40. "Stores to Integrate by April 1," *Louisville Defender*, March 2, 1961; "Deadline Set on Downtown Integration," *Louisville Courier-Journal*, February 24, 1961; "58 Demonstrators Arrested on Fourth," *Louisville Courier-Journal*, February 25, 1961; Hank Messick, "Integration in Downtown Seems Near," *Louisville Courier-Journal*, February 26, 1961. The members of the emergency committee were Dillman Rash of Louisville Title Company; Thomas Ballantine, vice president of Glenmore Distilleries; William Harrison, chair of Louisville Central Area Inc. and head of Taylor Drug Stores; George W. Norton, president of WAVE television; Barry Bingham, president of the *Louisville Courier-Journal, Louisville Times,* and WHAS; John M. Hennessey, Jefferson Circuit Court clerk; Henning Hilliard, broker; John Acree Jr. of Lincoln Life Insurance; Archibald P. Cochran, president of Anaconda Aluminum Company; and Henry Offert, president of Kentucky Trust Company.

41. Hank Messick, "Integration in Downtown Seems Near," *Louisville Courier-Journal*, February 26, 1961; "Full Desegregation Here within Month Predicted," *Louisville Courier-Journal*, February 28, 1961; "Orderly Integration Discussed at Meeting," *Louisville Courier-Journal*, March 1, 1961; "Stores to Integrate by April 1," *Louisville Defender*, March 2, 1961.

42. "Here Is the Text of Committee Report," *Louisville Courier-Journal*,

March 10, 1961; "Statement Is Presented by Negro Unit," *Louisville Courier-Journal*, March 10, 1961; "Negroes March and Sing Again on Fourth Street," *Louisville Courier-Journal*, March 10, 1961.

43. "Here Is the Text of Committee Report," *Louisville Courier-Journal*, March 10, 1961; "Time Enough Left for a Decent Human Influence," *Louisville Courier-Journal*, March 11, 1961; "Integration Situation Calm," *Louisville Courier-Journal*, March 11, 1961; "Statement Is Presented by Negro Unit," *Louisville Courier-Journal*, March 10, 1961; "Walker Says Integration Push Needed," *Louisville Defender*, March 15, 1961; Lynn Pfuhl to Gordon Carey, March 5, 1961, reel 20, file 38, CORE Papers.

44. "Negroes March and Sing Again on Fourth Street," *Louisville Courier-Journal*, March 10, 1961; "Integration Situation Calm," *Louisville Courier-Journal*, March 11, 1961; "Combs Joins Integration Talks as Committee Meets in Secret," *Louisville Courier-Journal*, March 17, 1961; "Mid-City Integration Talks Resume Today," *Louisville Courier-Journal*, March 18, 1961; "Integration Tension Appears to Be Easing," *Louisville Courier-Journal*, March 22, 1961; "Integration Committee Reports No Progress," *Louisville Courier-Journal*, March 29, 1961.

45. "Youth Endorse Rights Bill but 'Governor' Vetoes Plan," *Louisville Defender*, April 7, 1960; minutes of KCLU executive board meeting, February 15, 1960, box 1, folder "Minutes, 1956–1961," KCLU Papers; George Kimbrough to the editor, *Louisville Courier-Journal*, February 27, 1960; "Public Divided on Extent of Integration," *Louisville Defender*, March 17, 1960.

46. "Clergymen Here Delay Action on Desegregation," *Louisville Defender*, March 3, 1960; "Ministers Endorse City Ordinance," *Louisville Defender*, April 4, 1960.

47. "Segregation Protests Called Off," *Louisville Courier-Journal*, March 21, 1961; "Catholic Students Back Integration," *Louisville Defender*, April 27, 1961; "Integration Panel Convened by Mayor," *Louisville Courier-Journal*, April 29, 1961; James M. Rosenblum to the editor, *Louisville Defender*, March 23, 1961; Rosemary Payton to the editor, *Louisville Defender*, April 6, 1961; "Labor-Council Vote Supports Integration," *Louisville Courier-Journal*, June 21, 1961; Frank L. Stanley, Being Frank About, *Louisville Defender*, March 30, 1961.

48. "Group Advises Jailing Sit-In Demonstrators," *Louisville Defender*, May 12, 1960; "White Citizens Council Urges Use of Arms against Sit-Ins," *Louisville Defender*, May 12, 1960.

49. "Café, Tavern Groups Hold Closed Meeting," *Louisville Courier-Journal*, April 24, 1961; "New Group Opposed to Forced Integration," *Louisville Courier-Journal*, April 30, 1961.

50. "Committee Plans St. Louis Visit," *Louisville Courier-Journal*, April 15, 1961; George Gill, "10 Downtown Eating Places Hit as Negroes Resume Sit-In Plans," *Louisville Courier-Journal*, April 16, 1961; "Sit-Ins, Pickets Continue as 6 Firms Deny Service," *Louisville Courier-Journal*, April 18, 1961;

"149 Seized, Including 9 Adults, in Eating Place Demonstrations," *Louisville Courier-Journal,* April 21, 1961.

51. "Statement Is Presented by Negro Unit," *Louisville Courier-Journal,* March 10, 1961; Ora Spaid, "Dr. King Says 'Segregation Is Dead,'" *Louisville Courier-Journal,* April 20, 1961.

52. Joseph Perkins, news release, March 27, 1961, reel 20, file 38, CORE Papers; "NAACP Support Is Offered at Rally," *Louisville Courier-Journal,* March 20, 1961; "Freedom Riders Defy South; New Trips May Start from Here Next Month," *Louisville Defender,* June 1, 1961; "Shuttlesworth, ML King, Farmer to Speak Here," *Louisville Defender,* June 6, 1961.

53. Douglass Nunn, "New Plan Hinted on Integration," *Louisville Courier-Journal,* April 25, 1961; "Mayor Plans Tests for Desegregation," *Louisville Courier-Journal,* April 26, 1961; "This Is a Crucial Time for Decision on Desegregation," *Louisville Courier-Journal,* April 27, 1961.

54. "Restaurant Integration Fails," *Louisville Courier-Journal,* May 2, 1961; "Sit-Ins May Resume," *Louisville Defender,* May 4, 1961; "Racial-Protest Issue Unresolved," *Louisville Courier-Journal,* May 3, 1961; "Negroes Request Appeal by Mayor," *Louisville Courier-Journal,* May 4, 1961; "Negroes Call Off Boycott, Rule Out Demonstrations for Derby Weekend," *Louisville Courier-Journal,* May 6, 1961; "High Statesmanship," *Louisville Defender,* May 11, 1961.

55. "Next Desegregation Steps," *Louisville Defender,* May 4, 1961; "Negroes Seek Integration Law," *Louisville Courier-Journal,* May 18, 1961; "Hoblitzell Won't Force Integration," *Louisville Courier-Journal,* May 25, 1961; "Integration Leaders Ask Strong Accommodation Law," *Louisville Defender,* May 25, 1961; "Demonstrations Held Possible—Integration March on Aldermen Tuesday," *Louisville Defender,* June 8, 1961.

56. Minutes of board of aldermen meeting, June 13, 1961, project B, series II, reel 4, Louisville City Records.

57. Aubespin, interview, September 14, 1999.

58. John Briney, "Rocks, Eggs Thrown at Negroes Picketing Fontaine Ferry Park," *Louisville Courier-Journal,* June 20, 1961.

59. "Judge Curbs Picketing at Fontaine Ferry Park," *Louisville Courier-Journal,* June 21, 1960; "Freedom Marches On—Arrests, Fines Will Not Deter," *Louisville Defender,* June 22, 1961; "Negro Leaders Assail Judge, Democratic Organization," *Louisville Defender,* June 22, 1961; "Probation Voided in Stand-Ins," *Louisville Defender,* August 10, 1961.

60. "Mayor Group to Ask Talk on Rights," *Louisville Courier-Journal,* June 20, 1961; "Hoblitzell Forms New Integration Committee," *Louisville Defender,* July 13, 1961; "New Mayor's Group Comes under Fire," *Louisville Defender,* July 20, 1961; minutes of mayor's advisory committee on human rights meeting, July 18, 1961, box 13, file 7, Parrish Papers; "Mayor's Committee to Push Integration," *Louisville Defender,* July 27, 1961; Frank L. Stanley, Being Frank About, *Louisville Defender,* August 24, 1961.

61. Thornton Connell, "Negro Group Opposes Milburn and Ticket," *Louisville Courier-Journal,* February 9, 1961; "NAACP Unit Backs Dearing's View of Milburn," *Louisville Courier-Journal,* February 12, 1961; "Ministerial Alliance Opposed to Milburn," *Louisville Courier-Journal,* February 22, 1961.

62. "4 Candidates for Mayor Give Racial Views," *Louisville Courier-Journal,* February 24, 1961; "GOP Raps Mayor's Part in Integration," *Louisville Courier-Journal,* April 19, 1961; "Cowger Outlines Rights Position," *Louisville Defender,* July 7, 1961; "All Is Not Lost," *Louisville Defender,* June 22, 1961; "Cowger and Milburn Cut of Same Cloth," *Louisville Defender,* June 29, 1961.

63. "Voter Registration Drive Set," *Louisville Defender,* August 3, 1961; Raoul Cunningham, interview; "Parade Urges Voting," *Louisville Defender,* August 31, 1961.

64. Aubespin, interview, September 14, 1999.

65. "Cowger Wins by 16,581 in Big Upset," *Louisville Courier-Journal,* November 8, 1961; Fred Minshall, "Republicans Sweep City and County," *Louisville Courier-Journal,* November 8, 1961; "Democrats Win Only Fifth Ward as GOP Takes Rest, Plus County," *Louisville Courier-Journal,* November 8, 1961; "Republicans Sweep to Victory," *Louisville Defender,* November 9, 1961.

66. "Cowger Wins by 16,581 in Big Upset," *Louisville Courier-Journal,* November 8, 1961; Fred Minshall, "Republicans Sweep City and County," *Louisville Courier-Journal,* November 8, 1961; "Democrats Win Only Fifth Ward as GOP Takes Rest, Plus County," *Louisville Courier-Journal,* November 8, 1961; Dean Duncan, "Democrats Agree It Was Case of 'Time for a Change' Theme," *Louisville Courier-Journal,* November 8, 1961.

67. Aubespin, interview, September 14, 1999; Raoul Cunningham, interview; W. J. Hodge, interview.

68. Frank L. Stanley, Being Frank About, *Louisville Defender,* November 16, 1961; "Republicans Sweep to Victory," *Louisville Defender,* November 9, 1961; Nat Tillman, "Negroes Heed Battle Cry 'for Change,'" *Louisville Defender,* November 9, 1961; "Victory Challenges," *Louisville Defender,* November 16, 1961.

69. "BOP May Seek Relations Bill," *Louisville Defender,* November 16, 1961; "Cowger Still Favors 'Voluntary' Integration," *Louisville Defender,* December 7, 1961; minutes of board of aldermen meeting, March 27, 1962, project B, series II, reel 4, Louisville City Records; "City Passes Human Relations Law, Ordinance Established Committee," *Louisville Defender,* March 29, 1962.

70. "Human Relations Commission to Check Accommodations," *Louisville Defender,* July 12, 1962; "Letters to Outline Integration Survey," *Louisville Courier-Journal,* July 26, 1962; "Ohio Theater Opens Doors after Prodding," *Louisville Defender,* September 27, 1962; minutes of HRC research committee meeting, October 12, 1962, box 4, file "Research Committee/Civic Groups

Committee Minutes, 1962–1963," Louisville Human Relations Commission Papers, Louisville Metro Archives, Louisville, KY (hereafter cited as LHRC Papers); "Has Human Rights Commission Achieved Any Desegregation?" *Louisville Defender,* January 10, 1963; "Half Eating Places Found Integrated," *Louisville Courier-Journal,* January 12, 1963.

71. "Demonstrations Begin at West End Theater," *Louisville Defender,* May 10, 1962; "Order Hits Integration Picketing," *Louisville Courier-Journal,* June 8, 1962; Mary Hamilton to James McCain, December 19, 1962, reel 40, file 347, CORE Papers; "Five Face Demonstration Hearing," *Louisville Courier-Journal,* June 13, 1962; *News from SCEF,* June 13, 1962, clipping, box 55, file 3, Braden Papers.

72. Arthur Smith, "SNAC Fights Bias," *Louisville Defender,* August 9, 1962; Nancy Pennick Pollock, interview by the author, September 9, 1999, OHC; Cecil A. Blye, "Youth Says Official Twisted His Thumb," *Louisville Defender,* June 14, 1962; "Racial Ills Make Louisville Seem like Deep South City," *Louisville Defender,* July 5, 1962.

73. "Negro Leaders Reach Accord on Ordinance," *Louisville Defender,* December 21, 1961; "Desegregation Ordinance Called for by Integration Leaders at Meeting," *Louisville Defender,* June 28, 1962; "Some Businesses Prefer Integration Ordinance," *Louisville Courier-Journal,* August 3, 1962; "Those Seeking Ordinance Get Unexpected Help," *Louisville Defender,* August 9, 1962; "Leaders Want Accommodations Law in '63," *Louisville Defender,* January 3, 1963.

74. "Ordinance Asked on Integration," *Louisville Courier-Journal,* January 8, 1963; Vincent Crowdus, "Group Backs Integration Ordinance," *Louisville Courier-Journal,* January 10, 1963; "Civil Rights Law Is Urged," *Louisville Courier-Journal,* January 19, 1963; Vincent Crowdus, "Six Undecided about Racial Law," *Louisville Courier-Journal,* January 11, 1963.

75. "Bias Ordinance Goes to Aldermen, despite Dissents," *Louisville Courier-Journal,* April 10, 1963; "Aldermen Ponder Bias-Code Votes," *Louisville Courier-Journal,* April 11, 1963.

76. "The Limit of an Anti-bias Law," *Louisville Courier-Journal,* January 10, 1963; "The Clear Way to Eliminate Discrimination," *Louisville Courier-Journal,* January 12, 1963; "Negro Rights in Restaurants Can Be Established Now," *Louisville Courier-Journal,* February 12, 1963; "This Ordinance Will Achieve Its Purpose," *Louisville Courier-Journal,* April 12, 1963.

77. "Why the Aldermen Should Act Now on the Antibias Law," *Louisville Courier-Journal,* May 14, 1963; *LHRC Newsletter,* February 19, 1963, box 5, file "Open Housing/Public Accommodations, 1961–1967," Ray Bixler Papers, Ekstrom Library, University of Louisville, Louisville, KY; Ted Hightower to the editor, *Louisville Courier-Journal,* May 12, 1963; "CORE Pickets Dime Store in Sympathy," *Louisville Defender,* April 25, 1963; "ML King Calls for Louisville Help," *Louisville Defender,* May 9, 1963; "Birmingham Protest Figures to Speak," *Louisville Defender,* May 16, 1963; "White Ministers to

Support Mass Meeting," *Louisville Defender,* May 23, 1963; John E. Weir to the editor, *Louisville Courier-Journal,* May 16, 1963; "Bias Ordinance Discussed," *Louisville Courier-Journal,* May 11, 1963.

78. Johnson quoted in Morrison, "City That Integrated without Strife," 44.

79. "Cowger Calls for Passing Ban on Bias," *Louisville Courier-Journal,* May 10, 1963; "Bias Ordinance Discussed," *Louisville Courier-Journal,* May 11, 1963; minutes of board of aldermen meeting, May 14, 1963, project B, series II, reel 4, Louisville City Records; Victor Crowdus, "Aldermen Pass Ordinance Forbidding Discrimination in Public Accommodations," *Louisville Courier-Journal,* May 15, 1963.

80. Drew Pearson, "Louisville Makes Racial Progress," *Louisville Courier-Journal,* May 31, 1963; Reuben S. Turner to the editor, *Louisville Courier-Journal,* June 24, 1963; minutes of HRC civic groups committee meeting, June 28, 1963, box 4, file "Research Committee/Civic Groups Committee Minutes, 1962–1963," LHRC Papers; Hedrick Smith, "Effective Progress in Race Relations without Fanfare Is Found in Louisville," *New York Times,* reprinted in *Louisville Courier-Journal,* June 5, 1963; "Louisville Wins US City Award," *Louisville Defender,* April 2, 1964.

81. "Come Now, Mayor Cowger," *Louisville Defender,* June 20, 1963; C. H. Parrish to Leslie W. Dunbar, March 26, 1964, reel 1, folder 1904, SRC Papers; "Come Again, Roy Wilkins," *Louisville Defender,* January 30, 1964; "Integration—Still Our Most Urgent Need, " *Louisville Defender,* February 13, 1964; Frank L. Stanley, Being Frank About, *Louisville Defender,* June 15, 1964.

82. Tom Riner to the editor, *Louisville Courier-Journal,* April 22, 1963; Otto Langneks Jr. to the editor, *Louisville Courier-Journal,* May 2, 1963; James M. Donato to the editor, *Louisville Courier-Journal,* June 13, 1963; J. E. Wheeler to the editor, *Louisville Courier-Journal,* June 25, 1963; "Local Group Seeks Segregation Ticket," *Louisville Defender,* October 10, 1963; "Three Cafes Refuse Despite City Law," *Louisville Defender,* September 19, 1963.

83. "Suit Is Set by Taverns on Bias Law," *Louisville Courier-Journal,* June 19, 1963; Frank L. Stanley, Being Frank About, *Louisville Defender,* October 10, 1963; "Aldermen to Reconsider Ordinance," *Louisville Defender,* November 14, 1963; "Trial Date Set for Rights Law Appeal," *Louisville Defender,* January 9, 1964; "State Appeals Court Gets City Brief," *Louisville Defender,* October 8, 1964; Clarence L. Matthews, "Louisville Human Relations Commission Has Purpose Re-affirmed by Courts," *Louisville Defender,* February 4, 1965.

84. "Push Rights Bill, Wilkins Urges KY," January 24, 1964, clipping, box A148, file "Government, State, Kentucky, 1958–1964," group 3, NAACP Papers; Georgia Davis Powers, interview by the author, March 24, 2000, OHC; "AOCR Asks Vigorous Enforcement," *Louisville Defender,* June 18, 1964; *Kentucky's Black Heritage,* 119, 121; Mattie Jones, interview by the author,

March 3, 2000, OHC; Clarence L. Matthews, "Senate Passage of Civil Rights Bill Is Almost 'Anti-climatic,'" *Louisville Defender,* January 27, 1966. Barbers, beauty shops, and rooming houses were exempted from the public accommodations coverage of the act.

85. "Louisville Takes a Historic Stride in Race Relations," *Louisville Courier-Journal,* May 16, 1963; Drew Pearson, "Louisville Makes Racial Progress," *Louisville Courier-Journal,* May 31, 1963; Hedrick Smith, "Effective Progress in Race Relations without Fanfare Is Found in Louisville," *New York Times,* reprinted in *Louisville Courier-Journal,* June 5, 1963.

86. "Come Now, Mayor Cowger," *Louisville Defender,* June 20, 1963; "An Honor to Be Shared," *Louisville Defender,* April 6, 1964; "Come Again, Roy Wilkins," *Louisville Defender,* June 20, 1963; Aubespin, interview, September 14, 1999; Cecil Blye, "Accommodations Ordinance Assures a Rosy Future," *Louisville Defender,* May 23, 1963; Anne Braden to the editor, *Louisville Courier-Journal,* May 30, 1963.

87. Aubespin, interview, September 14, 1999; Hunter S. Thompson, "A Southern City with Northern Problems," *Reporter,* December 19, 1963.

4. The Battle for Open Housing

1. Roosevelt quoted in Meyer, *As Long as They Don't,* 161.

2. On the national open housing movement and for case studies of northern and western legislative battles, see ibid., chaps. 8–10; Juliet Saltman, *Open Housing: Dynamics of a Social Movement* (New York: Praeger, 1978); and Lynn W. Eley and Thomas W. Casstevens, *The Politics of Fair-Housing Legislation: State and Local Case Studies* (San Francisco: Chandler, 1968).

3. Meyer, *As Long as They Don't,* chap. 10.

4. "Housing Discrimination Gets Going Over in 13 States," *Louisville Defender,* March 14, 1963; "Equal Housing Push Is Mapped by Rights Group," *Louisville Courier-Journal,* May 14, 1963; "Race Group Finds National Spotlight," *Louisville Courier-Journal,* June 5, 1963; Hedrick Smith, "Effective Progress in Race Relations without Fanfare Is Found in Louisville," *New York Times,* reprinted in *Louisville Courier-Journal,* June 5, 1963; "Housing, Job Anti-bias Laws Expected," *Louisville Courier-Journal,* June 15, 1963; minutes of HRC civic groups committee meeting, June 28, 1963, box 4, file "Research Committee/Civic Groups Committee Minutes, 1962–1963," LHRC Papers; "Human Relations Group Would Survey Housing," *Louisville Courier-Journal,* June 7, 1963.

5. Charles H. Lamb, *Housing Segregation in Suburban America since 1960* (New York: Cambridge University Press, 2005), 14–15. For three views on urban renewal and its impact on inner-city neighborhoods, see Clarence N. Stone, *Economic Growth and Neighborhood Discontent: System Bias in the Urban Renewal Program of Atlanta* (Chapel Hill: University of North Carolina Press, 1976); Jon C. Teaford, *The Rough Road to Renaissance: Urban*

Notes to Pages 114–116

Revitalization in America, 1940–1985 (Baltimore: Johns Hopkins University Press, 1990); and E. Michael Jones, *The Slaughter of Cities: Urban Renewal as Ethnic Cleansing* (South Bend, IN: St. Augustine's Press, 2004).

6. "NAACP Asks Mayor to Name Negro to Urban Commission," *Louisville Defender,* April 5, 1962; F. W. Woolsey, speech before the National Council of Jewish Women, October 1963, box 1, file 1, F. W. Woolsey Papers, Ekstrom Library, University of Louisville, Louisville, KY; "Race Group Not Agreed on Housing," *Louisville Courier-Journal,* March 5, 1963.

7. Cecil Blye, "Block Busting, Panic Selling Laid to Negro Realtors," *Louisville Defender,* August 1, 1963; Cecil Blye, "White Brokers Control West End Property Sales; Negroes Give Aid," *Louisville Defender,* August 8, 1963. On blockbusting, see Amanda Irene Seligman, *Block by Block: Neighborhoods and Public Policy on Chicago's West Side* (Chicago: University of Chicago Press, 2005), chap. 6.

8. Anne Braden, interview the author, June 7, 2001, OHC; minutes of WECC founding meeting, [May 22, 1963], box 1, file 1, West End Community Council Papers, State Historical Society of Wisconsin, Madison (hereafter cited as WECC Papers).

9. "West End Council Seeks Racial Answers," *Louisville Courier-Journal,* August 4, 1963; WECC constitution and bylaws, n.d., Judy Hicks Papers, in the author's possession; "History and Intentions of the West End Community Council," March 1965, box 2, file "WECC, 1961–1968," Harvey C. Webster Papers, Ekstrom Library, University of Louisville, Louisville, KY; Anne Braden, typescript article, April 1970, box 1, file 4C, Woolsey Papers.

10. Anne Braden, typescript article, April 1970, box 1, file 4C, Woolsey Papers; *News from West End Community Council,* September 27, 1963, box 1, file 13, WECC Papers; "West End Council Seeks Racial Answers," *Louisville Courier-Journal,* August 4, 1963; *News from West End Community Council,* October 28, 1963, box 1, file 13, WECC Papers; "Prejudice Not Prevalent in West End Area," *Louisville Defender,* March 26, 1964; "Most Whites to Stay in West End," *Louisville Defender,* April 9, 1964; "Anti-Negro Feeling Found in West End," *Louisville Defender,* June 25, 1964; "Report Says City-Wide Open Occupancy Is Necessary," *Louisville Defender,* July 23, 1964; Mildred Robinson and Don Keller to committee on research and survey of Louisville Area Council of Churches, October 1, 1963, box 1, file 14, WECC Papers; Anne Braden, interview, June 7, 2001; Norbert Logsdon and Shirley Logsdon, interview by the author, October 25, 1999, OHC.

11. "Fair Housing Ordinance Recommended," *Louisville Defender,* April 23, 1964; *Commission on Human Relations Newsletter,* May 1964, box 7, file 14, WECC Papers; "Mayor Cowger Not to Back Housing Law," *Louisville Defender,* July 2, 1964; "Cowger Makes 3/4 Reversal on Housing," *Louisville Defender,* August 13, 1964; "Housing Progress Reported," *Louisville Defender,* March 11, 1965; "Housing 'Code of Ethics' to Take Ordinance's Place," *Louisville Defender,* May 6, 1965.

12. Clarence L. Matthews, "Housing Legislation Here May Be First Enacted in South If Passed," *Louisville Defender*, May 27, 1965.

13. "Local NAACP Studies Proposed Housing Law," *Louisville Defender*, May 27, 1965; Clarence L. Matthews, "Civil Rights Progress Continues," *Louisville Defender*, July 22, 1965; minutes of HRC housing committee meeting, May 20, 1966, box 5, file "Open Housing/Public Accommodations, 1961–1967," Bixler Papers; "The Need for a Fair Housing Law: A Report Submitted to the Human Relations Commission of the City of Louisville," n.d., box 8, file 15, WECC Papers; Clarence L. Matthews, "Crash Program for Integrated Housing Now Developing in City and County," *Louisville Defender*, March 24, 1966; "Racial Turmoil and the City," *Louisville Defender*, August 11, 1966; "Schmied Says Housing Law Lacks 'Teeth,'" *Louisville Courier-Journal*, October 2, 1965; "Mayor Seeks Housing Facts," *Louisville Defender*, September 1, 1966.

14. Clarence L. Matthews, "Leaders Present Housing Ordinance to Aldermen," *Louisville Defender*, September 15, 1966; "Draft Housing Law May Be Tested before Court," *Louisville Defender*, September 22, 1966; Clarence L. Matthews, "Open Housing Report Leaves Negro Leaders Optimistic but Quiet," *Louisville Defender*, October 20, 1966; minutes of HRC housing committee meeting, December 21, 1966, box 5, file "Open Housing/Public Accommodations, 1961–1967," Bixler Papers; Clarence L. Matthews, "Compromise on Penalties May Result in Ordinance," *Louisville Defender*, December 22, 1966; Clarence L. Matthews, "Compromise in Housing Sought; Jail Term Is Issue," *Louisville Defender*, December 29, 1966; "Housing Law Appears Likely; Weak Police Powers Feared," *Louisville Defender*, February 2, 1967.

15. "Open Housing Law Lack May Spark Demonstrations," *Louisville Defender*, November 3, 1966; "City, County Government Face Show Down with Rights Leaders," *Louisville Defender*, November 24, 1966; Clarence L. Matthews, "Stepped-Up Civil Rights Activity Predicted Locally Despite Gains," *Louisville Defender*, January 5, 1967; "Housing Group to Meet on 'Best Possible' Law," *Louisville Defender*, January 5, 1967.

16. On the Chicago Freedom Movement and SCLC's role in it, see David J. Garrow, ed., *Chicago 1966: Open Housing Marches, Summit Negotiations, and Operation Breadbasket* (Brooklyn, NY: Carson, 1989). For the first local use of "technician," see William Drummond, "Housing Demonstrations Possible in Two Weeks," *Louisville Courier-Journal*, February 21, 1967.

17. William Drummond, "Outside Demonstrators May Come," *Louisville Courier-Journal*, January 7, 1967; William Drummond, "SCLC Ready to March," *Louisville Courier-Journal*, January 24, 1967; William Drummond, "Housing Demonstrations Possible in Two Weeks," *Louisville Courier-Journal*, February 21, 1967; William Drummond, "Rights Workers Flowing In," *Louisville Courier-Journal*, March 7, 1967.

18. "An Explosive Lull," *Louisville Defender*, February 2, 1967; news release, February 26, 1967, box 82, file 3, Braden Papers; Clarence L. Mat-

thews, "Louisville in Limelight as Demonstrations Loom Again," *Louisville Defender,* March 2, 1967; "Top Leaders Urged to Meet on Open Housing," *Louisville Courier-Journal,* February 25, 1967.

19. Minutes of HRC housing committee meeting, December 29, 1966, box 5, file "Open Housing/Public Accommodations, 1961–1967," Bixler Papers; "Young to Request Housing Hearings," *Louisville Courier-Journal,* January 4, 1967; Kenneth Loomis, "Agency Offers Aid in Housing Debate, But . . . ," *Louisville Courier-Journal,* January 6, 1967; "Louisville Enters a Critical Period in Race Relations," *Louisville Courier-Journal,* January 20, 1967; "Housing Hearing Set on Original Proposal," *Louisville Courier-Journal,* February 1, 1967; William Drummond, "Open-Housing Plan Jeered," *Louisville Courier-Journal,* February 3, 1967; "A Hearing That Served Only to Make Matters Worse," *Louisville Courier-Journal,* February 5, 1967; "No Good to Come from Public Hearings," *Louisville Defender,* February 9, 1967; George Kimbrough and Sister Pauline Marie to the editor, *Louisville Courier-Journal,* February 11, 1967; John Finley, "Housing Hearing Boycott Backed," *Louisville Courier-Journal,* February 13, 1967.

20. Minutes of HRC housing committee meeting, July 11, 1963, box 7, file 14, WECC Papers; Robert Deitz, "Nunn against Any 'Forced' Open Housing," *Louisville Courier-Journal,* March 25, 1967; C. W. McFerran to the editor, *Louisville Courier-Journal,* January 13, 1967; Edwin T. Crumpton to the editor, *Louisville Courier-Journal,* February 5, 1967; Claude G. Files to the editor, *Louisville Courier-Journal,* February 9, 1967; Fred E. Riley to the editor, *Louisville Courier-Journal,* February 11, 1967; Arthur B. Prewitt to the editor, *Louisville Courier-Journal,* March 21, 1967; "Housing Opponents Call Public Meeting," *Louisville Courier-Journal,* March 29, 1967. On homeowners' rights, see Thomas J. Sugrue, *The Origins of the Urban Crisis: Race and Inequality in Postwar Detroit* (Princeton, NJ: Princeton University Press, 1996), chap. 8, and Durr, *Behind the Backlash,* chap. 4. For a discussion of white assumptions of the right to exclusivity, see MacLean, *Freedom Is Not Enough,* 46. Although MacLean focuses on conservative ideas about business and economic property rights, the idea was also used to defend exclusion of blacks from residential areas.

21. George Kimbrough and Sister Pauline Marie to the editor, *Louisville Courier-Journal,* January 15, 1967; P. W. Minshall to the editor, *Louisville Courier-Journal,* January 29, 1967; Philip Vernon Baker to the editor, *Louisville Courier-Journal,* February 26, 1967; Mrs. Edward Lesch to the editor, *Louisville Courier-Journal,* March 25, 1967; Dan Foley to the editor, *Louisville Courier-Journal,* February 18, 1967.

22. List of organizations endorsing open housing, January 23, 1967, box 8, file 15, WECC Papers. The list included civil rights groups such as the NAACP, WECC, and KCLC; religious organizations, including primarily white ones such as the Episcopal Diocese of Kentucky, West Louisville Cooperative Ministry, Louisville Conference of Jewish Organizations, National Council of

Christians and Jews, and Western District Pastors of the Methodist Church; the editorial boards of the major city papers; and student organizations from the University of Louisville, Louisville Presbyterian Theological Seminary, and Southern Baptist Theological Seminary.

23. *News from West End Community Council,* October 13, 1963, box 1, file 13, WECC Papers; "Open Occupancy Forum Set for Church Here," *Louisville Defender,* April 16, 1964; "Movement for Open Occupancy Is Receiving Growing Support," *Voice* (WECC newsletter), October 17, 1966, box 9, file 12, WECC Papers; "350 Hear Professor, Realtor Debate Housing," *Louisville Courier-Journal,* January 12, 1967; Brother John May to Hulbert James, April 26, 1967, box 1, file 18, WECC Papers.

24. WECC, news release, January 27, 1967, box 1, file 13, WECC Papers; Lester Pope, "Ministerial Group Proposes Open Housing Declaration," *Louisville Defender,* June 29, 1967; William H. Daniels to friends, May 8, 1967, box 1, file 18, WECC Papers; S. Arnold Lynch to all members, April 25, 1967, box 78, file 4, Braden Papers; Rod Wenz, "Actions—and Inactions—Are Assailed by West End Council's Leaders," *Louisville Courier-Journal,* May 20, 1967; *Voice,* March 28, 1966, box 9, file 12, WECC Papers; Cecil Blye, "Firm Announces Open Occupancy," *Louisville Defender,* January 19, 1964; Lester Pope, "Religion and Race Council to Open Housing Info Center," *Louisville Defender,* October 26, 1967.

25. Reverend William H. Daniels to members of council, March 28, 1966, file 26, LACRR and Project Understanding, Social Action Files; "Proposed Statement Regarding Equal Opportunities in Housing," [1967], box 8, file 15, WECC Papers; minutes of HRC housing committee meeting, September 15, 1965, box 5, file "Open Housing/Public Accommodations, 1961–1967," Bixler Papers; David Pollitt, Reverend Irvin S. Moxley, and Reverend William Daniels to friends, June 6, 1967, box 1, file 18, WECC Papers.

26. Pat Janensch, "Hunt for All-American Neighborhood Slated," *Louisville Courier-Journal,* June 6, 1966; "West End Neighborhoods Are Urged to Seek Awards for All-American Aspects," *Louisville Defender,* June 9, 1966; Lester Pope, "Interfaith Witness for Open Housing Brings Out 500 People," *Louisville Defender,* June 22, 1967.

27. Tom Moffett, interview by the author, February 16, 2000, OHC; Fred Hicks, interview by the author, September 15, 1999, OHC.

28. Reverend William H. Daniels to John Young, February 10, 1967, box 2, file 2, WECC Papers; Reverend Williams H. Daniels to friends, March 1, 1967, box 1, file 18, WECC Papers; minutes of ACOH meeting, March 3, 1967, box 78, file 2, Braden Papers.

29. Vincent Crowdus, "Aldermen Offered New Housing Plan, but Action Deferred," *Louisville Courier-Journal,* February 15, 1967; Clarence L. Matthews, "Aldermen Receive Revised Open Housing Ordinance," *Louisville Defender,* February 16, 1967; Clarence L. Matthews, "Bishop Tucker Favors Substitute Housing Law," *Louisville Defender,* February 23, 1967; "Housing

Ordinance's Author Defends Measure as 'Effective,'" *Louisville Courier-Journal*, March 13, 1967.

30. Bill Billiter, "Open Housing Group Denounces 'Substitute,'" *Louisville Defender*, February 14, 1967; COH, news release, February 28, 1967, box A33, file "Housing, Louisville, KY, 1967," group 4, NAACP Papers; Althea T. L. Simmons to Mildred Bond, March 1, 1967, box A33, file "Housing, Louisville, KY, 1967," group 4, NAACP Papers; William Drummond, "NAACP Attorney Attacks Proposed Housing Ordinance," *Louisville Courier-Journal*, March 11, 1967.

31. "New Marches Set to Protest Mayor's Stand," *Louisville Courier-Journal*, March 8, 1967; William Drummond, "Open Housing Protest Is Staged at City Hall," *Louisville Courier-Journal*, March 9, 1967; William Drummond, "NAACP Marchers Back Strong Housing Law," *Louisville Courier-Journal*, March 12, 1967; William Drummond, "Open Housers March on Alderman's Home," *Louisville Courier-Journal*, March 13, 1967; John Finley, "Open Housing Group Ejected," *Louisville Courier-Journal*, March 15, 1967; "Mayor Vows No Action Until 'Outsiders' Quit," *Louisville Courier-Journal*, March 16, 1967.

32. "Mayor Vows No Action Until 'Outsiders' Quit," *Louisville Courier-Journal*, March 16, 1967; "SCLC Plans Housing Push in Louisville," *Louisville Courier-Journal*, March 11, 1967; "Mayor Promises to Move Quickly on Open Housing," *Louisville Courier-Journal*, March 17, 1967; program for SCLC national executive board meeting, [March 1967], Hicks Papers; "King Leads March on Housing Foes after Arrest of 18," *Louisville Courier-Journal*, March 31, 1967; "Dr. King Has No Definite Plans to Return Here," *Louisville Times*, April 1, 1967, clipping, Hicks Papers.

33. Ray Bixler to the editor, *Louisville Courier-Journal*, [December 1966], clipping, box 5, file "Open Housing/Public Accommodations, 1961–1967," Bixler Papers; C. Eubank Tucker to the editor, *Louisville Courier-Journal*, January 9, 1967; "C. E. Tucker Lashes at 'Newcomers,'" *Louisville Defender*, January 26, 1967; "Statement on SCLC Group out of Chicago," n.d., box A33, file "Housing, Louisville, KY, 1967," group 4, NAACP Papers; William Drummond, "McAlpin-Led Group Rips Housing Protest Team," *Louisville Courier-Journal*, March 1, 1967; "Rights Leaders 'Split' over Methods," *Louisville Defender*, March 2, 1967.

34. William Drummond, "McAlpin-Led Group Rips Housing Protest Team," *Louisville Courier-Journal*, March 1, 1967; Bill Reddin and Harvey Webster, statement, March 1, 1967, box 1, file 13, WECC Papers; Ken Phillips, "The Case for Demonstrations," *Voice*, March 15, 1967, box 9, file 12, WECC Papers; "Ad Hoc Committee Issues Challenge on 'Newcomers' Tag," *Louisville Defender*, March 9, 1967.

35. Charles Tachau, interview by the author, August 16, 1999, OHC.

36. "'Uncle Tom' Labels Called Ridiculous for Rights Leaders," *Louisville Defender*, March 9, 1967; Lyman Johnson to the editor, *Louisville Defender*,

March 30, 1967; "Breach over Open Housing Tactics Still Unsettled," *Louisville Defender*, March 30, 1967; "Group of Negro Clergymen Attacks Housing Tactics," *Louisville Defender*, April 20, 1967; WAKY broadcast script, May 30, 1967, box 1, file 8, Braden Papers.

37. Vincent Crowdus, "Revised Housing Plan Taken Up; Critics Open Fire," *Louisville Courier-Journal*, March 1, 1967; "Housing Group to Reject Amended Ordinance," *Louisville Courier-Journal*, March 14, 1967; "King Leads March on Housing Foes after Arrest of 18," *Louisville Courier-Journal*, March 31, 1967; "The Case against Martin Luther King Jr." (broadside, n.p.: Truth about Civil Turmoil in Kentucky, [1967]), Hicks Papers; William A. Barnett to the editor, *Louisville Courier-Journal*, February 16, 1967; Ruth Rockwell Duffy to the editor, *Louisville Courier-Journal*, February 22, 1967.

38. "Open Housing—Nationally and Locally," *Louisville Courier-Journal*, February 16, 1967; "Let's Act Now on Open Housing While Compromise Is Feasible," *Louisville Courier-Journal*, February 23, 1967; "Act of Faith in Louisville's Good Will," *Louisville Courier-Journal*, March 2, 1967; "The High Cost of Inaction on Open Housing," *Louisville Courier-Journal*, March 16, 1967; "The Fever Rises on Open Housing in Louisville," *Louisville Courier-Journal*, March 31, 1967.

39. Frank L. Stanley, Being Frank About, *Louisville Defender*, February 23, 1967; "Delay Breeds More Open Housing Opposition," *Louisville Defender*, March 23, 1967.

40. "Housing Group Request Meeting with Schmied," *Louisville Courier-Journal*, March 2, 1967; Vincent Crowdus, "Group Seeks Housing Law Unanimity," *Louisville Courier-Journal*, March 3, 1967; "Mayor Promises to Move Quickly on Open Housing," *Louisville Courier-Journal*, March 17, 1967; Clarence L. Matthews, "Open Housing Ordinance Passage Seems Nearer as Mayor Reverses Stand," *Louisville Defender*, March 23, 1967; John Finley, "Schmied Housing Proposals Heard," *Louisville Courier-Journal*, March 29, 1967; Clarence L. Matthews, "Continued Demonstrations Appear Likely despite a Plea from Mayor Schmied," *Louisville Defender*, April 6, 1967; William Latham, "Aldermen May Act on Housing This Week," *Louisville Times*, April 4, 1967; "Gregory Coming Here, Housing Backers Say," *Louisville Times*, April 7, 1967; "Open Housing Now" schedule of events, April 9–11, [1967], Hicks Papers; Ellen Lake, "Hecklers Throw Rocks at Marchers," *Louisville Times*, April 8, 1967; "This Is a Week of Decision in Louisville's Race Relations," *Louisville Courier-Journal*, April 9, 1967.

41. Vincent Crowdus, "Open Housing Law Rejected; Aldermen Blame 'Disorders,'" *Louisville Courier-Journal*, April 12, 1967; "Text of Aldermanic Committee's Report on Open Housing," *Louisville Courier-Journal*, April 12, 1967.

42. "Marchers and Hecklers Demonstrate Downtown," *Louisville Courier-Journal*, April 12, 1967; Ellen Lake, "Marchers—Pro and Anti—Flood Downtown," *Louisville Times*, April 12, 1967; "Rights Leaders Ask Pledge of

Housing Law in Return for Leaving; City Says No," *Louisville Courier-Journal*, April 13, 1967; "Statement by Reverend A. D. King and Hulbert James," April 12, 1967, box 1, file 13, WECC Papers.

43. Ruth Bryant, interview by the author, September 27, 1999, OHC.

44. "2 Hurt, 5 Arrested as Marchers Pelted with Rocks, Bottles," *Louisville Courier-Journal*, April 14, 1967.

45. Don Bliss, "Open Housing Leaders Arrested before South End March Begins," *Louisville Times*, April 19, 1967; "Text of Mayor Schmied's Plea for Public Order," *Louisville Times*, April 15, 1967.

46. "Louisville: Whose Kentucky Home?" *Newsweek*, May 1, 1967, 27–28; Lawrence Grauman Jr., "The Derby Runs Scared," *Nation*, May 29, 1967, 689–92; "Louisville's Race: Derby Bogs Down," *Christian Century*, June 21, 1967, 817–18; "Open Housing," *New Republic*, January 13, 1968, 9–10.

47. "2 Hurt, 5 Arrested as Marchers Pelted with Rocks, Bottles," *Louisville Courier-Journal*, April 14, 1967; William Latham, "South End Parents Urged to Keep Children Away from Marchers," *Louisville Times*, April 14, 1967; "Backers of Open Housing Law Plan Another South End March Tonight," *Louisville Courier-Journal*, April 18, 1967; Virginia Delevan, "Hecklers Come Early, Leave Disappointed," *Louisville Times*, April 19, 1967; "Police Pelted, Car Tipped," *Louisville Courier-Journal*, April 21, 1967; William Latham, "Mayor Considers Curfew for City to Get Young Hecklers off Streets," *Louisville Times*, April 21, 1967.

48. "Marchers and Hecklers Demonstrate Downtown," *Louisville Courier-Journal*, April 12, 1967; "Text of Mayor Schmied's Plea for Public Order," *Louisville Times*, April 15, 1967; William Latham, "No March Set Tonight, but More Planned Later," *Louisville Times*, April 15, 1967; "Housing Group to Ask Reversal of Marching Ban," *Louisville Courier-Journal*, April 16, 1967; "Demonstrators Tell Court Ban Violated Their Rights," *Louisville Times*, April 17, 1967; "US Court Declines to Rule on March Ban," *Louisville Times*, April 20, 1967; "7 Demonstrators Begin 30-Hour Terms in Jail," *Louisville Times*, May 1, 1967.

49. "3 Hurt, 20 Arrested during March Headed by a New Set of Leaders," *Louisville Times*, April 18, 1967; Don Bliss, "Open Housing Leaders Arrested before South End March Begins," *Louisville Times*, April 19, 1967.

50. "Felony Charges Placed against 42 of 119 Arrested in Latest March," *Louisville Times*, April 20, 1967; William Latham, "Mayor Considers Curfew for City to Get Young Hecklers off Streets," *Louisville Times*, April 21, 1967; Jack Ayer, "1920 Great Red Scare Spawn," *Louisville Times*, April 28, 1967; Don Bliss, "Ex-Judge Arrested after Leading March," *Louisville Times*, April 22, 1967; "March Charges Naming Tachau Are Filed Away at Request of City," *Louisville Times*, April 29, 1967; Tachau, interview; Jack Ayer, "$20 Fine Assessed on March Count," *Louisville Times*, April 28, 1967; "Judge Colson Delays Demonstration Trials until November 10," *Louisville Defender*, July 13, 1967; Louisville COH to Parrish Kelly et al., October 23, 1967,

box 2, file 2, WECC Papers; "Judge M. Sternberg to Announce Civil Rights Fines February 29," *Louisville Defender,* February 8, 1968.

51. Harry Lewman, open letter, April 18, 1967, box 8, file 3, WECC Papers; William Latham, "Mayor Considers Curfew for City to Get Young Hecklers off Streets," *Louisville Times,* April 21, 1967; Don Bliss, "Ex-Judge Arrested after Leading March," *Louisville Times,* April 22, 1967; William Latham, "City, Rights Leaders to Try Again for Accord in Open-Housing Fuss," *Louisville Times,* April 26, 1967; Clarence L. Matthews, "Housing Controversy Moves toward Middle Ground and Moratorium," *Louisville Defender,* April 27, 1967; Don Bliss, "Court Procedure Blamed for Breakdown of Talks," *Louisville Times,* April 29, 1967; Jack Ayer, "Housing Leaders Respond Guardedly to Claim That Law Already Exists," *Louisville Times,* May 4, 1967; "Rights Group Asks New Housing Law," *Louisville Times,* May 5, 1967.

52. "NAACP Asks Boycott of Derby to Dramatize Open Housing Drive," *Louisville Times,* April 6, 1967; William Latham, "Mayor's Store Is Boycott Target," *Louisville Times,* April 13, 1967; Ad Hoc Committee on Open Housing to *Louisville Times,* April 14, 1967, box 78, file 4, Braden Papers; "NAACP Announces Boycott of Downtown Businesses in Open Housing Protest," *Louisville Defender,* April 20, 1967; "Downtown Boycott Shows Some Success," *Louisville Defender,* April 27, 1967; "56 Arrested, Ending Day's Second March," *Louisville Courier-Journal,* April 23, 1967; "Boycott Over; Registration Is Goal," *Louisville Defender,* July 20, 1967.

53. Ellen Lake, "Dr. King Due to Lead Drive against Derby," *Louisville Times,* April 25, 1967; Brian Purnell, "'Drive Awhile for Freedom': Brooklyn CORE's 1964 Stall-In and Public Discourses on Protest Violence," in *Groundwork: Local Black Freedom Movements in America,* ed. Jeanne F. Theoharis and Komozi Woodard (New York: New York University Press, 2005), 45–46; "Demonstrators May Try to Prevent Telecast of Derby, Leader Says," *Louisville Times,* April 27, 1967.

54. "Rights Leaders Ask Pledge of Housing Law in Return for Leaving," *Louisville Courier-Journal,* April 13, 1967; "Wrong Target and Time," *Louisville Defender,* April 13, 1967; "Derby Demonstrations Neither Prudent nor Helpful," *Louisville Defender,* May 4, 1967.

55. Virginia Delavan, "Cancellation of Derby Parade Is Big Disappointment to Bands," *Louisville Times,* May 2, 1967; "NAACP Offers to Stage Protest Pegasus Parade," *Louisville Times,* May 4, 1967; "City Makes Special Plea for Derby Security Help," *Louisville Times,* May 3, 1967; "Klan Ready to Help Police on Derby Day," *Louisville Times,* May 3, 1967; "1000 Police, Guardsmen to Protect Downs," *Louisville Times,* May 4, 1967.

56. "Derby Demonstrations Called Off," *Louisville Times,* May 6, 1967; Anne Braden, "Louisville," [1967], box 78, file 4, Braden Papers; Bill Billiter, "Tight Security Cuts Incidents at the Downs," *Louisville Courier-Journal,* May 7, 1967; "Good Judgement," *Louisville Defender,* May 11, 1967; anonymous letter to folks, May 11, 1967, Hicks Papers.

57. Don Bliss, "Another March Is Planned Tonight in South End," *Louisville Times*, May 9, 1967; Gerald Solomon, "Open Housing Group Marches on City Hall," *Louisville Times*, May 10, 1967; Don Bliss, "Dr. King, Grazed by Rock, Declares Marches Will Continue," *Louisville Times*, May 11, 1967.

58. Incidents during late May 1967 demonstrations (typescript, n.d.), Hicks Papers; Ellen Lake, "70 Marchers Are Egged, Jeered by Youthful Hecklers," *Louisville Times*, May 13, 1967; Don Bliss, "Police Crack Down on Hecklers; Autos of Marchers Are Sabotaged," *Louisville Times*, May 20, 1967; Don Bliss, "March Leader Taunts Small Band of Whites," *Louisville Times*, May 23, 1967; "Negro Open Housing Leader Pushed Her at March, White Woman Claims," *Louisville Times*, May 18, 1967; "Cowger Says Agitators Pose 'Greatest Threat,'" *Louisville Times*, May 12, 1967; Nat Tillman, "Riot Root Problems Exist Here in Louisville," *Louisville Defender*, July 27, 1967; "Police Permissiveness Adds Ugly Note to Open Housing Marches," *Louisville Defender*, June 8, 1967.

59. Ellen Lake, "70 Marchers Are Egged, Jeered by Youthful Hecklers," *Louisville Times*, May 13, 1967; Don Bliss, "Police Crack Down on Hecklers; Autos of Marchers Are Sabotaged," *Louisville Times*, May 20, 1967; "March Permit Is Denied Foes of Open Housing," *Louisville Times*, May 24, 1967; William Peterson, "Open Housing March Draws Complaint of Too Little Action from Teenager," *Louisville Courier-Journal*, May 25, 1967; "Open Housing Backers Plan March in Highlands Tonight," *Louisville Times*, June 1, 1967; "2 Men in Klan Garb Arrested at March Site," *Louisville Times*, May 31, 1967; "Klansman Seeks Permit for a March," *Louisville Times*, June 9, 1967; "City Turns Down Klan's Request for Permit to Parade Saturday," *Louisville Times*, June 14, 1967; "Robed Klansmen Stroll on Downtown Streets," *Louisville Courier-Journal*, June 18, 1967.

60. Don Bliss, "Dr. King Not Expected to Return till June," *Louisville Times*, May 19, 1967; "Picnic Replaces Demonstration," *Louisville Courier-Journal*, May 21, 1967; Priscilla Hancock, "Teenagers Wholeheartedly Support Open Housing Demonstrations Here," *Louisville Defender*, April 6, 1967; William Peterson, "Open Housing March Draws Complaint of Too Little Action from Teenager," *Louisville Courier-Journal*, May 25, 1967; "Open Housing Backers Map New Strategy," *Louisville Courier-Journal*, June 18, 1967; "Marchers Told Their Kitty Is in the Red," *Louisville Times*, June 24, 1967.

61. "Housing Backers Stress Registration of Voters," *Louisville Times*, June 26, 1967; "A Wiser Tactic," *Louisville Defender*, June 29, 1967; "NAACP Halts Boycott of Downtown Stores," *Louisville Times*, July 15, 1967; Lester Pope, "Martin L. King Urges Negroes to Use Vote to Combat Backlash," *Louisville Defender*, August 10, 1967; "Voter Registration Drive Has Enlisted 1,000 New Signees," *Louisville Defender*, August 24, 1967; "Voter Registration to End Saturday," *Louisville Defender*, September 7, 1967; "Voter Crusade Raps Clerk Hallahan," *Louisville Defender*, September 21, 1967.

62. Nat Tillman, "Commission Attempts to 'Outflank' Foes of Open Hous-

ing Law," *Louisville Defender,* May 18, 1967; Lester Pope, "Alderman Reynolds Says: Proposed New Housing Ordinance Needs 'Strong Criminal or Civil Penalties,'" *Louisville Defender,* September 7, 1967; Lester Pope, "Schmied Denies Any Commitment on Type of Ordinance," *Louisville Defender,* September 7, 1967; Lester Pope, "City Was Expected to Pass Open Housing Law Tuesday," *Louisville Defender,* September 14, 1967; Vincent Crowdus, "Aldermen Enact Housing Measure Despite Criticism," *Louisville Courier-Journal,* September 13, 1967.

63. "Open Housing Leaders, Mayor Hold Meeting," *Louisville Defender,* August 31, 1967; Cecil Blye, "Open Housing Supporters Map Massive Action Plan," *Louisville Defender,* September 7, 1967; "Open Housing Backers Get Aldermanic Rebuff," [1967], clipping, box 8, file 16, WECC Papers; "Demonstrations—Old Hat," *Louisville Defender,* September 21, 1967.

64. "A Political Dilemma," *Louisville Defender,* September 14, 1967; "Most Democratic Aldermanic Candidates Favor Some Open Housing Law Action," *Louisville Defender,* November 2, 1967; "It's Really 'Time for a Change' in Louisville Board of Aldermen," *Louisville Defender,* November 2, 1967; Cecil Blye and Lester Pope, "Light Turn Out Is Termed 'Bad News for Somebody,'" *Louisville Defender,* November 9, 1967; Nat Tillman, "Split Administration Seems Likely," *Louisville Defender,* November 9, 1967; WECC to Reverend Charles L. Glenn Jr., January 5, 1968, box 2, file 2, WECC Papers; "Mayor Faces 11 Democrats," *Louisville Courier-Journal,* November 8, 1967.

65. "Aldermen-Elect Expected to Immediately Pass Open-Housing Ordinance," *Louisville Defender,* November 16, 1967; "Open Housing a Certainty with Promising Aldermen and a Requesting Mayor," *Louisville Defender,* November 23, 1967; Lester Pope, "Open Housing Opponent Urges Aldermen Recall," *Louisville Defender,* November 30, 1967; "Small Crowd Hears Open Housing Law's First Reading Tuesday," *Louisville Defender,* December 7, 1967; Nat Tillman, "Louisville Passes Housing Law," *Louisville Defender,* December 21, 1967; "Strong Open Housing Ordinance Awaits Action by New Aldermen," *Louisville Defender,* November 20, 1967; "The Open Housing Ordinance: Its Provisions in Full," *Louisville Courier-Journal,* December 16, 1967.

66. Georgia Davis Powers, interview by Betsy Brinson, n.d., interview 21E6, Kentucky Oral History Collection, Kentucky Historical Society, Frankfort.

67. Priscilla Hancock, "Negro Family Is Stoned, Driven from New Home," *Louisville Defender,* July 25, 1968; "White Homeowner Offers Property to Black Buyer," *Louisville Defender,* July 3, 1969; Lester Pope, "Exposé of Trailer Park Segregation," *Louisville Defender,* August 14, 1969; "Former Resident Annoyed by Trailer Park Calls," *Louisville Defender,* August 21, 1969; "Racism May Have Been French Quarter Cancellation Cause," *Louisville Defender,* September 11, 1969; "Blacks Living in Areas Pleased," *Louisville Defender,* October 15, 1970; Priscilla Hancock, "City County Housing Found More Segregated than Ever," *Louisville Defender,* December 20, 1973; Juan

Williams, "Housing Segregation High in Louisville," *Louisville Defender,* November 14, 1974.

5. Building Bridges, Fighting Poverty, and Empowering Citizens

1. "Operation West End: A Proposal for a Community Action and Human Relations Project in Louisville's West End," [1965], box 1, file 1, WECC Papers.

2. See, for example, Timothy B. Tyson, *Radio Free Dixie: Robert F. Williams and the Roots of Black Power* (Chapel Hill: University of North Carolina Press, 1999); Rhonda Y. Williams, *The Politics of Public Housing: Black Women's Struggles against Urban Inequality* (New York: Oxford University Press, 2004); Countryman, *Up South;* and Annelise Orleck, *Storming Caesar's Palace: How Black Mothers Fought Their Own War on Poverty* (Boston: Beacon Press, 2005).

3. Frank L. Stanley, Being Frank About, *Louisville Defender,* June 12, 1958; "Louisville NAACP Urges Selective Buying Here," *Louisville Defender,* December 15, 1960.

4. "Protest Group Continues Selective Buying Here," *Louisville Defender,* September 22, 1960; "Leader Says Center Boycott Now Effective," *Louisville Defender,* September 9, 1960; "West End Group Seeks 'Selective Buying' Support," *Louisville Defender,* December 1, 1960; advertisement, *Louisville Defender,* August 17, 1961; "First Class Citizenship Includes Employment," *Louisville Defender,* August 24, 1961; "Sears, Sealtest, Coca Cola to Be Target of Louisville CORE," *Louisville Defender,* March 15, 1962; minutes of CORE meetings, March 30, 1962, April 12, 1962, reel 40, file 347, CORE Papers; "CORE Calls for Coca Cola Boycott," *Louisville Defender,* April 19, 1962; Andrew Edward Wade IV to the editor, *Louisville Defender,* April 26, 1962; "CORE Calls for a Non-buying Campaign against Sealtest Co," *Louisville Defender,* May 10, 1962; "CORE Meeting with Coca Cola Officials," *Louisville Defender,* July 5, 1972; "CORE Non-buying Movement Is Still Active," *Louisville Defender,* August 9, 1962; Henry Thomas, report on the Louisville CORE chapter, May 9, 1962, reel 40, file 347, CORE Papers; minutes of CORE meeting, June 15, 1962, reel 40, file 347, CORE Papers; Mary Hamilton to James McCain, December 19, 1962, reel 40, file 347, CORE Papers.

5. "Louisville Muffs Chance to Upgrade Negro Fire Captain," *Louisville Defender,* August 27, 1959; Cecil Blye, "Fire Chief Says Negroes Want Separate Stations," *Louisville Defender,* July 12, 1962; "Bishop Tucker Attacks Police Force 'Jim Crow,'" *Louisville Defender,* August 18, 1960; Shelby Lanier, interview by the author, September 29, 1999, OHC; "Human Relations Group to Probe Police Job Bias," *Louisville Defender,* January 14, 1965; "Rabb Charges Police Bias," *Louisville Defender,* February 11, 1965; "Long Over Due!" *Louisville Defender,* February 18, 1965; "Hoagland Denies Police Bias Charges; Committee Recommendations Are Made," *Louisville Defender,* February 25, 1965.

6. "New State Merit System to Halt Discrimination," *Louisville Defender*, January 26, 1961; "NAACP Asks City for Fair Job Practices," *Louisville Defender*, May 3, 1962; "Has Human Rights Commission Achieved Any Desegregation?" *Louisville Defender*, January 10, 1963; Clarence L. Matthews, "Equal Employment Law to Be Sought," *Louisville Defender*, March 19, 1964; "Rights Commission to Study Employment Laws," *Louisville Defender*, April 9, 1964; Mansir Tydings to Lee B. Thomas et al., memorandum, November 9, 1964, box 13, file 6, Parrish Papers; "City Sub-committee to Draft FEP Ordinance," *Louisville Defender*, December 10, 1964; "History Week Milestone? Job Ban Passes," *Louisville Defender*, February 11, 1965; "Businessmen to Welcome Hiring Law," *Louisville Defender*, February 25, 1965.

7. "Ky Rights Group Urges a Stronger Job Law for City," *Louisville Defender*, November 11, 1965; Clarence L. Matthews, "Few Job Bias Complaints Made: Retaliation Feared?" *Louisville Defender*, February 24, 1966; "Employment Bias Survey Shows Improvement Room," *Louisville Defender*, August 25, 1966; "Negroes Hold 1/5 of City, County Jobs," *Louisville Defender*, August 24, 1967; U.S. Department of Commerce, Bureau of the Census, *1970 Census of the United States: Characteristics of the Population*, part 19, *Kentucky* (Washington, DC, 1973), 44–45; "Bias Persists in Building Trades," *Louisville Defender*, May 9, 1968.

8. "Significant Breakthrough Hailed; Negro Craftsmen to Work on US Building," *Louisville Defender*, February 2, 1967; "Conferences Scheduled on Fair Employment," *Louisville Courier-Journal*, February 3, 1967; "Mayor Forbids Hiring Discrimination by Those Who Do Business in the City," *Louisville Defender*, February 29, 1968; "Rights Commission Exposes Discriminatory Employment," *Louisville Defender*, April 18, 1968; minutes of HRC meeting, June 6, 1968, Martin Perley Papers, Filson Historical Society, Louisville, KY.

9. "Ford Job Tests Biased, NAACP Official Claims," *Louisville Courier-Journal*, March 13, 1967; "NAACP Charges Discrimination at Olin Mathieson Arms Company," *Louisville Defender*, October 26, 1967; "Urban League Gets Job Training Contract," *Louisville Defender*, December 9, 1965; "Urban League Now Seeking Trainees," *Louisville Defender*, December 16, 1965; James L. Doyle to Arthur Walters, April 4, 1967, box 8, file 3, WECC Papers; "Operation Bread Basket Is Slated for Kentucky," *Louisville Defender*, September 23, 1965; "Operation Bread Basket Gets Mixed Reaction from Leaders," *Louisville Defender*, March 3, 1966; "Welcome into the Fray," *Louisville Defender*, March 3, 1966; "Sunday School Assn. to Support Employment Rally," *Louisville Defender*, June 2, 1966; "Religious Groups to Attack Negro Job Bias Problem," *Louisville Defender*, August 4, 1966.

10. Minutes of WECC human relations committee meeting, April 4, [1965], box 1, file 8, WECC Papers.

11. Program for first annual West End Arts and Talent Festival, July 1965, box 3, file 18, WECC Papers.

12. Minutes of WECC human relations committee meetings, June 1, 1965,

June 8, 1965, box 1, file 8, WECC Papers; "Fact Sheet: West End Arts and Talent Festival," [June 1965], box 3, file 18, WECC Papers; Phyllis Funke, "Arts, Talent Festival Scheduled in West End," *Louisville Courier-Journal,* June 27, 1965; minutes of WECC human relations committee meeting, July 6, 1965, box 1, file 8, WECC Papers; James E. Alsbrook, "West Enders Take Dose of Shakespeare," *Louisville Courier-Journal,* July 4, 1965.

13. West End Community Council to human relations committee, June 20, 1966, box 3, file 18, WECC Papers; art digest for "Living in a New World," [1966], box 3, file 18, WECC Papers; literary digest for "The Things We Share," [1967], Hicks Papers; literary digest for "Dream, Reality, and Renaissance," [1968], Hicks Papers. There are no figures available for the 1966 festival. In 1967 approximately two hundred people attended. See "Festival Festivities," *Louisville Courier-Journal,* August 11, 1967.

14. For the role of churches in the antiracism and antipoverty movements of the 1960s, see James F. Findlay Jr., *Church People in the Struggle: The National Council of Churches and the Black Freedom Movement, 1950–1970* (New York: Oxford University Press, 1993), 169–98; Friedland, *Lift Up Your Voice,* 93–112; Susan Youngblood Ashmore, "More than a Head Start: The War on Poverty, Catholic Charities, and Civil Rights in Mobile, Alabama, 1965–1970," in *The New Deal and Beyond: Social Welfare in the South since 1930,* ed. Elna C. Green (Athens: University of Georgia Press, 2003); and Mary L. Mapes, *A Public Charity: Religion and Social Welfare in Indianapolis, 1929–2002* (Bloomington: Indiana University Press, 2004), 61–90.

15. Reverend William H. Daniels to annual conference participants, January 24, 1965, box 2, file 1, WECC Papers; *Metropolitan Mission Newsletter,* June 1965, box 9, file 7, WECC Papers; "Louisville Race Relations Council Sponsors Seminar," *Louisville Defender,* June 17, 1965; minutes of WECC human relations committee meeting, February 28, 1966, box 1, file 8, WECC Papers.

16. Nat Tillman, "West Louisville Churches Unite in Cooperative Ministry to Aid Area," *Louisville Defender,* June 2, 1966; "West Louisville Cooperative Ministry Newly Organized," *Metropolitan Mission Newsletter,* Summer 1966, box 9, file 7, WECC Papers.

17. "West End Council Holds 'Peace and Brotherhood' Dinner," *Louisville Defender,* March 2, 1967; minutes of WLCM meeting, September 27, 1966, box 10, file 3, WECC Papers; "The Happening," n.d., clipping, WECC newsletter folder, Hicks Papers.

18. Marilyn Aycock, "Religious-Racial Conference Is Urged on Local Level," *Louisville Courier-Journal,* January 21, 1963; "Ministers' Study Group Is Formed," *Louisville Defender,* May 14, 1964; *Metropolitan Mission Newsletter,* June 1965, box 9, file 7, WECC Papers; "Louisville Race Relations Council Sponsors Seminar," *Louisville Defender,* June 17, 1965.

19. See, for example, the critique by the open housing ally Ray Bixler in "Fears and Fantasies" (paper presented to LACRR, April 19, 1967), box 5, file "Open Housing/Public Accommodations, 1961–1967," Bixler Papers.

20. "West End Council Seeks Racial Answers," *Louisville Courier-Journal,* August 4, 1963; Reverend Dalton Love and Norma Shobe to West End PTA presidents, February 4, 1964, box 1, file 12, WECC Papers; "West End Council Pushes Recreation," *Louisville Defender,* October 8, 1964.

21. "History and Intentions of the West End Community Council," [1965], box 1, file 1, WECC Papers.

22. This definition of community organizing draws on Charles M. Payne, *I've Got the Light of Freedom: The Organizing Tradition and the Mississippi Freedom Struggle* (Berkeley: University of California Press, 1995); Robert Douglas, interview by the author, September 10, 1999, OHC; and my own reading of WECC's work during this period.

23. Bryant, interview.

24. Report of WECC committee to study trash problem in Southwick, February 12, 1965, box 8, file 24, WECC Papers; minutes of WECC meetings, February 17, 1965, March 2, 1965, March 3, 1965, box 8, file 24, WECC Papers; [Sisters of Loretto], typescript, August 1965, box 1, file 1, WECC Papers; Bryant, interview.

25. "Southwick Club Takes Complaint to Mayor Cowger," *Louisville Defender,* May 31, 1962; "Southwick March to Seek Aid of Agency on Shop Facilities," *Louisville Courier-Journal,* May 1, 1963; minutes of WECC meeting with Southwick residents, March 3, 1965, box 8, file 24, WECC Papers; Edna Lee, interview by the author, October 27, 1999, OHC; Anne Braden to Mrs. Bryant, March 17, 1965, box 8, file 24, WECC Papers.

26. WECC, news release, November 21, 1965, box 1, file 13, WECC Papers; Robert L. Bennett and J. Thomas Meigs to LACRR, October 8, 1965, box 8, file 27, WECC Papers; "The Issue of New Housing in the Southwick Area," November 23, 1965, box 8, file 27, WECC Papers; "Mansir Tydings Opposes Southwick Units," *Louisville Defender,* October 28, 1965; "CORE Joins in Opposing More Housing in Southwick," *Louisville Defender,* August 11, 1966; "Southwick Units Are Held Up by Renewal Agency," *Louisville Defender,* August 11, 1966; Hulbert James to Robert Weaver, June 17, 1967, box 9, file 1, WECC Papers; "Kentucky Projects Sue Urban Renewal, Mayor, and Rev. King," *Louisville Defender,* August 10, 1967; Ruth Bryant, "Southwick Revisited," *People Speak* (Duvalle Area Council newsletter), February 21, 1966, box 7, file 1, WECC Papers.

27. "Summit Conference Scheduled May 29–30," *Louisville Defender,* May 14, 1964; Rt. Rev. Msgr. H. J. Lammers to Marlow Cook, September 14, 1964, with enclosure, "A Plan to Raise . . . ," September 8, 1964, file "Community Action Commission, October 7, 1964–December 29, 1966," box 104, Judges Files 510.1–510.4, Louisville Metro Government Archives, Louisville, KY. For an overview of the War on Poverty, see Irwin Unger, *The Best of Intentions: The Triumphs and Failures of the Great Society under Kennedy, Johnson, and Nixon* (New York: Doubleday, 1996).

28. "Arthur Evans Gets Youth Commission Job," *Louisville Defender,*

May 27, 1965; "Negroes, Poor Due More Youth Commission Seats," *Louisville Defender*, June 24, 1965; Connie Corteau, "US Poverty Officials to Hear Gripes Here," *Louisville Times*, July 1, 1965; Clarence L. Matthews, "War for Poor's Involvement in War on Poverty Shows Signs of Halting," *Louisville Defender*, July 8, 1965; "Local Youth Commission to Get More Members," *Louisville Defender*, July 15, 1965; Clarence L. Matthews, "New Anti-poverty Appointment Draws Fire," *Louisville Defender*, August 5, 1965; "Mayor Explains Anti-poverty Agency," *Louisville Defender*, August 12, 1965; Harold Yeager to directors of agencies to receive funds, November 18, 1965, box 4, file 11, WECC Papers; "Local War on Poverty Set to Go into Massive Action," *Louisville Defender*, December 2, 1965; "Area Councils Formed to Map Anti-poverty War," *Louisville Defender*, December 9, 1965; "Area Councils," n.d., box 7, file 1, WECC Papers.

29. Carol Stevens, "'Poverty Is Everybody's Business,' Expert Tells Local Group," *West Louisville Star*, December 17, 1964, box 8, file 14, WECC Papers; *Voice*, January 4, 1965, box 9, file 12, WECC Papers; "Community Mobilization through Neighborhood Councils," n.d., box 2, file "WECC, 1961–1968," Webster Papers.

30. Minutes of WECC executive meeting, February 25, [1965], box 64, file 4, Braden Papers; typescript, [March 12, 1966], box 64, file 5, Braden Papers.

31. "Operation West End: A Proposal for a Community Action and Human Relations Project in Louisville's West End," [1965], box 1, file 1, WECC Papers.

32. Tony Heitzman, interview by the author, May 26, 2000, OHC; David Gittleman, interview by the author, December 1, 1999, OHC; Kenneth Phillips and Tony Hason to George Wood, April 23, 1965, box 2, file 1, WECC Papers; Ken Phillips et al. to Dora Rice, December 8, 1965, box 2, file 1, WECC Papers; excerpts from minutes of United Church of Christ Committee on Church Renewal and Extension steering committee meetings, 1965, box 1, file 1, WECC Papers; Bernadine Stahl to businessmen, form letter, September 27, 1965, box 1, file 12, WECC Papers; WECC executive committee, statement, February 18, 1966, box 1, file 13, WECC Papers.

33. Minutes of WECC executive committee meeting, June 11, 1965, box 1, file 6, WECC Papers; *Voice*, July 1965, box 9, file 12, WECC Papers; Ken Phillips and Bernardine Stahl to Rev. C. Gresham Marmion, May 16, 1966, box 2, file 1, WECC Papers; Nat Tillman, "Hulbert James, a Man Who Has Known Poverty," *Louisville Defender*, June 22, 1967.

34. Report on first Duvalle Area Council meeting, November 29, 1965, box 7, file 2, WECC Papers; minutes of Duvalle Area Council meetings, January 10, 1966, February 14, 1966, August 22, 1966, September 12, 1966, December 19, 1966, box 7, file 2, WECC Papers; *People Speak*, March 3, 1967.

35. *Voice*, September 14, 1965, Hicks Papers; *Voice*, September 12, 1966, box 1, file 4B, Woolsey Papers; Douglas, interview.

36. Doris J. Calvin, reports, [October 1966, November 1966], box 6, file 3, WECC Papers.

37. Robert Douglas, "Community Organization in the Duvalle Area," [1966], box 7, file 1, WECC Papers; Fran S. E. Broaddus, memorandum to Duvalle Area Council members, February 14, 1966, box 7, file 1, WECC Papers; *People Speak,* February 21, 1966, February 17, 1967, box 7, file 1, WECC Papers; Henry Owens, interview by David Cline, May 31, 2006, SOHC.

38. Gail Evans, "Neighborhood Offers 'Constitution,'" *Louisville Courier-Journal,* January 1, 1968; "Pilot Cities Project," *Louisville Defender,* January 18, 1968; "$1.87 Million Allocated to Open Duvalle Project," *Louisville Courier-Journal,* January 9, 1968.

39. Bill Peterson, "Red Tape, Delays, Conflict Imperil the Pilot City Dream," *Louisville Courier-Journal,* June 18, 1969; Sterling Neal Jr., interview by David Cline, May 16, 2006, SOHC.

40. Sterling Neal Jr., interview by the author, April 21, 2000, OHC; Neal, interview by Cline.

41. Mary Goldsmith to Louisville and Jefferson County CAC, March 14, 1967, box 7, file 1, WECC Papers; *People Speak,* March 17, 1967, box 7, file 1, WECC Papers; Ben Cartinhour, "Parkland Health Center Building Plans Adopted," *Louisville Courier-Journal,* November 22, 1967; Paul Janensch, "Sound Effects Unnerving as Health Center Opens," *Louisville Courier-Journal,* February 6, 1968; Bill Peterson, "Red Tape, Delays, Conflict Imperil the Pilot City Dream," *Louisville Courier-Journal,* June 18, 1969: Gittleman, interview.

42. "Duvalle Health Center Study Asked," *Louisville Courier-Journal,* January 25, 1968; "Poverty Area Residents Quiz Club Women on Health Center," *Louisville Defender,* February 1, 1968; Cecil Blye, "Duvalle Health Center Board Told It's Sitting on a Powder Keg," *Louisville Defender,* January 25, 1968.

43. Neal, interview by Cline; Gittleman, interview; "Health Center Groundbreaking Marks Beginning of Unique West End Service," *Louisville Defender,* February 22, 1968.

44. "CAC Staff Recommends Retention of Dr. Yeager as Permanent Director," *Louisville Defender,* December 9, 1965; "West End Council Endorses Yeager for Anti-poverty Job," *Louisville Courier-Journal,* December 11, 1965; "Community Action Commission Chooses Neal S. Bellos to Serve as Agency Director," *Louisville Defender,* December 23, 1965; Paul Janensch, "Anti-poverty Dispute Flares Anew at West End Meeting," *Louisville Courier-Journal,* January 8, 1966; "CAC Still in Midst of Dispute," *Louisville Defender,* January 13, 1966; "CAC Gets Director but Differences Appear Unsolved," *Louisville Defender,* January 20, 1966.

45. "Structure Changes in CAC May Be Due," *Louisville Defender,* February 10, 1966; "Anti-poverty Programs to Be 'Streamlined,'" *Louisville Defender,* March 10, 1966; "Voice of the Poor to Be Heard during Evaluation

Meetings," *Louisville Defender,* April 21, 1966; Duvalle area evaluation, April 26, 1966, box 7, file 1, WECC Papers; Nat Tillman, "Poor Want Job Training, Jobs, Day Care Centers," *Louisville Defender,* May 5, 1966.

46. Clarence L. Matthews, "Expansion of Anti-poverty War Here Faces Obstacles," *Louisville Defender,* May 26, 1966; "Report on the Economic Opportunity Act Amendments of 1966," November 14, 1966, box 1, file 17, WECC Papers; "CAC Faces the Tough Task of Curtailing Anti-poverty Program," *Louisville Defender,* December 1, 1966.

47. "CAC Officials Seize Initiative to Head Off Pending Funds Cut," *Louisville Defender,* December 8, 1966; "Local CAC Officials Seek Grassroots Help against Program Cuts," *Louisville Defender,* December 22, 1966; WECC, news release, November 28, 1966, box 1, file 13, WECC Papers; "Local Anti-poverty War Keeps Its Major Projects," *Louisville Defender,* January 19, 1967.

48. "CAC Due for an Extensive Evaluation," *Louisville Defender,* January 12, 1967; L. V. Sanchez to Dr. C. H. Parrish, April 4, 1967, box 4, file 11, WECC Papers; "Poor to Have More Voice in Poverty Area," *Louisville Defender,* April 20, 1967.

49. Hulbert James, statement, May 15, 1967, box 82, file 3, Braden Papers; "Hearings Urged on Proposed CAC Charges," *Louisville Courier-Journal,* May 16, 1967; William Reddin and Harvey Webster to Community Action Commission, June 8, 1967, box 1, file 1, WECC Papers.

50. Unger, *Best of Intentions,* 184–85; Governor Edward Breathitt to Mr. Fergusson, September 28, 1966, box 9, file 8, WECC Papers; Hulbert James to Janet Buegli, October 31, 1966, box 2, file 1, WECC Papers; Richard Fine, report, December 6, 1966, box 9, file 11, WECC Papers; Beverly White, report, December 6, 1966, box 9, file 11, WECC Papers; P. Wagner, report, December 6, 1966, box 9, file 11, WECC Papers.

51. Minutes of WECC human relations committee meeting, January 31, 1966, box 1, file 8, WECC Papers; Dolores White Baker, interview by the author, May 18, 2000, OHC; Richard Fine to Janet Boegli, October 31, 1966, box 2, file 1, WECC Papers; *People Speak,* February 17, 1967, box 7, file 1, WECC Papers; "Local Organizer to Begin Arts and Crafts Center," *Voice,* February 12, 1968, Hicks Papers; Carroll Schempp, interview by the author, January 29, 2001, OHC.

52. White, report, December 6, 1966; report on VISTA volunteers in the Duvalle area, n.d., box 7, file 1, WECC Papers; Beverly White, report, February 20, 1967, box 9, file 11, WECC Papers; Judy Corse, reports, February 27, 1967, February 28, 1967, March 1, 1967, March 2, 1967, box 9, file 11, WECC Papers; anonymous report, February 27, 1967, box 9, file 11, WECC Papers; Ray Bixler to Hulbert James, April 13, 1967, box 5, file "Open Housing/Public Accommodations, 1961–1967," Bixler Papers.

53. "West Enders Seek Creative Approach to School Problems," *Louisville Defender,* February 10, 1966; "Panel Insists West End's Schools Equal," *Lou-*

isville Courier-Journal, February 5, 1966; Paul Janensch, "2 Groups to Seek School Reforms," *Louisville Courier-Journal,* July 2, 1966; "The West End Schools: A Time for Greatness," [1965–1966], box 7, file 3, WECC Papers; WECC education committee, "Statement to the Louisville Board of Education," n.d., box 1, file 5, WECC Papers; preliminary report on community school workshop, August 15, 1966, box 6, file 3, WECC Papers; Mrs. Thomas F. Moffett to members of the Kentucky legislature, February 4, 1968, box 2, file 2, WECC Papers.

54. Report of activities, June–September 1966, box 1, file 1, WECC Papers; "West Enders Seek End to Crime," *Louisville Defender,* May 5, 1966; "Attack on Teenage Girl Arouses Southwick," *Louisville Defender,* June 23, 1966; "Increased Protection Sought," *Louisville Defender,* June 30, 1966; "CAMP: Community Action on Metropolitan Problems," [November 4, 1966], box 6, file 1, WECC Papers; "CAMP Committee Meeting Report," June 13, 1966, box 6, file 1, WECC Papers.

55. "Report of the First Meeting of the Public Housing Tenants' Association," January 12, 1967, box 8, file 21, WECC Papers; "Martha Cunningham to Lead Tenants' Association," *Tenants for Action* (PHTA newsletter), March 1, 1967, box 8, file 21, WECC Papers; H. M. Booth to Hulbert James, September 2, 1966, box 1, file 16, WECC Papers; Anne Braden, "Eviction Threats Vindictive, Housing Tenants Charge," *Voice,* May 14, 1968, box 9, file 12, WECC Papers; H. M. Booth to Reverend Leo Lesser, March 27, 1969, box 7, file 11, WECC Papers. On organizing by public housing tenants, see Williams, *Politics of Public Housing.*

56. WECC, news release, June 28, 1966, box 1, file 13, WECC Papers; Pat Wagner, reports, February 4–17, 1967, February 20–March 3, 1967, box 9, file 11, WECC Papers; flyer for LWRO meeting, March 14, 1967, box 8, file 8, WECC Papers; "Welfare Rights Group Calls Mass Meeting," *Louisville Courier-Journal,* December 8, 1967; "Slave Bill 1967," box 8, file 8, WECC Papers; Shirley Small to CAC, February 7, 1968, box 8, file 7, WECC Papers. On the National Welfare Rights Organization, see Premilla Nadasen, *Welfare Warriors: The Welfare Rights Movement in the United States* (New York: Routledge, 2005).

57. "Operation West End: A Proposal for a Community Action and Human Relations Project in Louisville's West End," [1965], box 1, file 1, WECC Papers.

58. Lester Pope, "Meaningful Jobs Available for the 'Right Race,'" *Louisville Defender,* December 21, 1967; Cecil Blye, "Duvalle Health Center Board Told It's Sitting on a Powder Keg," *Louisville Defender,* January 25, 1968; Robert Cunningham, interview by the author, September 1, 1999, OHC.

59. Schempp, interview; F. W. Woolsey, "Say It with Theater," *Louisville Courier-Journal,* January 25, 1970.

60. Anne Braden to Joy and John, July 22, 1966, box 3, file 18, WECC Papers; art digest for "Living in a New World," [1966], box 3, file 18, WECC

Papers; Mervin Aubespin, interview by the author, January 22, 2002, in the author's possession; Douglas, interview.

6. Militancy, Repression, and Resistance in the Black Power Era

1. "West Enders Speak but Are Officials Listening," *Voice*, May 17, 1967; "Council Challenge to CAC," *Voice*, May 17, 1967; "There Is Need in West End for Both Parks and Schools," *Louisville Courier-Journal*, reprinted in *Voice*, May 17, 1967; J. Blaine Hudson, interview by the author, March 23, 2001, OHC; "James Resigns as West End Council Director," *Louisville Courier-Journal*, August 8, 1967.

2. "Hulbert James' Farewell Address to Highlight Council Workshop," *Louisville Defender*, September 14, 1967; Lawrence Pryor, "Black Power Policy Gains in West End," *Louisville Courier-Journal*, September 17, 1967.

3. "Rev. Tachau New West End Leader," *Louisville Courier-Journal*, September 18, 1967; WECC [Charles Tachau] to Reverend Charles L. Glenn, January 5, 1968, box 2, file 2, WECC Papers; "Council Adopts 'Black Power' but Names White Director," *Louisville Defender*, September 21, 1967.

4. For surveys of the black power movement, see Peniel E. Joseph, *Waiting 'til the Midnight Hour: A Narrative History of Black Power in America* (New York: Holt, 2006); William L. Van Deburg, *New Day in Babylon: The Black Power Movement and American Culture, 1965–1975* (Chicago: University of Chicago Press, 1992); and Jeffrey O. G. Ogbar, *Black Power: Radical Politics and African American Identity* (Baltimore: Johns Hopkins University Press, 2004). For stories of the black power movement specifically in southern communities, see, for example, Nahfiza Ahmed, "The Neighborhood Organization Workers of Mobile, Alabama: Black Power Politics and Local Civil Rights Activism in the Deep South, 1968–1971," *Southern Historian* 20 (1999), and Jeffrey A. Turner, "Student Power, Black Power, Class Power: Race, Class, and Student Activism on Two Southern Commuter Campuses," *Gulf South Historical Review* 16, no. 1 (2000).

5. "Muslims Express Beliefs," *Louisville Defender*, July 18, 1963; Hudson, interview. See chapter 5 for hints of black power philosophy in the War on Poverty and WECC's cultural programs.

6. Robert Cunningham, interview; Hudson, interview; Ken Clay, interview by the author, February 19, 2001, OHC.

7. Lawrence Pryor, "Black Power Policy Gains in West End," *Louisville Courier-Journal*, September 17, 1967.

8. Ibid.; Anne Braden to Reverend Gilbert Schroerlucke, May 5, 1968, box 1, file 4, Braden Papers.

9. "Robinson Becomes West End Community Council's Chairman," *Louisville Defender*, November 23, 1967.

10. Ongoing activity on all these issues is covered in the *Voice*. For specific cases, see "Welfare Recipients Plan Action," *Voice*, December 13, 1967;

"Parkway Place Residents Press Complaints," *Voice,* January 16, 1968; "West Enders Ask: Why Only One Pool?" *Voice,* June 18, 1968; "Council Works for More Black Jobs on Local Market Staff," *Voice,* December 19, 1968; and "Parents Confront School Board," *Voice,* May 14, 1968. See also "63 Given Employment in West End Job Drive," *Louisville Courier-Journal,* February 28, 1969, and "West End Council Wants Tenants on Housing Commission," *Louisville Courier-Journal,* February 14, 1969.

11. See articles in the *Voice,* for example, Pat Wagner, "Bread and Justice," *Voice,* June 14, 1967; "Welfare Recipients Plan Action," *Voice,* December 13, 1967; and "VISTA Ellen Barry Reports on WRO Work," *Voice,* March 12, 1968.

12. Margaret Roxga, "March on Milwaukee," *Wisconsin Magazine of History* 90, no. 4 (2007); Tachau, interview; "Youth Organizing," *Voice,* October 17, 1967; "Black Consciousness Goal of New Organizing Effort," *Voice,* February 12, 1968; Bill Peterson, "New Rights Group Urges Negroes to Think Black," *Louisville Courier-Journal,* February 26, 1968; Charles Tachau to Reverend Charles L. Glenn Jr., February 29, 1968, box 2, file 2, WECC Papers; "Introduction to the Black Unity League," [1968?], file 6, Black Unity League, Social Action Files; WECC, news release, May 23, 1968, box 1, file 13, WECC Papers; Charles Tachau, "Black Unity League . . . a Force against Racism," *Voice,* March 12, 1968.

13. Charles Tachau to Reverend Charles L. Glenn Jr., February 29, 1968, box 2, file 2, WECC Papers; plan for BULK black history program, [1968], box 4, file 1, WECC Papers; Cecil Blye, "Black Unity League Formed to Further Black Culture," *Louisville Defender,* February 29, 1968; Bishop Marmion to clergy of Diocese of Kentucky, July 1, 1968, box 4, file 1, WECC Papers; "A Plea for Direct Help by the Administration" (addressed to administration of Louisville Male High School), May 28, 1968, file 26, Louisville Housing Projects, Social Action Files; "A Soul Session," *Voice,* May 14, 1968; "African Topics Dominate Black Arts Festival," *Louisville Defender,* July 11, 1968.

14. "SCLC's Sims' Arrest Termed 'a Mistake,'" *Louisville Defender,* August 2, 1967; Charles Tachau, "Innocent Men Jailed Two Months," *Voice,* October 17, 1967; "Charles Tachau Criticizes Bonds in Fire-Bombing Case," *Louisville Defender,* October 26, 1967; Charles Tachau, "Most Important Lessons for Louisville," *Voice,* December 13, 1967; Charles Tachau and Neville Tucker to . . . , form letter, March 28, 1968, box 1, file 11, WECC Papers.

15. Clarence L. Matthews, "New York's Youth Unrest Absent Here," *Louisville Defender,* June 11, 1964; "Police Quell Pending Racial Outburst Here," *Louisville Defender,* July 16, 1964; "West End Riot Averted," *Louisville Defender,* September 23, 1965; "Trouble Erupts in West End over Weekend," *Louisville Defender,* August 25, 1966; "No Racial Violence Expected in Louisville," *Louisville Defender,* August 13, 1964; Clarence L. Matthews, "Civil Rights Leaders, Experts Have No Fear of Riots Here," *Louisville Defender,* September 9, 1965; Nat Tillman, "Riot Root Problems Exist Here in Louisville," *Louisville Defender,* July 27, 1967.

16. "Black Unity Leaguers Are Bitter and Angry," *Louisville Defender,* April 11, 1968.

17. Manfred Reid, interview by James Braden, n.d., partial transcript of audiotape with notes by James Braden, box 16, file 4, Braden Papers.

18. Morris Jeff, "Police Incident Adds to Tension," *Voice,* May 14, 1968; Carl Braden, interview by James Braden, April 4, 1969, partial transcript of audiotape with notes by James Braden, box 16, file 4, Braden Papers; Eugene Robinson, interview by James Braden, n.d., partial transcript of audiotape with notes by James Braden, box 16, file 4, Braden Papers; Cecil Blye, "Rep. McGill Leads Protest Delegation to City Hall," *Louisville Defender,* May 16, 1968; "Police 'Strike' Talked as Civil Service Board Dockets Appeal," *Louisville Defender,* May 23, 1968; Jim Braden, "Civil Disorders," box 16, file 2, Braden Papers; "Absence 'Sways' Civil Service Board," *Louisville Defender,* May 30, 1968.

19. Bill Peterson, interview by James Braden, [1968], partial transcript of audiotape with notes by James Braden, box 16, file 4, Braden Papers; Bryant, interview; Carl Braden, interview by James Braden, April 4, 1969, partial transcript of audiotape with notes by James Braden, box 16, file 4, Braden Papers; Eugene Robinson, interview by James Braden, n.d., partial transcript of audiotape with notes by James Braden, box 16, file 4, Braden Papers. On SCEF, see Fosl, *Subversive Southerner,* 305–6.

20. Bill Peterson, interview by James Braden, [1968], partial transcript of audiotape with notes by James Braden, box 16, file 4, Braden Papers; Carl Braden, interview by James Braden, April 4, 1969, partial transcript of audiotape with notes by James Braden, box 16, file 4, Braden Papers; Eugene Robinson, interview by James Braden, n.d., partial transcript of audiotape with notes by James Braden, box 16, file 4, Braden Papers; partial transcript of speeches, May [27], 1968, box 1, file 8, Martha Leslie Allen Papers, State Historical Society of Wisconsin, Madison; Bill Peterson with Mervin Aubespin, notes on rally, [1968], box 16, file 4, Braden Papers; Jay Thomas, interview by James Braden, n.d., partial transcript of audiotape with notes by James Braden, box 16, file 4, Braden Papers; Florian Meeks and Reginald Meeks, interview by James Braden, n.d., partial transcript of audiotape with notes by James Braden, box 16, file 4, Braden Papers; Robert "Kuyu" Sims, interview by James Braden, April 4, 1969, partial transcript of audiotape with notes by James Braden, box 16, file 4, Braden Papers.

21. Bill Peterson, interview by James Braden, [1968], partial transcript of audiotape with notes by James Braden, box 16, file 4, Braden Papers; Bill Peterson with Mervin Aubespin, notes on rally, [1968], box 16, file 4, Braden Papers; Jay Thomas, interview by James Braden, n.d., partial transcript of audiotape with notes by James Braden, box 16, file 4, Braden Papers; Florian Meeks and Reginald Meeks, interview by Jim Jordan, n.d., partial transcript of audiotape with notes by Jim Jordan, box 16, file 4, Braden Papers; Manfred Reid, interview by James Braden, n.d., partial transcript of audiotape with

notes by James Braden, box 16, file 4, Braden Papers; Jim Braden, "Civil Disorders," 89, box 16, file 2, Braden Papers.

22. Jim Braden, "Civil Disorders," 1, 89–137, box 16, file 2, Braden Papers; Bill Peterson, interview by James Braden, [1968], partial transcript of audiotape with notes by James Braden, box 16, file 4, Braden Papers; Jay Thomas, interview by Jim Jordan, n.d., partial transcript of audiotape with notes by Jim Jordan, box 16, file 4, Braden Papers; Clay, interview; Cecil Blye, "West End Riot Laid to Officer Clifford's Reinstatement," *Louisville Defender,* May 30, 1968.

23. Anne Braden, "A Mother's Story," [July 16, 1968], box 78, file 3, Braden Papers; Duwaine McElroy, "Mrs. Groves Demands Officer's Suspension," *Louisville Defender,* June 6, 1968.

24. Charles B. Tachau to Manley N. Feinberg, memorandum, August 3, 1968, box 1, file 9, WECC Papers.

25. Jim Braden, "Civil Disorders," 96, 122–28, box 16, file 2, Braden Papers; transcript of hearings before the Joint Legislative Committee on Un-American Activities, September 24–25, 1968, Louisville, KY, box 16, file 4, Braden Papers; Carl Braden, interview by James Braden, April 4, 1969, partial transcript of audiotape with notes by James Braden, box 16, file 4, Braden Papers; Eugene Robinson, interview by James Braden, n.d., partial transcript of audiotape with notes by James Braden, box 16, file 4, Braden Papers.

26. Louisville staff of the SCEF, "Lessons of Louisville: White Community to Black Rebellion," June 14, 1968, in the author's possession.

27. Jim Braden, "Civil Disorders," 117–18, box 16, file 2, Braden Papers; "Schmied Hears Complaint of Slain Youth's Mother," *Louisville Defender,* June 13, 1968; Cecil Blye, "Mrs. Groves Asks for FBI Help," *Louisville Defender,* June 27, 1968; Priscilla Hancock, "BULK Demands Charges against Officer Noe," *Louisville Defender,* July 4, 1968; "Mayor Rejects Groves Plea," *Louisville Defender,* August 8, 1968; "Council in Joint Reply to Mayor Seeks Action on Killing," *Voice,* August 16, 1968.

28. On the nature of government repression of activists in general and black militants in particular, see, for example, Robert Justin Goldstein, *Political Repression in Modern America from 1870 to 1976* (Urbana: University of Illinois Press, 2001); Nelson Blackstock, *COINTELPRO: The FBI's Secret War on Political Freedom* (New York: Anchor Foundation, 1988); and Dhoruba Moore, "Strategies of Repression against the Black Movement," *Black Scholar* 12, no. 3 (1981). On the conspiracy trials, see, for example, Timothy Dean Draper, "Revisiting 1968," *Chicago History* 31, no. 1 (2002); J. Christopher Schutz, "The Burning of America: Race, Radicalism and the 'Charlotte Three' Trial in 1970s North Carolina," *North Carolina Historical Review* 76, no. 1 (1999); Ian F. Haney-López, *Racism on Trial: The Chicano Fight for Justice* (Cambridge, MA: Belknap Press of Harvard University Press, 2003); and John William Sayer, *Ghost Dancing the Law: The Wounded Knee Trials* (Cambridge, MA: Harvard University Press, 1997).

29. Carl Braden, interview by James Braden, April 4, 1969, partial transcript of audiotape with notes by James Braden, box 16, file 4, Braden Papers; transcripts of hearings before the Joint Legislative Committee on Un-American Activities, September 24–25, 1968, box 16, file 4, Braden Papers; "City Shifts Blame for Civil Disorders: Frames Black Leaders," [1968], box 1, file 9, WECC Papers; "A Dangerous Manipulation of Bail Power," *Louisville Courier-Journal,* June 5, 1968.

30. Pollock, interview; William C. Sullivan, *The Bureau: My Thirty Years in Hoover's FBI* (New York: Norton, 1979), 133–34.

31. "A Scapegoat Hunt Is Not the Answer," *Louisville Courier-Journal,* June 4, 1968; "A Dangerous Manipulation of Bail Power," *Louisville Courier-Journal,* June 5, 1968; George Gibson, "Ky. Liberties Unit Raps Colson," *Louisville Defender,* June 13, 1968; "City Shifts Blame for Civil Disorders: Frames Black Leaders," [1968], box 1, file 9, WECC Papers; Fred Hicks, "Speakers Stress Unity at West End Protest Rally," *Voice,* June 18, 1968; "National Militants to Convene in City," *Louisville Defender,* June 6, 1968.

32. "Sims, Hawkins, Make Bond; Cortez Is Still in Jail," *Louisville Defender,* June 13, 1968; SCEF to friends, action memorandum, July 26, 1968, box 75, file 4, Braden Papers; "Jail Dissenters, Don't Bother with Proof," *Voice,* August 16, 1968; "Foot-Dragging on the Plot Charges," *Louisville Courier-Journal,* October 8, 1968.

33. Paul M. Branzburg, "West Enders to Reconsider Boycott," *Louisville Courier-Journal,* October 23, 1968; Manfred Reid, interview by James Braden, n.d., partial transcript of audiotape with notes by James Braden, box 16, file 4, Braden Papers; Cecil Blye, "Mrs. Ruth Bryant Aided Black Arts and Culture," *Louisville Defender,* October 24, 1968.

34. Thomas Moffett, "What about the Conspiracy" (speech, October 22, 1968, printed and distributed by WECC), box 1, file 9, WECC Papers; WECC to members and friends, statement, October 19, 1968, box 1, file 9, WECC Papers; Manfred Reid, interview by James Braden, n.d., partial transcript of audiotape with notes by James Braden, box 16, file 4, Braden Papers; Bryant, interview.

35. Cecil Blye, "Black League Paid Expenses for Cortez," *Louisville Defender,* June 6, 1968.

36. Notes from WECC meeting to support the Black Six, October 29, 1968, box 1, file 9, WECC Papers; WECC, news release, January 2, 1969, box 1, file 13, WECC Papers.

37. [Ad Hoc Committee for Justice], news release, November 7, 1968, box 75, file 4, Braden Papers; "Council Initiates City-Wide Action Movement," *Voice,* November 12, 1968.

38. "Attorneys Ask Federal Court to Free Cortez," *Louisville Defender,* December 12, 1968; Carl and Anne Braden to Joseph Forer and David Rein, January 20, 1969, box 75, file 4, Braden Papers; David Rein to Carl Braden, February 12, 1969, box 75, file 4, Braden Papers; "What's the Truth about Charges against Cortez," *Voice,* February 22, 1969; "Cortez Called 'Life Crim-

inal,'" *Louisville Defender,* February 6, 1969; "Conviction of Cortez Raises Serious Questions," *Voice,* April 17, 1969; Jimmy [Braden] to Anne and Carl [Braden], March 27, 1969, box 67, file 3, Braden Papers. Attorney Dan Taylor attempted to have the conviction overturned because Cortez had not been read his rights. In mid-July 1970, the U.S. Court of Appeals for the Sixth Circuit in Cincinnati upheld the conviction, and Taylor asked the Supreme Court to review the case. At the same time, Cortez had a partial victory; his bond was reduced enough that he was able to get out of prison pending the outcome of the appeal. As a condition of the decision, however, district court judge James F. Gordon ordered Cortez to return to his last permanent residence—St. Louis—and remain in the jurisdiction of the district court there, in effect removing him from the Louisville scene. Thereafter Cortez's predicament dropped out of the concern of Louisville activists, and the local media ceased to report on his case. See "James Cortez Enters U.S. Penitentiary," *Louisville Defender,* June 5, 1969; "Cortez Appeal Undecided," *Louisville Defender,* January 1, 1970; SCEF, news release, July 15, 1970, box 75, file 5, Braden Papers; "Cortez Wins 'Bail Battle,'" *Louisville Defender,* July 23, 1970.

39. Charles Tachau to Taylor, Tucker, and Delahanty, memorandum, January 11, 1969, box 75, file 4, Braden Papers; Anne Braden to Jim Braden, January 19, 1969, box 1, file 5, Braden Papers; "Official Louisville Tried to Unload Case It Can't Win," *Voice,* January 22, 1969; Cecil Blye, "Black Six—Alabammy Bound; Lawyers Appeal Change of Venue," *Louisville Defender,* January 23, 1969; Lester Pope, "'Black Six' Unwanted by Hart Countians," *Louisville Defender,* January 30, 1969; Ed Ryan, "Black Six Trial Bounced Back to Louisville," *Louisville Courier-Journal,* January 6, 1970.

40. Ben Johnson, "Black Six Jury Selected; Cortez Offers Objections," *Louisville Defender,* June 25, 1970; *News from SCEF,* July 5, [1970], box 1, file 14, Allen Papers; Ben Johnson, "Directed Verdict Ends Trial of the Black Six," *Louisville Defender,* July 9, 1970; handwritten notes on Black Six trial, June 29–July 7, 1970, box 1, file 15, Allen Papers; "'Big Frame' Claimed by Sims, Reid," *Louisville Defender,* July 9, 1970; SCEF to Louisville friends, memorandum, July 1970, box 75, file 5, Braden Papers.

41. "Complaint for Declaratory Judgment and Injunction Relief," 1968, box 4, file 2, WECC Papers; "West End Council Votes to Join Suit against KUAC," *Louisville Defender,* April 11, 1968; *Voice,* April 16, 1968, box 9, file 12, WECC Papers; minutes of Kentuckians against KUAC meeting, July 13, 1968, file 24, Kentuckians against KUAC, Social Action Files; Judy Hicks to plaintiffs and supporters, April 21, 1968, July 13, 1968, file 24, Kentuckians against KUAC, Social Action Files; "For What Good Purpose," *Louisville Defender,* June 20, 1968.

42. "Federal Judge Dismisses Suit Attacking State Probe Unit," *Louisville Times,* May 27, 1968; Paul Bergner, "State Groups Protest KUAC Proceedings," *University of Louisville Cardinal,* December 6, 1968; *A Political Fable: How the People of Can-Talk Joined Hands and Quashed the Quack-Quacks*

(pamphlet, n.p., n.d.), Hicks Papers; William Bradford, "House Defeats Bid to Finance Group for State Probes," *Louisville Times,* January 27, 1970; Anne Braden, interview by the author, September 18, 2001, OHC.

43. Lester Pope, "State to Be 'Tried' Next Month," *Louisville Defender,* January 15, 1970; John Ernst and Yvonne Baldwin, "The Not So Silent Minority: Louisville's Antiwar Movement, 1966–1975," *Journal of Southern History* 73, no. 1 (2007): 124; "Mock Trial Charges Are Listed by WECC, Front," *Louisville Defender,* February 5, 1970; Carol Cavanough, "Nunn, Hyde 'Tried' Friday," *Louisville Defender,* February 12, 1970.

44. "Bishop Tucker Denounces Black Militants at Jackson, Mississippi Church Meeting," *Louisville Defender,* December 19, 1968; Lyman Johnson to the editor, *Louisville Defender,* May 15, 1969; "Sound Advice for Anarchists," *Louisville Defender,* May 15, 1969; Lester Pope, "Memorial Rites Become Black Militancy Forum," *Louisville Defender,* April 10, 1969; Cecil Blye, "Reverend W. J. Hodge Calms Unrest at City Rites," *Louisville Defender,* April 10, 1969.

45. Roy C. Snyder to Charles Tachau, June 13, 1968, box 1, file 19, WECC Papers; Bishop Marmion to clergy of Diocese of Kentucky, July 1, 1968, box 4, file 1, WECC Papers; David Holt, "West End Council Dies; Few Attend Its 'Funeral,'" *Louisville Courier-Journal,* March 23, 1970; Priscilla Hancock, "Father Tachau Resigns from West End Council," *Louisville Defender,* July 11, 1968; Paul Branzburg, "Reverend Leo Lesser Named West End Council Head," *Louisville Courier-Journal,* August 24, 1968; Paul M. Branzburg, "Rev. Lesser Challenges Racial Integration Goal," *Louisville Courier-Journal,* September 7, 1968; notes on WECC workshop, September 14, 1968, box 10, file 5, WECC Papers; Carl Braden, report, March 23, 1970, box 1, file 1, WECC Papers; "West End Community Council 'Fades Away,'" *Louisville Defender,* March 26, 1970; Bill Peterson, "Once a Vigorous Force, West End Council Folds," *Louisville Courier-Journal,* April 20, 1970.

46. Bill Peterson, "Child of Controversy: The West End Council," *Louisville Courier-Journal,* July 27, 1968; David Holt, "West End Council Dies; Few Attend Its 'Funeral,'" *Louisville Courier-Journal,* March 23, 1970; Carl Braden, report, March 23, 1970, box 1, file 1, WECC Papers; "West End Community Council 'Fades Away,'" *Louisville Defender,* March 26, 1970; Bill Peterson, "Once a Vigorous Force, West End Council Folds," *Louisville Courier-Journal,* April 20, 1970; Anne Braden, "A Dream That Failed," April 1970, box 1, file 4C, Woolsey Papers.

47. On the history of black studies programs and campus black power activism, see Peniel E. Joseph, "Black Studies, Student Activism, and the Black Power Movement," in *The Black Power Movement: Rethinking the Civil Rights–Black Power Era,* ed. Peniel E. Joseph (New York: Routledge, 2006).

48. Hudson, interview.

49. Ibid.; "Black Student Union at UofL Wins Fight for Negro Courses," *Louisville Defender,* June 13, 1968; "The Black Student Union" (flyer, Octo-

ber 1968), file 3, Black Student Union Papers, Ekstrom Library, University of Louisville, Louisville, KY (hereafter cited as BSU Papers); "In the Revolution," *Ahead in the Revolution,* December 1968, file 3, BSU Papers.

50. "Recruiting Proposal to the University of Louisville," March 1969, file 1, BSU Papers; Cecil Blye, "'Proposals' Are Wide-Sweeping," *Louisville Defender,* March 6, 1969; Hudson, interview; Anne Braden to Jim Braden, March 6, 1969, box 15, file 10, Braden Papers.

51. BSU Community News Service, "Fact Sheet," May 1969, box 1, file 4B, Woolsey Papers; Lester Pope, "Black Students Make 16 Demands at UofL," *Louisville Defender,* March 6, 1969; minutes of HRC meeting, March 6, 1969, Perley Papers; "A Good Beginning," *Louisville Defender,* March 13, 1969; "Black Coalition, University of Louisville Come to Terms," *Louisville Defender,* March 13, 1969.

52. Hudson, interview; BSU Community News Service, "Fact Sheet," May 1969, box 1, file 4B, Woolsey Papers; BSU executive committee, news release, April 23, 1969, file 1, BSU Papers.

53. "Strickler 'Reads Riot Act,'" *Louisville Defender,* May 15, 1969; BSU Community News Service, "Fact Sheet," May 1969; Hudson, interview; Bob Winlock, interview by the author, March 13, 2001, OHC; Joe Hoban, "The University of Louisville Crisis: Background and Analysis," May 4, 1969, box 1, file 4B, Woolsey Papers.

54. Joe Hoban, "The University of Louisville Crisis: Background and Analysis," May 4, 1969, box 1, file 4B, Woolsey Papers; John Filiatreau, "UL Re-admits 3 of 8 Dismissed Blacks," *University of Louisville Cardinal,* May 16, 1969, box 5, file "Open Housing/Public Accommodations, 1961–1967," Bixler Papers; "Expelled UofL Students Claim Rigged Hearing, Double Jeopardy," *Louisville Defender,* May 22, 1969; Hudson, interview; Odell McCollum, "Seven Blacks Acquitted in UofL Takeover Case," *Louisville Defender,* April 16, 1970; "Expelled Black Students Are Readmitted by UofL," *Louisville Defender,* November 27, 1969.

55. "Street Poll Reveals Mixed BSU Sentiments," *Louisville Defender,* May 15, 1969; Joetta Harrington, "Tell It Like It Is," *Louisville Defender,* May 15, 1969; Cecil Blye, "Bishop C. E. Tucker Raps Proposed Protest March by West End Council," *Louisville Defender,* May 15, 1969; "West End Community Council Pledges Support to Black Students," *Louisville Defender,* May 15, 1969; SCEF to white friends in the Louisville community, memorandum, May 4, 1969, box 75, file 4, Braden Papers; Ad Hoc Committee for Justice, memorandum regarding demonstration, May 26, [1969], box 1, file 4B, Woolsey Papers.

56. Anne Braden to Jimmy Cortez, May 22, 1969, box 1, file 5, Braden Papers; "UofL Black Affairs Coordinator Makes Big Hit with Community," *Louisville Defender,* June 12, 1969; "Black Affairs Program Begins in Five City Poverty Areas," *Louisville Defender,* July 10, 1969; "Shawnee Festival Planned by Black Affairs Office," *Louisville Defender,* July 17, 1969;

"An Experience in Self-Expression," *Louisville Defender,* August 14, 1969; "Screening Committee Appointed by Black Affairs Office at UofL," *Louisville Defender,* July 24, 1969; Cecil Blye, "Black Affairs Program Model for Southeast," *Louisville Defender,* September 4, 1969; "UofL Releases Final Progress Report on Blacks," *Louisville Defender,* September 25, 1969; "UofL Increases Black Recruitment, Admissions," *Louisville Defender,* September 17, 1970; Department of Pan-African Studies, University of Louisville, http://louisville.edu/panafricanstudies.

57. Lester Pope, "BSU Joins Park-Duvalle 'Paint Program,'" *Louisville Defender,* August 7, 1969; "Black Art Festival Scheduled by BSU," *Louisville Defender,* February 19, 1970; Ray Bixler, "Psychology Head Pleads for Support of UofL's Black Student Union," *Louisville Defender,* February 12, 1970; "Bishop Tucker Denounces BSU Position," *Louisville Defender,* December 25, 1969; "Black Students Demonstrate at University of Louisville," *Louisville Defender,* April 29, 1971; Priscilla Hancock, "Black Student Unions Join," *Louisville Defender,* November 22, 1973.

58. Hudson, interview; Neal, interview by the author; Howard Owens, interview by the author, February 28, 2000, OHC; *The World in Revolution—Our Black Thing* (pamphlet, n.p., n.d.), file 26, Louisville Miscellaneous, Social Action Files; Henri Williams Jr. to brothers and sisters, [1970], file 6, Black Unity League, Social Action Files.

59. Henri Williams Jr. to brothers and sisters, [1970], file 6, Black Unity League, Social Action Files; "14 Steps to Equality—What JOMO Believes," *Louisville Defender,* December 24, 1970; "Black Solidarity Week," *Louisville Defender,* April 22, 1971; Hudson, interview.

60. Neal, interview by the author; "Our Black Thing Brings Kent State Drama Here," *Louisville Defender,* July 16, 1970; Priscilla Hancock, "WATU—Our Black Thing Scores," *Louisville Defender,* July 23, 1970; "Our Black Thing Presents Show," *Louisville Defender,* August 20, 1970.

61. "Moja Enia Odun Dudu" (festival program, September 28–30, 1973), private collection; "African Liberation Day Scheduled for May," *Louisville Defender,* May 6, 1976.

62. Neal, interview by the author; "Dope Program Seeks Funds to Combat Narcotics Wave," *Louisville Defender,* December 10, 1970; Susan Brown, "Bullets Deface Bldg of Com for Self Defense," *Louisville Defender,* February 24, 1972; Jason Williams, "New 'Rights' Coalition Decries 'R' and 'X' Films," *Louisville Defender,* April 4, 1974; Ron Long, "Stop Dope Now Director Charges Conflict of Interest," *Louisville Defender,* October 7, 1976.

63. Cecil Blye, "Black Panthers to Organize Here?" *Louisville Defender,* February 27, 1969; Susan Brown, "Panthers Initiate Sickle Cell Clinic," *Louisville Defender,* August 3, 1972; Pollock, interview; Susan Brown, "Free Breakfasts Become a Reality," *Louisville Defender,* September 28, 1972; "Panthers Picket Film 'Superfly,'" *Louisville Defender,* January 11, 1973.

64. "Black Panthers: Intensify Lou. Action," *Louisville Defender,* May 18,

1972; "Over 100 Protest Lou. '7' High Bonds and Nixon War," *Louisville Defender,* May 25, 1972; Louisville Seven Defense Fund Committee, "Press Statement on Behalf of the Louisville 7," [1972], file 26, Louisville Seven Defense Fund, Social Action Files; confidential report, September 14, 1972, box 1, folder "FBI Files," KCLU Papers; Meryl Thornton, "Panthers Trial Set for Monday," *Louisville Defender,* September 21, 1972; "Free Blakemore" (flyer, n.d.), file 24, Kentucky Political Prisoners' Committee, Social Action Files; Meryl Thornton, "Panthers Vow to Free Member," *Louisville Defender,* October 5, 1972; William Allison, interview by the author, September 21, 2001, OHC.

65. "Over 100 Protest Lou. '7' High Bonds and Nixon War," *Louisville Defender,* May 25, 1972; confidential report, September 14, 1972, box 1, folder "FBI Files," KCLU Papers; Meryl Thornton, "Panthers Trial Set for Monday," *Louisville Defender,* September 21, 1972; flyer, January 1973, file 24, Kentucky Political Prisoners' Committee, Social Action Files.

66. Confidential report, July 25, 1973, box 1, folder "FBI Files," KCLU Papers; "Kentucky Political Prisoners' Committee to Hold Rally Saturday," *Louisville Defender,* July 12, 1973; Meryl Thornton, "Cedric Wilson Jury Holds Long Verdict Discussions," *Louisville Defender,* April 4, 1974; Meryl Thornton, "Lack of Evidence Acquits Wilson," *Louisville Defender,* April 11, 1974.

67. Anne Braden, interview, September 18, 2001; Fosl, *Subversive Southerner,* 317, 323, 327.

68. The Bradens left SCEF in part because it had become increasingly white and riven with ideological debate. They spent their energy on the Southern Student Organizing Committee regionally and the Kentucky Alliance locally. Eventually SCEF was take over by the October League and disintegrated. Allison, interview; Anne Braden, interview, September 18, 2001.

69. For a summary and critique of the narrative, see Peniel E. Joseph, introduction to Joseph, *Black Power Movement;* on the overlap between the black power and civil rights movements, see Tyson, *Radio Free Dixie.*

7. Making Civil Rights Gains Real

1. *A Community Study among Whites and Negroes in Louisville* (New York: Roper Research Associates, 1969).

2. Although many studies of the freedom struggle in the South come to a close in the late 1960s, a few recent examinations of southern urban areas in the 1970s and beyond affirm that the same issues dominated the movements there. See, for example, J. Mills Thornton III, "Aftermath," in *Dividing Lines: Municipal Politics and the Struggle for Civil Rights in Montgomery, Birmingham, and Selma* (Tuscaloosa: University of Alabama Press, 2002), 500–564, and David A. Harmon, *Beneath the Image of the Civil Rights Movement and Race Relations: Atlanta, Georgia, 1946–1981* (New York: Garland, 1996).

Although his study is not confined to one urban area, Timothy Minchin demonstrates the focus on labor and economic issues across the region in *From Rights to Economics*.

3. For a study of the rise of the law-and-order philosophy in the late 1960s, see Michael W. Flamm, *Law and Order: Street Crime, Civil Unrest, and the Crisis of Liberalism in the 1960s* (New York: Columbia University Press, 2005).

4. "Tension High in Jackson Area," *Louisville Defender*, August 7, 1969; Cecil Blye, "Youth Shot, Mother Beaten in East End," *Louisville Defender*, August 7, 1969; HRC special committee on police practices, report, August 1969, Perley Papers. Other cases in the next year included the shooting of an African American Vietnam War veteran, Stanley Ledford; a beating of a postal worker; and a beating of a black woman, who called the police to arrest the offending officers. See "Moderates Meet; Call for Action in Ledford Killing," *Louisville Defender*, July 31, 1969; "Youth's Shooting Clouded by Conflicting Statements," *Louisville Defender*, July 31, 1969; "Postal Clerk Alleges Brutal Beating by West End Officers," *Louisville Defender*, August 21, 1969; "West End Woman Calls Police to Arrest Police," *Louisville Defender*, September 4, 1969.

5. "The True Facts behind the Greenwell Market Case," n.d., file 26, Louisville Housing Projects, Social Action Files; "White Trio Exposes Brutality," *Louisville Defender*, June 10, 1971; "Equal Justice Committee Decries Police Brutality," *Louisville Defender*, June 24, 1971.

6. Jones, interview; "Defense Begins Case for Tinsley Brothers," *Louisville Defender*, October 28, 1971; "Tinsleys' Retrial Sought," *Louisville Defender*, November 4, 1971; "Tinsley's [*sic*] May Escape Death Penalty," *Louisville Defender*, February 10, 1972. During the year, other incidents of police brutality in the west end were reported. For examples, see Ben Johnson, "Young Black Woman Allegedly Abused during Shoplifting Arrest," *Louisville Defender*, December 24, 1970; "Black Youth, Mother Beaten by Policemen," *Louisville Defender*, September 16, 1971; and "Claude Woods Charges Police Brutality," *Louisville Defender*, September 30, 1971.

7. Martin Perley, interview by the author, February 23, 2000, OHC; "Rights Unit to Continue Police School," *Louisville Defender*, August 1, 1968; minutes of HRC meetings, June 29, 1968, August 1, 1968, September 5, 1968, Perley Papers; Barbara Stallard, "Policemen Tell of Dislike for Sensitivity Training," *Louisville Defender*, August 8, 1968; Barbara Stallard, "Police Training Failed?" *Louisville Defender*, September 5, 1968.

8. Lester Pope, "Rights Commissioners Want Gun-Play Rules," *Louisville Defender*, August 21, 1969; "Report of the Special Committee on Public Police Practices," [August 1969], Perley Papers; minutes of HRC meetings, September 3, 1970, November 5, 1970, Perley Papers; HRC director's reports, December 3, 1970, November 4, 1971, Perley Papers.

9. "Police Version of Killing Questioned," *Voice*, August 13, 1969, Hicks Papers; Charles Tachau, "Laws May Help Curb Police Violence," *Voice*, Au-

gust 13, 1969, Hicks Papers; "Community Groups Issue Ultimatum to Police Chief," *Louisville Defender,* September 23, 1971; "NAACP Calls Mass Membership Rally," *Louisville Defender,* October 14, 1971.

10. Marilyn Johnson, *Street Justice: A History of Police Violence in New York City* (Boston: Beacon Press, 2003), 232; "Why Not?" *Louisville Defender,* August 21, 1969; Suzy Post, interview by the author, April 3, 2000, OHC; "Does Louisville Need a Civilian Review Board?" (flyer, [February 1972]), file 26, Louisville Miscellaneous, Social Action Files; "Is the Policeman Your Friend?" (flyer, [1972]), file 26, Louisville Housing Projects, Social Action Files; HRC director's report, June 1, 1972, Perley Papers.

11. Robert McConnell, "City Police Union Pledges to Fight Civilian Review," *Louisville Courier-Journal,* May 19, 1972; Tinsley Stewart, "Accord on Upgrading Police Stops at Review by Civilians," *Louisville Courier-Journal,* June 16, 1972; Tom Denton, "Viewpoints on a Civilian Police Review: Against," *Louisville Courier-Journal,* June 27, 1972. For an example of the law enforcement fight against civilian review, see Michael W. Flamm, "'Law and Order' at Large: The New York Civilian Review Board Referendum of 1966 and the Crisis of Liberalism," *Historian* 64 (2002).

12. HRC director's report, June 1, 1972, Perley Papers; Susan Brown, "Review Ordinance 'Lacks Uniformity,'" *Louisville Defender,* June 22, 1972; Susan Brown, "Morris Charges Public Is Misled," *Louisville Defender,* July 6, 1972; "Not the Democratic Way," *Louisville Defender,* July 6, 1972; "Important Meeting" (flyer, November 29, 1972), file 24, Kentucky Women's Political Caucus, Social Action Files.

13. See, for example, Meryl Thornton, "Woman Claims Eye Loss from Police Brutality," *Louisville Defender,* September 7, 1972; Susan Brown, "Mother Charges Brutality," *Louisville Defender,* September 14, 1972; Meryl Thornton, "Countian Arrested Alleges Brutality," *Louisville Defender,* September 21, 1972; Priscilla Hancock, "Deadly Weapon Charge Dropped against Paraplegic," *Louisville Defender,* August 9, 1973; Meryl Thornton and Priscilla Hancock, "Youth Dies; Shot in Back," *Louisville Defender,* January 31, 1974; Meryl Thornton, "Coroner's Jury to Review Shooting of 17-Year-Old," *Louisville Defender,* February 14, 1974.

14. Louis Coleman, interview by the author, March 5, 2001, OHC.

15. Priscilla Hancock, "LUL to Screen Police Brutality Complaints," *Louisville Defender,* February 21, 1974; Jason Williams, "Blacks Explain Concept of a Good Police," *Louisville Defender,* October 10, 1974; "Urban League Releases Monthly Police Report," *Louisville Defender,* September 30, 1976; Susan Brown, "Black Police Officers Organization to Hold 'Police Brutality' Hearings," *Louisville Defender,* June 14, 1973; "Police-Community Relations Sessions," *Louisville Defender,* March 18, 1976.

16. Jason Williams, "County Policemen Who Used Mace on Black Youth Suspended," *Louisville Defender,* March 14, 1974; Jason Williams, "Alleged Beating Still under Investigation," *Louisville Defender,* April 17, 1975; Ja-

son Williams, "Policemen Named in Brutality Case, Still Patrol Community," *Louisville Defender,* April 24, 1975; minutes of HRC meeting, April 21, 1975, Perley Papers; Ron Long, "Task Force on Police Conduct Prepares to Include Citizens," *Louisville Defender,* June 3, 1976; Jason Williams, "Aldermen Call Temporary Halt to Police Probe," *Louisville Defender,* March 3, 1977.

17. "Col. Richmond Asks for More Negro Recruits," *Louisville Defender,* May 30, 1968; Priscilla Hancock and Ben Johnson, "Safety Director Lists Black Recruitment as Top Priority," *Louisville Defender,* July 2, 1970; Ben Johnson, "Black Recruiting Troubles Local Police Departments," *Louisville Defender,* September 3, 1970.

18. Cecil Blye, "Rights Official Charges Unfair Police Hiring," *Louisville Defender,* June 4, 1970; "Ministers Seek More Black Police," *Louisville Defender,* June 18, 1970; "Local Urban League Seeks to Enroll Black Policemen," *Louisville Defender,* January 6, 1972; "Urban League Sponsors Black Police Intern Program with Department," *Louisville Defender,* May 10, 1973; "Urban League Position Paper on Policemen in City Graduating Class," *Louisville Defender,* July 12, 1973; Susan Brown, "UL Wants More Black Police," *Louisville Defender,* July 19, 1973.

19. Meryl Thornton, "Sloane Says No to Black Officer Training Class," *Louisville Defender,* March 28, 1974; Jason Williams, "Civil Service and Police Stymie Black Recruitment," *Louisville Defender,* October 17, 1974; Meryl Thornton, "Record Number of Blacks Pass Police Written Exams," *Louisville Defender,* November 7, 1974.

20. "Black Police Suit Has Many Merits," *Louisville Defender,* March 21, 1974; Jason Williams, "Black Police File Suit: Charge City Police with Discrimination," *Louisville Defender,* March 21, 1974; W. Marvin Dulaney, *Black Police in America* (Bloomington: Indiana University Press, 1996), 75–78.

21. Frank L. Stanley, Being Frank About, *Louisville Defender,* September 17, 1970, September 24, 1970; Stan MacDonald, "Black Policemen Face Two 'Fronts,'" *Louisville Courier-Journal,* May 17, 1971; Mervin Aubespin, "Black Cops . . . They Feel Race Raises Problems," *Louisville Courier-Journal,* November 26, 1973; "White Officers' Harassment," *Louisville Defender,* May 16, 1974. For a study of the experiences of black officers during this period, see Kenneth Bolton Jr. and Joe R. Feagin, *Black in Blue: African-American Police Officers and Racism* (New York: Routledge, 2004).

22. Lanier, interview.

23. Dulaney, *Black Police in America,* 74.

24. "Black Cop's Hearing Cont'd," *Louisville Defender,* June 1, 1972; Vincent Crowdus, "US Charges Official Bias against Black Police," *Louisville Courier-Journal,* December 14, 1974; Meryl Thornton, "Black Officer Accuses City of Dual Standard," *Louisville Defender,* January 11, 1973; Meryl Thornton, "Policeman's Suspension Believed Racially [Inspired]," *Louisville Defender,* December 13, 1973; Meryl Thornton, "Black Police Fund Begun," *Louisville Defender,* December 20, 1973.

25. Vincent Crowdus, "US Charges Official Bias against Black Police," *Louisville Courier-Journal,* December 14, 1974; Meryl Thornton, "EEOC Charges City Police with Racial Discrimination," *Louisville Defender,* December 19, 1974.

26. For studies of the *Griggs* case and its impact on equal employment cases, see Robert Samuel Smith, "Race, Labor and Civil Rights: *Griggs v. Duke Power* and the Expansion of Equal Opportunity" (PhD diss., Bowling Green State University, 2002), and Michael Peter Benver, "Preparatory Programs, Banding, and Affirmative Action in an Urban Police Department" (EdD diss., University of Louisville, 1996), 17.

27. Benver, "Preparatory Programs," 24–25; Ben Johnson, "New Police Test Is Job-Related, but It's Still Tough," *Louisville Courier-Journal,* December 25, 1975.

28. Minutes of HRC meeting, November 4, 1976, Perley Papers; Mervin Aubespin, "Louisville Police Officially Charged with Discrimination," *Louisville Courier-Journal,* November 5, 1976; Ben Johnson, "Recruiters Are Searching for Blacks to Apply to Be Louisville Policemen," *Louisville Courier-Journal,* January 10, 1977; minutes of HRC meeting, March 3, 1977, Perley Papers; Vincent Crowdus and Ben Johnson, "FOP Sues to Halt Naming of Black Officer as Major," *Louisville Courier-Journal,* October 21, 1976; Benver, "Preparatory Programs," 24–25.

29. For the story of the Louisville suit and court orders, see Benver, "Preparatory Programs," 22–25.

30. For a description of this transition, see Paul D. Moreno, *From Direct Action to Affirmative Action: Fair Employment Law and Policy in America, 1933–1972* (Baton Rouge: Louisiana State University Press, 1997).

31. Minutes of HRC meetings, August 1, 1968, January 2, 1969, February 6, 1969, Perley Papers; HRC director's reports, February 6, 1969, July 12, 1973, Perley Papers.

32. "Rights Commission Hears L&N Discrimination Case," *Louisville Defender,* July 3, 1969; "Dupont Ruling May Affect L&N Race Bias Case," *Louisville Defender,* July 24, 1969; Jason Williams, "L&N to Pay Blacks $7440 in Back Pay," *Louisville Defender,* September 19, 1974.

33. "Rights Commission Orders Philip Morris Policy Change," *Louisville Defender,* April 20, 1970; "Local Hotel to Upgrade Blacks," *Louisville Defender,* October 30, 1969; "Black Complainant Wins $400 from Theater," *Louisville Defender,* January 20, 1972. During this period, the HRC director's reports and meeting minutes show that discrimination complaints were filed and investigated, but they do not list details about individual cases.

34. MacLean, *Freedom Is Not Enough,* 96–97. On the Philadelphia Plan, see Sugrue, "Affirmative Action from Below," and Dean J. Kotlowski, "Richard Nixon and the Origins of Affirmative Action," *Historian* 60 (1998).

35. Ben Johnson, "Ad Hoc Coalition Demands More Blacks in Construction," *Louisville Defender,* April 2, 1970; Cecil Blye, "United Blacks Demand

Firing of Action Now Program Chief," *Louisville Defender,* April 16, 1970; "United Blacks Walk Out on Rights Unit," *Louisville Defender,* April 23, 1970; HRC director's report, May 1970, Perley Papers.

36. HRC director's reports, May 7, 1970, May 1970, Perley Papers; minutes of HRC meeting, October 2, 1970, Perley Papers; "United Blacks, County Judge Sign Labor Pact," *Louisville Defender,* January 6, 1972.

37. "Dupont Employees Attack Job Bidding Procedure," *Louisville Defender,* October 10, 1968; "Dupont Ruling May Affect L&N Race Bias Case," *Louisville Defender,* July 24, 1969; "NAACP Plans Voter Drive," *Louisville Defender,* January 30, 1969; "NAACP Files Bias Complaint against UofL Medical School," *Louisville Defender,* February 26, 1970; "NAACP Files Complaint against Olin Corp.," *Louisville Defender,* February 11, 1971.

38. "NAACP Charges A&P Bias," *Louisville Defender,* May 25, 1972; "NAACP Ends A&P Boycott," *Louisville Defender,* September 7, 1972; "NAACP Urges Chain Stores to Hire More Blacks," *Louisville Defender,* December 7, 1972; Jason Williams, "NAACP Files EEO Complaint against A&P," *Louisville Defender,* January 9, 1975.

39. "Kroger Co. to Upgrade and Add Black Workers," *Louisville Defender,* May 1, 1969; "NAACP Cracks Down Hard on Local Chain Grocery Stores," *Louisville Defender,* November 16, 1972; Meryl Thornton, "NAACP Initiates Kroger Boycott," *Louisville Defender,* December 28, 1972; "NAACP Rejects Kroger Proposal; Boycott Continues," *Louisville Defender,* January 18, 1973; "NAACP Rejects Kroger Plan," *Louisville Defender,* February 1, 1973.

40. Susan Brown, "NAACP Opposes HRC Kroger Conciliation," *Louisville Defender,* June 28, 1973; Jason Williams, "NAACP Files Complaint against KYHRC," *Louisville Defender,* October 17, 1974.

41. Robert Cunningham, interview; "Black Workers' Coalition Plans to Check Businesses," *Louisville Defender,* April 9, 1970; "Black Coalition Calls for Separate Black Union," *Louisville Defender,* September 17, 1970.

42. Ben Johnson, "Black Employees Take Day Off at Ford to Dramatize Company's Racial Problems," *Louisville Defender,* November 19, 1970; "Black Board Members at Ford Resign," *Louisville Defender,* April 27, 1972; HRC director's reports, July 12, 1973, September 6, 1973, Perley Papers; "Attention All Black Employees" (flyer, [April 1971]), file 6, Black Worker's Coalition, Social Action Files; Susan Brown, "Blacks Picket Distillery for Firing 15," *Louisville Defender,* August 3, 1972; Margaret Pankey to the editor, *Louisville Defender,* October 5, 1972; Susan Brown, "Distillery to Rehire Fired 15 Blacks," *Louisville Defender,* August 10, 1972; Susan Brown, "Black Workers Continue Picketing McCrory's; No Agreement Reached," *Louisville Defender,* June 7, 1973; Susan Brown, "McCrory's New Manager Welcomed to City," *Louisville Defender,* October 11, 1973.

43. Robert Cunningham, interview.

44. Meryl Thornton, "Tobacco Workers Protest Small Numbers; Only 2 Black Supers," *Louisville Defender,* August 30, 1973; Meryl Thornton, "Lo-

rillard Workers Fewer than 1931," *Louisville Defender,* September 27, 1973; Meryl Thornton, "Local Civil Rights Groups Join Tobacco Workers' Fight," *Louisville Defender,* September 6, 1973.

45. Meryl Thornton, "Local Civil Rights Groups Join Tobacco Workers' Fight," *Louisville Defender,* September 6, 1973; "NAACP Files Suit for Lorillard Workers," *Louisville Defender,* January 31, 1974; "Lorillard Boycotted," *Louisville Defender,* September 13, 1973; Meryl Thornton, "Fired Lorillard Workers Call for 'Black Friday,'" *Louisville Defender,* September 20, 1973; minutes of HRC executive committee meetings, October 4, 1973, November 1, 1973, Perley Papers; Priscilla Hancock, "State NAACP Supports Tobacco Workers' Fight," *Louisville Defender,* October 11, 1973; Meryl Thornton, "Tobacco Workers Held to Grand Jury," *Louisville Defender,* October 18, 1973; Priscilla Hancock and Meryl Thornton, "Four Get Suspended Sentences," *Louisville Defender,* December 20, 1973.

46. "LG&E, Coca-Cola Charged with Racial Discrimination," *Louisville Defender,* February 19, 1970; minutes of HRC meeting, January 6, 1972, Perley Papers; minutes of HRC executive session, August 2, 1973, Perley Papers; minutes of HRC meeting, February 4, 1971, Perley Papers.

47. Cheri Bryant Hamilton, interview by the author, October 23, 1999, OHC; minutes of HRC meetings, July 1, 1976, August 5, 1976, October 7, 1976, Perley Papers.

48. W. J. Hodge, "Hodge Forms Committee to Spotlight Lack of Jobs," *Louisville Defender,* May 13, 1978; "Disgraceful, Deceptive Is the Word for City's Affirmative Action Plan," *Louisville Defender,* May 13, 1978.

49. Jason Williams, "Blacks Disgusted as Mayor Vetoes City Affirmative Action Ordinance," *Louisville Defender,* July 6, 1978.

50. Courtney Barrett, "Affirmative Action Law to Be Signed," *Louisville Courier-Journal,* August 8, 1978; Elaine Kramer, "Mayor Signs Ordinance on Affirmative Action," *Louisville Courier-Journal,* August 9, 1978.

51. "Opinion Backs Position Stansbury Took on Veto," *Louisville Courier-Journal,* September 1, 1978; Courtney Barrett, "New City Law on Affirmative Action Not Free of Problems," *Louisville Courier-Journal,* March 12, 1979.

52. "Record Number of Black Candidates Face Tuesday's Primary with Optimism," *Louisville Defender,* May 22, 1969; "Record Number of Black Aspirants Enter Primary," *Louisville Defender,* April 1, 1971; Georgia Davis Powers, *I Shared the Dream: The Pride, Passion, and Politics of the First Black Woman Senator from Kentucky* (Far Hills, NJ: New Horizon Press, 1995); "Chas. Anderson, Local Attorney, Opens Campaign," *Louisville Defender,* March 6, 1969; Cecil Blye, "Attys. Turner, Owens May Get Judgeships," *Louisville Defender,* November 13, 1969; Meryl Thornton, "First Local Black Files for Sheriff," *Louisville Defender,* January 25, 1973; Susan Brown, "Crumlin Seeks Police Judgeship," *Louisville Defender,* February 8, 1973; "Black Elected Officials in Kentucky Total 35," *Louisville Defender,* November 13, 1969; "Six out of Ten Black Win," *Louisville Defender,* November 8, 1973.

53. Lester Pope, "Unity Democrats Seek Black-White Coalition," *Louisville Defender*, March 27, 1969.

54. "Colonial Park Sponsors Unity," *Louisville Defender*, May 15, 1969; "Unity Fund Drive Soul Supper Is Saturday," *Louisville Defender*, May 15, 1969; "Concept of Unity Slate: Power for the People," *Voice*, April 17, 1969, box 9, file 12, WECC Papers; Lester Pope, "'Tucker Is Being Used as Pawn': Morris Jeff," *Louisville Defender*, April 17, 1969; "Black Unity Slate Picks Thornberry," *Louisville Defender*, May 1, 1969.

55. "Neville Tucker Rallies, Wins Court Nomination," *Louisville Defender*, June 5, 1969.

56. Cecil Blye, "White Delegation Hit; Blacks Seek Bigger Role," *Louisville Defender*, August 8, 1968; Cecil Blye, "Black Republicans Wanted Crumlin to Replace Dearing," *Louisville Defender*, September 11, 1969; "'Minimum Effort' Planned by Black Precinct Captains," *Louisville Defender*, October 9, 1969.

57. Cecil Blye, "Democrats Pick 7 Negro Delegates," *Louisville Defender*, August 1, 1968; Dunnigan, *Fascinating Story of Black Kentuckians*, 367; Hamilton, interview.

58. Lester Pope, "Burke Hopes to 'Depolarize' the Races in Louisville," *Louisville Defender*, December 4, 1969; "A New Administration . . . a New Hope," *Louisville Defender*, December 4, 1969; "Mayor Burke's Administration," *Louisville Defender*, November 15, 1973.

59. Lester Pope, "Burke Hopes to 'Depolarize' the Races in Louisville," *Louisville Defender*, December 4, 1969; "A New Administration . . . a New Hope," *Louisville Defender*, December 4, 1969; "Mayor Burke's Administration," *Louisville Defender*, November 15, 1973; "Dr. Carroll Witten's Leadership," *Louisville Defender*, November 29, 1973; "Public Safety Demands Black Representation," *Louisville Defender*, November 15, 1973.

60. Susan Brown, "Mayor-Elect Sloane Says He Will Appoint More Blacks," *Louisville Defender*, November 15, 1973; Priscilla Hancock, "Sloane Names Black Aide," *Louisville Defender*, December 6, 1973; "Three Programs Geared to Aid Blacks," *Louisville Defender*, June 6, 1974; Hamilton, interview.

61. Aubrey Williams, interview by the author, May 17, 2000, OHC.

62. "Leo Lesser Will Run," *Louisville Defender*, March 8, 1973; "24 Blacks Seek Office in Tuesday Primary," *Louisville Defender*, May 24, 1973; Frank L. Stanley, Being Frank About, *Louisville Defender*, May 24, 1973; Susan Brown, "Lesser: 'Campaign's Beneficial,' Plans for Whole Community," *Louisville Defender*, May 31, 1973; "Black Candidates Win a Measure Even in Defeat," *Louisville Defender*, May 31, 1973.

63. Jason Williams, "Aldermen Lois Morris and Ace Brown Not Slated by Sloane," *Louisville Defender*, March 6, 1975; Jason Williams, "Lois Morris Announces Candidacy for Mayor," *Louisville Defender*, June 5, 1975; Jason Williams, "Milburn Maupin Hopes to Succeed in Mayor's Race," *Louisville*

Defender, September 23, 1976; "Lois Morris Discusses Upcoming Mayoral Race and Candidacy," *Louisville Defender,* October 7, 1976; Ron Long, "Black Caucus to Build Political Power," *Louisville Defender,* October 28, 1976; Charmaine Bissell and Jason Williams, "Voters Call for One Black Candidate in Mayoral Race," *Louisville Defender,* February 10, 1977.

64. Ben Johnson, "Black Vote Power: Numbers Are There but Not the Clout," *Louisville Courier-Journal,* May 26, 1977; Jason Williams, "Black Caucus Endorses Stansbury," *Louisville Defender,* May 5, 1977. By 1970, blacks made up 24 percent of the city's population. The rise from 15 percent in 1950 is attributable in part to white migration out of the city. In that time the white population declined by approximately 35,000. The result is also due to some in-migration of African Americans. Luther Adams has calculated that between 1930 and 1970, Louisville gained a net of 17,000 African American migrants. Luther Adams, "'It Was North of Tennessee': African American Migration to Louisville and the Meaning of the South," *Ohio Valley History* 3 (Fall 2003): 37. On the one other major black campaign for mayor, in 1985, see Sharon D. Wright, "Electoral and Biracial Coalition: Possible Election Strategy for African American Candidates in Louisville, KY," *Journal of Black Studies* 25 (1995).

65. Carl Hines, interview by the author, September 21, 1999, OHC; Williams, interview.

66. *Kentucky Directory of Black Elected Officials* (Frankfort: Kentucky Commission on Human Rights, 1976), 1; Ben Johnson, "Black Vote Power: Numbers Are There but Not the Clout," *Louisville Courier-Journal,* May 26, 1977; Lois Morris to volunteers, March 14, 1977, box 4, folder "Correspondence," Lois Morris Papers, Ekstrom Library, University of Louisville, Louisville, KY.

8. The Busing Crisis

1. On busing and school desegregation, see Nicolaus Mills, ed., *Busing U.S.A.* (New York: Teachers College Press, 1979); Ronald P. Formisano, *Boston against Busing: Race, Class, and Ethnicity in the 1960s and 1970s* (Chapel Hill: University of North Carolina Press, 1991); Steven J. L. Taylor, *Desegregation in Boston and Buffalo: The Influence of Local Leaders* (Albany: State University of New York Press, 1998); and Richard A. Pride and J. David Woodard, *The Burden of Busing: The Politics of Desegregation in Nashville, Tennessee* (Knoxville: University of Tennessee Press, 1985).

2. "Teacher Integration Increases to 36 Here," *Louisville Defender,* May 25, 1961; "220 Negro Teachers Are Integrated," *Louisville Defender,* September 24, 1964; "Integration Rises in City Schools," *Louisville Defender,* October 22, 1964; Benjamin Muse, "Louisville," May 1964, box 1, file 4A, Woolsey Papers; "Local NAACP Says School Heads Trying to Achieve Desegregation," *Louisville Defender,* May 6, 1965; "Five Local Schools Would Be

'Segregated' under State Board of Education Proposal," *Louisville Defender,* July 2, 1964; "City School System under Criticism; Noe Defensive," *Louisville Defender,* April 7, 1966; Kentucky Commission on Human Rights, *Louisville School System Retreats to Segregation: A Report on Public Schools in Louisville, Kentucky, 1956–1971* (Frankfort: Commonwealth of Kentucky, 1971).

3. "Louisville School System May Be Legal Action Target," *Louisville Defender,* April 14, 1966; "Supt. Noe Reaffirms Open Plan," *Louisville Defender,* November 25, 1966; "Louisville NAACP Attacks City Schools' Imbalance," *Louisville Defender,* March 6, 1969; "NAACP May Take Action If HEW Doesn't End Segregation," *Louisville Defender,* May 29, 1969; "Samuel Noe Ends Career," *Louisville Defender,* July 3, 1969; "Walker Pledges to Work with NAACP," *Louisville Defender,* August 21, 1969.

4. "Teacher Integration up to County Staff," *Louisville Courier-Journal,* June 2, 1963; Reverend Thurmond Coleman to the editor, *Louisville Courier-Journal,* May 30, 1963; "County Integrates 5 Teachers; Newburg Considered Problem," *Louisville Defender,* June 26, 1963. For a review of the history of county actions, see John L. Ramsey, "County School System Integrates Following Court Decision," *Louisville Defender,* February 14, 1974.

5. Jack Lyne, *Schoolhouse Dreams Deferred: Decay, Hope, and Desegregation in a Core-City School System* (n.p.: Phi Delta Kappa International, 1998), 159–61; "County and City Schools Both Must Be Completely Desegregated," *Louisville Defender,* July 1, 1971; "Emotion Not the Answer," *Louisville Defender,* July 29, 1971; "Van Hoose Must Stand Tall," *Louisville Defender,* August 5, 1971; "Newburg Children—the Real Victims," *Louisville Defender,* August 12, 1971; "County School Board Elects to Defy HEW," *Louisville Defender,* August 12, 1971.

6. "Redistricting Asked for Newburg Schools," *Louisville Defender,* September 3, 1971. For a brief overview of the legal history of the school desegregation suits against the city and county from 1971 to 1974, see Robert A. Sedler, "The Louisville–Jefferson County School Desegregation Case: A Lawyer's Retrospective," *Register of the Kentucky Historical Society* 105, no. 1 (2007).

7. Linda Raymond, "US Court Asked to Order City School Desegregation," *Louisville Times,* June 23, 1972; "Three School Suits Filed," *Louisville Defender,* June 29, 1972; Galen Martin to June Shagaloff Alexander, June 19, 1972, box C134, file "*Haycraft v. Board of Education,* 1972–76," group 5, NAACP Papers; "A Capsule of School Case Litigation," *Louisville Defender,* January 3, 1974; Sedler, "Louisville–Jefferson County School Desegregation Case," 14; James Nolan, "School Desegregation Suits in Louisville Area Dismissed," *Louisville Courier-Journal,* March 9, 1973.

8. James Nolan, "School Desegregation Suits in Louisville Area Dismissed," *Louisville Courier-Journal,* March 9, 1973; James Nolan, "Judges Question Louisville, County on Merger, Busing for Integration," *Louisville Courier-Journal,* October 4, 1973; James Nolan, "Louisville-Area Schools

Told to Draft Desegregation Plan," *Louisville Courier-Journal*, December 29, 1973; Susan Brown, "City Board Won't Appeal Decision," *Louisville Defender*, January 10, 1974; "Our BofE's Challenge," *Louisville Defender*, January 17, 1974; "Act Illegally," *Louisville Defender*, February 7, 1974.

9. Bob Hill, "Sue Connor Plans to Be Around Awhile," *Louisville Times*, September 9, 1975; Jim Adams, "Joyce Spond: Antibusing Leader with a 'Reasoned' Approach," *Louisville Courier-Journal*, October 6, 1975.

10. "Priddy Asks Convention to Discuss Busing," *Louisville Defender*, February 7, 1974; "Representative Kidd Warns against Inflamed Passions Urging Anti-busing," *Louisville Defender*, February 14, 1974; Meryl Thornton, "Adult Anti-busing Furor Prompts Student Tensions," *Louisville Defender*, February 21, 1974; Jason Williams, "County School Board Meets; Residents Oppose Busing, Merger, and Walker," *Louisville Defender*, March 28, 1974.

11. Draft of pamphlet, 1972, file 1, Ad Hoc Committee for School Integration, Social Action Files; "False Busing Fears," *Louisville Defender*, February 14, 1974; board of directors of Eastern Area Council to the editor, *Louisville Defender*, March 7, 1974; "Civic Groups Sponsor Desegregation Panels," *Louisville Defender*, April 4, 1974.

12. Jason Williams, "Pro-busing Cohorts Swarm County Board," *Louisville Defender*, April 25, 1974.

13. Jason Williams, "School Boards Petition to Stay Desegregation," *Louisville Defender*, September 5, 1974; Sedler, "Louisville–Jefferson County School Desegregation Case," 18–19.

14. Chronology of merger plans, 1975, box 4, file "Brown School Ad Hoc Committee on School Merger," Progress in Education Papers, Ekstrom Library, University of Louisville, Louisville, KY (hereafter cited as PIE Papers).

15. Ibid.; Priscilla Hancock, "Finances Force City BofE to Seek Merger with County," *Louisville Defender*, February 28, 1974; "Third Party Needed to Arbitrate Merger," *Louisville Defender*, May 16, 1974; Jason Williams, "City Schools Try to Force Merger with County," *Louisville Defender*, November 14, 1974; Jason Williams, "County Board of Education Denies City's Merger Request," *Louisville Defender*, November 28, 1974; Jason Williams, "Louisville School Board Ends Years of Educating," *Louisville Defender*, April 3, 1975.

16. "Plantation Mentality Afflicts Judge Gordon," *Louisville Defender*, June 12, 1975; Jason Williams, "School Desegregation," *Louisville Defender*, July 24, 1975; Jason Williams, "Gordon's Desegregation Plan Has Special Requirements for Black Students," *Louisville Defender*, August 7, 1975.

17. Mr. and Mrs. R. J. Maynard to the editor, *Louisville Times*, August 12, 1975; Kenneth A. Tyler to the editor, *Louisville Times*, August 13, 1975. For more critiques, see the letters to the editor of the *Louisville Times* from Mrs. Joseph Phillips, August 6, 1975; G. Terry Minton, August 12, 1975; Gerard W. De Boer, August 12, 1975; Doris Rachilla, August 12, 1975; and Mrs. H. J. Sears, August 15, 1975. See also, for example, William Kellerman,

Sue Connor, and Robert Deprez, testimony, *Hearing before the United States Commission on Civil Rights: Held in Louisville, Kentucky, June 14–16, 1976* (Washington, DC, 1976), 26–39, 427–29.

18. On the link between antibusing and the rise of modern conservatism and the New Right, see, for example, Matthew D. Lassiter, *The Silent Majority: Suburban Politics in the Sunbelt South* (Princeton, NJ: Princeton University Press, 2006), part 2 (on the Charlotte busing debate); Durr, *Behind the Backlash,* 166–73; and Lisa McGirr, *Suburban Warriors: The Origins of the New American Right* (Princeton, NJ: Princeton University Press, 2001), 239–40.

19. Carolyn Colwell, "Union Members Opposed to Busing," *Louisville Courier-Journal,* August 5, 1975; Ronald Harsh (president of District 27 International Association of Machinists and Aerospace Workers) to the editor, *Louisville Courier-Journal,* August 25, 1975, clipping, box 4, file "ULAB," PIE Papers; "Labor Groups Oppose School Busing Plan," *Louisville Courier-Journal,* August 26, 1975; Jim Adams, "Leaders of Union Join Two Groups in Busing Protest," *Louisville Courier-Journal,* August 24, 1975; Jim Adams, "Plants Plan Normal Business," *Louisville Courier-Journal,* September 3, 1975. See also advertisements for numerous union resolutions, *Louisville Courier-Journal,* September 1975, box 4, file "ULAB," PIE Papers.

20. Richard Manning, "Klan Leaders to Be Featured Speakers at Anti-busing Rally," *Louisville Times,* July 15, 1975; Robert T. Garrett, "Induction of Members, Rallies Are Planned by Klan," *Louisville Courier-Journal,* August 21, 1975; Carol Hardison, "Klan Plans to Disrupt School Opening," *Louisville Defender,* August 21, 1975; "Will the Klan Gain a Foothold in Louisville," *Louisville Defender,* July 17, 1975; Jason Williams, "Klan Preaches Race Hate," *Louisville Defender,* July 24, 1975; Betty Lacer to the editor, July 31, 1975, clipping, box 4, file "Ku Klux Klan, 1976–1976," PIE Papers.

21. "Workshop on Integration Set," *Louisville Defender,* August 21, 1975; "School Officials Say Busing Will Succeed," *Louisville Defender,* August 28, 1975; "Peaceful Desegregation," *Louisville Defender,* July 24, 1975; Ben Johnson, "Black Parents, Youth Hear Speakers Ask Support of Integration Plan," *Louisville Courier-Journal,* August 20, 1975; "CALM Bumper Stickers Ready" and "Neighborhood News" announcements, *Alert* (Task Force for Peaceful Desegregation newsletter), August 22, 1975, box 4, file "Taskforce for Peaceful Desegregation," PIE Papers; Lyne, *Schoolhouse Dreams Deferred,* 278; advertisement, *Louisville Defender,* August 28, 1975; "Open Letter to Parents," *Louisville Defender,* September 4, 1975.

22. "Demonstrate against the Klan" (flyer, August 1975), box 4, file "Ku Klux Klan, 1976–1976," PIE Papers; Kentucky Alliance, statement, August 15, 1975, box 4, file "Ku Klux Klan, 1976–1976," PIE Papers; Ben Johnson, "March Set to Show Concern for Children's Safety," *Louisville Courier-Journal,* August 29, 1975; James Parks, "Panthers Prepare to Protest Community," *Louisville Defender,* August 28, 1975; "Unity Rally and March" (flyer, August 1975), box 1, file "Newsletters," PIE Papers.

23. Doris Johnson, "Black Parents Voice Busing Concern," *Louisville Defender,* August 21, 1975; James Parks, "Two Local Leaders Discuss Busing," *Louisville Defender,* September 4, 1975; Larry Basham, "West End YWCA Holds Desegregation Meeting," *Louisville Defender,* September 4, 1975; Marsha Rhea, "Students Express Fear of Parents' Reaction to Busing," *Louisville Courier-Journal,* August 19, 1975; Jason Williams, "Local Officials Warn against School Desegregation Violence," *Louisville Defender,* August 14, 1975; John Nevin, interview by Ethel White, May 2, 1988, OHC.

24. William K. Stevens, "Louisville, Suburbs Integrate Schools," *New York Times,* September 5, 1975; Judith Ann Birkhead, "Consolidation and Desegregation of Public Schools in Jefferson County, Kentucky" (EdD diss., University of Cincinnati, 1978), 335–38; Anne Braden to Pete [Seeger], October 6, 1975, box 2, file "PIE Rally," PIE Papers; "The First Day: Much Evidence of a Community's Good Sense," *Louisville Courier-Journal,* September 5, 1975.

25. Dianne Aprile, Mike Wines, and Ira Simmons, "At Fairdale High, a Quiet Day Turned Sour," *Louisville Times,* September 5, 1975; Martin E. Biemer, "Officials Thankful Pupils Left before Riots Began," *Louisville Times,* September 6, 1975. The violence of September 5 was reported in numerous articles in the local papers and in the national media. The most comprehensive and detailed description is in "Dozens Hurt, 192 Arrested in Riots; 800 Guardsmen Called to Duty," *Louisville Times,* September 6, 1975. I would like to thank Elizabeth Gillespie McRae for sharing her insights on the contrast between nonracial claims and the use of racial rhetoric in Boston. Elizabeth Gillespie McRae, "White Women, Massive Resistance, and the Boston Anti-busing Crusade" (paper presented at the annual meeting of the Southern Historical Association, Richmond, VA, October 31–November 3, 2007).

26. "Dozens Hurt, 192 Arrested in Riots; 800 Guardsmen Called to Duty," *Louisville Times,* September 6, 1975.

27. Ibid.; Judith Rosenfeld, "Everyday People," *Louisville Times,* September 6, 1975; Jerry Hicks, "Anti-busing Rioters Scar Southern High Area," *Louisville Times,* September 6, 1975.

28. "Dozens Hurt, 192 Arrested in Riots; 800 Guardsmen Called to Duty," *Louisville Times,* September 6, 1975; William K. Stevens, "Violence Breaks Out in Louisville after 2d Peaceful Day of Cross-District Busing," *New York Times,* September 6, 1975; Nevin, interview; Birkhead, "Consolidation and Desegregation," 341–42.

29. "At Least 60 Arrested Downtown," [September 1975], clipping, box 2, file "ESAA Grant Application," PIE Papers; William K. Stevens, "School Buses in Louisville Will Carry Guards Today," *New York Times,* September 8, 1975; William K. Stevens, "Louisville Busing Resumes as More Students Enroll," *New York Times,* September 9, 1975; "Protesters Drive through Western Part of Louisville," *Louisville Courier-Journal,* September 11, 1975; William K. Stevens, "Quiet Louisville Accepting Busing," *New York Times,* September 11, 1975.

30. "Protestors Drive through Western Part of Louisville," *Louisville Courier-Journal*, September 11, 1975; "8000 in Louisville March to Protest School Bus Order," *New York Times*, September 28, 1975; typescript of antibusing activities, [September 1975], box 5, file "Anti-busing Activities," PIE Papers; Mike Brown and Dick Kaukas, "Busing Protest Includes Incidents of Racial Discord," *Louisville Courier-Journal*, December 7, 1975; Jason Williams, "Black Officer Defends against Accusations," *Louisville Defender*, December 8, 1975; James Parks, "Officer Brown Reprimanded by Chief Nevin," *Louisville Defender*, January 1, 1976.

31. "High Absenteeism at GE Curtails Some Production," *Louisville Courier-Journal*, September 13, 1975; "Boycott Shuts One Ford Plant," *Louisville Courier-Journal*, October 2, 1975; Donald M. Houghton, "Unions Plan Anti-busing March," *Louisville Times*, October 1, 1975; Richard Stockman, "Unions Fund Racist Rally," *Workers' Power*, October 31, 1975, box 4, file "ULAB," PIE Papers; Jim Adams, "Labor Union Antibusing Leaders Note," *Louisville Courier-Journal*, November 21, 1975; "Anti-busers Wrong in Knocking Out Windows at Louisville Courier-Journal," *Louisville Defender*, November 27, 1975; Jason Williams, "Anti-busing Demonstrators Attack Black Man," *Louisville Defender*, November 27, 1975. On the conflict within the labor movement over ULAB's participation in the antibusing movement, see Minchin, *From Rights to Economics*, 134–50.

32. Nancy Gall-Clayton to editors and broadcasters, September 11, 1975, box 1, file "Notices and Statements," PIE Papers; "An Invitation for Your Involvement and Support," [Fall 1975], box 1, file "PIE Literature," PIE Papers; "Story Dictated," September 17, 1975, box 1, file "Notices and Statements," PIE Papers; "Coalition Formed to Oppose Racism," *Louisville Defender*, September 18, 1975; Dick Kaukas, "Pro-busing Leader Doesn't Like to See People 'Stepped On,'" *Louisville Courier-Journal*, n.d., clipping, box 1, file "Clippings," PIE Papers.

33. Suzy Post et al. to friend, open letter, October 4, 1975, box 2, file "PIE Rally," PIE Papers; PIE, news release, October 6, 1975, box 1, file "Notices and Statements," PIE Papers; "Pro-busing March Slated," *Louisville Defender*, October 9, 1975; [Anne Braden] to Pete [Seeger], September 15, 1975, box 1, file "General Correspondence, 1975," PIE Papers; Mervin Aubespin, "Downtown March Backs Integration," *Louisville Courier-Journal*, n.d., clipping, box 1, file "Clippings," PIE Papers; "Story Phoned to World, October 15, 1975," box 1, file "Notices and Statements," PIE Papers.

34. Jim Adams, "Busing Foes Peaceful at 2 Klan Rallies," *Louisville Courier-Journal*, September 7, 1975; "Protesters Drive through Western Louisville," *Louisville Courier-Journal*, September 11, 1975; Jason Williams, "White Service Stations Boycott," *Louisville Defender*, September 11, 1975; Carolyn Colwell and Ed Ryan, "Antibusing Speaker Renews Plan for Business Boycott," *Louisville Courier-Journal*, September 29, 1975; *Hearing before the United States Commission on Civil Rights*, 73–77.

35. Leslie Ellis and Lynn Bynum, "Some Flee Busing by Crossing River into Indiana," *Louisville Courier-Journal,* August 21, 1975; Bonita Emerick, interview by Elizabeth Gritter, August 2, 2005, SOHC; Judy Rosenfield, "Getting Away from It All," *Louisville Times,* October 28, 1975; Dale Moss, "Clarksville Blocks Busing Transfers," *Louisville Times,* August 20, 1975; "Nearby School Districts Won't Welcome Transfers," *Louisville Times,* August 27, 1975; Pat Delahanty, interview by the author, September 3, 1999, OHC.

36. David Creed, "Integration Spurs Private Schools," *Louisville Courier-Journal,* September 15, 1975; David Creed, "A Profile of Five New Private Schools," *Louisville Courier-Journal,* September 15, 1975; Sheldon Shafter, "40 Louisville Churches Trying to Establish Independent Schools," *Louisville Courier-Journal,* October 7, 1975. On the rise of private schools and "segregation academies," see Carrie Faulk, "The First Line of Defense: The Battle to Preserve Segregation through Clairborne Academy, 1969–1970," *North Louisiana History* 37, no. 4 (2006), and Margaret Rose Gladney, "I'll Gladly Take My Stand: The Southern Segregation Academy Movement" (PhD diss., University of New Mexico, 1974).

37. Charles W. Ranney to the editor, *Louisville Courier-Journal,* September 12, 1975; Ed Ryan, "Antibusing Fervor Has Incumbents Running Scared," *Louisville Courier-Journal,* September 29, 1975; Jim Adams, "New Antibusing Group Organizes in Louisville," *Louisville Courier-Journal,* October 9, 1975; Sheldon Shafer, "Busing Group Gives a List for Voters," *Louisville Courier-Journal,* November 4, 1975.

38. Anne Pardue, "Jefferson Legislators Meet with Carroll on Busing," *Louisville Courier-Journal,* September 12, 1975; Ed Ryan, "Carroll Asks to Testify before Congress in Favor of Busing Ban," *Louisville Courier-Journal,* October 3, 1975; Ed Ryan, "Carroll Steps Up Criticism of School Busing," *Louisville Courier-Journal,* October 9, 1975; Ken Loomis, "Antibusing Groups Urge More School Boycotts," *Louisville Courier-Journal,* September 15, 1975; Ed Ryan, "Gable Having Problems Drawing Crowds," *Louisville Courier-Journal,* October 16, 1975; Ed Ryan, "Carroll Wins in Democratic Sweep," *Louisville Courier-Journal,* November 5, 1975; Jim Adams, "Legislature: Jefferson County Democrats Lose Two Seats in House," *Louisville Courier-Journal,* November 5, 1975.

39. Jim Adams, "Busing Foes Peaceful at 2 Klan Rallies," *Louisville Courier-Journal,* September 7, 1975; Tom Van Howe and J. Stephen Fagan, "Klan Chiefs Eye Area's Busing Strife," *Louisville Times,* September 26, 1975; Jim Adams and David Creed, "Rift in Ku Klux Klan," *Louisville Courier-Journal,* September 11, 1975; Jim Adams, "Klan Inducts Group, Hears National Chief at Rally in Bullitt," *Louisville Courier-Journal,* November 2, 1975.

40. Jim Adams, "Busing Foes Peaceful at 2 Klan Rallies," *Louisville Courier-Journal,* September 7, 1975; Jim Adams, "Klan Inducts Group, Hears National Chief at Rally in Bullitt," *Louisville Courier-Journal,* November 2, 1975; "Remark Aired at Judge Is Probed," *Louisville Courier-Journal,* Sep-

tember 19, 1975; Jim Adams, "Fraternity of the Klan," *Louisville Courier-Journal*, December 22, 1975. For the *Louisville Courier-Journal*'s coverage of dissension and legal problems in the Klan, see, for example, "Klan Official Faces Charges in Cycle Incident," *Louisville Courier-Journal*, September 30, 1975, and Jim Adams, "Klan Flap, National and State KKK Exchange Charges," *Louisville Courier-Journal*, August 30, 1975.

41. *American Mercury*, Fall 1975, reprint, Perley Papers; flyer announcing Constitution Farm, n.d., Perley Papers; Reverend L. W. Hughes, open letter, n.d., Perley Papers; Parents for Freedom flyer, n.d., Perley Papers; NAPF newsletters, October 1975, November 23, 1975, box 4, file "NAPF," PIE Papers.

42. Jim Adams, "Living in Fear," *Louisville Courier-Journal*, October 2, 1975; Ben Johnson, "Targets of Hate," *Louisville Courier-Journal*, November 19, 1975; Jason Williams, "Whites Try to Run Black Family out of Okolona," *Louisville Defender*, November 20, 1975; "Important News from Progress in Education," [November 1975], box 1, file "Newsletters," PIE Papers; Alvis Bond, "Local Rights Organizations Demand Arrest, Conviction of South End Terrorists," *Louisville Defender*, March 25, 1976.

43. Jason Williams, "Whites Try to Run Black Family out of Okolona," *Louisville Defender*, November 20, 1975; PIE, news releases, November 24, 1975, March 15, 1976, box 1, file "Notices and Statements," PIE Papers; PIE, statement to [Russell] McDaniels (county police chief), November 26, 1975, box 1, file "Notices and Statements," PIE Papers; "7 Criticize Police on Protection for Black Family," *Louisville Times*, November 26 1975; Alvis Bond, "Local Rights Organizations Demand Arrest, Conviction of South End Terrorists," *Louisville Defender*, March 25, 1976; PIE to people who volunteered to spend . . . , memorandum, December 2, 1975, box 1, file "PIE Literature," PIE Papers.

44. "Mayor Harvey Sloane," *Louisville Defender*, September 19, 1975; PIE to Mayor Harvey Sloane, statement, October 27, 1975, box 1, file "Notices and Statements," PIE Papers; Jim Rennessen, "Proponents Urge Sloane to 'Tell Nation Busing Is Working in Louisville,'" *Louisville Times*, October 27, 1975.

45. "County Judge Todd Hollenbach," *Louisville Defender*, September 18, 1975; PIE to County Judge Todd Hollenbach, statement, October 24, 1975, box 1, file "Notices and Statements," PIE Papers; Anne Braden, "Progress in Education Charges Hollenbach with 'Spending Tax Money Wrongly,'" *Louisville Defender*, October 23, 1975; Lynn Bynum, "PIE Burns," *Louisville Courier-Journal*, October 25, 1975; "Let Your Voice Be Heard" (flyer, [January 1976]), box 1, file "Announcements of Meetings," PIE Papers; "United Black Protective Parents Petition," May 1976, box 1, file "PIE Literature," PIE Papers; "UBPP Visits Hollenbach," *News from PIE*, March 1976, box 1, file "Newsletters," PIE Papers.

46. Wanda Nichols, "Proposals Offered in Busing Hearing," *Louisville Courier-Journal*, November 11, 1975; Bob Hill, "Busing Protestors Shut

Down Speakers at Alternative Hearing," *Louisville Times,* November 20, 1975; Mike Wines, "Busing Alternatives Hearing in Fairdale Ends in Bedlam," *Louisville Times,* November 21, 1975; PIE to County Judge Todd Hollenbach, statement, November 26, 1975, box 1, file "Notices and Statements," PIE Papers; Ben Johnson, "No Apology: Hollenbach Hears Complaint of Pro-busing Group," *Louisville Courier-Journal,* November 27, 1975; "Important News from Progress in Education," [November 1975], box 1, file "Newsletters," PIE Papers.

47. "Busing Issue," *Louisville Defender,* October 24, 1974; Meryl Thornton, "Group Joins Effort to Stop Racist Attacks on Black School Children," *Louisville Defender,* November 21, 1974; Mervin Aubespin, "Black Leader Says Races Now at Odds over Boston Busing," *Louisville Courier-Journal,* November 22, 1975; Louisville Student Coalition against Racism to friends, November 1975, box 4, file "SCAR," PIE Papers; "Students Attend Antiracism Meeting," *Louisville Defender,* June 3, 1976; "National Conference against Racism," *News from PIE,* October 1976, box 1, file "Newsletters," PIE Papers.

48. Jane Ramsey, "Racism in the Schools or in the Community: Same Issue Same Fight," *News from PIE,* February 1977, box 1, file "Newsletters," PIE Papers.

49. Jason Williams, "Fairdale Student Injured," *Louisville Defender,* September 11, 1975; Keith Runyon and Mike King, "Scattered Violence Reported in County," *Louisville Courier-Journal,* September 8, 1975; "Missile Strikes Bus; 3 Students Hurt," *Louisville Courier-Journal,* October 11, 1975; Mervin Aubespin, "Black Parents Air Complaints about Pupil Transportation," *Louisville Courier-Journal,* September 20, 1975; Jason Williams, "Blacks Demand Better Bus Service," *Louisville Defender,* September 25, 1975.

50. Ralph Campbell, "Two Charge Gun Held on Them," *Louisville Defender,* November 13, 1975; Ben Johnson, "Black Students Say the Hate Was Unexpected," *Louisville Courier-Journal,* September 11, 1975; David Creed, "9 Arrested, 2 Injured in Iroquois Fight," *Louisville Courier-Journal,* October 15, 1975; Chris Morris, "Racial Fighting Erupts at Durrett High School," *Louisville Courier-Journal,* November 8, 1975; Dick Kaukas, "Black Students, White Youths Throw Objects," *Louisville Courier-Journal,* October 2, 1975; Jason Williams, "Students Discuss Violence in Schools," *Louisville Defender,* October 2, 1975.

51. Ben Johnson, "Black Students Say the Hate Was Unexpected," *Louisville Courier-Journal,* September 11, 1975; Jason Williams, "Atherton Students Walk Out, Cite Harassment, Suspensions," *Louisville Defender,* May 6, 1976; Jason Williams, "Parents Seek Removal of Assistant Principal," *Louisville Defender,* October 21, 1976; Jason Williams, "Black Manual Student Disputes School Official and Media Coverage," *Louisville Defender,* November 18, 1976; Lynn Bynum, "Ballard High Principal Has Suspended 20 Black Students since Monday," *Louisville Courier-Journal,* September 11, 1975;

"School Suspensions Running 40% ahead of Last Year's Rate," *Louisville Courier-Journal,* October 13, 1975; Linda Stahl, "Pupil Suspensions up 82% from '74," *Louisville Courier-Journal,* December 12, 1975; Jason Williams, "It's Pitiful How Unconcerned Blacks Are," *Louisville Defender,* December 18, 1975; Jason Williams, "Atherton Students, Parents Seek Remedy," *Louisville Defender,* May 13, 1976; "Black School Suspensions," *Louisville Defender,* April 15, 1976; Milburn Maupin, testimony, *Hearing before the United States Commission on Civil Rights,* 324–25.

52. Jason Williams, "Blacks Plan Mass Busing March," *Louisville Defender,* October 9, 1975; Jason Williams, "Black March for Busing," *Louisville Defender,* October 16, 1975; Jason Williams, "Pro-busing March Fizzles Out," *Louisville Defender,* November 27, 1975.

53. Jason Williams, "KSCLC Calls for Coke Boycott," *Louisville Defender,* September 25, 1975; Jason Williams, "Black Workers' Coalition Boycotts Coca Cola," *Louisville Defender,* March 18, 1976.

54. Benitha Ellis, interview by the author, September 4, 2000, OHC; UBPP statement of purpose, n.d., box 4, file "UBPP," PIE Papers; Jason Williams, "Black Parents to Go to Washington to Talk about Busing," *Louisville Defender,* October 23, 1975.

55. Jason Williams, "Black Parents to Go to Washington to Talk about Busing," *Louisville Defender,* October 23, 1975; Anne Braden, "Kentucky Parents Hit Anti-busing Hearing," *Daily World,* October 38, 1975, clipping, box 1, file "1975," PIE Papers; "Pro-busing Groups Testify before Senate," *Louisville Defender,* October 30, 1975; "Important Sunday Rally" (flyer, [November 1975]), box 1, file "Announcements of Meetings," PIE Papers.

56. Sister Eileen M. Egan to Spaulding College faculty and staff, March 19, 1975, exhibit no. 21, *Hearing before the United States Commission on Civil Rights,* 521; Martin Perley, "Now Our Job Begins," *Alert,* September 9, 1975, box 4, file "Task Force for Peaceful Desegregation," PIE Papers; "Task Force Urges Support," *Alert,* September 19, 1975, box 4, file "Task Force for Peaceful Desegregation," PIE Papers; notices, *Alert,* November 5, 1975, February 23, 1976, box 4, file "Task Force for Peaceful Desegregation," PIE Papers; "Congratulations Winners," *Alert,* June 14, 1976, box 4, file "Task Force for Peaceful Desegregation," PIE Papers; master lists of member groups, n.d., box 4, file "Task Force for Peaceful Desegregation," PIE Papers; Samuel Robinson to representatives of member organizations, October 19, 1976, box 4, file "Task Force for Peaceful Desegregation," PIE Papers.

57. Lois Cronholm, testimony, *Hearing before the United States Commission on Civil Rights,* 162–63.

58. Brochures and materials on Project Connection in the author's possession; Alfred Horrigan et al. to the editor, *Louisville Defender,* October 9, 1975; *Alert,* September 9, 1975, box 4, file "Task Force for Peaceful Desegregation," PIE Papers; Louisville Presbyterian Theological Seminary, notice, *Alert,* September 19, 1975, box 4, file "Task Force for Peaceful Desegregation," PIE

Papers; "The A to Z History and Present Work of the Interfaith Task Force on School Integration," exhibit 27a, *Hearing before the United States Commission on Civil Rights,* 670–75.

59. Jim Adams, "Rally Told Court-Ordered Busing Is Only One of Country's Ills," *Louisville Courier-Journal,* February 26, 1976; "Antibusing Demonstrators Stage Orderly Downtown Protest," *Louisville Courier-Journal,* February 13, 1976; "Group Weighs Busing Protest for Derby Day," *Louisville Times,* December 31, 1975; "ULAB Is Denied Permit for March," *Louisville Courier-Journal,* March 11, 1975; Jason Williams, "ULAB March: 1967 Revisited, Reversed," *Louisville Defender,* April 15, 1976; "Busing Foes March Peacefully on Preston; Others Gather Elsewhere," *Louisville Times,* September 6, 1976; "Tear Gas Used to Disperse Protesters," *Louisville Courier-Journal,* September 6, 1976; Patrick Howington, "Violence, Numbers at Busing Protests Less than in Past," *Louisville Times,* September 6, 1977; Jim Adams and Bill Osinski, "Busing Protesters March on Dixie; Blacks Are Harassed," *Louisville Courier-Journal,* September 6, 1977; "Antibusing Group Plans July 4 Rally on Preston Highway," *Louisville Times,* June 29, 1978; Leslie Ellis, "'Dedicated' Busing Protesters Stage Pre-election March without Incident," *Louisville Courier-Journal,* November 7, 1978.

60. Minutes of HRC executive committee meeting, June 10, 1976, Perley Papers; "Dear Brothers and Sisters," *News from January 1977,* box 1, file "Newsletters," PIE Papers; "Racist Attacks Continue—Still No Arrests," *News from February 1977,* box 1, file "Newsletters," PIE Papers.

61. David Tachau, "Both County Police and School System Say They Have Agents in Busing Groups," *Louisville Times,* August 10, 1976; R. G. Dunlop, "Grenades, Dynamite Found in Probe of Anti-busing Group," *Louisville Courier-Journal,* August 18, 1976.

62. Anne Braden to Ron, October 1, [1976], box 4, file "Ku Klux Klan, 1976–1976," PIE Papers; Jason Williams, "Five Cars Set Afire within 30 Minutes," *Louisville Defender,* October 7, 1976; "8 Foot Cross Burned on Lawn of Residence," *Louisville Courier-Journal,* April 1, 1976; Nancy Gall-Clayton, interview by the author, September 13, 1999, OHC.

63. "Sloane, Hollenbach Condemn Racism, Anti-Semitism," *Louisville Defender,* April 8, 1976; "Text of Declaration of Independence of Bigotry," *Louisville Defender,* April 15, 1976; minutes of HRC meeting, May 6, 1976, Perley Papers; Carolyn Colwell, "Antibigotry Services to Be Held June 26–27," *Louisville Courier-Journal,* April 24, 1976; Kate Parry, "'Silent People' Are Asked to Sign Anti-bigotry Pact," *Louisville Courier-Journal,* June 9, 1976; "News Conference against Bigotry," *News from PIE,* April 1976, box 1, file "Newsletters," PIE Papers; "PIE Statement for News Conference against Bigotry," April 8, 1976, box 1, file "Notices and Statements," PIE Papers.

64. Wanda Nichols, "Busing Opponents, Supporters Meet to Try to Ease Differences," *Louisville Courier-Journal,* August 31, 1976; Ben Johnson, "Busing Foes, Supporters to Keep Talking," *Louisville Courier-Journal,* Sep-

tember 8, 1976; Dick Kaukas, "Busing Session Peaceful; Uproar Was All Out-side," *Louisville Courier-Journal,* September 30, 1976; Dick Kaukas, "New Anti-busing Group Separates Itself," *Louisville Courier-Journal,* September 26, 1976; Patrick Howington, "Busing Foes Take Aim," *Louisville Times,* November 4, 1976; Mervin Aubespin, "Group of Busing Advocates, Opponents, State Goals for Resolving Differences," *Louisville Courier-Journal,* October 26, 1976.

65. "Spring Workshop Planned," *News from PIE,* January 1976, box 1, file "Newsletters," PIE Papers; "Community Workshop on the Rights and Responsibilities of Students and Parents" (flyer, March 21, 1976), box 4, file "UBPP," PIE Papers; "Spread the Word: People's Workshop on the Schools," *News from PIE,* April 1976, box 1, file "Newsletters," PIE Papers; "People's Workshop a Success," *News from PIE,* May 1976, box 1, file "Newsletters," PIE Papers; "Black Protective Parents, PIE Cosponsor Workshop," *Louis-ville Defender,* May 6, 1976; "PIE Plans New Workshop," *News from PIE,* October 1976, box 1, file "Newsletters," PIE Papers; "School Workshop Plans Grow," *News from PIE,* February 1977, box 1, file "Newsletters," PIE Papers.

66. "From the Trauma of Busing, an Opportunity for Change," *Louisville Courier-Journal,* June 12, 1976; Jason Williams, "Busing—the First Year," *Louisville Defender,* June 10, 1976; Carol Thomas to the editor, *Louisville Defender,* September 2, 1976; Ralph Campbell, "Teachers and Students Say 'Things Are Better This Year,'" *Louisville Defender,* September 9, 1976; "Black Parents Give Failing Grade to Human Relations in the Schools," *Louisville Defender,* November 18, 1976.

67. "Decisions on Our Work," June 8, 1976, box 3, file "Statewide March," PIE Papers; "Students Rights," *News from PIE,* July 1976, box 1, file "Newsletters," PIE Papers; "Lay Advocacy Project Planned," *News from PIE,* August 1976, box 1, file "Newsletters," PIE Papers; "Urgent Notice," [August 17, 1976], box 3, file "United Action Opening Day," PIE Papers; Jason Williams, "UBPP Opens Office for School Woes," *Louisville Defender,* September 2, 1976; Mattie Mathis, "Discrimination in Schools: Black Parents Fight Back," *News from PIE,* February 1977, box 1, file "Newsletters," PIE Papers; Gregory D. Jones, "Board Votes to Close Five Schools at End of Year," *Louisville Defender,* April 29, 1976; "Protest School Closings," *News from PIE,* April 1976, box 1, file "Newsletters," PIE Papers; "Demand Funds for Roosevelt," *News from PIE,* October 1976, box 1, file "Newsletters," PIE Papers.

68. Frank Ashley, "Jefferson County Judge's Race," *Louisville Courier-Journal,* November 6, 1977; Frank Adams, "Hollenbach Is Defeated by Mc-Connell," *Louisville Courier-Journal,* November 9, 1977.

69. Jane Ramsey, "Racism in the Schools or in the Community: Same Issue Same Fight," *News from PIE,* February 1977, box 1, file "Newsletters," PIE Papers.

Conclusion

Epigraphs: Amos Oz, "Il Big Bang di Ogni Storia," *La Repubblica*, December 3, 1997, 40, translated and quoted in Alessandro Portelli, *The Order Has Been Carried Out: History, Memory, and Meaning of a Nazi Massacre in Rome* (New York: Palgrave Macmillan, 2003), 24; Suzy Post, interview by Sarah Theusen, June 23, 2006, SOHC.

1. Hamilton, interview; Porter, interview.

2. Dolores Delahanty, interview by the author, April 14, 2000, OHC; Hicks, interview; Coleman, interview.

3. Mayraj Fahim, "Louisville Metro Has Shown Other Regions How Mergers Can Change Balance of Power," *City Mayors*, December 24, 2006, http://www.citymayors.com/government/louisville.html.

4. Galen Martin, interview by the author, November 11, 1999, OHC.

5. On the elite nature of pre–World War II civil rights work in Louisville, see Wright, *Life behind a Veil*, esp. 262–82.

6. On the role of life histories of activists in revealing the connections among movements across time, I am indebted to Kathryn L. Nasstrom, "Beginnings and Endings: Life Stories and the Periodization of the Civil Rights Movement," *Journal of American History* 86 (1999).

7. For examples of the Popular Front as the roots of the civil rights movement, see chapter 1, note 6. For an example of a community study that pushes the story into the 1980s, see J. Todd Moye, *Let the People Decide: Black Freedom and White Resistance Movements in Sunflower County, Mississippi, 1945–1986* (Chapel Hill: University of North Carolina Press, 2004). For examples of community studies that emphasize the overlap between issues, see Christina Greene, *Our Separate Ways: Women and the Black Freedom Movement in Durham, North Carolina* (Chapel Hill: University of North Carolina Press, 2005); Peter B. Levy, *Civil War on Race Street: The Civil Rights Movement in Cambridge, Maryland* (Gainesville: University Press of Florida, 2003); and Skotnes, "Black Freedom Movement." On the overlap between movements, see Tyson, *Radio Free Dixie*, and Williams, *Politics of Public Housing*. For a description and critique of the traditional civil rights narrative, see Brian Ward, "Forgotten Wails and Master Narratives," introduction to *Media, Culture, and the Modern African American Freedom Struggle*, ed. Brian Ward (Gainesville: University Press of Florida, 2001); Renee C. Romano and Leigh Raiford, *The Civil Rights Movement in American Memory* (Athens: University of Georgia Press, 2006), xiv; and Peter Lau, *Democracy Rising: South Carolina and the Fight for Black Equality since 1865* (Lexington: University Press of Kentucky, 2006).

Bibliography

Archival Collections

Martha Leslie Allen Papers, State Historical Society of Wisconsin, Madison.

Ray Bixler Papers, Ekstrom Library, University of Louisville, Louisville, KY.

Black Student Union Papers, Ekstrom Library, University of Louisville, Louisville, KY.

Anne and Carl Braden Papers, State Historical Society of Wisconsin, Madison.

Congress of Racial Equality Papers, State Historical Society of Wisconsin, Madison (microfilm edition, University of Louisville, Louisville, KY).

Mark F. Ethridge Papers, Wilson Library, University of North Carolina, Chapel Hill.

Judy Hicks Papers, in the author's possession.

Judges Files, Louisville Metro Government Archives, Louisville, KY.

Kentucky Civil Liberties Union Papers, Ekstrom Library, University of Louisville, Louisville, KY.

Kentucky Oral History Commission Collection, Kentucky Historical Society, Frankfort.

Louisville City Records, Louisville Metro Government Archives, Louisville, KY.

Louisville Human Relations Commission Papers, Louisville Metro Government Archives, Louisville, KY.

Lois Morris Papers, Ekstrom Library, University of Louisville, Louisville, KY.

National Association for the Advancement of Colored People Papers, Manuscript Division, Library of Congress, Washington, DC (original and microfilm editions).

National Urban League Papers, Manuscript Division, Library of Congress, Washington, DC.

Oral History Collection, Ekstrom Library, University of Louisville, Louisville, KY.

Charles H. Parrish Papers, Ekstrom Library, University of Louisville, Louisville, KY.

Martin Perley Papers, Filson Historical Society, Louisville, KY.
Progress in Education Papers, Ekstrom Library, University of Louisville, Louisville, KY.
Social Action File, State Historical Society of Wisconsin, Madison.
Southern Oral History Collection, Wilson Library, University of North Carolina, Chapel Hill.
Southern Regional Council Papers, Robert W. Woodruff Library Archives, Atlanta University Center, Atlanta (microfilm edition, University of North Carolina, Chapel Hill).
Harvey C. Webster Papers, Ekstrom Library, University of Louisville, Louisville, KY.
West End Community Council Papers, State Historical Society of Wisconsin, Madison.
F. W. Woolsey Papers, Ekstrom Library, University of Louisville, Louisville, KY.

Books, Articles, and Other Published Materials

Adams, Frank T. *Unearthing Seeds of Fire: The Idea of Highlander.* Winston-Salem, NC: Blair, 1975.
Adams, Luther. "'It Was North of Tennessee': African American Migration to Louisville and the Meaning of the South." *Ohio Valley History* 3 (Fall 2003): 37–52.
Adams, Patricia L. "Fighting for Democracy in St. Louis: Civil Rights during World War II." *Missouri Historical Review* 80 (1985): 58–75.
Ahmed, Nahfiza. "The Neighborhood Organization Workers of Mobile, Alabama: Black Power Politics and Local Civil Rights Activism in the Deep South, 1968–1971." *Southern Historian* 20 (1999): 25–40.
Ashmore, Susan Youngblood. "More than a Head Start: The War on Poverty, Catholic Charities, and Civil Rights in Mobile, Alabama, 1965–1970." In *The New Deal and Beyond: Social Welfare in the South since 1930,* edited by Elna C. Green, 196–238. Athens: University of Georgia Press, 2003.
Bartley, Numan V. *The Rise of Massive Resistance: Race and Politics in the South during the 1950s.* Baton Rouge: Louisiana State University Press, 1969.
Blackstock, Nelson. *COINTELPRO: The FBI's Secret War on Political Freedom.* New York: Anchor Foundation, 1988.
Bolton, Kenneth, Jr., and Joe R. Feagin. *Black in Blue: African-American Police Officers and Racism.* New York: Routledge, 2004.
Borstelmann, Thomas. *The Cold War and the Color Line: American Race Relations in the Global Arena.* Cambridge, MA: Harvard University Press, 2001.
Braden, Anne. *The Wall Between.* Knoxville: University of Tennessee Press, 1999.

Brown, Cynthia Stokes. *Refusing Racism: White Allies and the Struggle for Civil Rights*. New York: Teachers College Press, 2002.

Brown, Sarah Hart. "Congressional Anti-communism and the Segregationist South: From New Orleans to Atlanta, 1954–1958." *Georgia Historical Quarterly* 80 (1996): 785–816.

Carmichael, Omer, and Weldon James. *The Louisville Story*. New York: Simon and Schuster, 1957.

Carson, Clayborne. *In Struggle: SNCC and the Black Awakening of the 1960s*. Cambridge, MA: Harvard University Press, 1981.

Chafe, William H. *Civilities and Civil Rights: Greensboro, North Carolina, and the Black Struggle for Freedom*. New York: Oxford University Press, 1980.

Chappell, David L. *Inside Agitators: White Southerners in the Civil Rights Movement*. Baltimore: Johns Hopkins University Press, 1994.

A Community Study among Whites and Negroes in Louisville. New York: Roper Research Associates, 1969.

Cottrol, Robert J., Raymond J. Diamond, and Lelande B. Wave. *"Brown v. Board of Education": Caste, Culture, and the Constitution*. Lawrence: University Press of Kansas, 2003.

Countryman, Matthew J. *Up South: Civil Rights and Black Power in Philadelphia*. Philadelphia: University of Pennsylvania Press, 2006.

Cox, Dwayne D., and William J. Morison. *University of Louisville*. Lexington: University Press of Kentucky, 2000.

Crews, Clyde F. *An American Holy Land: A History of the Archdiocese of Louisville*. Wilmington, DE: Glazier, 1987.

Cummings, Scott, and Michael Price. "Race Relations in Louisville: Southern Racial Traditions and Northern Class Dynamics." Policy Paper Series, Urban Research Institute, University of Louisville, Louisville, KY, June 1990.

Deslippe, Dennis A. "'Do Whites Have Rights?' White Detroit Policemen and 'Reverse Discrimination' Protests in the 1970s." *Journal of American History* 91 (2004): 932–60.

Dittmer, John. *Local People: The Struggle for Civil Rights in Mississippi*. Urbana: University of Illinois Press, 1994.

Draper, Timothy Dean. "Revisiting 1968." *Chicago History* 31, no. 1 (2002): 4–25.

Dudziak, Mary L. *Cold War Civil Rights: Race and the Image of American Democracy*. Princeton, NJ: Princeton University Press, 2000.

———. "Desegregation as a Cold War Imperative." *Stanford Law Review* 41, no. 1 (1988): 61–120.

Dulaney, W. Marvin. *Black Police in America*. Bloomington: Indiana University Press, 1996.

Dunnigan, Alice Allison. *The Fascinating Story of Black Kentuckians: Their Heritage and Traditions*. Washington, DC: Association for the Study of Afro-American Life and History, 1982.

Durr, Kenneth D. *Behind the Backlash: White Working-Class Politics in Bal-timore, 1940–1980*. Chapel Hill: University of North Carolina Press, 2003.

Egerton, John. *Speak Now against the Day: The Generation before the Civil Rights Movement in the South*. Chapel Hill: University of North Carolina Press, 1994.

Eick, Gretchen Cassel. *Dissent in Wichita: The Civil Rights Movement in the Midwest, 1954–1972*. Chicago: University of Illinois Press, 2001.

Eley, Lynn W., and Thomas W. Casstevens. *The Politics of Fair-Housing Legis-lation: State and Local Case Studies*. San Francisco: Chandler, 1968.

Ernst, John, and Yvonne Baldwin. "The Not So Silent Minority: Louisville's Antiwar Movement, 1966–1975." *Journal of Southern History* 73, no. 1 (2007): 105–42.

Evans, Sara. *Personal Politics: The Roots of Women's Liberation in the Civil Rights Movement and the New Left*. New York: Vintage Books, 1979.

Fahim, Mayraj. "Louisville Metro Has Shown Other Regions How Mergers Can Change Balance of Power." *City Mayors*, December 24, 2006. http://www.citymayors.com/government/louisville.html.

Fairclough, Adam. "The Costs of *Brown*: Black Teachers and School Integra-tion." *Journal of American History* 91 (2004): 43–55.

Faulk, Carrie. "The First Line of Defense: The Battle to Preserve Segregation through Clairborne Academy, 1969–1970." *North Louisiana History* 37, no. 4 (2006): 218–35.

Feldman, Glenn, ed. *Before "Brown": Civil Rights and White Backlash in the Modern South*. Tuscaloosa: University of Alabama Press, 2004.

Findlay, James F., Jr. *Church People in the Struggle: The National Council of Churches and the Black Freedom Movement, 1950–1970*. New York: Oxford University Press, 1993.

Flamm, Michael W. *Law and Order: Street Crime, Civil Unrest, and the Crisis of Liberalism in the 1960s*. New York: Columbia University Press, 2005.

———. "'Law and Order' at Large: The New York Civilian Review Board Referendum of 1966 and the Crisis of Liberalism." *Historian* 64 (2002): 643–65.

Flug, Michael. "Organized Labor and the Civil Rights Movement in the 1960s: The Case of the Maryland Freedom Union." *Labor History* 31 (1990): 322–46.

Formisano, Ronald P. *Boston against Busing: Race, Class, and Ethnicity in the 1960s and 1970s*. Chapel Hill: University of North Carolina Press, 1991.

Fosl, Catherine. *Subversive Southerner: Anne Braden and the Struggle for Racial Justice in the Cold War South*. New York: Palgrave Macmillan, 2002.

Frazier, E. Franklin. *Negro Youth at the Crossways: Their Personality Devel-opment in the Middle States*. New York: Schocken Books, 1967.

Friedland, Michael B. *Lift Up Your Voice like a Trumpet: White Clergy and the Civil Rights and Antiwar Movements, 1954–1973.* Chapel Hill: University of North Carolina Press, 1998.

Garrow, David J., ed. *Chicago 1966: Open Housing Marches, Summit Negotiations, and Operation Breadbasket.* Brooklyn, NY: Carson, 1989.

Goldfield, Michael. "Race and the CIO: The Possibilities for Racial Egalitarianism during the 1930s and '40s." *International Labor and Working-Class History* 44 (1993): 1–31.

Goldstein, Robert Justin. *Political Repression in Modern America from 1870 to 1976.* Urbana: University of Illinois Press, 2001.

Greene, Christina. *Our Separate Ways: Women and the Black Freedom Movement in Durham, North Carolina.* Chapel Hill: University of North Carolina Press, 2005.

Grimshaw, William J. *Bitter Fruit: Black Politics and the Chicago Machine, 1931–1991.* Chicago: University of Chicago Press, 1992.

Gruenwald, Kim. "Space and Place on the Early American Frontier: The Ohio Valley as a Region, 1790–1850." *Ohio Valley History* 4 (Fall 2004): 31–48.

Hall, Jacquelyn Dowd. "The Long Civil Rights Movement and the Political Uses of the Past." *Journal of American History* 91 (2005): 1233–63.

Hall, Wade H. *The Rest of the Dream: The Black Odyssey of Lyman Johnson.* Lexington: University Press of Kentucky, 1988.

Haney-López, Ian F. *Racism on Trial: The Chicano Fight for Justice.* Cambridge, MA: Belknap Press of Harvard University Press, 2003.

Hardin, John A. *Fifty Years of Segregation: Black Higher Education in Kentucky, 1904–1954.* Lexington: University Press of Kentucky, 1997.

Harmon, David A. *Beneath the Image of the Civil Rights Movement and Race Relations: Atlanta, Georgia, 1946–1981.* New York: Garland, 1996.

Harrison, Lowell H., and James C. Klotter. *New History of Kentucky.* Lexington: University Press of Kentucky, 1997.

Heaney, Gerald W., and Susan Uchitelle. *Unending Struggle: The Long Road to an Equal Education in St. Louis.* St. Louis: Reedy Press, 2004.

Honey, Michael. "Operation Dixie: Labor and Civil Rights in the Postwar South." *Mississippi Quarterly* 45 (1992): 439–52.

Jackson, Kenneth T. *Crabgrass Frontier: The Suburbanization of the United States.* New York: Oxford University Press, 1985.

Jacoway, Elizabeth, and David R. Colburn, eds. *Southern Businessmen and Desegregation.* Baton Rouge: Louisiana State University Press, 1982.

Johnson, Marilyn. *Street Justice: A History of Police Violence in New York City.* Boston: Beacon Press, 2003.

Jolly, Kenneth S. *Black Liberation in the Midwest: The Struggle in St. Louis, Missouri, 1964–1970.* New York: Routledge, 2006.

Jones, E. Michael. *The Slaughter of Cities: Urban Renewal as Ethnic Cleansing.* South Bend, IN: St. Augustine's Press, 2004.

Joseph, Peniel E. "Black Studies, Student Activism, and the Black Power Movement." In *The Black Power Movement: Rethinking the Civil Rights–Black*

Power Era, edited by Peniel E. Joseph, 251–77. New York: Routledge, 2006.

———. *Waiting 'til the Midnight Hour: A Narrative History of Black Power in America.* New York: Holt, 2006.

Kentucky Commission on Human Rights. *Louisville School System Retreats to Segregation: A Report on Public Schools in Louisville, Kentucky, 1956–1971.* Frankfort: Commonwealth of Kentucky, 1971.

Kentucky Directory of Black Elected Officials. Frankfort: Kentucky Commission on Human Rights, 1976.

Kentucky's Black Heritage: The Role of the Black People in the History of Kentucky from Pioneer Days to the Present. Frankfort: Kentucky Commission on Human Rights, 1971.

Kerns, J. Harvey. *A Survey of the Economic and Cultural Conditions of the Negro Population of Louisville, Kentucky.* N.p.: Department of Research and Community Projects, National Urban League, 1948.

Kesselman, Louis C. "Negro Voting in a Border Community: Louisville, Kentucky." *Journal of Negro Education* 26 (Summer 1957): 273–80.

Kimbrough, Mary, and Margaret W. Dagen. *Victory without Violence: The First Ten Years of the St. Louis Committee of Racial Equality, 1947–1957.* Columbia: University of Missouri Press, 2000.

Kleber, John E., ed. *Encyclopedia of Louisville.* Lexington: University Press of Kentucky, 2001.

Klibaner, Irwin. *Conscience of a Troubled South: The Southern Conference Educational Fund, 1946–1966.* Brooklyn, NY: Carlson, 1989.

K'Meyer, Tracy Elaine. *Interracialism and Christian Community in the Postwar South: The Story of Koinonia Farm.* Charlottesville: University of Virginia Press, 1997.

———. "The Louisville Civil Rights Movement's Response to the Southern Red Scare." *Register of the Kentucky Historical Society* 104, no. 2 (2006): 217–48.

Korstad, Robert Rodgers. *Civil Rights Unionism: Tobacco Workers and the Struggle for Democracy in the Mid-Twentieth-Century South.* Chapel Hill: University of North Carolina Press, 2003.

Korstad, Robert, and Nelson Lichtenstein. "Opportunities Lost and Found: Labor, Radicals, and the Early Civil Rights Movement." *Journal of American History* 75 (1988): 786–811.

Kotlowski, Dean J. "Richard Nixon and the Origins of Affirmative Action." *Historian* 60 (1998): 523–41.

Krueger, Thomas A. *And Promises to Keep: The Southern Conference for Human Welfare.* Nashville, TN: Vanderbilt University Press, 1967.

Lamb, Charles H. *Housing Segregation in Suburban America since 1960.* New York: Cambridge University Press, 2005.

Landau, Herman. *Adath Louisville: The Story of a Jewish Community.* Louisville, KY: Landau, 1981.

Lassiter, Matthew D. *The Silent Majority: Suburban Politics in the Sunbelt South*. Princeton, NJ: Princeton University Press, 2006.

Lassiter, Matthew D., and Andrew B. Lewis, eds. *The Moderates' Dilemma: Massive Resistance to School Desegregation in Virginia*. Charlottesville: University Press of Virginia, 1998.

Lau, Peter. *Democracy Rising: South Carolina and the Fight for Black Equality since 1865*. Lexington: University Press of Kentucky, 2006.

Levy, Peter B. *Civil War on Race Street: The Civil Rights Movement in Cambridge, Maryland*. Gainesville: University Press of Florida, 2003.

Lewis, George. *The White South and the Red Menace: Segregationists, Anticommunism, and Massive Resistance, 1945–1965*. Gainesville: University of Florida Press, 2004.

Lutz, Paul. "Desegregation: A Crisis without Drama." *Journal of the West Virginia Historical Association* 10, no. 1 (1986): 16–33.

Lyne, Jack. *Schoolhouse Dreams Deferred: Decay, Hope, and Desegregation in a Core-City School System*. N.p.: Phi Delta Kappa International, 1998.

MacLean, Nancy. *Freedom Is Not Enough: The Opening of the American Work Place*. Cambridge, MA: Harvard University Press, 2006.

Mapes, Mary L. *A Public Charity: Religion and Social Welfare in Indianapolis, 1929–2002*. Bloomington: Indiana University Press, 2004.

McGirr, Lisa. *Suburban Warriors: The Origins of the New American Right*. Princeton, NJ: Princeton University Press, 2001.

Meier, August, and Elliott Rudwick. *CORE: A Study in the Civil Rights Movement, 1942–1968*. New York: Oxford University Press, 1973.

Meyer, Stephen Grant. *As Long as They Don't Move Next Door: Segregation and Racial Conflict in American Neighborhoods*. Lanham, MD: Rowan and Littlefield, 2000.

Mills, Nicolaus, ed. *Busing U.S.A.* New York: Teachers College Press, 1979.

Minchin, Timothy J. *From Rights to Economics: The Ongoing Struggle for Black Equality in the U.S. South*. Gainesville: University Press of Florida, 2007.

Moore, Dhoruba. "Strategies of Repression against the Black Movement." *Black Scholar* 12, no. 3 (1981): 10–16.

Moreno, Paul D. *From Direct Action to Affirmative Action: Fair Employment Law and Policy in America, 1933–1972*. Baton Rouge: Louisiana State University Press, 1997.

Morris, Aldon D. *The Origins of the Civil Rights Movement: Black Communities Organizing for Change*. New York: Free Press, 1986.

Moye, J. Todd. *Let the People Decide: Black Freedom and White Resistance Movements in Sunflower County, Mississippi, 1945–1986*. Chapel Hill: University of North Carolina Press, 2004.

Nadasen, Premilla. *Welfare Warriors: The Welfare Rights Movement in the United States*. New York: Routledge, 2005.

Nasstrom, Kathryn L. "Beginnings and Endings: Life Stories and the Periodization of the Civil Rights Movement." *Journal of American History* 86 (1999): 700–711.

Ogbar, Jeffrey O. G. *Black Power: Radical Politics and African American Identity.* Baltimore: Johns Hopkins University Press, 2004.

Orleck, Annelise. *Storming Caesar's Palace: How Black Mothers Fought Their Own War on Poverty.* Boston: Beacon Press, 2005.

Patterson, James T. *"Brown v. Board of Education": A Civil Rights Milestone and Its Troubled Legacy.* New York: Oxford University Press, 2001.

Payne, Charles M. *I've Got the Light of Freedom: The Organizing Tradition and the Mississippi Freedom Struggle.* Berkeley: University of California Press, 1995.

Plummer, Brenda Gayle. *Rising Wind: Black Americans and U.S. Foreign Affairs, 1935–1960.* Chapel Hill: University of North Carolina Press, 1996.

Portelli, Alessandro. *The Order Has Been Carried Out: History, Memory, and Meaning of a Nazi Massacre in Rome.* New York: Palgrave MacMillan, 2003.

Powers, Georgia Davis. *I Shared the Dream: The Pride, Passion, and Politics of the First Black Woman Senator from Kentucky.* Far Hills, NJ: New Horizon Press, 1995.

Price, Margaret. *The Negro and the Ballot in the South.* Atlanta: Southern Regional Council, 1959.

Pride, Richard A., and J. David Woodard. *The Burden of Busing: The Politics of Desegregation in Nashville, Tennessee.* Knoxville: University of Tennessee Press, 1985.

Purnell, Brian. "'Drive Awhile for Freedom': Brooklyn CORE's 1964 Stall-In and Public Discourses on Protest Violence." In *Groundwork: Local Black Freedom Movements in America,* edited by Jeanne F. Theoharis and Komozi Woodard, 45–76. New York: New York University Press, 2005.

Reed, Merl E. *Seedtime for the Modern Civil Rights Movement: The President's Committee on Fair Employment Practice, 1941–1946.* Baton Rouge: Louisiana State University Press, 1991.

Romano, Renee C., and Leigh Raiford. *The Civil Rights Movement in American Memory.* Athens: University of Georgia Press, 2006.

Roxga, Margaret. "March on Milwaukee." *Wisconsin Magazine of History* 90, no. 4 (2007): 28–39.

Salmond, John A. "'The Great Southern Commie Hunt': Aubrey Williams, the Southern Conference Educational Fund, and the Internal Security Subcommittee." *South Atlantic Quarterly* 77 (1978): 433–52.

Saltman, Juliet. *Open Housing: Dynamics of a Social Movement.* New York: Praeger, 1978.

Sayer, John William. *Ghost Dancing the Law: The Wounded Knee Trials.* Cambridge, MA: Harvard University Press, 1997.

Schutz, J. Christopher. "The Burning of America: Race, Radicalism and the 'Charlotte Three' Trial in 1970s North Carolina." *North Carolina Historical Review* 76, no. 1 (1999): 43–65.

Sedler, Robert A. "The Louisville–Jefferson County School Desegregation Case: A Lawyer's Retrospective." *Register of the Kentucky Historical Society* 105, no. 1 (2007): 3–32.

Self, Robert O. *American Babylon: Race and the Struggle for Postwar Oakland.* Princeton, NJ: Princeton University Press, 2003.

Seligman, Amanda Irene. *Block by Block: Neighborhoods and Public Policy on Chicago's West Side.* Chicago: University of Chicago Press, 2005.

Sewell, Stacy Kinlock. "Left on the Construction Bench: The New York Construction Trades and Racial Integration, 1960–1972." *New York History* 83 (2002): 203–34.

Share, Allen J. *Cities in the Commonwealth: Two Centuries of Urban Life in Kentucky.* Lexington: University Press of Kentucky, 1981.

Sosna, Morton. *In Search of the Silent South: Southern Liberals and the Race Issue.* New York: Columbia University Press, 1977.

Stone, Clarence N. *Economic Growth and Neighborhood Discontent: System Bias in the Urban Renewal Program of Atlanta.* Chapel Hill: University of North Carolina Press, 1976.

Sugrue, Thomas J. "Affirmative Action from Below: Civil Rights, the Building Trades, and the Politics of Racial Equality in the Urban North, 1945–1969." *Journal of American History* 91 (2004): 145–73.

———. *The Origins of the Urban Crisis: Race and Inequality in Postwar Detroit.* Princeton, NJ: Princeton University Press, 1996.

Sullivan, Patricia. *Days of Hope: Race and Democracy in the New Deal Era.* Chapel Hill: University of North Carolina Press, 1996.

Sullivan, William C. *The Bureau: My Thirty Years in Hoover's FBI.* New York: Norton, 1979.

Taylor, Henry Louis, Jr., ed. *Race and the City: Work, Community and Protest in Cincinnati, 1820–1970.* Chicago: University of Illinois Press, 1993.

Taylor, Steven J. L. *Desegregation in Boston and Buffalo: The Influence of Local Leaders.* Albany: State University of New York Press, 1998.

Teaford, Jon C. *The Rough Road to Renaissance: Urban Revitalization in America, 1940–1985.* Baltimore: Johns Hopkins University Press, 1990.

Theoharis, Jeanne F., and Komozi Woodard, eds. *Freedom North: Black Freedom Struggles outside the South, 1940–1980.* New York: Palgrave Macmillan, 2003.

Thompson, Becky. *A Promise and a Way of Life: White Antiracist Activism.* Minneapolis: University of Minnesota Press, 2001.

Thornton, J. Mills, III. *Dividing Lines: Municipal Politics and the Struggle for Civil Rights in Montgomery, Birmingham, and Selma.* Tuscaloosa: University of Alabama Press, 2002.

Turner, Jeffrey A. "Student Power, Black Power, Class Power: Race, Class, and

Student Activism on Two Southern Commuter Campuses." *Gulf South Historical Review* 16, no. 1 (2000): 48–70.

Tyson, Timothy B. *Radio Free Dixie: Robert F. Williams and the Roots of Black Power.* Chapel Hill: University of North Carolina Press, 1999.

Unger, Irwin. *The Best of Intentions: The Triumphs and Failures of the Great Society under Kennedy, Johnson, and Nixon.* New York: Doubleday, 1996.

U.S. Commission on Civil Rights. *Hearing before the United States Commission on Civil Rights: Held in Louisville, Kentucky, June 14–16, 1976.* Washington, DC, 1976.

U.S. Department of Commerce, Bureau of the Census. *Census of Population, 1950.* Vol. 2, *Characteristics of the Population, Kentucky.* Washington, DC, 1952.

———. *1970 Census of the United States: Characteristics of the Population.* Part 19, *Kentucky.* Washington, DC, 1973.

———. *Population and Housing Statistics for Census Tracts, Louisville, Ky., and Adjacent Area.* Washington, DC, 1942.

Van Deburg, William L. *New Day in Babylon: The Black Power Movement and American Culture, 1965–1975.* Chicago: University of Chicago Press, 1992.

Ward, Brian, ed. *Media, Culture, and the Modern African American Freedom Struggle.* Gainesville: University Press of Florida, 2001.

Warnock, Henry U. "Prophets of Change: Some Southern Baptist Leaders and the Problem of Race, 1920–1921." *Baptist History and Heritage* 7 (1972): 172–83.

Webb, Clive, ed. *Massive Resistance: Southern Opposition to the Second Reconstruction.* New York: Oxford University Press, 2005.

Williams, Rhonda Y. *The Politics of Public Housing: Black Women's Struggles against Urban Inequality.* New York: Oxford University Press, 2004.

Woods, Jeff. *Black Struggle, Red Scare: Segregation and Anti-communism in the South, 1948–1968.* Baton Rouge: Louisiana State University Press, 2004.

Wright, George C. *A History of Blacks in Kentucky.* Vol. 2, *In Pursuit of Equality, 1890–1980.* Frankfort: Kentucky Historical Society, 1992.

———. *Life behind a Veil: Blacks in Louisville, Kentucky, 1865–1930.* Baton Rouge: Louisiana State University Press, 1985.

Wright, Sharon D. "Electoral and Biracial Coalition: Possible Election Strategy for African American Candidates in Louisville, KY." *Journal of Black Studies* 25 (1995): 749–58.

Dissertations, Theses, and Unpublished Papers

Banks, Nancy A. "'The Last Bastion of Discrimination': The New York City Building Trades and the Struggle over Affirmative Action, 1961–1976." PhD diss., Columbia University, 2006.

Benver, Michael Peter. "Preparatory Programs, Banding, and Affirmative Action in an Urban Police Department." EdD diss., University of Louisville, 1996.

Birkhead, Judith Ann. "Consolidation and Desegregation of Public Schools in Jefferson County, Kentucky." EdD diss., University of Cincinnati, 1978.

Collins, Ernest. "The Political Behavior of the Negroes in Cincinnati, Ohio, and Louisville, Kentucky." PhD diss., University of Kentucky, 1950.

Free, Jonathan M. "Life, Liberty, and Recreation: Louisville Park Desegregation, 1947–1955." Honors thesis, University of Louisville, 2007.

Gilpin, Toni. "Left by Themselves: A History of the United Farm Equipment and Metal Workers Union, 1938–1955." PhD diss., Yale University, 1992.

Gladney, Margaret Rose. "I'll Gladly Take My Stand: The Southern Segregation Academy Movement." PhD diss., University of New Mexico, 1974.

Hudson, James Blaine. "The History of Louisville Municipal College: Events Leading to the Desegregation of the University of Louisville." EdD diss., University of Kentucky, 1981.

Lang, Clarence E. "Community and Resistance in the Gateway City: Black National Consciousness, Working Class Formation, and Social Movements in St. Louis, Missouri, 1941–1964." PhD diss., University of Illinois, Urbana-Champagne, 2004.

Marshall, Anne Elizabeth. "'A Strange Conclusion to a Triumphant War': Memory, Identity and the Creation of a Confederate Kentucky, 1865–1925." PhD diss., University of Georgia, 2004.

McElhone, Patrick S. "The Civil Rights Activities of the Louisville Branch of the National Association for the Advancement of Colored Persons: 1914–1960." Master's thesis, University of Louisville, 1976.

McRae, Elizabeth Gillespie. "White Women, Massive Resistance, and the Boston Anti-busing Crusade." Paper presented at the annual meeting of the Southern Historical Association, Richmond, VA, October 31–November 3, 2007.

Newberry, Anthony Lake. "Without Urgency or Ardor: The South's Middle of the Road Liberals and Civil Rights, 1945–1960." PhD diss., Ohio University, 1982.

Skotnes, Andor. "The Black Freedom Movement and the Workers' Movement in Baltimore, 1930–1939." PhD diss., Rutgers University, 1991.

Smith, Robert Samuel. "Race, Labor and Civil Rights: *Griggs v. Duke Power* and the Expansion of Equal Opportunity." PhD diss., Bowling Green State University, 2002.

Symon, Robert Bruce. "'Child of the North': Louisville's Transition to a Southern City, 1879–1885." Master's thesis, University of Louisville, 2005.

Terry, David Taft. "'Tramping for Justice': The Dismantling of Jim Crow in Baltimore, 1942–1954." PhD diss., Howard University, 2002.

Newspapers and Magazines

American City
Business Week
Christian Century
Cub
Daily Worker
Look
Louisville Courier-Journal
Louisville Defender
Louisville Leader
Louisville News
Louisville Times
Nation
New Republic
Newsweek
New York Times
Reporter
Shively (KY) Newsweek
Southern Patriot
University of Louisville Cardinal
U.S. News and World Report
Voice

Interviews

Unless otherwise noted, all interviews are by the author.

Kentucky Oral History Collection, Kentucky Historical Society, Frankfort.

Powers, Georgia Davis, by Betsy Brinson. N.d.

Oral History Collection, Ekstrom Library, University of Louisville, Louisville, KY.

Allison, William. September 21, 2001.
Aubespin, Mervin. September 14, 1999.
Baker, Dolores White. May 18, 2000.
Barnett, Henlee, by Linda White. March 28, 1984.
Beckett, Goldie Winstead, by Kenneth Chumbley. September 12, 1978.
Braden, Anne. March 22, 2001; June 7, 2001; September 18, 2001.
Bryant, Ruth. September 27, 1999.
Clay, Ken. February 19, 2001.

Coleman, Louis. March 5, 2001.
Cunningham, Raoul. June 19, 1996.
Cunningham, Robert. September 1, 1999.
Delahanty, Dolores. April 14, 2000.
Delahanty, Pat. September 3, 1999.
Douglas, Robert. September 10, 1999.
Ellis, Benitha. September 4, 2000.
Gall-Clayton, Nancy. September 13, 1999.
Gaslinger, Chris. February 7, 2000.
Gittleman, David. December 1, 1999.
Hamilton, Cheri Bryant. October 23, 1999.
Heitzman, Tony. May 26, 2000.
Hicks, Fred. September 15, 1999.
Hines, Carl. September 21, 1999.
Hodge, Philip. February 8, 2001.
Hodge, W. J., by Chuck Staiger. December 14, 1977.
Hudson, J. Blaine. March 23, 2001.
Jackson, Evelyn, by Darlene Eakin. N.d.
Jones, Mattie. March 3, 2000.
Lanier, Shelby. September 29, 1999.
Lee, Edna. October 27, 1999.
Logsdon, Norbert, and Shirley Logsdon. October 25, 1999.
McMillan, Joseph. September 23, 1999.
Martin, Galen. November 11, 1999.
Maupin, Milburn, by Darlene Eakin. October 2, 1978.
Moffett, Tom. February 16, 2000.
Neal, Sterling, Jr. April 21, 2000.
Nevin, John, by Ethel White. May 2, 1988.
Owens, Howard. February 28, 2000.
Patterson, William, by Darlene Eakin. N.d.
Perley, Martin. February 23, 2000.
Pollock, Nancy Pennick. September 9, 1999.
Porter, Woodford. September 9, 1999.
Post, Suzy. April 3, 2000.
Powers, Georgia Davis. March 24, 2000.
Robinson, Runette. September 9, 2000.
Schempp, Carroll. January 29, 2001.
Shobe, Benjamin. August 27, 1999.
Tachau, Charles. August 16, 1999.
Thomas, Lee. April 10, 2000.
Walls, John, by Patrick McElhone. July 31, 1973.
Walls, Murray, by Dwayne Cox. July 27, 1977.
White, Gerald. August 29, 2000.

Williams, Aubrey. May 17, 2000.
Winlock, Bob. March 13, 2001.
Yeager, Margaret, by Darlene Eakin, July 1, 1973.

Southern Oral History Collection, Wilson Library, University of North Carolina, Chapel Hill

Emerick, Bonita, by Elizabeth Gritter. August 2, 2005.
Johnson, Lyman, by John Egerton. July 12, 1990.
Neal, Sterling, Jr., by David Cline. May 16, 2006.
Owens, Henry, by David Cline. May 31, 2006.
Post, Suzy, by Sarah Theusen, June 23, 2006.
Wyatt, Wilson, by John Egerton. July 12, 1990.

In the Author's Possession

Atwood, Kenton. November 6, 1996.
Aubespin, Mervin. January 22, 2002.
Poignard, Arminta, by Gwen Potts. [1996].
Tinsley, Deanna Shobe. July 16, 1996.
Wade, Andrew, by Catherine Fosl. November 8, 1989.

Index